ALSO BY SHARON R. KAUFMAN

The Healer's Tale: Transforming Medicine and Culture

The Ageless Self: Sources of Meaning in Late Life

...AND A TIME TO DIE

How American Hospitals
Shape the End of Life

SHARON R. KAUFMAN

A LISA DREW BOOK

SCRIBNER

NEW YORK   LONDON   TORONTO   SYDNEY

A LISA DREW BOOK/SCRIBNER
1230 Avenue of the Americas
New York, NY 10020

SCRIBNER and design are trademarks of
Macmillan Library Reference USA, Inc., used under license
by Simon & Schuster, the publisher of this work.

A LISA DREW BOOK is a trademark of Simon & Schuster, Inc.

For information about special discounts for bulk purchases,
please contact Simon & Schuster Special Sales:
1-800-456-6798 or business@simonandschuster.com.

Designed by Kyoko Watanabe
Text set in Minion

Manufactured in the United States of America

1   3   5   7   9   10   8   6   4   2

Library of Congress Cataloging-in-Publication Data
Kaufman, Sharon R.
—And a time to die: how American hospitals shape the end of life/Sharon R. Kaufman.
p. cm.
"A Lisa Drew book."
Includes bibliographical references and index.
1. Terminal care—United States. 2. Hospital care—United States.
3. Death—Social aspects—United States. I. Title.

R726.8.K385   2005
362.17'5'0973—dc22   2004052530

ISBN 0-7432-6476-2

For my parents

" 'This is the nature of modern death,' Murray said. 'It has a life independent of us. It is growing in prestige and dimension. It has a sweep it never had before. We study it objectively. We can predict its appearance, trace its path in the body. We can take cross-section pictures of it, tape its tremors and waves. We've never been so close to it, so familiar with its habits and attitudes. We know it intimately. But it continues to grow, to acquire breadth and scope, new outlets, new passages and means. The more we learn, the more it grows. Is this some law of physics? Every advance in knowledge and technique is matched by a new kind of death, a new strain. Death adapts, like a viral agent. . . .' "

Don DeLillo
White Noise

CONTENTS

...AND A TIME TO DIE

INTRODUCTION

"The job of ethnography, or one of them anyway, is indeed to provide, like the arts and history, narratives and scenarios to refocus our
attention; not, however, ones that render us acceptable to ourselves
by representing others as gathered into worlds we don't want and
can't arrive at, but ones which make us visible to ourselves by representing us and everyone else as cast into the midst of a world full of
irremovable strangeness we can't keep clear of."

Clifford Geertz
Available Light

This is a book about time and death. It is about the bureaucracy, rhetoric,
machines, and procedures that define American hospitals and structure
time and death within their walls, creating a new reality—death brought
into life. It is also about the culture that predominates in the hospital and
its deep, internal ambivalence about death. That ambivalence arose with
the coming together of three elements: the work and goals of medicine,
American individualism, and the market-oriented health care delivery
system. It confronts patients, families, and hospital staff with the need to
make seemingly impossible choices. Together, these elements have contributed to a vociferous nationwide conversation about "the problem of
death," a problem that is manifested most visibly and dramatically by
patients who have entered what I call the gray zone at the threshold
between life and death. This book maps the journeys such patients take

1

into and through that zone as well as the culture that surrounds it. Throughout my two years of on-site research, I sought to learn how doctors, nurses, patients, and families experience the hospital and the deaths that occur there. I wanted to understand why hospital death is considered by so many to be "a problem" and to explore the nature of that problem's recalcitrance. This book traces—through the experiences of the doctors and nurses who work in hospitals, the very sick patients who enter them, and the family members who must decide what to do—the ways in which hospitals shape the deaths that happen within their walls and the social sources upon which those configurations are founded.

Beginning in the 1980s, "the problem of death" emerged as a new topic, part of a broad public discourse in the United States. In front-page news articles, op-ed pages, and popular magazines, on radio and television, people were talking about it. Ordinary individuals were disturbed about the ways their loved ones died in hospitals—connected to tubes and machines, following endless procedures, disoriented and in pain. In general, they died after too much technological intervention and with too little personal say. Doctors made public their dissatisfaction with losing their authority to freely determine the care of their dying patients. Health economists, policymakers, and hospital administrators bemoaned the fact that dying cost too much and went on for too long. Throughout the 1980s and into the 1990s it became increasingly clear to critics and analysts of the health care system that large numbers of people had become critical of the management of dying, the procedures for dying, and the institutional circumstances in which dying was taking place.

American understanding of the relationship between medical care and the dying transition has come to hinge largely on the structure of health care delivery, and that structure has consequences for health professionals, patients, and their families. The ways we think and talk about the "dying process" and the dying person and the ways we prepare for death, stave it off, and respond to medical treatments for those near death are all shaped by social institutions and bureaucratic practices.[1] And that led me to ponder the circumstances in which the American health care system allows us to classify people as *dying* and the ways in which hospital death has come to be understood as a problem. Today, more than twenty years after the public discussion began about the difficulty of dying in American hospitals, the conversation remains heated and the "problem" affects more patients, families, and health professionals than ever before.

Death today is medically and politically malleable and open to end-less negotiation. This means that death can be timed, and timing has become the crux of the matter. While the primary task of medicine is to deny death, everyone also knows that, ultimately, death cannot be denied. But medicine can manipulate when death occurs. Cardiopul-monary resuscitation (CPR), mechanical ventilators, feeding tubes, and powerful medications, for example, are all tools that, if applied, can slow death's arrival and, if withheld or withdrawn, can speed it up. Because these tools are ubiquitous in the hospital and natural to it, the com-pelling, inescapable questions when death seems near become whether to start or continue their use, when to stop their use, and on what grounds these steps should be taken. Attention is focused on the timing of events and procedures, and this has determined the possibilities avail-able for approaching life that is near its end and, ultimately, death.

Yet medical tools and procedures are not the only contributors to the way hospital deaths happen, and they are not the only contributors to the widely felt disquiet. In American society, with its strong emphasis on the ideal of individual rights, the decision-making power of a person facing death is deemed necessary and central. The importance of listen-ing to the patient's point of view, the need for others to intuit that view when the patient's voice is silenced by disease, and judgments about how long the life of a very sick patient should be maintained by medical means all become essential factors in the timing of his or her death. A specific rhetoric—of "suffering," "dignity," and "quality of life"—shapes those judgments and is deployed often in hospital discussions about what to do for and about the critically ill individual. That rhetoric emerges as a strong determinant of when death occurs.

People today want things from death, and their desires are both con-tradictory and unprecedented. Many want dying to be an experience that can be characterized as "good," yet persons near death and those who care for them often perceive it as difficult or painful, harrowing or humil-iating. People want death to be made comfortable by the tools of medi-cine, which they expect can eliminate both the disturbing visible signs of the body's disintegration and the patient's experience of suffering. Yet they also hold vague ideas that death can somehow be "natural"—and by that they usually mean peaceful and easy, like the sleep of a child—and without the overuse of drugs or machines. People want the medical profession to offer hope and compassionate intervention, but they are distraught when death is preceded by "too much" invasive medical technology. Many want to control the way death happens for themselves and their loved ones by planning ahead for it, yet few are actually prepared for the moments when decisions must be made or for the kinds of questions that will emerge when death is near.

Hospital death is framed as a problem in the United States because, while many claim to want that elusive "good" death for themselves and their loved ones, they also want—equally or more strongly—that their loved ones *not* die. These contradictory emotions emerge from a particular view of medical progress—that the tools of contemporary medicine can effect more and more cures, stop (for a while at least) the process of growing old or repair the failing bodily systems that accompany very late life, and deny death indefinitely. Thus a great many people experience—as patient, family member, friend, or clinician—the seemingly insoluble tension between, on the one hand, the desire to extend someone's life and the expectation that it can and should be extended using the tools of medicine and, on the other, the contrasting value of allowing death to occur "with dignity" or without "artificial" technological prolongation. The ways we respond, inside the hospital, to the contradictory emotions, and to the conditions of the very sick people who inspire those emotions, result from the manner in which the hospital system structures treatments and organizes the experiences of patients and their families. Our responses result, too, from historical developments in the doctor-patient relationship, the institutionalization of "patient autonomy," and the cultural traditions we as individuals draw on to invest with meaning the "appropriate" moment for death.

Struggling to find ways to either stave off death or arrange for "good" deaths, hospital staff, together with the powerful technologies that are part of hospitals today, can also allow a third possibility—a prolonged hovering at the threshold between life and death. Instead of death, the hospital opens up an indefinite period of waiting during which patients do not cross that threshold until it is decided when it is *time* for them to die. Scenarios of patients being maintained at the threshold, and of dilemmas that arise there about what to do and when, are common.

I carried out my research at three community hospitals in California for a total of two years (1997 and 1999–2000).[2] I observed the course of over a hundred critically ill patients who died (and many more who did not). I followed them through procedure after procedure, day after day and sometimes week after week, and spoke with about a third of them—with most, quite briefly. I talked, generally repeatedly, with scores of family members whose relatives were hospitalized. I stood with families at patients' bedsides for brief chats, sat in waiting rooms with them while they cried, paced, made phone calls, and wrung their hands, and had coffee with them in hospital cafeterias as they talked at length about the patient's history and condition and the dilemmas they faced while trying to fit this hospitalization into their lives and think about long-term caregiving. They constructed hypothetical scenarios of recovery or decline that changed, sometimes daily, as the patient's condition improved or worsened. They considered choices they might have to make soon, whether they would discuss those choices with other family and friends, whether others were capable of hearing and talking about the situation. Some spoke with conviction about doing everything they could to keep their relative alive. Some said they did not know what they wanted for the patient or what the patient would want now. I watched them react to information from doctors—information that meant a decision had to be made about, for example, amputating a gangrenous limb in order to give the patient more time, or transferring a relative from the intensive care unit to a hospital for long-term, ventilator-dependent patients, or arranging for death as soon as all the relatives were able to assemble, or the need to bring an end to suffering. Often I watched family members slowly change their minds about their relative's condition, saw them realize, after days or weeks and after many conversations with physicians and nurses, that their relative was now, in fact, dying.

At each of the hospitals, I also interviewed, watched, followed around, listened to, and talked about patients' conditions and treatments with health professionals: doctors, nurses, social workers, and respiratory, physical, occupational, and speech therapists. Almost everyone showed compassion. Almost everyone was efficient. I had access to patients' medical charts, to rounds on various hospital units, and to some staff meetings and family-staff conferences. I attended team meetings on some medical units every week for a year. In one ICU, I accompanied the medical team on bedside rounds several times a week for eighteen months.

I listened to nurses talk to family members and respond to their questions but never state outright that a patient would soon die. I watched as nurses tried to communicate with very sick patients who could barely speak. In the ICU, nurses monitored machines, gave intravenous medications, never took their eyes off a patient (even while writing in the medical chart), and spoke reassuringly to patients and families. They were a conduit of information to doctors. They told me how their day-to-day tasks of making patients comfortable and keeping them alive worked as advocacy on behalf of patients. On the medical floors, nurses gave medications, organized the flow of patients from procedure to procedure and out of the hospital, and explained what was going on to families. They joked at the impossible circumstances of their work—when, for example, they learned that impoverished homeless patients who required extensive medical follow-up had been discharged to the streets, or when very old people clearly at the end of their lives were given life-prolonging treatments. They complained often that they had too many patients to give them the kind of care they wanted to give.

I listened as doctors asked nurses, respiratory therapists, and other hospital staff about patients' physiological functions and asked nurses and social workers about how families were coping. I watched them do surgical procedures on patients in the ICU. I listened to their deliberations about what to do next and when, often when all the options seemed hopeless. I stood with them in the hallways when they told family members what they wanted to do next to a patient, and why. When families asked questions about life support and prognosis, I listened to doctors explain why, for example, a comatose patient connected to a mechanical ventilator would not recover, or how medicine could not know for sure if a condition was irreversible but felt strongly that it was. I watched them tell extremely ill patients who would not recover that staff could make them comfortable with medications and allow them to die, and then I listened to them explain to families how dying would physiologically occur and what it would look like.

I followed respiratory therapists as they watched mechanical ventilators and adjusted oxygen flow. I stood at bedsides while they worked with doctors to put breathing tubes carefully, correctly, but swiftly down patients' windpipes. I accompanied them as they calmed patients and tried to make the oxygen masks more comfortable, tested lung capacity, wrote everything into the medical chart.

I sat in social workers' offices as they talked on the phone with families about meetings with doctors, nursing home placement, taking the patient home to die, and the necessity of filling out Medicaid forms. I walked the hospital corridors with them as they sought out discharge planners and physicians, and I sat in on their visits with patients. Sometimes they acted as patients' counselors or therapists, talking about what was meaningful at this time in their lives, simply being present to listen. Often, too, they worked as bureaucrats, trying to assess which less-costly unit the patient could be moved to and talking with patients and families about the timing for a move to a nursing home or hospice care.

I stood at bedsides with chaplains who led prayer services for patients who were close to death. I listened as they asked families what was important about their faith, what was important for the patient, and what they would like to do to mark the passing of their relative.

I sat with discharge planners as they complained that a patient's care was no longer reimbursed by Medicare and that the hospital would have to cover the costs. I listened as they talked about the inherent conflict in their job—the pressure to move patients out of the hospital in a cost-effective manner even as doctors refused to discharge very sick patients.

After my two years of observation, I learned that each patient's hospital stay is seen by medical personnel through the lens of the passage of time, through the institutional demand to move through time with economic and clinical efficiency. For doctors and nurses in the hospital, the timing of decisions and procedures (that is, the speed or slowness with which they occur), the ability to get things done in a timely way, the obstacles to that timeliness, and the timing of death all represent overarching concerns. Time is the marker for things health professionals think should happen and for things that must get done, and it weighs heavily on everyone who works in a hospital.

The scenes I witnessed were sometimes unsettling, yet it is important to emphasize that nothing was unique or unusual. People who work in hospitals across the United States will recognize these scenarios—dependence on the mechanical ventilator, extended periods of watching a patient hover at the threshold of death, endless and perhaps "futile" procedures, the decision to insert a feeding tube or withdraw life support, and all manner of dying itself. Many doctors and nurses have written about these things in their own books and articles as ordinary occurrences, all part of hospital routine. They are all considered "normal" because they have been *normalized* over time. In each of the twenty-seven patients' stories I reconstruct, the death scenario—or the *death-in-life* scenario—is clearly the inevitable outcome of ways in which the hospital system guides events and individual choices. I have chosen these particular stories because, taken together, they represent a range of hospital phenomena and patient and family experience that are considered problematic in the public discourse. They are not meant to be considered, individually or as a group, "typical" of adult deaths or of medical care in hospitals across the United States. In my years of observations, *I saw an equal proportion of hospital deaths that no one considered problematic.* Yet, the events I describe here are common. And that is troubling.

My experience in these hospitals led me to recognize and consider four topics that have been missing from the growing conversation about problematic death, and this book aims to describe them. First, the hospital system shapes medical practice and practitioner and patient experience, yet that system has not often been acknowledged in the ongoing lay discussion of problematic dying. (Health care policy analysts, health economists, and a few outspoken physician critics have, however, long been concerned with the ways in which the health care system operates to determine forms of dying.) The hospital system organizes how lifesaving biomedical technologies are used as well as the ways in which day-to-day activities are carried out. Together the bureaucracy, the technologies, and ordinary medical practices create the phenomenon of the threshold between life and death, and the *waiting* that occurs there, and thus spark the conversation of complaint. At that threshold, the hospital acts as a laboratory, an experimental space in which new kinds of persons, new forms of life itself, are made and questions are raised about what it is to be alive and to be human.

Second, the rhetoric used by hospital staff, families, and patients to make sense of an individual life when it hovers at the gray zone is not acknowledged in the public conversation for its powerful role in determining when to allow death to happen. Though that rhetoric circulates widely in American society and thus seems "natural" in the hospital setting, it is deployed and negotiated at the bedside of very sick patients to control the dying transition.

The next overlooked topic concerns the hidden kinds of knowledge that doctors, nurses, and other health professionals share among themselves about hospital procedures, hospital routines, and what needs to be done at the threshold between life and death. The information they possess stands in sharp contrast to what patients and families experience and grasp when they enter the hospital and confront critical illness. Despite the widespread critique of the overuse of medical treatments and the apparent desire for change, professional knowledge of what goes on in the hospital when death is near and why, as well as hospital staff's expectations about patient and family responsibility, remains sequestered there.

Lastly, neither the management of the threshold nor the way death occurs in the hospital is inevitable. Both are complicated cultural fabrications. Our understandings of how hospital death occurs and is staved off, and of what is "right" and "wrong" with either, are determined by historical trends in politics, medicine, and social life. Those include the changing power relations among the institutions of science, religion, and the law; the ways in which biomedical technologies have come to be used and valued; developments in Medicare and other federal regulations and policies; the transformation over the twentieth century of ideas about the body, the person, and old age; and the evolving roles of medical specialists, ethicists, legal experts, managers, hospital patients, and families in that transformation.

Like the ordinary hospital practices that have become cause for so much complaint, medicine, too, derives from complex social sources that contribute to the tenacity of ideas about "how things are done." Medicine today is a web of complex social institutions, diverse kinds of knowledge, fragmented systems of care, and a broad array of clinical practices. In all those ways, it has become the most powerful framework in the United States for understanding critical illness and for approaching the dying. There is a widespread demand to have control at the end of life through having greater choice. This presents a paradox, for medicine both provides and constrains that choice. It offers an abundance of treatments. But it also organizes—perhaps in the hospital most dramatically—how one can know the problems of the body, what makes a person alive or dead, what the role of the family should be, and the relations among patients, families, and health professionals. It declares what is important to know and what needs to be imagined. Then, it ignores other, perhaps equally important things. Thus, it produces particular forms of dying.

With the tools of anthropology, by traveling into the hidden yet taken-for-granted world of the hospital and by closely observing what occurs in territory both familiar and strange, I wanted to dismantle any simple views of technological overload and lack of personal command that so commonly characterize how American hospital dying is understood and to expand the concept to include the institutional structures and cultural forces that shape it. I wanted to understand what goes on at the threshold between life and death, to see if I could discern the range of activities that makes hospital patients poised there such a common, and yet unwanted, occurrence. I also wanted to investigate some of the paradoxes that the hospital world sets up, both for the people who work there and for the patients and families who come through it, because, like any highly complex institution, the hospital is a frustrating and demanding place, full of contradictions and practices that seem to serve only the bureaucracy itself. Finally, I wanted to explore the historical sources of hospital culture that have shaped the way people see the pressure of time, the patient's condition, what must be done, and what cannot be done, and that have forced so many to make what seem to be impossible choices.

In the hospitals I saw several phenomena in play—the work of medicine and the workings of the hospital, the dominant ethics of individualism that gave rise to the public conversation about control and "better dying," and the myriad individual responses to critical illness and to the hospital itself—and I wanted to understand how, together, they are implicated in how we come to assess and negotiate what to do when a person is at the threshold. But I also realized that an even broader concern is at stake for everyone in American society; for entangled with shifting notions of life at the end of life and the limits and promise of medical care is an ambivalent social responsibility toward the very vulnerable in our midst.

Natives and Strangers in the Territory of Dying

As an anthropologist, I wanted to try to understand and then describe how the American hospital organizes dying, how it makes certain kinds of deaths possible and inevitable, and to do so, I entered the lives of patients and families and the workplaces of hospital staff. But every time I entered that strange world where treatments, rules, technologies, expertise, compassion, and tragedy combine, I felt caught in the conceptual conundrum that anthropologist Clifford Geertz has described (now famously) as "a scientistic worry about being insufficiently detached" and a simultaneous "humanistic worry about being insufficiently engaged."[3] There are two tensions that characterize anthropological work: tensions that arise between immersion and detachment and between engaged participation and dispassionate reporting. These have been framed traditionally in "insider/outsider" terms, with "insider" awareness and unself-conscious response on the one hand and "outsider" analytic discovery that enables comparison on the other. These tensions are thought to be productive, eventually yielding interpretive insights through the "double consciousness" produced by tacking between different realms of understanding—insider and outsider, native and stranger.[4] When I entered the world of hospital medicine, I began to wonder, who is insider, who outsider—and where did I, the anthropologist, fit? What did the answer to these questions mean for what I was seeing and for how I was interpreting hospital practices and the dramas surrounding them?

These questions nagged at me because I was troubled about my own relationship to what I wanted to learn. I felt myself to be both insider and outsider. The lack of a suitable label for my position in relation to the hospital and to the people I met and the practices I observed made me somewhat uneasy every time I walked through hospital doors. Yet my uneasiness, my lack of definitive status, helped me think through the contradictions I encountered, the differences of feeling and understanding between doctors and nurses, between health professionals and families, indeed, among all the players. My fluctuating position enabled me to hear the cacophony of their voices—all their different kinds of truths—and to explore the criteria on which those truths were established.

I was studying phenomena characterized as problematic in my own society, and I was observing activities considered troublesome yet ordinary, expected yet feared. Since much of what I saw seemed routine to me (after all, the hospitals are in "my culture"), and since the rhetoric that shapes the practices surrounding dying was part of my own, ordinary vocabulary (I, too, favor "dignified" dying and a high "quality of life"), I initially wondered how I could achieve an outsider's "objective" distance to appraise what was going on. Like most Americans, I am generally familiar with the workings of the hospital, any hospital. I have been a hospital patient, though not with a life-threatening illness, and have visited friends and relatives there. I had also conducted research in hospitals prior to this project. Most important, I am a participant in the widespread dialogue about problematic death. I share with many others the wish for a death (far in the future) that is somehow *natural*, whatever that means, and not fraught with dilemmas about maintaining the body when consciousness and *life* seem gone. I participate in the making of the tension that is at the heart of the "problem" of death because I, too, want what is considered "the best" medical treatment (perhaps high-tech, definitely scientifically informed) for family and friends who become ill. More broadly, I am native to a culture that values individualism, the necessity of speaking and being heard, the right to know about disease and treatment and to have options. There is no doubt that I am deeply entrenched here, an insider/native in the land of biomedical explanation and an only-sometimes critic within its logic.

On the other hand, at the start of my research at least, I was also an outsider to the organizational principles of hospital treatment and a stranger to what health professionals are thinking when death seems near. I did not have the knowledge of disease, physical decline, and treatments that doctors and nurses have. I did not know how many lifesaving procedures existed or what regulations and policies guided hospital activity. I was ignorant about the constant change and turmoil in the world of health care finance and of the extent to which those changes affect hospital work and patients' experiences. I was unaware of the extent to which, in the hospital, choice is inevitably encumbered by bureaucracy. Like any sick person's family member, I learned the rules of the institution, the reasons for specific procedures, the limits and powers of technology, and some things about bodily systems and disease processes by sitting with patients and talking with the nurses, doctors, and social workers who came by. But unlike family members, I sat by hundreds of beds, and I began to learn how health professionals think about what they do and how they decide what is important. And so, at some level, I became an insider to two ways of knowing the hospital world—the staff's and the family's.

Eventually, I came to wonder whether anyone was entirely comfortable, entirely an insider in such an out-of-this-world place. From one perspective, all hospital staff are insiders. They have daily and weekly routines that they take for granted. They have specialized languages. They know the rules and rituals, the shortcuts, the machinery and the symbols, the ways to get around. They know what counts as normal and ordinary in terms of the progress of disease, medicine's responses, coworkers' activities, and institutional procedures. They know the policies that affect their particular jobs, even if they balk at some of them. Though much must be learned—from knowledge of the sick body to the uses of medical equipment, from the etiquette of doctor-nurse and staff-patient interactions to hospital rules governing patient placement and movement—those things are, ultimately, assumed by hospital staff to be natural to the place, to be part of its very constitution.

But even what seems "natural" can undergo change, and hospitals are places of ongoing social change and reorganization. During my observations, hospitals in the greater metropolitan area where I work merged and closed, and new arrangements for patient treatment were forged between and among hospital groups. Certain specialized units closed in some hospitals; others opened or expanded in size. Nurses periodically went on strike. In one hospital, physicians changed the lines of authority and communication in the intensive care unit, and the organizational hierarchy and the role of ICU nurses changed twice. In another hospital, ethics committee members proposed new guidelines for Do Not Resuscitate orders that were debated throughout the hospital for months. In yet another, "palliative care" became a distinctive form of end-of-life medical practice. All of these changes became part of the "insider" knowledge held by health professionals.

Hospitals, however, are highly complex, small societies, unknowable by any one individual. So when, for example, the frame of reference shifts to include the changes in power relations between administrators and medical staff that are brought about by health care finance reforms, doctors and nurses, too, feel that they are outsiders. They feel alienated and marooned in a corporate business landscape where they have no authority to care for patients in the ways they were taught were ideal. For a long time, and certainly during my research, physicians and nurses have felt besieged by corporate cost-saving demands. Across the United States, hospitals' first cost-cutting measure seems to be to reduce the number of nurses they employ. Thus, nurses are the most vulnerable "natives" in the system because their employment is frequently at stake.[5] Physicians experience a different sort of vulnerability and alienation. They feel like expendable commodities at the service of the bureaucracy and thrust into unwanted negotiations with hospital administrations and managed care companies about how fast they can discharge patients and how few procedures (and which ones) they can prescribe. Their work is under constant surveillance by utilization review committees, risk management departments, and those whose job it is to watch the bottom line. Both nurses and doctors complain about working in a system that above all does not respond to their professional priorities, a system that is no longer deemed habitable by those whose job it is to treat and care for patients. One young physician I spoke with characterized the first year of her residency training in internal medicine as a period of learning to be disciplined by the bureaucracy to be a cog in the system. Patients were merely an epiphenomenon, she remarked, the objects acted on to ensure the smooth running of the institution.

And what about the patients and families who come and go, who enter the hospital once or circulate through it repeatedly? To what degree are they insiders or outsiders? On the one hand, they are definitely outsiders. Most of them have only vague knowledge, if any, of human physiology and disease, medical procedures, or those organizational features of the hospital that determine what happens to patients. Most patients and families struggle to make sense of the routines, sights, sounds, language, and personnel inside what they see as a strange and sometimes terrifying place. They are visitors, travelers outside their own lives and severed by medical necessity from their own biographies. Yet, on the other hand, whether patients and families are born in the United States or are recent immigrants, whether they are highly educated or not, most want access to the hospital's tools when they are in crisis. Medicine, the dominant system by which we understand the human organism and its malfunctions and diseases, can stave off death regardless of the patient's condition, age, or degree of frailty. *Almost everyone knows this*, and this knowledge is always in the background of people's awareness when they are in the hospital environment. In that sense, patients and families are insiders indeed. They are also true insiders in another sense—they are participants in the dying. Although they are not native to the complex ways the hospital works, they are the real stakeholders—in how death is made and how the hospital makes death—in a way that the hospital staff and that I, the anthropologist, could not be.[6]

While doing my research, I felt more *like* the professional staff than like the patients and families for a variety of reasons. I was not ill or receiving treatment. Unlike a patient's family member, my observations and questions were not clouded by worry, anxiety, grief, or emotional turmoil, nor was I faced with monumental decisions. For staff, the hospital is a fixed, permanent place and patients are transitional objects that must be moved along; for staff, as for me, the hospital is where they go on a regular schedule to do a known job. For patients and families, the hospital is the transitional thing—a stressful limbo—and being there heightens their sense of physical and emotional vulnerability and lack of control.

I could empathize with patients and families whenever I recalled the hospitalizations of my own relatives, but my empathy could go only so far because I lived outside their experience and suffering and nothing was presently at stake for me. I was aware that at any time I could be in their shoes, but unless that happened, I could not share the intensity of their feelings or the meanings they derived from their only-partial understanding of the hospital environment and what went on in it. For them everything that happened in the hospital was unwanted and disconnected from their ordinary lives. In contrast, like hospital staff, I quickly learned that everything was routine, many things were predictable, and I could interpret as ordinary occurrences the crises and dislocations that patients and families faced. And I realized that, along with staff, I am implicated in the normalizing of hospital routines simply because, after a few months of observations, I, too, came to view the routines and events and bureaucratic logic as ordinary and as "natural" to the place.

Emotion and the Ethnographer

When I told people I was studying how death occurs in the hospital, the most frequent response was "How could you do that? Isn't it depressing?" I replied that I had great empathy for the very ill patients and shocked and grieving families I came to know, as well as for the doctors and nurses, who carry enormous responsibility. I also had my own fears and sense of horror that arose in the face of terrible disease and sometimes equally terrible treatments. But these were tempered, for me, by the analytic challenge each case presented: Why is this scene unfolding in this way? How is the hospital making this death? What are the sources of ambivalence and contradiction—about treatment, death, and life itself? Most important, I was observing strangers. I had no special bond with any of the patients or families, nor was I acquainted with any of the hospital staff before my research began. Because I was emotionally detached, watching hospital activity did not depress me.

Nonetheless, repeatedly watching death, and watching people poised on the threshold between life and death, from so close a perspective has had an emotional impact on me that is difficult to describe because those scenes were both hard and not hard to observe. I remained emotionally detached in part because I was privy to such an essential moment without being a player in the decisions that surrounded it and without experiencing the grief and guilt that accompanied it. Task-oriented, I was trying to understand what I was seeing by comparing different points of view within a disjointed system. One can look at language, and perhaps especially the language of emotion, in two ways. One is to view language as *representing experience,* and from that perspective my vocabulary to describe the impact of what I witnessed seems impoverished. My struggle to articulate my emotions reveals that my "feelings" and "thoughts" cannot so easily be separated. How to describe witnessing young and old deaths, expected and unexpected deaths; watching health care professionals stave death off or acknowledge its inevitability and prepare for it; seeing the surprise, incomprehension, and chaos that arise within families; being in the presence of dead bodies? I was simultaneously sad and curious, anxious for families, apprehensive about diagnoses, appalled at what patients went through, and at times very uncomfortable about interfering (sometimes simply by being present, sometimes by asking questions) in others' work and lives. My emotions regarding patient and family suffering were inseparable from my emotions about being a careful researcher, constantly on guard about the impact of my intrusion on staff routines and into patient and family privacy.

Much of the time emotions did not arise from "inside" me but were generated by a particular situation—the tense conference in which the medical team asked for a decision, but the family could not possibly choose; the exhausted family members waiting anxiously at the bedside; the technical, purposeful, and tension-filled lifesaving activity that gave rise to ethical dilemmas for some hospital staff and hope for families; the humorous banter and macabre jokes shared among medical and nursing staff; the frustration everyone felt when things did not go well; the immense sadness felt by doctors and nurses when their patients died unexpectedly; the shock and grief that families experienced when their relatives died without, seemingly, any warning signs. In such instances, I absorbed the feelings in the room, though I did not fully share them.

The second way to view language is that it actually *creates experience and emotion,* that our vocabularies shape and in fact give us what we feel and what we know. The language of medicine and of hospital routines and hospital death is deeply entrenched in the way things work there, and it guides what families, especially, are expected to feel. It is rational and instrumental. It forces objectivity and decisiveness. Frustration, grief, uncertainty, fear, and surprise are given voice (occasionally by hospital staff as well as by patients and families), but through a vocabulary of pragmatism that emphasizes problem-solving and decision-making. Such language ignores or redirects incoherence, anxiety, breakdown, diffuse suffering, and any other expression of affect that lacks rationality. Similarly, the talk about "control" and "dignity" as death approaches, about "the good death," that is common among staff, patients, and families can only be known through institutional activity that organizes how these terms are given shape within the hospital world. Talk about grief and "grief work" operates in a similar fashion. Therapy, support groups, and self-help books are available to help manage and structure the stages of grief and thus to define it. Emotional understanding of dying and grieving is shaped through phrases such as "being ready to die," "knowing it is time to die," and "accepting death," phrases that delimit emotion as instrumental and organized—not inchoate and overwhelming— experience. That kind of language normalizes hospital deaths. In addition, the particular language used to describe the existential features of the patient's condition—especially his "quality of life" and degree of "suffering"—shapes and even determines the time for his death. And it was the vocabulary through which I experienced—and thus wrote about—the dying transition.

There is another difficulty in describing what I feel about all of this. My opinions, indeed my moral stance and my values, regarding what I observed are not firm. Though I began my research holding the common, negative opinion about "being attached to machines," and I was against "artificially prolonging death," I quickly learned that it is not simple to make those stock phrases—and the assumptions that surround them—specific. For example, "life support" is not a discrete activity or procedure, and thus its presence and role are not always easy to discern. "Artificial life prolongation," though seldom wanted in the abstract, is rarely perceived as such by the family at the bedside. Hope for a return to "normal" is ever-present while there is life. Yet *life* itself can be a matter of debate. Faith in medical treatment is tenacious and powerful, and hope for continued life usually trumps the desire to bring an end to suffering. Family feelings for the person-now-patient are sometimes expressed as demands that physicians extend treatments past the point of effectiveness. For their part, doctors often use equivocal language when speaking with families about the chance for "meaningful" survival. Thus, emotion, opinion, and "fact" become impossible to separate.

If emotions can be conceptualized as an expression of values or apprehensions, as anthropologist Catherine Lutz suggests,[7] then mine, given what I have seen, remain decidedly mixed and unresolved. I learned, while I watched many "life-and-death" dramas unfold, that I could not possibly stand in judgment of other people's decisions. What if the person lying in that bed, attached to tubes, unconscious, on the brink of death, were my parent or my child? After two years of observing such scenes, I think I know what I would want or what I would do, how long I would ask for life-sustaining procedures, and how long I would maintain hope—but I learned also that I cannot be so sure. I have learned enough to know that if something like this happens to me or my loved ones, I'll be equally unnerved, equally caught up in the pathways, the waiting, and the rhetoric that this book details. At some level, I learned that all you can do is the best you can do at the moment, and if you love the person who lies in a hospital bed at the threshold, you want that person's life to be longer.

The medical, nursing, and social work staff welcomed me to their units and graciously and thoughtfully responded to my queries. No one ever asked me to stop observing them. Acutely aware of how hospitals make death problematic, they hoped that an anthropologist, someone with an outsider's critical eye, would be able to suggest some solutions. They were not opposed to criticism of hospital practice. "How can we make death better?" was the question they posed to me. Like staff, families and patients also welcomed me and my research endeavors. Only a few patients who were able to talk did not want to do so, and only three families did not want me present at the bedside or at conferences with the medical team. After a meeting with the health care team or after the tape-recording of a private conversation, family members sometimes asked, "Did you get the information you needed?" Even in their grief and exhaustion, they, like the staff, hoped I would be able to learn things that might ease the treacherous journey through the hospital, might provide some guidelines that would help "make death better."

I had intruded on patients' privacy and on staff work routines, and I felt I owed all of them something—some sort of translation of their experience into a practical solution for the sorrows of families and the burdens of hospital staff. Part of me wanted to be an engaged activist and work toward the worthy goal of "improving" hospital death. But that would have meant paying closest attention to an agenda for political and social change and compromising my goal of "seeing," as comprehensively as one person working alone could, the multiple strands of cultural formation, institutional constraint, and production of power that make hospital death happen. To the extent I could, I needed to stand outside the logic of the hospital world, including its desire for change. I thought that if I was able to pay attention to the activism I encountered but remain distanced from it, to be sympathetic to the activists' goals while also being critical of the context of their work, and to concentrate on looking at how cultural forms emerge and are organized, my study had the potential to be more analytically useful for a practical reconsideration of the ways American death is made.[8]

My research made it clear that I could not provide direct solutions to the "problem" of hospital dying—that problem is deeply, perhaps inextricably embedded in the political and economic organization of American medical care, the logic of hospital routines, the values and language associated with individualism, and a complex history of the ways in which doctors have come to understand both disease and their patients and in which medical practices have shaped the nature of relationships among disease, its management, old age, and the end of life. Within this complex context, I map for readers the routes toward dying in American hospitals. I show what the different roads to that destination look like, their impact on those who travel them, and some of the cultural foundations on which they were built. I show how all individual decisions about travel on those roads (which byway to take, when to stop, when to speed up) are mostly not "decisions" at all, but rather are determined by the existing grid—the structural patterns of the hospital system. That system works by forcing decision-making on us all, by claiming that we have choices to make; and my discussion of how the system operates does not and cannot change that, for the ideologies and values that support the system reach deep into American society. My discussion does show, however, how we got into the present dilemma and what its contemporary features look like. The web of routines, regulations, and finance mechanisms that both coordinate and fragment the health care delivery system, of which the hospital is one part, cannot easily be dismantled or abandoned. And the values of individualism and individual rights, along with the powerful rhetoric that supports those values and guides many of us in deciding what to do at the threshold of death, cannot easily be ignored. But they can be described. My aim is to show why the so-desired "unproblematic" death is so hard to attain. My hope is that what I reveal can be a useful guide for all who face a journey through the hospital in the future.

PART I

The Predicament

Death Becomes a New Kind of Problem

"Consider modern medicine, a practical technology which is highly developed scientifically. The general 'presupposition' of the medical enterprise is stated trivially in the assertion that medical science has the task of maintaining life as such and of diminishing suffering as such to the greatest possible degree. Yet this is problematical. By his means the medical man preserves the life of the mortally ill man, even if the patient implores us to relieve him of life, even if his relatives, to whom his life is worthless and to whom the costs of maintaining his worthless life grow unbearable, grant his redemption from suffering. . . . Yet the presuppositions of medicine, and the penal code, prevent the physician from relinquishing his therapeutic efforts. Whether life is worth while living and when—this question is not asked by medicine. Natural science gives us an answer to the question of what we must do if we wish to master life technically. It leaves quite aside, or assumes for its purposes, whether we should and do wish to master life technically and whether it ultimately makes sense to do so."

Max Weber
"Science as a Vocation," 1919

"Following social conventions, we avoid labeling persons as being 'near the end of life' unless they are unambiguously very close to death. Regardless, most of us will die following a course of illness with a persistently ambiguous prognosis."

J. Lynn, A. Wilkinson, F. Cohn, and S. B. Jones
"Capitated Risk-Bearing Managed Care Systems
Could Improve End-of-Life Care," 1998

"My mother, Georgia Hansot, died recently in the intensive care unit of a major hospital in the eastern United States. She was 87 years old. . . . As I think back on it, I am astounded that I had so little inkling of how hard it would be to help my mother have the death she wanted. . . . I tried to accompany her into the intensive care unit but could not. . . . An hour later, when I was allowed to see her, she was attached to a respirator and had a feeding tube inserted down her throat. What had happened? . . . Exactly the opposite of what she had wished had occurred; the living will had become invisible just when it was needed most. . . . I found that I was dealing with a bewildering array of medical specialists trained to prolong lives, not to let patients die. . . . My mother's wishes, as they were understood by her family physician and her daughter, were now subject to the approval of strangers: the cadre of cardiologists, neurologists, and pulmonologists who attended her. None of these specialists knew my mother, and they all had their convictions about how to do best by her. . . . My stress built over the ensuing 5 days as mother's distress was palpable. She successfully tore out her feeding tube only to have it reinserted and her restraints tightened. An attempt to remove my mother from the ventilator failed; her swollen larynx prevented her from breathing on her own. . . . The hospital came to feel like alien territory, full of medical strangers intent on maintaining my mother's vital signs at all costs. During her ordeal, my mother became increasingly frantic. . . . My sense of being trapped in a nightmare intensified. . . . In the long days that I spent with her . . . I was able to ask my mother twice—with her nurse as a witness, and with 4 hours between each question—whether she wished to die. My very clearheaded and determined mother thus was able, finally, to assert herself for the necessary last time. . . . The hours dragged by as the specialists were persuaded, one by one, to give their consent. Finally, a technician was allowed to pull the tube from my mother's throat. . . .

"In retrospect, as I review the events of those painful 5 days, there seems to be no simple explanation for what happened. . . . All told, I think my mother was fortunate. In the long run, her wishes were followed; 5 days in the intensive care unit compares favorably with the experiences of many other elderly persons. But the experience was harrowing, for her and for me. What is routine for hospital staff is all too often the first experience of its kind for critically ill patients and their families. . . . This essay is written in the hope that hospitals will devise procedures so that patients and their families can, with less pain and perplexity than I experienced, decide when and how death arrives."

Elisabeth Hansot
"A Letter from a Patient's Daughter"

DEATH AND HOSPITAL CULTURE

"... What death is becomes a matter of deciding at what point a person should be treated as having died, in respect of the cessation of various types of bodily function. . . . Death becomes a point zero: it is nothing more or less than the moment at which human control over human existence finds an outer limit."

Anthony Giddens
Modernity and Self-Identity

The Emerging Conversation of Complaint

In the United States during the twentieth century, death moved out of the home and into medical institutions. Today, more Americans die in hospitals than anywhere else,[1] and the most frequent response to critical illness there is to try to stave off death with the most sophisticated technological means available. Approximately one-quarter of all hospitalized patients are treated in intensive care or cardiac care units before they die.[2]

Not all family members experience the death of a loved one as Elisabeth Hansot did, yet over the past twenty-five years many like her—family members and health professionals alike—have contributed to a conversation that has become increasingly prominent in American life. The discourse about the problem of death has been promulgated and spread by articulate and activist health care consumers and by growing numbers of physicians, nurses, ethicists, health care economists, and others critical of hospital practices. Its essential feature is the notion—

born of the values of autonomy and individual rights—of patient control over decision-making at life's end. Patient (and family) control is considered essential for reducing or eliminating the pain, suffering, loneliness, and humiliation that are perceived to accompany life-prolonging (or death-prolonging) medical treatments. Inevitably, conflict arises between patient determination of the extent of medical intervention and physician or institutional domination of treatments near death. This conflict is played out in countless daily hospital scenarios as health professionals, patients, and families struggle in the face of tensions that have been created in choosing treatments labeled "heroic" or "humane" and in defining responsible, ethical medical care.

In efforts to reform the way Americans die, proponents of patient control and choice have focused their attention mostly on individual initiative—for example, choosing home hospice over hospital care, writing living wills or other advance directives, and participating in grassroots efforts to supplant or enhance standard medical care with family and community involvement. All of those efforts are based on the activities of an educated, informed middle class, and they have generated a great deal of media attention. Another example of individual initiative is evident in the widely felt need to stockpile sleeping pills, sedatives, or other medications so that death can be timed according to one's desires.

But the problem of death is broader and deeper than the widely publicized quandaries of individual choice-making. Public discussion has much less often engaged the impacts of the structural environment in which most deaths occur—a patchwork health care delivery system designed to save life and to treat patients with acute, short-term medical problems. Nor does that public discussion engage the absence of access to medical services among the poor. However, a number of physicians, health care analysts, and other observers are drawing attention to the economic structure of health care delivery, asserting that dying can only be made "better" by instituting significant changes in the financing of end-of-life medical care.[3] To a great extent, current payment schemes guide treatments and shuttle patients from institution to institution.

The focus on individual autonomy and on reforms to enhance self-determination also downplays the voices of those without adequate access to medical services and/or without political and media clout. Many marginalized people, for example, are worried about the widespread debate surrounding the right to euthanasia. Their anxiety, that the legalization of euthanasia could lead to the unwanted deaths of persons deemed "less worthy" by others, gets far less attention in public discourse than the cry for the right to control the time of one's own dying.[4]

Though it expressed only certain concerns and reflected only some voices, by 1990 the public discourse about the problem of death and the desire to make it better was loud and clear. Throughout the 1990s it grew ever louder and was given substance in law, medicine, media reports, the arts, and many kinds of professional and lay activity. It was apparent, for example, in legal decisions such as the federal Patient Self-Determination Act of 1990 (a result of the influence of academic bioethics on hospital policy, in which all hospital patients must be informed of their right to make treatment choices) and in the U.S. Supreme Court's consideration of physician-assisted suicide in 1997. It was heard in the vote of the people in Oregon to legalize euthanasia in 1994 (reaffirmed in 1997). Television and radio also took up the subject, airing programs in which dying persons and their families and friends were interviewed on such topics as family care of a dying relative, advance directives, and euthanasia. Newspapers across the country ran articles about lack of communication between patients and doctors, the overuse of technology, and the problems of managed care. Popular books were published, advocating personal control of one's own death. The hospice movement became better known as an alternative to the high-tech hospital. Jack Kevorkian inspired both fascination and ambivalence. Many case studies in medical journals and personal testimonials in newspaper opinion pages told of "unwanted" kinds of dying.

The conversation about problematic dying also led to a plethora of community education efforts to change the ways in which death occurs and to new medical school and medical residency curricula to sensitize students and young doctors to the inevitability and naturalness of death. It was the subject of a Pulitzer Prize–winning play, Wit (first performed in 1997 in theaters, later in academic medical centers, and eventually made into a television movie), depicting the tyranny and humiliation of aggressive treatment for those who die in teaching hospitals. Public policy organizations developed goals for improved end-of-life care that does not prolong agonized dying. By now there is exceptionally far-reaching discussion about the tensions created by standard medical practice thought to have run amok in an obsolete health care delivery system designed only for the diagnosis and treatment of acute medical problems.

The end of life in the hospital cannot be disentangled from the operational details of a complex social/legal/medical institution that strictly guides the flow of events and how they are understood. The hospital is a place of disconnection. When a death is near, it is a place of bureaucratic logic without logical purpose, a place where everyone muddles through regulated-yet-improvised, routine-yet-disquieting arrangements of medical algorithms, professional relations, and strategies for getting patients through the system. The contemporary hospital, with its remarkable tools and complicated ways of organizing health professionals' work and moving patients and families through the system, is on the cutting edge of culture-making. Its systems, techniques, and logic shape the forms of dying that occur there.

All cultures contain contradictions and hospital culture is no exception. I encountered four striking examples of this. First, though patient autonomy (and its extension, in practical terms, to family members) serves as one important source of an ethic of medical practice,[5] the notion of patient autonomy is actually applied only within a narrow sphere— decision-making about specific medical treatments offered by individual physicians. Further constraint comes from a constellation of institutional imperatives. Thus, while patient and family decision-making is considered paramount, decisions, when they are made at all, are constrained by hospital rules, reimbursement mechanisms, and standards of care. The onus of responsibility for deciding what to want often is on the patient or family, yet they rarely have an informed sense of what is best. Scenarios in which families are offered choice about the goals of medical treatment when death is near reveal the dark side of autonomy—full of anguish, guilt, and above all the absence of knowledge about medical outcomes. Patients and families are given choices but only among the options made available by hospital norms and regulations and within the framework of the almost unstoppable march of treatment. Patients and families do not know and cannot know what to want when reacting to a complicated system of rules that is strange to them. Given this system, patients only want to breathe, to escape the place, to get better, or to die.

Second, other than in relation to certain kinds of diseases (e.g., terminal cancer or end-stage AIDS), death is rarely spoken of or foreseen until shortly before it occurs. Medical care emphasizes the stabilization and normalization of organ systems and the gathering of laboratory data in service of that stabilization. Especially in the intensive care unit, concrete life-sustaining activities (e.g., mechanical ventilation,[6] medication to stabilize blood pressure) preclude the anticipation of death. Clinical medicine in the ICU is like surgery—its gaze falls only on a carefully circumscribed field, the analyzable interior of the body. A waning *life* is rendered invisible, or nearly so, in the reading and then treating of signs of the body's pathology. Disease is treated until there is no more physiologic response to therapy. Only then is death expected. Only then does it "need" to be acknowledged by hospital staff.

The third contradiction is that heroic, aggressive medical care now exists alongside "palliative care," a relatively new approach in which the reduction of pain, anxiety, and other symptoms of distress and the goal of overall comfort replace curative or stabilizing treatments when disease is no longer responsive to those treatments.[7] However, the switch from curative to palliative activity is often fraught with conflict because the core purpose of hospital medical care is to maintain life. The organization of the institution pushes everyone toward lifesaving treatment, even when hospital staff, patients, or their families do not want to prolong dying.

Finally, although most people die in hospitals, hospitals are not structured for the kinds of deaths that people claim to want. For example, Medicare's reimbursement methods dominate what happens to the majority of hospital patients at the end of life. In its attempt to control spending over the last two decades, Medicare has systematically been eliminating its cost-based payments to hospitals and nursing homes, and hospitals are not explicitly reimbursed for providing palliative care.[8] The institutional response to these cutbacks has been for nursing homes to transfer dying patients to hospitals to avoid the cost of intensive treatments, and for hospitals to discharge patients, once they are labeled "dying," so as not to incur the cost of palliative care.[9] Simply put, at this point in history, dying people are not wanted in medical institutions, and it shows.[10]

The wake-up calls from various sectors of society—for advance directives (bioethicists and health professionals), for better doctor-patient communication (patients, families, media, medical and sociological research), for revision of treatment policies (hospital committees and medical organizations), and for health care finance reform (doctors, health economists, politicians, consumers)—are all important. However, the broadly acknowledged quandary over dying is more complex than any single change of policy or behavior can address. Medicine's techno-logical and bureaucratic imperatives are coupled with its lack of clear social obligations. The pervasive quest for an emotionally satisfying death exists uneasily with the fact that dying has become a technical endeavor, a negotiated decision and a murky matter biologically. Poten-tial litigation hangs over and even guides health practitioner activity. These developments have an enormous impact on how life at the end of life is made and interpreted.

The acute care hospital is merely one piece of a larger system, one piece of an extremely complex bureaucracy. The ways in which that sys-tem operates largely determine when health professionals label some-one as dying, how *life* and *death* sometimes come to be interpreted as matters of family responsibility, and the ways in which *being alive* and the value of *life* and of *a particular life* are debated and decided.

The Facts of Death: The Data Speak

The most comprehensive study ever conducted on dying in the United States was carried out in five university hospitals over four years beginning in 1989. The SUPPORT study (Study to Understand Prog-noses and Preferences for Outcomes and Risks of Treatment) docu-mented in considerable detail that many critically ill hospitalized people undergo prolonged deaths characterized by the use of invasive life-sustaining medical technologies.[11] When the results of the study were published in 1995, health care analysts and consumers alike agreed that much of end-of-life hospital care was neither appropriate nor satisfac-tory and that major changes in business-as-usual needed to be imple-mented. To understand the character of hospital dying, forty-three hundred patients diagnosed with life-threatening illnesses were enrolled in the first, two-year phase of the project. Their average age was sixty-five. The study investigators concluded, as most any collection of personal tes-timonials would reveal during the 1990s, that dying in the hospital is not comfortable or supportive and may be the cause of suffering for patients. Investigators found, for example, that only 47 percent of physicians knew when their patients wanted to avoid cardiopulmonary resuscitation (CPR); that 38 percent of patients who died spent ten or more days in an intensive care unit immediately preceding death; that 46 percent of Do

Not Resuscitate (DNR) orders were written within two days of death even though 79 percent of the patients had a DNR request somewhere in the medical record;[12] and that for 50 percent of conscious patients, families reported moderate to severe pain at least half the time in the three days preceding death.

A subsequent second, two-year intervention phase of the SUPPORT study was intended to have a positive effect on medical care and the perceived quality of hospital deaths by enhancing the flow of information between doctors and patients. It involved approximately five thousand additional patients, about half in a control group, half in an intervention group. Nurses—not physicians—were trained to carry out the intervention through various intermediary means: by providing information to physicians about patient preferences regarding resuscitation and other interventions; by providing information to patients and families about prognoses and treatments; by facilitating conversations between patients and physicians; and by providing emotional support to patients and families. The results were startling. The interventions aimed at improving physician-patient communication and physician knowledge of prognosis and patients' end-of-life wishes did not change the use of aggressive intensive care treatments, the timing of DNR orders, avoidance of CPR, or provision of pain relief. Nor did those interventions alter the quality of patient and family experience.[13] Even where a focused and concerted effort was made to reduce pain and to respect patient wishes regarding limiting the use of high-technology measures that prolong dying, no overall improvement was made, either toward reducing the level of pain or toward reducing the use of high-tech interventions.[14]

A plethora of related studies conducted since that landmark project have attempted to document and understand the hospital barriers to doctor-patient communication, standard end-of-life treatments for a variety of medical conditions, the uses (and nonuse) of pain medications, patient and family decision-making, the training needs of physicians and nurses, and the financial basis for uncoordinated end-of-life medical services and for lack of services. Their findings have shown that some of the difficulties surrounding end-of-life medical care are intractable indeed. For example, one difficulty is the practical matter of how physicians can know and then honor patient preferences when patients themselves do not know what to want. It is impossible for many, if not most, people to itemize in advance of critical illness what they will "want" in the way of specific interventions (ventilator? defibrillator? vasopressors? emergency surgery?) if they fall seriously ill. A second intractable problem arises from the limits of medical knowledge—it is not possible to prognosticate accurately about the nearness of death and then to assess which treatments are excessive or inappropriate. Both these difficulties are rooted in the widespread contemporary idea that *death can be disciplined*—that is, that it can be planned in conjunction with medical treatments and can and should be managed well.

Years ago, policymakers and bioethicists thought that the existence of documents stating preferences about end-of-life medical intervention would ameliorate the problem of "too much" or inappropriate hospital treatment, and they advocated their use. Yet less than 10 percent of the general population has written advance directives, that is, a written "living will" or more formalized legal document such as the durable power of attorney for health care.[15] The SUPPORT study investigators found that having an advance directive had no significant effect on limiting the use of resuscitative efforts at the time of death. Indeed, most patients' advance directives (61 percent) did not explicitly state a preference to forgo CPR. Advance directives were, in general, found to be too vague to be relevant to medical decision-making about resuscitation.[16] Those documents that do exist are noted to be vague and uninformed about a person's current medical condition.[17] Some studies show that large percentages of people do not necessarily want their future treatment to be determined by previously written documents,[18] and thus directives specified in advance of need cannot and do not resolve many dilemmas about how aggressive to be with treatments at the bedside.

Physicians, too, encounter intractable end-of-life problems, perhaps chief among them the problem of prognosis about death. For the most part, physicians avoid making such prognoses, and when they do, their accuracy is poor. Physician-sociologist Nicholas Christakis notes in his study of medical prognosis among American doctors that the lack of accuracy has two components: "First, physicians' prognoses are prone to error, meaning that they tend not to be correct for any given individual. Second, their prognoses are prone to bias, meaning that they err in a systematic way—exhibiting, for example, a tendency to overestimate survival in their ... prognoses."[19] Physician Joanne Lynn and her colleagues have shown that the course of most diseases and the timing of most deaths simply are too unpredictable for accurate prognoses.[20]

The most common popular understanding of "the dying process" is that there will be a relatively long period of stability followed by a short period (sometimes only hours long) of physical decline. While that trajectory often characterizes cancers, it does not, in fact, characterize most disease that precedes death. A more common situation is one of long-term disability, with periods of acute symptom exacerbation that may or may not be accompanied by obvious decline. Patients, families, and sometimes physicians expect that, given the right medical treatment, patients will survive each exacerbation, and the patient frequently does survive many flare-ups or acute episodes. Thus, when death finally occurs, it seems "sudden." This protracted dying trajectory is typical of chronic heart failure and chronic lung disease, which together account for about a quarter of all deaths annually in the United States.[21] Lynn reports that in the case of advanced heart failure, for example, the vast majority of patients who were thought by physicians to have at least a 50 percent chance of living six months died the day after that prognosis was made.[22] Persons with strokes, dementia, or degenerative disease often follow yet a third trajectory, one of increasing frailty and diminished function. Yet prognosis about death does not seem to be any more accurate for that category of patients.[23]

In an attempt to show that not all medical care at the end of life is excessive and inappropriate, even in intensive care units, groups of physician investigators have responded both to the widely expressed wish for "death with dignity" and to the SUPPORT study findings and have documented that the frequency of withholding and withdrawing life-supporting measures in ICUs has increased among physicians.[24] However, in a national survey of end-of-life care for critically ill patients, investigators found extremely wide variations in the types of interventions used, whether aggressive or not. This underscores the absence of any national consensus about end-of-life care, and the fact that there are no shared standards of practice. For example, among patients who died in 131 intensive care units in thirty-eight states, the median frequency of CPR was 23 percent, but in some ICUs more than 75 percent of deaths were associated with failed CPR attempts.[25] In a survey of CPR use among emergency room physicians in all fifty states, researchers found that although 78 percent of survey respondents honor legal advance directives regarding resuscitation (when those are available), only 7 percent will follow unofficial documents or verbal wishes. Many (62 percent) make the decision to do CPR because of fear of litigation or professional criticism, and 55 percent had attempted numerous resuscitations despite physician expectations that those attempts would be "futile."[26] In a study conducted at a university-affiliated public hospital, 52 percent of participating physicians felt that CPR should be "offered" to all patients regardless of its potential benefit and despite a hospital policy allowing them to do otherwise.[27]

Private Anguish: Taking It Public

Patients' and doctors' individual experiences are not visible in the SUPPORT study, but they are poignantly expressed in the thousands of personal testimonials and confessions that appear regularly in the media—most often from family members of persons who have died, but also from doctors. Taken together those stories describe the full range of disquieting features of hospital dying and point to complicated gray areas of treatment that the SUPPORT study only alludes to: What kinds of treatments get defined as aggressive, as "artificially" life-prolonging, as inhumane, and under what circumstances? Is use of the mechanical ventilator always a heroic measure? What about medications that stabilize blood pressure? What about dialysis or feeding tubes? When is using any of these considered "comfort care" and by whom? Under what circumstances does using them change from being the standard of care (that is, assumed to be appropriate) to constituting an *unnatural* (that is, inappropriate) prolongation of life? Then there are gray areas of clinical/moral understanding about "suffering" and "quality of life," the rhetoric within which family members, especially, try to make sense of the patient's future and "what should be done." Is there a moment when life is no longer worth living or worth preserving—for instance, when a person suffers great pain that cannot be relieved? Or becomes comatose? Or has been comatose for a week or a month or a year? Are antibiotics or antidepressants—when given to comatose or near-comatose patients—contributing to a better quality of life? Or are they prolonging suffering? Who or what defines "quality of life" and "suffering"? The list goes on . . . and on.

The testimonials also highlight two important facts that the SUPPORT survey could not reveal. First, they underscore that patients and families, when faced with health crises and the surrounding plethora of medical options, *do not know what to want,* other than recovery or an end to suffering in a general sense. Second, it is clear that the hospital is a setting in which health professionals' ability to act with conviction is constrained by professional relations, hospital regulations, standards of practice, finance arrangements, the legal implications of their treatment choices, and the demands made by patients' families. Both groups must act and respond within the institution, and they do so with different sorts of knowledge and priorities.

The media abound with stories about the inability to categorize medical treatments as good or bad, appropriate or not, and whether a family member should "assist death." For example, in a newspaper opinion piece the daughter of an elderly man with advanced lung cancer writes that she asked for antibiotics to fight his infection. She wondered, when told by a physician that the patient would only get repeated infections and die soon anyway, whether withholding antibiotics was a form of assisted suicide. Her father had instructed her to "make sure they keep giving me antibiotics, even if they don't want to" when he regained consciousness following another bout of pneumonia. She authorized the antibiotics, then was plagued by the next set of questions: "Did we want a feeding tube if it came to that? Did we want to withhold his insulin? His potassium? Would we agree to stop having his blood tested?" She noted that her father "had made me promise not to stop treatment. He was a man who did not want to die, even then." "Slowly," she wrote as she acknowledged his decline, "we agreed to stop the blood tests, the potassium, the insulin. We agreed to give him morphine in anticipation of his suffering. . . . Perhaps foolishly, we kept our promise: the IVs of antibiotics and fluids and nutrients did not stop."[28] Such confusion is commonly felt by family members who enter the hospital only to be overwhelmed by the seemingly endless treatments available there. Which procedures prolong life? Which are only prolonging pain and dying? Is one complicit in causing death if one refuses the insulin or the antibiotics? What does it mean to say yes or no to a certain treatment or procedure?

There are stories from the doctor's point of view as well, stories of too much treatment, of attempting to modify or resist the technological imperative despite overwhelming pressures from a variety of sources to use the most advanced technologies all the time. A doctor writes of wanting to remove the ventilator that was only postponing the death of an elderly man who had been fighting cancer: "Organ by organ, the Unit had taken over his life functions. The ventilator served as his lungs, the dialysis machine his kidneys, transfusions his bone marrow." The doctor, knowing that resuscitation would not restore health or life in this case, and wanting to spare the dying patient a final violent intervention, urged the patient's wife to issue a Do Not Resuscitate order. But the wife said to him, "I know he's going to die, but I can't tell you to stop trying." The wife did not issue the order and was resentful of the "pressure" the physician exerted on her. The doctor informs the reader that a few days later, when the patient's blood pressure dropped, he "began a 20-minute exercise of pounding on the ribs, pushing pressors, and drawing blood from the lifeless corpse." The patient did not survive the procedure, and the physician bemoans the fact that he was powerless to stop it.[29]

Though physicians claim in newspaper and magazine articles that patients and families want procedures that will neither restore health nor help at all, the greatest number of personal stories are about unwanted treatments and come from the family perspective. There are many reports of relatives who were resuscitated, had surgery, or underwent "aggressive" procedures against their wishes, only to die anyway—frequently in a hospital intensive care unit—hours, days, or weeks later and following pain, fear, and suffering. The following examples are typical: A man writes poignantly of three relatives who received "too much care." A doctor insisted that the writer's ninety-seven-year-old grandmother have her gangrenous leg amputated, or she would die a painful death. Though the patient did not want the surgery, the leg was amputated, and she died following three days of searing pain. The angry author of the tale questions the medical judgment that would authorize the procedure. Then he wrote of his eighty-four-year-old stepfather, who, following two strokes, had placed a notarized Do Not Resuscitate order with both his doctor and the hospital. When he had another stroke, the patient's wife (the author's mother) told the attending physician about his wish not to be resuscitated and that a DNR order was on file. The doctor responded, "You want to kill him?" The stroke patient was resuscitated and spent a week in the intensive care unit and two more weeks in the hospital. Then, with the encouragement of family and friends, the patient's wife "got up the gumption" to ask the doctor to disconnect the mechanical ventilator. The patient died a few hours later. A third family member, who had had cardiac bypass surgery in the past, was told at age seventy-eight by his physician that he needed another bypass operation. The man refused the surgery, but the doctor persuaded his wife of more than fifty years "to talk him into the operation." During the surgery the doctors realized the man had a failing kidney. Though this patient also had a notarized DNR order in his medical chart, "the doctors used a defibrillator on him five times to bring him back to what they call life. He spent his last days in intensive care, kept alive on tubes for his family's last good-byes, which he probably didn't hear."[30]

Similar accounts have been appearing in the popular media and in health professional journals with growing frequency for more than two decades. They attest to the difficulty of bringing about change either in the complex environment where deaths mostly occur or in the expectation that something can and should be done about dying. "Death with dignity" is difficult or impossible to achieve in the hospital, according to these reports, because of the compelling pressure on everyone there— medical staff, patients, and families—to employ the most sophisticated technologies and to make choices among them. The pressures are insidious, and their far-ranging sources include the American attraction to and reliance on powerful and costly medical equipment and procedures, public and private health care finance arrangements, and a history of ambiguous information, both in the medical community and in the general public, about the relationships among aging, disease, decline, and mortality.

Staff Tensions at the Threshold: A Web of Dilemmas
Doctors' Voices

When physicians speak about the tensions the hospital produces, they reveal the troubled clinical and moral reflection they bring to problem-solving. Physicians are not always sure how to act, or which treatment, if any, is best in the long run, yet usually they are compelled to make a choice and do something. The autonomous and unencumbered doctor-as-decision-maker—characteristics that simultaneously describe the ideal physician (even in the era of managed care) and constitute a source of consumer dissatisfaction—no longer exists because the responsibility for decisions is today embedded in the structural components of medical practice. For example, physicians are dependent on referrals from their peers. Thus, a gastroenterologist will insert a feeding tube in a ninety-five-year-old, frail, bed-bound, and demented patient to extend life, not necessarily because that physician thinks the feeding tube is appropriate medical treatment in this case, but rather because the patient's internist has asked him to do the procedure. For another example, physician

choices regarding the costs of medical procedures are overseen by hospital utilization review committees that urge physicians to choose the least
expensive treatment options and to discharge their patients as quickly as
possible. The constraints of hospital oversight come up against physicians' felt need to pursue diagnoses as well as therapies through whatever
tests and procedures they deem necessary. In addition, doctors feel pressured, sometimes by families of patients, sometimes by their physician
colleagues, to pursue aggressive treatments that they may personally consider inappropriate, nonbeneficial, and a potential cause of pain and suffering. These and similar very real forces influence how doctors practice
their craft.

Beyond such considerations, it is also important to note that actual
decision-making by an individual clinician is often not a deliberate and
premeditated act. And a "decision" may have no practical impact. Events
sometimes simply unfold. Sometimes decisions emerge during negotiations with patients, family members, other health professionals, and
occasionally hospital administrators. They may also occur without overt
discussion. Many patients who require emergency lifesaving treatments
are not considered terminally ill at the start of those interventions.
Treatments are not thought, initially, to be prolonging only the end
phase of a dying process that is already under way. Also, doctors are
trained to respond in an emergency *as though death were not inevitable.*

Even when physicians' decision-making is an explicit act, it can be a
murky enterprise. A critical care specialist was well aware of his position
in a much larger system of health care delivery when he described to me
what is, for him, a common decision-making quandary: What to do
about the frail, demented patient who "ends up" in an intensive care
unit? His description provides a good example of how one practitioner's
ideals about treatment must continually be negotiated amid pressures
from institutional forces.

"A typical situation here is that a demented person in a nursing home
can't swallow very well, food goes down his lungs, he gets pneumonia,
the people in the nursing home panic, they send the patient to the hospital, the doctor panics, the patient goes to the intensive care unit, and
the whole sequence of events and interventions gets played out.

"I might have a lot of judgments about the demented person with
pneumonia who comes in from the nursing home. This person shouldn't
be in the intensive care unit, shouldn't be in the hospital. Probably should

be back at the nursing home, probably should be allowed to die. But he is the person who is in the intensive care unit and you are stuck with him. So the best thing, the most efficient thing, to do is to try and get him well as quick as possible so you can reverse the process and get him going back to the nursing home. So what that means is doing a certain amount of aggressive or active work. Instead of withdrawing, you might actually think, 'Well, the quickest way out of this is to get him over these little humps so then I can get him out of here.' So it gets tricky sometimes."

In many instances the line between some ideal notion of "humane" end-of-life care and aggressive medical intervention that delays death is not clear to physicians *in practice*. Confusion over what actually constitutes comfort care or palliation, and whether that set of practices can be separated from unnecessary, optional, or unwanted life-prolonging interventions, creates dilemmas for physicians. Many physicians see their ideal role in caring for the terminally ill as providing comfort. But some of them note that it is the physician who must assess *how* to provide comfort and point out that diagnosing disease and treating acute problems, even if that requires the use of intensive care procedures, may be the best way to achieve that goal. Thus, palliative or comfort care is not really a discrete activity that can be identified in the abstract. It is defined by physicians, on the ground, in relation to kinds and degrees of treatment. "Comfort" has to be continually redefined in the context of a treatment-oriented health care delivery system. In that system, immediate aggressive intervention is sometimes rationalized as the most efficient way for the patient to receive palliation at some later point.

Ambivalence about what to do as a patient's condition deteriorates and ambiguity about medical goals as death approaches are common. The actual unfolding of activities that give form to hospital dying is, in many cases, much less purposeful and much more muddled than either the public conversation about problematic dying or the clear-cut goals of patient autonomy in decision-making, comfort, and pain relief suggest.

A community geriatrician told this story when asked to describe the kinds of dilemmas she faces regularly:

"To me the most difficult decisions are those that involve someone who is so frail that it's difficult to know how aggressive to be for the treatment. It's also very difficult if it's a patient I'm not familiar with. I took care of a woman in her nineties, very demented, with Parkinson's disease. I was told that when she heard that others had died, she said,

'Could they move over so I can lay down with them and die also?' She wasn't very happy about being alive in this state. She developed a fever and very low blood pressure, and I was told that she did this occasionally and it was usually because of an upper-respiratory infection. By the end of the day she was doing very poorly. I wondered what we should do because she was so sick and frail; maybe it was just best to keep her comfortable at home.

"But not knowing her well and not knowing how the family would feel, I admitted her to the hospital and I did everything I could do on the day of admission to make sure she would stay alive. I checked her blood for evidence of infection; I started her on antibiotics and gave her a lot of fluids so the blood pressure would come up, but she remained comatose. The next day I didn't really do much. She wasn't turning around. I made a decision not to look into what was wrong, figuring that if it was something that needed an operation, I didn't think she would be operated on.

"Another physician took over her case three days after she was hospitalized. Some information accumulated and that physician decided to progress further. In an abdominal ultrasound we found that there were gallstones despite the fact that the woman had had her gallbladder removed. Some of the staff thought, 'We wouldn't operate on her but maybe we can do a relatively safe procedure and try to get those stones out because then she might improve.' That's not what I would have done. As it turned out, there were some stones removed and she was discharged from the hospital, but she expired the day she was discharged.

"I felt that no matter what was done it wouldn't have helped because she was so malnourished and frail. But I have a lot of trouble with situations like that, not knowing how far to push when I'm really very confident the situation is dismal. How hard should I try to maintain someone's life when I think my intervention will only have the person last a few days longer? It's also difficult when you're working with a group of physicians and each physician might treat a case in a different way. . . . Sometimes it's very difficult to know when to stop being very aggressive because you get very attached to people. We care a lot about them, and I can make the mistake of thinking that keeping them alive is good for them. When it may not be."

The technological imperative in medicine—to order ever more diagnostic tests, to perform procedures, and to intervene with ventilators and feeding tubes to prolong life or stave off death—is one of the most important variables in contemporary medical practice and is the source of innumerable clinical-moral qualms. It determines thought and action, and it provides a restrictive language—"do everything," "not very much," "only a little"—through which choices are framed and dilemmas are understood. By confining choice to either/or terms and by forcing physicians to equate good, appropriate care with maximum intervention, the technological imperative narrows doctors' field of possibilities and thus removes options. When the patient is old and has multiple, complex medical problems, the impact of the technological imperative is especially destabilizing, both to ideas of good medical care and to the idea that certain conditions should not be prolonged. The geriatrician's personal preference was to forgo invasive treatment because of the patient's frailty and advanced age as well as her understanding that any procedure she ordered might add to the patient's pain; but it distressed her to know that her opinion differed from that of other physicians. Her fundamental uncertainty about medicine's uses of aggressive treatment "to keep them alive" and about her own responsibility "in situations like that" is powerfully expressed at the close of her story: "I can make the mistake of thinking that keeping them alive is good for them."

Nurses' Voices

Like physicians, nurses function in a world of clinical and moral ambiguity when it comes to dying patients, but their mandate is different and so, therefore, is their focus when talking about end-of-life care. The nurses' role is to make the patient as comfortable as possible, while at the same time ensuring the best possible medical outcome. Nurses use the word *comfort* more often than doctors do and in a different sense. For nurses it simultaneously encompasses a moral stance, clinical knowledge, and the tangible, practical skills in which they have developed expertise. They also use specific words such as *torture* and *suffering* to define the opposite of comfort, words that physicians use much less often. When doctors use the term *comfort,* especially as an alternative to invasive interventions at the end of life, it remains secondary to locating disease and dysfunction and discovering, through clinical skill and diagnostic procedures, what is hidden in the body. Those tasks almost always take priority in the physician's perspective, especially in the ICU (at least until multiple-system organ failure can no longer be ignored). The primacy of the need for diagnostic discovery and then for medical action contributes to the unease many doctors experience when death is near. In contrast, nurses have a clear mandate to alleviate pain and suffering, especially in the intensive care unit. This presents them with ongoing challenges, both for working well with physicians and for creating a space in which the well-being of the patient can be demonstrated to their own satisfaction.

When I asked nurses to talk about how they handle those challenges, they responded with portraits of how they see their work, their patients, and the practices that define comfort. A nurse with sixteen years' experience in intensive care units talked about her goals of care for patients who spend days or weeks in the ICU but neither recover enough to leave nor die:

"Well, for the most part what I say is, this is my opportunity to practice good nursing so that when someone comes along who can be saved, I'll be really good at my job. And I do mean that. The fact that these people are there, that they are sort of trapped in their disease, in their bodies, in the ICU, isn't my fault. And it isn't up to me to change it. So my goal for those people is that they have the most comfortable day possible. Whether that means being left alone, and sometimes it does, or getting a nice bath, or helping their families come to terms, or whatever. Maybe tune up their pain meds. Pain that isn't obvious and that isn't being addressed. My moral sense of it is to say, I just want my patients to be more comfortable at the end of the day, when I leave them, than when I found them in the morning.

"That can be a challenge in the ICU. To just help this purgatory that they are in—to use this ever so Catholic term—to be tolerable, to be somewhat more manageable at some level. And for myself, to have the opportunity to be really good at what I do. I get to sit down and listen to a daughter or wife or mother or lover and let them talk and let them cry. And I try to do that, to just be there, because if it were up to me, I would probably change it. I would say, what are the chances of this person living? At what point are we being futile? How many days are we going to pursue this treatment? And if we really did something less elaborate, maybe one out of a hundred would live, but the other ninety-nine would not be tortured."

Another experienced critical care nurse spoke about the tension between technology and care and creating comfort in its midst: "I think nurses go into critical care and get into that environment because there's a sort of rush they get by taking care of someone who is not doing well, and there's this constant emotion and they're involved and really active. The doc and the nurses work very well together, so there's this collegiality that goes on differently than it does in other units, and that is very appealing to the nurses. Technology can sometimes be a bad thing in the critical care environment because the more technology you have, the more people want to try and use it in situations where it's not necessarily advantageous. When I'm taking care of really sick patients, I want them to be comfortable. I want families to be comfortable, and I want them to trust that I know what I'm doing and will do my best to make sure that they get what they need. So if they're going to improve, they'll do it, and if they're not going to improve, then they'll be comfortable, and I'll be honest about what's going on with them. It's a tough question because technology is so much what we do. Critical care nurses are very technology-oriented, very task-oriented. We've come a long way about thinking about what the plan is for this patient. Forget about the monitor, forget about the IV, forget about this stuff. What is the plan? Where are we going? What's the ultimate goal here, the goal for the patient? Is the goal to get them home? Is the goal to let them die in peace? Is the goal to get them to a med-surg unit? What is the goal here? And to that end, what are all the steps we need to take to get there—to get away from thinking about the monitor that they're on, or the IV that they're hooked to, or the machine that they're attached to."

A third nurse described her responsibility to create comfort in the presence of physical suffering:

"You have a responsibility to sedate people. But there are people who are undersedated. On a routine basis, undersedated. You have a huge tube in your mouth. When I talk to people afterward who have been through it, I love to hear what they have to say, because I don't know at the time, and I'll ask, 'How was that for you? What were your perceptions of it?' because that's what's real, what they're perceiving. And people have said, 'Oh, it felt like there was a shoe in my mouth, this huge thing was in my mouth.' You're not eating, you're not breathing on your own, all the things that you take for granted. You're not clean. People don't get their hair washed, you're just laying there matted, and that's sort of the baseline discomfort. But if you add on to it their aches and pains and the inability to communicate, which in and of itself is one of the biggest stressors any human being could go through. Imagine if nobody could hear what you said, or you were voiceless, how impotent and frustrated you would feel. So that's just your basic baseline suffering. And then you can add on to it the uncertainty of your family. If you're a mother, and your children are unattended, and you've got cancer, or you're bleeding for some reason, and you can't get out, then utter panic.

"And so all that is there. It's just a given. But we don't see it, we're immune. And you have to sort of think about it as a given, all the time. If you forget that, then you're doing everybody a disservice. If you remember, then you're going to talk to everybody very, very differently. You're not going to be put out to do something for them—put a cool cloth on their head or wipe their face or do their mouth care—because it's the least you can do.

"Suffering beyond that is subjective. And I've had to convince doctors on occasion. I had a young man, a thirty-five-year-old man, who had arteriovenus malformation. That's like a freeway in your brain, an intersection of vessels in there, and sometimes you get these things from birth, and they have many weak walls, and they can rupture. It's like a time bomb if you have one. And his had ruptured. And he was young and energetic and full of life going into it. And the pain. When he was awake and going downhill, he was holding his head and said it felt like a balloon bursting and there was just this horrible pain. The next day, it made him unable to talk, and we were sitting there watching the death, and there was nothing we could do. He had already bled and they couldn't get in there to repair it because he would die on the [operating] table. You don't take anybody to surgery if they're not going to survive the surgery. At that point he hadn't had anything, no pain medicine whatsoever. The doctor on call didn't know him, and he wasn't thinking about the long night that this human being was going to have. But then every five-, ten-minute increment, if you're standing there, you can see it, and you just, all you have to do is put your hand there, you can just feel the suffering, you don't have to even hear him say it. The doctor said, 'Well, his blood pressure is fine and his heart rate isn't high,' and I just knew he had the worst headache of his entire life. And I said, 'You know, if he is in fact dying, couldn't we just give him something?' And they don't want to because it's a neural injury and then you would obscure further decline. There are many times when nurses intervene.

"So he did get something and he did relax, visibly relax. And at that point, you have to think what it would be like to be alone, dying, in the middle of the night. If there was no one there to hold his hand, and you could have held his hand [but didn't], then it makes you less of a person."

Nurses describe a tension between the "purgatory" of invasive medicine on the one hand and their mandate and ability to reduce suffering on the other. Those who choose to work in intensive care can articulate (more easily than physicians, it seems) a critique of medicine's most sophisticated tools when those tools interfere with the patient's need for comfort and nurses' deeply felt imperative to provide it. Nurses sometimes worry about what kind of people they are as they struggle to work amid the conflicts generated by hospital, and especially ICU, medicine.

Evasiveness about Death and the Problem of Prognostication

Both nurses and doctors are evasive about death—the nurses because they do not want to overstep their authority, the doctors for more complex reasons. Physician evasiveness is a major factor in heightening the tensions families and patients sometimes feel at the threshold and in maintaining the illusion that they have "choices" about what to do. Doctors are particularly evasive when discussing death. Filmmaker Frederick Wiseman has made an extraordinary six-hour documentary film, *Near Death*,[31] about minute-to-minute decision-making, deliberation, and treatment in the intensive care unit at Beth Israel Hospital in Boston. Wiseman lets viewers observe the private bedside conversations between physicians and critically ill patients about their precarious conditions and their treatment options as well as the long deliberations in the ICU corridors among the doctors and nurses about how much to do, which treatments to employ and when, and what the patient and the patient's family want to do next. We, the film's audience, become privy to the language physicians and nurses use when they talk to and about very sick patients, and we hear how patients and families respond. This is not like the television show *ER*. The conversations are not short, dramatic, authoritative, or to the point. In fact, they are the opposite—long, tedious, equivocal, repetitive, and without resolution.

The camera follows four very sick patients and their families. In each case the physicians spend considerable time at the bedside and in the hallways in earnest discussion about what to do with patients, families, and other medical staff. In each case they claim to want to be guided by

patient and family decision-making. The physicians in the film continually ask patients and families what they want to do next—about specific
treatments, about whether the patient wants to stop treatment, about
whether the patient wants to "live" indefinitely on a ventilator in the ICU.
(Physician to patient with end-stage heart disease: "There are very few
people who could make as informed a judgment as you can with everything that you've been through.") But doctors and nurses are often
ambivalent about how, and whether, patients or families should actually
be in charge of decision-making regarding the withdrawal, continuation,
or start of new treatments. (Nurse to doctor: "Include them, but do not
let them make the decision. Families have way too much responsibility.")

The filmed physicians are articulate and compassionate. They come
across as sincere and knowledgeable. Their talk seems endless. Yet in
each case, regardless of the hours and hours of talk with and about
patients, the physicians remain entirely evasive about death. Instead
they talk extensively about stabilizing the medical condition or about
potential organ system recovery, and that talk misleads patients. (Doctor to patient: "Your lungs aren't going to get better, and so the act of
putting you on the machine is almost a futile effort. We'd use the tube if
you got worse, if something went wrong with your heart. We only want
to do what you want to do—if you want to live.") They rarely mention
death per se. They never tell patients that no matter which treatments
they choose, their medical condition will lead to death, or that death is
imminent. (Physician to medical team: "We can probably drag this out
for a week. That's okay with me if that's what he wants. But let's get the
cardiologist up here to make sure there isn't something else we can do."
Or, nurse to wife of patient: "We can expect him to get worse, to decline.
But we can still look for treatable things.")

Doctors in the film insist over and over that they do not know what
will happen and that they cannot predict the future. ("You're in a bor-
derline situation between surviving and not surviving." And, "God
decides. We don't. These things have a life of their own, they really do.")
They talk almost exclusively about treatment options for the control of
disease and regulation of specific systems, and the fact that patients (or
families) have the right to choose among those options. With other
medical staff they speak about organs and organ systems and what they
could do to reverse a particular problem. And they confuse patients and
families by telling them that they can, at any time, change their minds

about their advance directives and, specifically, about emergency CPR, thus intimating that resuscitation could "save" their lives.

The physicians in the film believe in hope, and they say repeatedly that there is always hope. To families and to each other they speak about hope in terms of percentages—Mr. Smith has a one-in-a-million chance. They never speak about decision-making in the face of death.

The film's final credits report that all the patients profiled died either in the ICU or within a week of being discharged from the ICU. None ever left the hospital.

In his study of medical prognosis, Nicholas Christakis ponders deeply the ways in which prognostication about death is avoided in clinical medicine and notes that prognosis is surrounded by a "structured silence" that is learned and then cultivated in everyday medical practice.[32] Physicians talk about prognosis only when it is unavoidable, and when they do, they tell "bad news" in highly formulaic ways. They favor a "staged, statistical, and optimistic form of prognostication"[33] in which an unfavorable prognosis is given to patients in stages, is couched in optimism and hope, is influenced by what doctors think patients want to hear, and refers to statistics about similar patients. Physicians tend to overestimate survival both to themselves and to patients.[34] Furthermore, they are inadequately trained in prognosis. They tend to experience emotional stress when they feel forced to predict the future, and they fear that blatant prognostication can harm patients.[35] Physicians are mindful of the ways in which information is delivered to patients and families, and they understand "truthfulness" in prognosis to have many forms of expression, depending on their reading of how severe the patient perceives his or her disease to be as well as on their own need to deliver a sense of hope. Most do not view "truth" as a single fact, disconnected from the ways in which patients express a need to know things and with only one form of telling. It is an exceptional doctor who talks about death straight on, before visible signs of dying are evident, even when patients or family members start to ask questions around it.

Illusions of Choice

Patient and family participation in decision-making has been hailed as a positive development in contemporary medicine. In the context of serious illness and decline in the hospital, however, it is a distortion or misrepresentation because the choices available are actually guided and limited by the options physicians and others present. Those, in turn, exist within a system of institutional directives. In addition, patient and family "decision-making" when death is or seems to be near confounds notions of physician responsibility and good communication. Critics of medical practice suggest that, in seeming to offer multiple treatment choices for end-of-life conditions, physicians' expertise and experience are devalued and their accountability is potentially or actually abdicated and eroded.[36] Patients and families are thus thrust into choice-making situations for which they are entirely unprepared. At the same time, patients assume that physicians have a great deal of authority and expertise and want them to use it to decide what is best. A recent Harris poll found that two-thirds of Americans desire "personal choice" at the end of life.[37] But inside the hospital such choice is elusive, far from simple, and it fuels the "problem" of death.

Two ubiquitous features of the hospital world, the mechanical ventilator and the ever-present possibility of emergency resuscitation, figure prominently in the widespread conversation of complaint and contribute to impossible choices for patients and families, and sometimes, to disagreement among physicians.

Imagining Imminent Death:
Code Status and Emergency Resuscitation

One tension that permeates hospital culture is created by the possibility of employing emergency cardiopulmonary resuscitation, CPR, a potentially lifesaving, yet always dreaded, procedure. The issue of "code status"—determining whether a patient wishes to have cardiopulmonary resuscitation attempted in the event of cardiac or respiratory arrest—looms large in hospital culture, and it is frequently a dominant preoccupation of doctors and nurses when death seems near. While in the popular view CPR "can bring the dead back to life," this is not actually the case. In cardiac arrest, the heart is unable to effectively maintain the blood flow and blood pressure necessary to sustain life. In respiratory arrest, the patient is unable to move enough air to oxygenate the blood supply and tissues and thus to sustain life. In both situations, at the moment of arrest, *the patient is in danger of imminent death* unless something is done to reverse the problem.

Performing emergency CPR is called a *code* in hospital jargon, and if seriously ill hospital patients do not state that they wish to forgo a resuscitation attempt in the case of cardiac or respiratory arrest (or their family members do not speak up for them in this regard), the default procedure in nearly every American hospital is to attempt resuscitation in emergency life-threatening situations. To change the default "code status" of performing emergency resuscitation (referred to in the medical chart as "full code"), a written order stating "no CPR" or "no code" or "DNR" must be in the medical chart instead.[38] Thus to override the default action, patients must decide at some point prior to or during a hospitalization whether, during an emergency that threatens their survival, they would want medical personnel to thrust a breathing tube down their windpipe, perform chest compressions (possibly breaking ribs), and electrically shock the heart *in the hope* that a life-sustaining heart rhythm would be restored. Patients, and often their families, must envision a medical crisis in the future based on a hypothetical scenario. This, of course, is impossible to do. But this is what the hospital system sets up for people. Choice about a code status designation is not really open. Doctors often do not want to talk about code status to desperately sick persons or their families and frequently do not do so. Very sick patients usually do not initiate or wish to have those discussions either. So CPR is typically performed if no one speaks up against it, if the physician in charge of the case does nothing to prevent it, and if there is no DNR statement included in the patient's medical chart.

Hospitalized patients and their families generally do not realize that they must speak up if they do not want emergency resuscitation attempted. Most are unaware of the code status designation in the first place and have no idea what the term *code status* refers to. They do not think in terms of the specific, technical jobs that their doctors and nurses may perform to "save" their lives. After all, one comes to the hospital to turn care over to professionals, to relinquish the enormous responsibility for sustaining life and for making medical decisions. Medical treatment is always invested with a sense both of possibility and of foreboding because the interventions that may cause "miracles" also take place in a Kafkaesque setting where events unfold in ways one hardly understands. The result is that most of the time very sick persons do not really "decide" about resuscitation efforts at all.

Doctors do broach the topic of code status with patients and families when they feel strongly that a resuscitation attempt would be unsuccessful and would be terrible to perform prior to death—for instance, on those who have a terminal diagnosis and are thought to be near death anyway, as in the story below about Carol Jones, or on those frail elderly who have multiple, serious medical conditions indicating that the end of life is near. In such cases that I observed, physicians work to convince the patient or family "to choose" against a resuscitation attempt, and their efforts in that regard are a significant topic in the medical literature.[39] Since cardiac arrest often occurs at the end stage of an illness and is, under those circumstances, almost inevitably fatal, the standard to perform CPR is no small matter.

One of the most striking paradoxes of this feature of hospital culture is that the pressure physicians sometimes experience—to make sure patients or family understand that resuscitation will be attempted in an emergency if no one speaks up against it—makes families feel coerced, guilty, and without control. When presented with a mandatory "choice" of CPR or DNR, families infer that they have been handed the responsibility for determining the "life" or "death" of their relative. Many think that "choosing" to forgo a resuscitation attempt on their relative means that they are choosing the patient's death.

Resisting Choosing: The Family of Carol Jones

The CPR or DNR choice becomes important, indeed central, for Carol Jones's physicians when they recognize that she will soon die despite their efforts to treat her. They confront the patient's family with the request for a "decision" because they want to organize the least traumatic death possible. Having recognized the inevitability of death, the doctors want to avoid a resuscitation attempt, which they are certain will not succeed. In contrast, the physicians' moment of recognition comes as a shock to the family members, who, two weeks after the patient is hospitalized, apparently face for the first time both that the patient is unequivocally near death, regardless of her code status, and that they are responsible for choosing either a resuscitation attempt (with unknown outcome) or death without such an attempt.

Background: Carol Jones, age fifty, had not seen a doctor in ten years. When her abdomen swelled considerably, she went to her physician, who drew off a gallon of fluid, examined it, and found cancer cells. Her husband, brother, and three (young adult) children were shocked by the cancer diagnosis and could not imagine what the future would hold. They hoped and assumed that her condition could be treated; that is, that it could be made to go away. Mrs. Jones was hospitalized, and then things happened fast from the family's point of view. The surgeons found extensive cancer that was impossible to treat. They were not sure where the primary site had been, where it had begun.

After the surgery the physicians found they could not remove Mrs. Jones from the ventilator. Her condition was too precarious and she could not breathe without it. Following ordinary hospital protocol, Mrs. Jones was sent to the intensive care unit so that medical staff could attempt to stabilize her condition. Their goal was to allow her some time to live, and hospital staff hoped she could be removed from the mechanical ventilator and sent home, if only for a few days, to be with her family before she died.

Day 14: Two weeks after surgery Mrs. Jones is still in the intensive care unit, her life sustained by powerful medications, delivered intravenously, that keep her blood pressure at a viable level, and by the mechanical ventilator that breathes for her. She is not getting well enough to go home. She cannot be removed from the ventilator. All her organ systems are failing despite the stabilizing treatments, and so the physicians feel the time has come to shift their strategy. It is time for Mrs. Jones to die. The physicians want the family to acknowledge that the patient is dying and give the go-ahead to stop the treatments, which, staff now acknowledge, are only postponing her death. But the family, as is so typical, *does not know what to want.* They certainly do not want Mrs. Jones to die. They do not understand her condition in the same way the doctors do, and they have not been informed yet about her impending death.

Carol Jones's surgeon, family doctor, oncologist, and critical care specialist meet with the family to get their permission to stop what the physicians now consider to be death-prolonging treatments and to avoid what they are certain would be unsuccessful emergency resuscitation. The following conversation ensues:

Surgeon: Things seem to have taken a turn for the worse, all over. She has a fever; that means infection. She has lots of strikes against her: malnourished, cancer, pneumonia, poor lung function. Never able to get water off the lungs. Not absorbing anything in her gut. And now her heart. We're using medications that we only use in cardiac arrest patients. These are major problems. . . . I think you have to be involved. This is the 1990s, not the 1930s or '40s or '50s when doc-

tors just decided everything. And you have to make a decision. We
can discontinue antibiotics. . . .

Family physician: If you do decide to let go, if you do decide to accept
the inevitable, is another way to say it, to give her dignity.

Surgeon: As her primary surgeon, I need from you the code status. She
is being resuscitated right now with drugs. She can't make an
informed decision. Should she be shocked? Defibrillated? We need
to know yes or no. You can say, "Don't go higher on the drugs." We
could dial them down. For me, the main issue is shocking the
heart. It's not active, it's just saying if her heart stops, you wouldn't
want to do this. I'd like a decision from you before this conference
is over.

Daughter: We need time to think about that and we'd like to consult
with you. (She breaks down and cries.)

Family physician (contradicting the request of the surgeon): We respect
that. You don't have to make that decision now.

The meeting concludes with no resolution for the doctors either
about avoiding a routine attempt at CPR in the case of cardiac arrest or
about allowing her to die with the modicum of "dignity"—always a relative term—they could conjure up by withdrawing respiratory and pharmacological support before she has a feared cardiac arrest.

Later the same day, the surgeon tells me that if even one family member does not agree with the others about code status, it is best to wait, so
that that family member does not feel railroaded into making a decision
that he "killed the patient." I learn from Mrs. Jones's nurse that the
patient's daughter came to Mrs. Jones's bedside a few hours after the conference, in tears. She stayed for nearly a half an hour and then went to talk
with the surgeon. The nurse informs me that shortly afterward Mrs. Jones
was made No Code, that is, no CPR in the event of a cardiac arrest. The
daughter made the decision the physicians hoped she would make, and at
their insistence, but it was impossible for her to do so when, surprising
her, they first broached the topic during the conference.

Day 28: Mrs. Jones has experienced more irreversible medical complications during the past two weeks. Two intensive care physicians
speak with Mrs. Jones's husband at length, letting him know that "it is
time for her to die." That is, it is time to remove life-sustaining medications and allow her to die from her advanced disease—before she has a

cardiac arrest. A nurse mentions to me that the patient's husband is finally "ready to let her go." He tells her, "I don't want to see her suffer anymore." The doctors tell Mr. Jones their plan for a death as dignified as possible given the circumstances: to lower, over a period of hours, the powerful blood-pressure medications that are keeping the patient alive. They will do this, they say, after the family arrives at the bedside tomorrow so that they can be with the patient during her last moments of life. They start an intravenous morphine drip, to reduce any pain the patient might experience.[40]

Day 29: The doctors gradually reduce the life-sustaining medications Mrs. Jones is receiving. Mrs. Jones dies five hours later, with her husband and children at her bedside and with all her intravenous lines and the mechanical ventilator still in place.

During my research, I attended many conferences and bedside conversations in which I listened to physicians offer families information about the diseased body and the hospital and the way things work. It was information that they, the medical team, took for granted but that families had great difficulty interpreting. Yet, though doctors are authoritative and possess knowledge that patients and families do not have, they are not all-knowing, and only when they anticipate or fear a death do doctors want to focus on their potential next move—getting a code-status decision, giving more life-prolonging treatments or withdrawing them, and preparing the patient and family for death. And so, when they know the patient is at the threshold of death, they speak loosely about a kind of "death with dignity" that they understand is merely a decision to stop life-prolonging medical procedures *before* a cardiac arrest or other form of death can occur. That, in their opinion, would be less dignified for the patient and certainly more messy and intensive for the staff.

The family, on the other hand, may not be aware of the potential for cardiac arrest and is usually not concerned about the urgency of decision-making. (Family members with previous hospital experience or who are health care professionals themselves are exceptions.) Mrs. Jones's family was not informed about the importance, for the doctors, of a code status until she had been in the hospital for two weeks.[41] Until the conference with the doctors, they did not know that the technologies keeping Mrs. Jones alive were only postponing her death and not contributing either to the reduction of suffering or to recovery. Families like the Joneses are thrust into a disorienting world that presents them with disquieting dilemmas: If Carol is already being "resuscitated" with drugs, does that mean she is only alive "artificially"? Why are the doctors demanding a family decision right now about defibrillation? If the first procedure (blood-pressure-stabilizing drugs) is standard of care—that is, no one asks the family for its opinion; it's just what is done—why must the second procedure be determined by family? And why at that particular moment? Families are called upon to respond quickly to complex information that is emotionally overwhelming. They never want to "choose" death, though many accept death, usually after speaking with doctors, when they realize that it is inevitable. It is no wonder that some do not easily accept the logic of hospital-mandated choice.

Physician Disagreement about Code Status Designation: Sam Martin

Sometimes doctors disagree among themselves about the inevitability of death and about whether a resuscitation attempt should be avoided. One physician may think that a potential resuscitation attempt could maintain life, while another is confident that it would not be successful. They disagree about whether a patient's choice, made before the current crisis, for no emergency CPR should be disregarded. I observed, though only a few times, changes in a patient's code status that had been recorded in the medical chart, changes that reflected physician disagreement about what should be done if the patient suffered a cardiac or respiratory arrest. Patients and families are usually not aware of such differences of opinion or of changes made to the code status designation.

One significant factor in physician disagreements is that the hospital bureaucracy seems to prohibit any official memory of a patient's desired code status. Even when advance directives are already in the medical chart, potential resuscitation terms are often renegotiated. However, individual physicians who know particular patients do remember previous code status decisions and write them in the medical record. Thus physicians are able, in many cases, to provide continuity from one hospitalization to the next even when a patient's voice is silenced by disease. The following story provides one example of the way a code status "decision" unfolds.

Sam Martin, who had congestive heart failure, was moved to the ICU five days after admission to the general medical ward. Already hospitalized several times, Mr. Martin was knowledgeable about the institution's need for a code status decision and said, in no uncertain terms, that in the event of a massive brain injury he did not want his life prolonged and did not want to be resuscitated if he suffered a cardiac arrest. "Do Not Resuscitate" was written in his medical chart, as it had been during each of his previous hospitalizations that year. Once admitted to the ICU, however, Mr. Martin's code status became a zone of struggle for the hospital physicians. The cardiologist wanted to treat him with certain drugs under certain circumstances, thereby making him a "pharmacological code." That is, Mr. Martin would receive vasopressor medications if the cardiologist thought those were medically indicated to "get him over this hump," but, abiding by his wishes, physicians would not shock his heart and his chest would not be pounded. Emergency resuscitation has subdivisions.[42] Another doctor, who had been in charge of Mr. Martin's care on the medical floor, insisted that the No Code status be retained in the ICU. The designation was changed several times in the medical chart over the next two days. Mr. Martin, though seriously ill, remained alert and entirely competent during that period. His medical chart did not indicate whether he was aware of the repeated changes. Finally, the cardiologist capitulated and Mr. Martin was made No Code. He got somewhat better and was discharged from the hospital several days later.

Two years later, when Mr. Martin was admitted to the hospital for the last time, his code status was contested anew. He had had a cardiac arrest at home, and a friend who was there performed emergency CPR. The paramedics arrived a few minutes later and shocked Mr. Martin several times, finally normalizing his cardiac rhythm. He was put on a respirator to aid his breathing and taken to the hospital emergency department, where he remained unresponsive. When hospitalized for congestive heart failure just three weeks earlier, Mr. Martin had again requested that "Do Not Resuscitate" be written in his medical chart. Despite those consistent documents, his only living relative, characterized as "distant" by hospital staff, stated that Mr. Martin "would wish full support in the event of some reversible brain injury."

Because no one could predict with absolute certainty that Mr. Martin's condition was irreversible, mechanical ventilation was continued and he was transferred to the ICU. There he was designated Full Code, to be resuscitated in the event of a cardiac arrest "pending further discussions with the family and primary team." The consulting neurologist wrote in the medical record, "He has sustained anoxic brain injury. The magnitude of this injury is profound. Given his history, it is my impression that the likelihood of his making a meaningful recovery from this event is small. . . . I understand that the patient had a prior directive that indicated that should he sustain irreversible brain injury, he would not want to be maintained on a ventilator. Given this, if the family wishes to withdraw him from the ventilator, this would be appropriate." The hospital social worker said that the patient's relative "was aware of the patient's wishes" and that "she will need to sign another DNR form today because the last DNR was signed by the patient on the last hospital admission." To complicate matters, Mr. Martin began to breathe, though weakly, on his own.

A few hours after the neurologist added his note, the ICU physician wrote "Do Not Resuscitate" in the medical chart. Mr. Martin was cared for aggressively for another forty-eight hours, in hopes of improvement. Two days after his admission to the ICU, Mr. Martin's only relative had a long discussion with the intensive care physician. Together they confirmed that Mr. Martin did not want to be kept alive if he was in a permanent coma or was neurologically devastated. Life-sustaining blood pressure medications and the mechanical ventilator were withdrawn, and the physician wrote "according to the patient's wishes" in the medical chart. Mr. Martin died shortly thereafter.

The Mechanical Ventilator: "Deciding" to Use a Powerful Tool

The negative public reaction to the mechanical ventilator has sparked the "right to die" movement across the United States and inspired the widespread cry for "death with dignity." The mechanical ventilator is a machine that "breathes," by forcing air directly into the lungs of patients who cannot breathe for themselves due to a loss of lung or brain function. It is standard practice in American hospitals to use mechanical ventilation if the patient would otherwise die immediately without it. It will be employed, if needed, unless patients make it clearly known, through living wills or other written documents if they cannot communicate, that they do not want their bodily functions thus sustained, or unless they have advocates who can persistently and effectively express this wish to hospital staff.

"Deciding," when one is not in a medical crisis, that one does not want this life-sustaining tool may seem relatively straightforward. But forgoing air when one is desperate for it is another matter. Then the abstract, before-the-fact opinion that a ventilator is "unwanted life support" becomes irrelevant. And often the ventilator is in place before one is even capable of "deciding." Patients, families, and health professionals will face more "choices" when they learn that it cannot be removed because the patient will not be able to breathe "naturally." Then the choices are constructed around the problems of when, why, and how to withdraw ventilator support so that the patient can "be allowed" to die. These choices must also be made in the face of a trap that the mechanical ventilator has created: it confers upon the decider a perceived responsibility for either "unnaturally" prolonging dying or proactively "causing" death.

Choosing Breath: Bertha Hanson

Before her admission to the hospital, Bertha Hanson, eighty-four years old and frail, was becoming increasingly short of breath. She had pneumonia and a high fever. On admission she agreed to aggressive medical treatment and a feeding tube, if that became necessary, because she was not eating much and was losing strength. But she had made it clear she did not want anyone to try to resuscitate her if she had a cardiac arrest or to place her on a mechanical ventilator if she stopped breathing.

At the end of Mrs. Hanson's second week in the hospital, I went to her room with a respiratory therapist, who wanted to see if Mrs. Hanson would breathe more easily if her nasal cannulas were replaced with a mask that pushes oxygen into the nose and lungs. The therapist spent about half an hour gently, cautiously putting the mask on Mrs. Hanson, adjusting the elastic straps on her cheeks. She set the pressure and volume levels, hoping to make Mrs. Hanson comfortable by increasing the oxygen supply, but Mrs. Hanson was exceedingly uncomfortable and grew agitated with the mask strapped to her face. To me, she looked as if she were suffocating, and she struggled against the oxygen flow rather than relaxing into it and letting the machine breathe for her, as she was prompted to do. Utterly exhausted, Mrs. Hanson finally told the therapist to take the mask off.[43]

Later the same night Mrs. Hanson's oxygen level desaturated to about 60 percent (a normal saturation level is in the high nineties). "Not compatible with life for very long," one physician explained.[44] She was simply not getting enough air and was in "respiratory distress." Her daughter, who had been at her bedside all day, asked her, "Should we help you breathe?" and Mrs. Hanson nodded yes. She was moved immediately to the ICU, where a mechanical ventilator tube was inserted down her windpipe and where she and the ventilator could be monitored. The medical chart stated that she "had a near respiratory arrest. At that time she was profoundly short of breath and did agree to be intubated and placed on mechanical ventilator."

Mrs. Hanson's fever persisted and she continued to receive antibiotics, but after two days in the ICU, she slipped into unconsciousness. After diagnostic tests did not reveal anything that could lead to curative therapies, the critical care physicians explained to the patient's daughter that nothing would reverse Mrs. Hanson's condition or "save" her life. Mrs. Hanson's daughter then "decided" to have her mother removed from the ventilator, allowing her to die. Mrs. Hanson died in the ICU about an hour later.

Mrs. Hanson wanted, and chose, to breathe. Her daughter assumed that the mechanical ventilator would be, simply, a short-term solution to her mother's medical crisis. She, like many other family members I observed, could not imagine that the patient's respiratory distress indicated the end of her life.

Mrs. Hanson's move from the medical floor to the ICU was not unusual, and neither was her death there. In the panic of respiratory distress, the need to breathe overwhelms any prejudgment about what one "wants." Once someone is in the hospital, treatments to alleviate respiratory distress are instantly available, and mostly, their use prolongs wanted life and is much appreciated. Respiratory distress is, however, also a visible and traditional indicator of dying, though it is no longer assumed to signify or precede inevitable death, and so it is not widely tolerated. It is no wonder that so many Americans' lives end in an intensive care unit.

Failure to Imagine

Of all the players in the hospital, patients and families know the least about the way the hospital works and the limits of therapy. Many, perhaps most, people do not know what *life support* entails operationally and do not understand the limits of cardiopulmonary resuscitation or mechanical ventilation. They have little knowledge of human physiology or the processes of serious disease and their treatments or physical markers, such as shortness of breath or the dying transition. They do not understand the institutional rules that drive much of medical practice in the hospital: patients must be discharged as quickly as possible; patients can remain on particular hospital units only if they are receiving specific therapies; someone has to choose whether resuscitation or the ventilator is wanted; physicians often decide the right moment for dying.[45] Families are not prepared for the emotional turmoil and guilt that arise when they are confronted with complex, apparently life-or-death options—whether to start or stop life-sustaining drugs, or, in an emergency with no time to reflect, to begin artificial ventilation with a breathing machine.

Modern hospital practices place physicians, patients, and families each in quite different but equally untenable positions. Physicians I observed feel a strong pressure from the hospital, the law, and contemporary norms to ask patients—or family members if the patient is silenced by illness—to express an opinion about actions the consequences of which neither patient nor family can anticipate.[46] Sometimes, as we saw in the case of Carol Jones, physicians back down about the urgency of their requests when confronted with grief, shock, confusion, refusal, and what I observed to be a striking inability to cope with making "choices" about procedures. Many families demonstrated this inability, regardless of education level or any other sociodemographic feature. It is ironic that the American health care system's emphasis on "patient autonomy" includes, in a practical sense, the need for families to speak for patients who are too ill to express an opinion about how they want to die. But families sometimes resist speaking for patients (or sometimes contradict patients who can speak), and that frustrates physicians. Families rarely want to shoulder medical decision-making responsibility, and they view procedural choices ("Should she be defibrillated?" or "Should she be placed on or removed from a ventilator?") not as options for managing death but as assuming responsibility for "killing" the patient.

Despite the abundance of personal accounts in the media about what happens to critically ill and dying persons in the hospital, it struck me throughout my research that people newly immersed in the hospital world have not absorbed lessons from those stories. They have not been meaningfully forewarned about the way hospital treatment and hospital logic work to prolong life, stave off dying, and then make death happen. Though poignant, detailed, and far-reaching, the now-so-public conversation of control and complaint simply has no effect at the existential moment of confrontation with critical care medicine and hospital bureaucracy. For most patients and families the experience of hospitalization is disorienting and all-consuming. They cannot imagine that they are enmeshed in a phenomenon made up of an institutionalized pathway of treatments, a trajectory of disease, rules about hospital finance, and the press to use aggressive interventions. Most people cannot imagine either hospital procedures that stave off death but do not restore health or the terrible responsibility for turning off life support. Neither can they imagine death itself.

DEATH IN LIFE

The "Person" and the Experience of Dying

"... Life and death are not properly scientific concepts but rather political concepts, which as such acquire a political meaning precisely only through a decision."

Giorgio Agamben
Homo Sacer

Central to the discourse about hospital dying is a deep, often anguished concern about what happens to the "person" who is a patient at the threshold between life and death. Hospital practices and treatments for critically ill patients who are near death raise questions about what it means to be fully "alive," to be fully a "person." Several features of hospital practice invite investigation of how the *person* and *life* come to be understood and evaluated; the most compelling among them are the intensive care unit and the routines and dramas that dominate it; the feeding tube and the controversies and symbols that surround it; the prolonged comatose state and the technological and institutional apparatuses that support it; and the fact that in the hospital the relationship between disease in late life and "normal" old age—when it approaches death—is not at all straightforward. Taken together, these four features of medical practice within the hospital have opened a realm in which the distinction between *life* and *death* becomes blurred and contested—

for clinical expertise, biomedical technologies, and hospital routines can sustain essential aspects of biological existence even when signs of a unique, valuable *individual's life* are absent or questionable. The physiological processes that indicate some degree of *aliveness* can medically be sustained in a body that would die without technological and institutional support. Thus the bureaucratic imperatives of the hospital, when combined with medicine's management of the end of life, can bring *death into life* in a manner impossible to achieve before the recent era, and *life* and *death* have become entangled to the point that they are now indistinguishable.

The on-the-ground organizational activities associated with the intensive care unit, the ventilator, the feeding tube, the prolonged comatose state, and states of being that are neither "comatose" nor "awake" or "alert," taken together, have created this zone of indistinction[1] that is now a normal part of the American hospital world and a commonplace creation of medical work. It is a gray zone between health, awareness, function, and viable *life* on the one hand, and "no longer a person," "death in life," or *death* on the other hand. This gray zone has become exquisitely complex during the past thirty years and has spread—into new kinds of hospitals, into more patients' lives and families' worlds, to more medical conditions and corporeal states. Though the zone of indistinction is by now considered a normal and ordinary hospital phenomenon, its emergence and broadening have deepened societal anxiety about how we can recognize the end of an individual's life or the end of a *natural* life and about how we can recognize the presence of suffering.[2] The existence of this zone, born of the confluence of routine medical practice, hospital organization, and the cultural force of respect for individual rights, creates a pervasive predicament. The anxiety it provokes is inescapable. It has led us to ask, *What can we do about dying? What actions can and should we take?*

Death Moves into the Body

Death is shaped, known, defined, and disputed through the varied forms of human activity that surround it. Thus death is not a natural phenomenon; it is made. And the ways in which death is made vary tremendously culturally and historically. There is no such thing as a death that occurs beyond the boundaries of society and historical moment, social norms and expectations, tradition and cultural innovation. In his comprehensive history of death in the Western world, Philippe Ariès traces relationships among religious rituals, community practices surrounding the dying, the corpse and the bereaved, and emerging notions of disease to show how knowledge of death and practices surrounding it have changed over two thousand years. For most of that span of time, doctors were rarely at the bedside and death was not associated with medical treatments.

For well over a thousand years, death was a public event rather than the private family matter it has now become. Until the nineteenth century, the *ars moriendi* (dying well, the art of dying) of the fifteenth century provided the model of how a spiritual passage—of crossing a critical threshold from life into the unknown—should unfold. Though the deathbed scene was a drama that unfolded in public view—the deathbed chamber was freely entered by family and neighbors as they all waited for death to arrive—it nonetheless embodied a private, intimate relationship between the act of crossing that threshold and the dying individual. Ariès writes, "The fate of the dying man was decided for the last time, in which his whole life and all his passions and attachments were called into question."[3]

By the end of the eighteenth century, death began to be understood as located in the body, as resulting from something that happened to the body. Philosopher-historian Michel Foucault describes the emergence of anatomic understandings of the body together with clinical understandings of disease in his history of modern medicine's "gaze," that is, its apprehension of relationships among disease symptoms, internal organs, and medical knowledge and practice.[4] That new gaze became more focused and elaborated during the nineteenth century's developments in the biological sciences, and soon death was seen to result from disease or some natural process or anomaly, located deep within the body, to be known and attended to by doctors. New, clinical understandings of pathology established an unprecedented, previously inconceivable relationship between death and life—death was an aspect of life and it was encompassed by life. Medicine made death visible to the doctor. *The dying person was transformed into the patient.* The most powerful terms in which death was understood shifted from religion and the invisible, fateful crossing at the deathbed to medicine's attendance at, and more recently intervention in, the disease process. Modern medicine's task vis-à-vis death has been ironic from the start: to understand how disease works in the body and to deny the power of death, a power that for millennia had been understood as a "natural" truth.

The legendary physician William Osler was the first in the United States to ask how death enters the body. He conducted a study of "the sensations of the dying" at Johns Hopkins University Hospital between 1900 and 1904. His was the first modern, systematic attempt to learn what happens to the person and the body as death approaches. Osler asked nurses to monitor and document the signs of distress and physical decline among a group of almost five hundred patients. "Ninety suffered bodily pain or distress of one sort or another, eleven showed mental apprehension, two positive terror, one expressed spiritual exaltation, one bitter remorse. The great majority gave no sign one way or the other; like their birth, their death was a sleep and a forgetting," Osler wrote.[5] Most people died peacefully, he claimed, because most were in some sort of coma. His project was a pathbreaking attempt to understand the physiology of the dying transition and its expression in individual difference.

Karen Quinlan: New Kind of Person, New Kind of Problem

It is difficult to pinpoint an exact moment when dying emerged publicly as being problematic in American life. However, the 1975–76 publicity surrounding the court case of Karen Ann Quinlan moved the topic of medical decision-making—the question of who best represents the patient's interest and, most important, the fear of a lingering and grotesque death—squarely into the public domain. Karen Quinlan, a comatose woman, became famous when her parents, after months of deliberation and soul-searching, sought to have her removed from the mechanical ventilator that was enabling her to breathe, thus keeping her alive.[6] When Karen's doctor and the hospital administration refused to disconnect the machine, fearing criminal prosecution or other sanctions, her parents petitioned first the Superior Court of New Jersey and then that state's supreme court to have it withdrawn. The supreme court eventually ruled in favor of the Quinlans. (After the ventilator was removed, Karen existed in an unresponsive condition for nine years before she finally died.)

The Quinlan case opened a door to a new world of medical challenges and, most important, forced everyone involved with her to ask a new question: What shall we do about her? This comatose young woman tethered to a breathing machine was a new kind of person—not fully alive and not quite dead—created by the confluence of high-tech machinery, attentive medical and nursing care, and the influence of the law on medical practice. She was also a new kind of problem, a dilemma that burst out of the borders of traditional clinical medicine and into other domains, including the existential. *What to do?* perplexed everyone. Debates about who had the right to prolong or end her life moved from private conversations at her hospital bedside into professional journals, the courts, and the media. Discussion about who is in charge of a person in a coma, what constitutes a life worth living, who authorizes death, and the dark side of advanced technologies that can foster a new state of being—*death-in-life*—emerged into national consciousness. The case of Karen Ann Quinlan made two troubling issues apparent to a broad public: First, medical technology could contribute to, could in fact create, bizarre and unnatural forms of human life and could foster new kinds of suffering for the family and medical staff and perhaps for the machine-dependent person. Second, "death" could become *a matter of deciding when a person should die and when a person should be considered dead.*[7]

The Quinlan case was emblematic of the most recent shift in the public perception of dying—from something inevitable that simply happens, to an event to be staved off, an act over which one must assert control, a clinical dilemma and a technical decision. Yet that shift actually came about somewhat gradually, beginning in the 1950s and continuing through the 1970s and 1980s, with a number of changes in both the medical and social landscapes. Chief among these changes were developments in the ways physicians *saw* their patients (including the identification of the patient-as-person in clinical medicine), the broadening location of disease, and a dramatic change in what the physician *heard* when a patient spoke about himself and his illness. These developments were to become central to the perception that death is problematic.

From Disease to Life: The Emerging Patient-as-Person in Medicine

In their social history of the changing power of clinical intervention, William Ray Arney and Bernard J. Bergen (a sociologist and psychiatrist, respectively) describe how, during the mid–twentieth century, medical thinking and practice regarding what troubles the patient became restructured.[8] Clinical medicine began to order patients' lives in a new way—by managing and delineating the entire life cycle, including death. This was medicine's "new revolution," one that Arney and Bergen claim was as significant a transformation as the one described by Foucault that brought scientific medicine into existence around 1800.[9] In this most recent revolution, medicine's dominance as a framework for understanding what constitutes treatment and the focus of that treatment reached deep into every crevice of life, shaping our notions of disease, of the self, and of the purpose of clinical medicine. "Around the middle of the twentieth century the object of medicine's attention changed. The patient's subjective experience of disease became an integral part of the object medicine practiced on. This change is marked by replacement in medical practice of the 'anomaly' by the 'chronic patient' and by the merging of two discourses on life—the medical discourse concerned principally with curing disease and the socio-moral discourse concerned principally with extending compassion to the person living with the disease—that were separate but parallel during the nineteenth century."[10]

The idea that the patient is an *experiencing person*—someone with a deep, psychic interior who lives in and is shaped by a social world and who must articulate needs, desires, and an identity—had been developing for several decades in American psychiatry and psychology as the influence of Freud's work was taken up in clinical practice. His work began to influence general medical practice as well.[11] Arney and Bergen mention the 1950 publication of the medical textbook *Principles of Internal Medicine* as a prominent sign of new developments in ways of thinking about the patient. That well-regarded text, they claim, expanded the field of medicine's concern from diseases of the body to *the whole person*. It was organized around the notion that the patient *is* a person: "The art of medicine is not confined to organic disease; it deals also with the mind of the patient and with his behavior as a thinking, feeling human being."[12]

This reconstruction of the patient and movement of disease away from his body's interior space out into his social relationships and psycho-emotional world had actually started to occur even before 1950.[13] (Several physicians with whom I spoke recalled books, written by physicians in the 1920s and 1930s, that urged doctors to consider the "whole patient.") By midcentury, the patient's disease could no longer be separated either from the dialogue about the disease, into which both doctor and patient entered, or from what the physician was starting to hear about psychosocial elements—e.g., behavior patterns, family and community relations, and psychological processes. The patient and the illness coexisted, were cocreated, within a larger social and psychodynamic system. Patients had diseases; patients had problems as well.

British psychoanalyst Michael Balint was instrumental during the 1950s in forging a powerful link between a patient's symptoms and his feelings, biography, and social life. His book, *The Doctor, His Patient and the Illness*, was widely read and cited by physicians.[14] Balint advocated that general practitioners work like psychoanalytic psychiatrists. Physicians' own thoughts and feelings, he proposed, could themselves be diagnostic tools, not to locate corporeal pathology of course, but rather to identify the scope of the human problem, including illness. Physicians' insights into and knowledge of patients as whole persons could be instruments in a new and therapeutic alliance with patients, an alliance that required patients to have needs.

Two things changed in the middle years of the twentieth century. The first was that patients now had a voice within a medical discourse; the patient was now the patient-as-person. They expressed their symptoms and, importantly, their feelings, verbally. The second change was related to the context in which physicians placed what they heard about their patients' problems. Physicians began to locate problems within systems—within cells, tissues, and organ systems in the body and within the worlds of family, community, and cultural and ecological environments. Once physicians were able to perceive patients as individuals whose diseases were located in the matrix of a life, medicine began to manage that life, including its end.

The historical development of the patient-as-person is to be distinguished from a more widely understood, parallel development: the way in which therapeutics, diagnostic technologies, and developments in the burgeoning specialty fields began to change mid-twentieth-century medical practice and led to the now decades-old complaint that doctors treat patients like objects and see only diseases (or body parts) and not whole persons. Early in the twentieth century doctors cared for patients in their homes and knew patients in relation to their families and communities. They could cure relatively few diseases. When therapeutic advances led to a shift from caring for the patient to a focus on specific organ systems and curing disease, clinics and hospitals, rather than home and community, became the primary locations in which physicians examined and knew patients, their symptoms, and their problems. Doctors specialized and then subspecialized. Fragmentation of care and of the patient became popular complaints. By the late 1960s, there was a cry among some physicians to remember the whole patient,[15] and the consumer movement for "person-centered" treatment in health care emerged.

By the 1970s more doctors were indeed becoming sensitive to the patient's subjective point of view. Many began to work as members of teams that included the patient and the family. The new medical discourse about life and its need for management increased the importance of pain and suffering and gave rise to a new language to talk about them.[16] In the 1970s "birth" and "death" were replaced by "birthing" and "dying." Those were newly conceived socio-medical processes in which the subjective, experiencing person became the new object of medical knowledge and work. The support group was born, a place of near equality in which the physician-expert empathizes with the suffering patient-as-person. The support group has a dual purpose: to hear the patient's unique troubles and needs, which the doctor acknowledges and affirms, and also to submerge individuality to an ordered, routine way of knowing and coping.[17]

According to these (and other) new ways of ordering patients' lives and conditions, the patient must speak about the problems he or she is experiencing because treatment depends on doctor-patient mutual engagement. This was an unprecedented kind of partnership, and it took shape in the context of the growing impact on all physicians of the law (following the Quinlan case), new federal regulations about informed consent for medical treatments, and an emerging demand for patient autonomy. By the end of the 1970s, when paternalism in medical practice declined significantly as a result of the rise of consumer activism and rights movements of all kinds, physicians were required by the new logic to speak truth to the patient, including disclosing the "facts" about impending death.[18]

Truth and Need Appear on the Scene: The Psychological Process of Dying

Thus death became, according to the new logic, a management problem, a part of life that needed to be ordered and orderly. It could no longer be understood outside the realm of medical treatment. And so death moved into the American hospital, where, in their pioneering studies conducted during the early 1960s, sociologists Barney Glaser, Anselm Strauss, and David Sudnow showed the uneven development of "truth speaking." Hospital staff rarely named death during those years, and doctors and nurses almost never discussed the topic of impending death with patients. Sociologists were the first to investigate empirically how mid-twentieth-century dying was, in fact, organized and understood through hospital activities, especially the medical and nursing staff's interactions with patients and families. Who can speak about death and to whom, the ways in which awareness about death is revealed or concealed, the strong concern for silence about death, and expectations about the timing and certainty of death all were shown to be socially elaborated, that is, to be organized by the norms of medical and nursing practice and the dominant values of the era. Glaser and Strauss found that dying had a "trajectory," a duration and shape that were determined both by disease and by the way medical care and communication worked. The patient's dying trajectory became important for knowing which signs of the patient's condition designated the passage from life to death.[19]

Psychiatrist Elisabeth Kübler-Ross extended the transformed medical logic about "speaking truth" and "hearing experience" to the *dying* person, who, she emphasized, is more than just a body in physiological decline. After conducting more than two hundred interviews with hospitalized terminally ill patients, she concluded that a dying person is a self-aware and, most important, an interactive and psychological being.[20] Dying is a psychological process in which a narrating self is central and essential. The physician, Kübler-Ross informed us, not only can assist that process but also has the responsibility to do so. Nearness to death does not obliterate personal identity, the essential quality of being human. In fact nearness to death can be a catalyst for expressing some of our most human qualities, such as compassion, forgiveness, and the review of one's life course.

Karen Quinlan's comatose condition was all the more troubling in the context of Kübler-Ross's work (published a few years before that case became public) because the young woman's voice, her identifiability as a unique human being, was absent. Without the ability to express herself or state her opinion about her condition, she was no longer quite, or fully, human. Her condition was frightening to us. Though the

well-known five-stage theory Kübler-Ross postulated[21] has been criticized for overdetermining the progress of the dying transition and experience, its underlying message—that the dying person has an authentic
voice that must speak—had a profound influence. It helped form the
American understanding, first, of the relationship of the dying person to
being fully human and, second, of the person's experience of dying.
Kübler-Ross's theory taught us that dying is an experiential process that
could and must in fact be observed, expressed, and monitored through
supportive care. And the interior world of emotions, psychic need, and
spirituality came to be an important aspect of optimally organized
dying, mapped and managed by medicine.[22]

The modern hospice movement was fueled by the emerging expression of desire for individual control over the dying experience, by
Kübler-Ross's generally accepted-as-given five stages of dying, and by
symptom management techniques that were becoming available outside the hospital (especially the use of intravenous pain medication and
patient-controlled release pumps). It is generally considered to have
started with the founding of St. Christopher's Hospice in Great Britain
in 1967; hospice care for dying people began in the United States in
1974. Hospice soon became a means for combining modern medical
knowledge and practice with an institutional response to the expression
of individual need and with an imagined tradition of family and community that was considered to be an alternative to the growing bureau-
cratization, patient alienation, and use of technology found in the
hospital.[23]

Yet hospice has been slow to establish and gain in popularity in the
United States. Of those people who die each year in the United States, just
one-quarter, or fewer, do so in hospice programs,[24] and many people are
not even familiar with the term.[25] Nevertheless, hospice has become the
contemporary symbol of the Anglo-American, middle-class idea of
"the good death"—a "patient and family–centered process" in which the
foci of attention are personal comfort for the patient and material and
emotional support for family and friends, while the patient knowingly
and reflexively declines toward death. A distinction between "good" and
"bad" deaths has existed historically. Sociologist Tony Walter traces the
change in the meanings of "good death" and notes that, in premodern
times, the good death consisted of the opportunity to say farewell to one's
family and prepare to cross the threshold to the afterlife. In the modern

era, death should be quick, unconscious, or at least painless. Most recently, in the period Walter calls the neo-modern era, the emphasis is on individual patient control of the style of death, and "good" mostly indicates a death that is aware, pain-free, and in which psychological and worldly business are completed.[26] Symptom control is the highest priority, and it is sometimes considered to be in the service of psychological insight (and its expression) and spiritual transcendence.

Like the abstraction of "death with dignity," hospice—as it is commonly understood—has also become an abstraction, the quintessential, metaphorical place for the reduction of suffering, fulfilled dying, and ultimate individualism—all values articulated by the educated middle class. Ironically, hospice is now mostly bureaucratized. It is paid for by Medicare, but only if the patient who is referred to hospice is considered by doctors to have less than six months to live. As a result, it is mostly cancer patients and others with a clear terminal trajectory who can anticipate death who receive hospice services of any kind.[27]

Patients Acquire Autonomy

The ideas of patient autonomy and patient self-determination have their own history vis-à-vis American medical practice and the American hospital. Without doubt, the foundation for the ascendance of patient self-determination as a value in health care was laid with the Nuremberg Code, a response of the Nuremberg Tribunal to the Nazi atrocities carried out in the name of medical research during the Second World War. A year prior to its publication in the United States, the *Journal of the American Medical Association* printed an editorial written by physician Andrew C. Ivy that responded to a report of war crimes, "The Brutalities of Nazi Physicians." That editorial anticipated the ten articles of the Nuremberg Code in its outline of basic ethical standards for medical research.[28] The Nuremberg Code was published in the *Journal of the American Medical Association* on November 29, 1947. It focused public attention, for the first time, on the conduct of modern medical research, the rights of sick patients and healthy subjects to voluntarily engage in medical science, and the need for professionals in medicine, science, and the law to examine the entire research endeavor—from recruitment of patients to the medical outcomes of experiments.

Yet historian David Rothman notes, "Well into the 1960s, the American research community considered the Nuremberg findings, and the

Nuremberg Code, irrelevant to its own work."[29] Few investigators seriously or deliberately followed the 1946 AMA guidelines, and then the Nuremberg Code, in their actual research practices, especially the directives that subjects must knowingly volunteer and be informed about the nature of a study and its risks.[30] Following an exposé in 1966 of ethically troublesome research practices at American universities, hospitals, and medical centers, Americans in many fields (medicine, social science, law, theology, and philosophy) finally acted on the goadings of the Nuremberg Code and began to scrutinize the realm of medical experimentation.[31] Over the next two decades, patient rights, patient autonomy, and patient self-determination became dominant features of the American doctor-patient relationship. No other society considers the autonomy of the patient to be as essential a priority when determining choices of medical treatments.[32]

The federal government became involved. The National Commission for the Protection of Human Subjects of Biomedical and Behavioral Research was created by the U.S. Congress in 1974 to establish practical and ethical guidelines for the conduct of medical research and, more broadly, to ensure that all patients would be able to make their own decisions regarding therapeutic matters. The creation of the commission was a response to several developments, including the rapidly expanding scope of biomedical research that used sick patients as experimental subjects; the revelations in the medical literature (beginning with the 1966 exposé) and popular press about morally abhorrent clinical research practices in the none-too-distant past;[33] and the changing character of the doctor-patient relationship. That national commission and another one that followed it in 1980 issued a series of reports (in the late 1970s and the 1980s) that emphasized the principles of patient autonomy and patient rights in biomedical research and clinical practice.[34] Importantly, members of both commissions included more lawyers and academically trained philosophers than physicians. They were concerned foremost with the ethics of experimentation, but their reports also considered medical decision-making in general and the importance of informed consent in all clinical work.[35]

The growing influence of these ethicists lent intellectual and pragmatic authority to the idea of patient autonomy in physician-patient communication and in medical decision-making. "Patient autonomy" became a guiding principle—some claim it was the dominant principle—

of the physician-patient relationship in American medicine, largely (though never completely) displacing the physician authority and paternalism that had earlier characterized the clinical encounter.

From her perspective as both physician and philosopher, Jodi Halpern offers a summary of the way autonomy is interpreted today in American medical practice:

> The term *autonomy* refers both to a psychological capacity to make decisions that reflect one's own goals and an ethical ideal of self-determination. The term is used in medicine to describe an evolving set of patients' rights, extending from rights to determine what happens to one's own body, to rights to informed consent and refusal of treatment, to rights to participate more fully in medical decision-making. Many of these rights have emerged through lawsuits, and hence it is through a legalistic prism that physicians understand their obligations to respect autonomy.[36]

Sociologist Renée Fox puts the concept into the broader context of the bioethical values that have shaped the ways Americans conceptualize medical care delivery:

> From the outset, the conceptual framework of bioethics has accorded paramount status to the value-complex of individualism, underscoring the principles of individual rights, autonomy, self-determination, and their legal expression in the jurisprudential notion of privacy. By and large, what bioethics terms *paternalism* is negatively defined, because however well-meaning, and concerned with the good and the welfare of another person it may be, it interferes with and limits an individual's freedom and liberty of action.[37]

The Patient Self-Determination Act, which became federal law in 1990, further institutionalized the values promoted by bioethics. The act legally mandated the "right" of all hospital patients to be informed about and to determine their own medical treatments, including the refusal of treatments.[38] The act illustrates the institutional dominance that the ideal of autonomy had attained in ordinary medical practice by the end of the 1980s. That ideal underlies all the patient and family testimonials about problematic dying that began to appear with greater frequency during those years. The act is also yet another iteration of the "rights discourse" that since the 1960s has become the dominant (and widely criticized) framework for considering controversy in American social and political life.[39] "Patients' rights" quickly joined civil rights, women's rights, gay and lesbian rights, disability rights, the rights of the fetus, prisoners, animals, etc.

What the constellation of values, ideologies, and practices that has come to be known as the autonomy paradigm[40] ignores, and what the Patient Self-Determination Act itself could not possibly encompass, is that neither patients nor families are unencumbered actors. They are not making treatment choices that are "rational" (that is, made according to a philosophically based calculus of moral reasoning), "informed" (in a medical sense), or uninfluenced by class, race, religion, or the social conditions and webs of power in which they actually live. Moreover, autonomy is not a dominant value or concern for everyone in American society.[41] And as we saw in the story of Carol Jones and her family, most patients and families do not know what to want when faced with specific directives about options that are generated by institutional routines. Some refuse to decide. Some make choices that, because of the way the health care delivery system works, cannot be implemented. Always their points of view are determined and constrained by the fabric of their lives, by their degree of religious faith, and by what they come to know about disease, the body, how near their relative seems to death, and the way the hospital works. So while "patient autonomy," in some diffuse and abstract sense, is now federal policy, and though many physicians work hard to allow for its specific expression (especially, as we shall see, in ways that keep patients moving smoothly through the hospital's established routines and pathways of care), it is never enacted in some pure, unfettered form in the hospital, nor can it ever be.[42]

American ideals about autonomy and individual rights are joined by notions of *dignity* as those notions circulate—without shared understanding or precise meaning—through the hospital world.[43] All three concepts have further expanded the scope of the patient-as-person's identity—the identity upon which medicine practices. Importantly today, the patient's identity as a rights-bearing subject, along with his subjectivity and his medical condition, all need equal attention from health professionals. For its part, talk about dignity is often connected to ideas of *suffering*, especially in attempts to assess the role suffering plays in a patient's experience of critical illness and of hospitalization (whether or not the patient can articulate his or her suffering). Dignity is also invoked in the deliberations among staff and family about *whether there has been enough suffering.* Dignity may refer both to the practical impacts of medical treatments on the patient's body and existence *and* to the intrinsic value of *life,* regardless of its condition. In addition, the inclusion of dignity as one of its primary components makes self-determination a complex matter indeed because dignity encompasses both the ways in which others act toward the patient and the degree to which the patient's desires regarding treatment and life-prolongation are fulfilled.

Brain Death and the Mechanical Ventilator: Complicating the "Person"

The changing perceptions about the scope of dying patients' problems worked their way into the fabric of standard medical practice over several decades; but another event had an immediate, if not immediately visible, effect on how death is made and understood. This event took place in 1968, at the same time as the "discovery" of the experiential process of dying and the start of the hospice movement. While Kübler-Ross was interviewing dying hospital patients to learn about their psycho-emotional experience, the Ad Hoc Committee of the Harvard Medical School to Examine the Definition of Brain Death was formed to respond to two new technologies—organ transplantation and the mechanical ventilator or respirator.[44] To solve practical, clinical problems that accompanied the use of these powerful tools, the Harvard committee created a new definition of death: *brain death.* It determined that a person crosses the threshold from life to death when there is irreversible and permanent cessation of function of the *entire* brain, that is, of both consciousness and reflexive activity.

With this new definition, the "person" could be declared dead while at the same time the internal organs could be kept viable by machines. The mechanical ventilator was coming into widespread use in intensive care units in industrialized countries, and it could keep the heart pumping and the lungs "breathing" so that tissues and organs would continue to receive oxygenated blood and would not "die." This would facilitate transplants and increase their success. Most important, transplant surgeons would not be accused of taking organs from "living" persons.[45] This new, legal definition of brain death was never subject to widespread public debate in the United States. The Harvard committee decision was followed by the creation of the Uniform Determination of Death Act, passed by the U.S. Congress in 1981 and followed by similar legislation in European countries. That act outlined the clinical criteria that determine brain death.[46]

"Brain death" was problematic from the start for two reasons. First, the distinction was never clear between the clinical criteria used to make a diagnosis of death and the conceptual basis for a definition of death. Historian Martin Pernick explains, "A capacity like the ability to breathe, to integrate bodily functions, or to experience consciousness can be seen simply as a marker that indicates whether a more basic something else called *life* is still present. But the ability to perform these very same functions can also be considered not the indicator but the essence of life. Or these abilities may be regarded as necessary for life, without explicitly saying whether they are criteria or definitions. Thus, when someone identifies a particular capacity as vital, without explicitly stating whether it is the essence or merely a criterion of life, there is no unambiguous way to determine which conceptual role is being claimed."[47] Second, the 1981 law incorporated two distinct concepts of death. The first focused on the physiological breakdown of the entire organism, the second on the cessation of function throughout the brain: "Death . . . can be demonstrated either on the traditional grounds of irreversible cessation of heart and lung function or on the basis of irreversible loss of all function of the entire brain."[48] The absence of breath and heartbeat, historically the defining features of death—features that anyone could note—was no longer the only, or the most comprehensive, or the correct criterion. It was now one of two "correct" criteria.

Within a few years, troubling ramifications of the Harvard committee decision and the 1981 law began to ripple through the medical community. Evidence of confusion regarding how to speak about the brain-dead condition began to appear in studies of health care professionals who worked with organ donors. Were potential donors on mechanical respirators really dead? How dead were they? Doctors and nurses sometimes noted that donors died twice—first from trauma or disease and then again when respirators were removed. Dead persons who are connected to mechanical ventilators do not look dead, which causes unresolved distress for some families and health professionals. The very existence of brain-dead persons who were kept in such a life-like condition on the ventilator suggested that there was more than one kind of death, or that brain death was not actual, final death.

Rather than serving to specify and clarify the moment and conditions of death, the notion of brain death made death more indeterminate (and disquieting) because brain death was defined via transplant technologies. Brain death was not a *natural* phenomenon. Rather, it was an event that could be—and was—decided through clinical and political negotiation.[49] Philosopher Giorgio Agamben goes so far as to say that with the Harvard committee decision, *death* "becomes an epiphenomenon of transplant technology."[50] Whether brain death *is* death has been murky ever since. By the 1990s, confusion and debate about brain death extended beyond the world of organ transplants, spilling over into wider discussions among health professionals about the nature of consciousness, the degree to which brain-dead individuals can be distinguished from corpses, and the moral ambiguity posed by bodies that are neither persons nor cadavers.[51]

Definitions of death aside, the mechanical ventilator contributed generously to the new problem of what to *do* about death. By the early 1970s, the "breathing machine" was standard equipment in all major medical centers and most community hospitals in the United States. Through the application of positive pressure, the mechanical ventilator forces air directly into the lungs at a volume and rate adjusted by medical practitioners and maintained by the machine. Like many technologies before it, the development of the mechanical ventilator was applauded. It enabled new forms of treatment such as coronary artery bypass graft surgery; it prolonged the life of persons with neuromuscular diseases or adult respiratory distress syndrome; it made recovery from life-threatening pneumonia and chronic lung disease possible. The mechanical ventilator also sparked the creation of the intensive care unit and was immediately considered essential technology there.[52] By 1975, mechanical ventilation was indicated for a long list of diseases and health problems and was available in most U.S. hospitals.[53]

But from the very beginning of its association with intensive care medicine, the mechanical ventilator created at least two troubling new outcomes in addition to the ambiguities surrounding brain death. The ventilator is capable of keeping alive for months and years people who are in a "vegetative" or comatose state. And it also keeps people alive who may be conscious but whose vital organ systems have failed to sustain life. The ventilator thus brought into existence three varieties of death-in-life—the brain dead, the comatose, and the inhabitants of some other location in the gray zone of indistinction.[54]

Indeterminate Old Age: The Quandary of the "Person" in Late Life

The definition of *brain death* complicated the idea of the "person"-acted-on-by-medicine by opening up a category of patients who seem to observers to be not fully alive but not quite dead. Old age—when it becomes part of the equation when considering *what to do* about allowing or staving off death—further troubles the idea of the "person" because medical science is equivocal about whether old age is fundamental to a person's identity as a patient. That is, if old age is an essential, descriptive feature of all human personhood in the last part of life, then one cannot treat it via medical means, and, indeed, it is a phenomenon outside the realm of medical action. If, on the other hand, old age is to be understood in terms of disease processes rather than in terms of the natural, inevitable end to the arc of a life in time, then it can (and should) be acted on by the tools of medicine.

The gray zone between life and death that the hospital creates and biomedical technologies perpetuate is further troubled by an indistinct area of clinical and scientific understanding regarding relationships among normal old age, disease, and "natural" death at the end of a life span. Especially when an old person is frail and disabled, the vague areas of clinical knowledge are joined by an unclear ethics. In that clinical-ethical morass, medicine asks, what shall we do about very old people who are no longer the way they were? The gray science and ethics of old age come together in the hospital in two ways. First, although decline of bodily functions leads, inevitably, to death, death is not necessarily inevitable, even at the end of life, during any given medical crisis or any given hospitalization (as we shall see). Second, in geriatrics, the medical specialty focusing on old age, the task of disentangling pathology from normal decline at the end of life is far from simple. The question of whether *old age* is a disease and the problem of what normal, natural decline *all the way to death* looks like are both tenacious, unresolved themes in geriatric medicine and have a history in clinical science. Those themes and their history have considerable impact at the bedside, especially when death may be near but the tools of medicine and the hospital's routines are moving patients along from treatment to treatment in the hope of avoiding death. Medical discourse, over the twentieth century, focused its gaze on a rights-bearing, experiencing person, whose life and problems could be mapped and treated. The conundrum of old age as it appears in hospital medicine today affects the idea of the patient-as-*person*. For if old age is viewed primarily as the effects of disease processes on the body, then the person-in-the-patient tends to be effaced, and then, most important, the old are not seen to be, nor allowed to be, *dying persons*.

It is significant for the broadly perceived problem of what to do about dying that both the nature of aging and the relationship of old age to disease have been debated for well over a century. Whether aging is disease, whether *normal* aging is *pathological*, and whether aging per se leads inevitably to death have been persistent questions that emerged long before contemporary high-tech medicine. The terms of the debate have shifted with the growing sophistication of biological knowledge and with changes in the politics of medical science and the delivery of health care, but the debate itself is ongoing.[55] It is made manifest at the hospital bedsides of old patients when families and doctors must decide whether to allow death because its time has come, or to stave death off because something can be done to ameliorate disease or stabilize the patient's condition.

In 1909, I. L. Nascher, a New York physician, proposed the term *geriatrics* to designate a new scientific specialty. His aim was to separate the concepts of old age and disease from one another and at the same time to legitimate and institutionalize the medical study of both.[56] From the dawn of geriatrics as a specialty, a clinical distinction between *normal* and *pathological* was acknowledged to be difficult, if not impossible, to discern, and theories about the nature of old age conflicted. Some believed that old age was an infectious, chronic disease and proposed that new discoveries in medical science be applied in the search for cures. Others doubted that old age could be cured, precisely because it was a progressive disease. Still other medical scientists claimed the pathological degeneration of aging to be the result of normal, natural developmental processes, unrelated to specific diseases.[57] Whether old age could be cured became the subject of intense medical debate at the beginning of the twentieth century.

Nascher cut through those debates with the assumption that old age is a normal condition. His text, *Geriatrics,* appeared in 1914 and became the major authority on geriatrics in the United States.[58] Nascher contended that *normal* and *pathological* were as distinguishable in old age as in earlier periods of life. This separation of the normal from the pathological structures Nascher's text, which is divided into two parts, "Physiological Old Age" and "Pathological Old Age." However, as anthropologist Lawrence Cohen notes, the same syndromes and symptoms are described in both sections. Nascher's separation of *normal* and *pathological* collapses in his own analysis.[59]

Nascher's work, though authoritative, did not provide definitive clarification about relationships among advanced age, disease, and decline at the end of life. Debates about pathology and normalcy in old age continued. One theory of aging as a chronic disease was taught in American medical schools at least until the late 1930s.[60] Historian Andrew Achenbaum notes that by the period between the First and Second World Wars, two opposing views of old age were competing for acceptance in the American medical profession. "One school considered 'senility' a pathological disorder; the other described it as a normal physiological state. In 1941, it remained 'a major problem for science to determine which is correct.'" [61] The distinction between normal old age and disease, though a powerful and long-lasting idea, could not be clinically perceived.

Today aging *during the later years* is not considered a disease.[62] The distinction between normal, progressive, and universal aging and externally caused disease is firmly entrenched in the gerontological sciences (which include the biological, behavioral, and social studies of aging). Physicians who specialize in geriatric medicine, as well as many internists and family practitioners, work hard to separate normal aging from disease when they consider their patients' problems. In general, practitioners in the field of geriatrics claim that identifying disease is important; once it has been treated, it need no longer interfere with a person's normal aging.[63] Yet in ordinary medical practice it is extremely difficult to firmly categorize as either normal or pathological such common late-life symptoms as, for example, memory loss, vision and hearing impairments, appetite and bowel disorders, and walking and balance difficulties. And in the gerontological sciences—where there is a great deal of interest in the role of genetic or cellular changes that cause disease in late life—many acknowledge that there is a "continuum" between aging and disease, that is, an inability to completely separate the two notions.[64]

Together with ordinary medical care, gerontological research has fostered ambiguity about where aging ends and disease begins and what role each plays in human decline and mortality. In the hospital, the physiological characteristics that signify decline in advanced age are complicated by disease. Both are treated in an effort to simultaneously rid the body of disease *and* stave off the declining function of organ systems, which, in the final analysis, is normal in advanced age.

Like medicine's, the public's understandings of the relationships among the old person, aging, disease, and death are infinitely tangled. A Harris poll on aging conducted during the 1980s found that in general Americans believe that the primary cause of disability in later life is old age itself—which was viewed in the poll as "a kind of disease."[65] Yet no definitive connection is drawn by poll takers or their respondents between disease in late life and death. The idea of *age-related disease* also confounds public understanding because aging and disease, separately or together, can cause death. Arteriosclerosis and the decalcification of bone, for example, are expressions of normal, ordinary human aging "until they progress to a point at which they lead to diseases such as heart attacks, strokes, osteoporosis, and renal disorders. How one identifies the point of transition is not clear."[66] Arteriosclerosis can be thought of as disease or as normal aging, depending on the definition of aging.[67] Some biologists note that making a distinction between biological and pathological aging is sometimes not possible.[68] Others propose that aging and disease be viewed as a continuum rather than as discrete categories, using the example that there may be a continuum of brain lesions from normal aging to Alzheimer's disease just as there is a continuum of arteriosclerotic changes from normal to disease entity.[69] Lay confusion about whether old age is characterized primarily by disease, coupled with medicine's history of debate about the relationship of normal to pathological aging, together provide one important reason why so many hospitalized old people receive aggressive medical treatments, enabling them to hover on the threshold of death for days or weeks before they die. Elisabeth Hansot's story of her mother, which opens Part I, results from the indeterminate relationship between old age and disease.

Thus even in late life, death has come to be considered an option, one of several available to practitioners and consumers of health care.[70] Philosopher Daniel Callahan noted in 1987 that many in American society, including the institution of medicine itself, had lost a sense of the normal and natural life span that includes the inevitability of decline and death.[71] He called for a societal dialogue that would result, he hoped, in a broad consensus about the inevitability in old age of death following decline so that Americans could set limits on the technological imperative and the widespread angst it has produced at hospital bedsides. His discussion provoked more than a decade of debate about the rationing of health care to the elderly and their right to unlimited medical services in very late life. It also created a great deal of consternation among professionals in geriatrics and gerontology who feared that the proposals to "set limits" on the amount of medical treatment older people would receive and to reconsider the meaning of the "natural" arc of the life course would lead to rampant discrimination against older people.[72]

One of the reasons people do not know what dying *as a natural phenomenon in late life* looks like is that frailty, debility, and decline are today defined—and thus constrained—by the language of medicine. That language describes discrete diseases, which can be treated to prolong decline—sometimes for a long time. There is simply no escaping modern medicine's diagnostic categories for knowing what is wrong with old bodies. The final outcome of old age—death—is seen in the hospital almost exclusively as the end point of effective medical treatment. No one dies of old age there. In scientific debates about the likelihood or even the impossibility of death in the absence of disease, the inevitability of organ failure in old age—i.e., parts simply wearing out— is ignored, muted, or denied, and death that is precipitated by old age itself is rarely acknowledged.[73] Old-age-as-disease has become a more compelling truth than old-age-as-a-normal-developmental-process that includes decline toward death. And, most important, old-age-as-disease drives hospital practice.

That no one dies of old age is a "fact" created by national and international classification systems in an effort to systematize mortality statistics. Bureaucratically created categories of causes of death prevent physicians from writing "old age" on death certificates and force them, instead, to use the clinical-pathological designations that the modern culture of medicine has developed over time.[74] According to the International Classification of Diseases (ICD), a disease classification and coding scheme developed in the late nineteenth century to coordinate information about worldwide morbidity and mortality, old age is not a disease or a cause of death. The last year in which one could die from "old age," or from being simply "worn-out," was 1913.[75] Those designations no longer exist. The classification system has been redrawn many times in the past century to reflect changing understandings of disease.

Today, the ICD codes are ubiquitous in medical information systems generally and in hospital diagnosis specifically. What is listed in the codes becomes *real* in a pragmatic sense—medical conditions, forms of treatment, and ways of categorizing the patient emerge from the ICD listings.[76] Hospital reimbursement schemes (both Medicare and private insurance) are determined by them. What is not listed cannot be used in day-to-day medical work, either to classify and thus interpret patients' maladies or to be financially remunerated. The ICD codes are, in fact, tightly constrained (though modifiable) organizational rules. People die only of discrete diseases, the rules proclaim, and thus a rationale is created not only for labeling diseases as the cause of death in old age, but also for understanding death as only possible in terms of disease categories. The bureaucracy of the health care system does not allow the *person* to age and then die. One physician who has many elderly patients remarked to me, "There is simply no way out—aging is thought of as a disease."[77]

By the 1980s the question "What can we do about dying?" was being posed with great regularity both within and beyond the confines of the medical establishment. The question could be raised only when several cultural facts had come together, and it continues to be asked because that configuration has not changed: First, death has been brought into life through the decision-making required by medicine and the hospital system, thus creating a zone of indistinction between *life* and *death*. Second, dying has become a psychodynamic process, and the dying person is assumed to need support during the experience—support in terms of medical procedures (especially symptom relief) and emotional or spiritual care. Third, *normal old age* and *disease* are hopelessly entangled and both are treated medically. Yet the longer the patient is medically maintained at the gray zone through ordinary hospital activities that avert death, the more troubling the condition of the patient-as-person becomes, both for hospital staff and for families.

The question of what to do about death remains pervasive because the relationship of the *person* to *life* is so intricate yet indeterminate.

Political debate coupled with biomedical technologies has upset the definition of death and fostered new kinds of persons and new modes of life in the zone of indistinction. Medical discourse has shaped the contemporary patient into a person who suffers and speaks, and whose condition across the life span is perceived and understood through engagement with clinical medicine. When the debatable character of old age itself, as seen through the lens of medical science and hospital practice, is added to this "shaped" patient, it threatens to erode the whole idea of the person—a human being who will naturally face a dying transition—because diseases can be treated without taking that particular definition of personhood into consideration.

As human beings who care both for and about others, when we confront hospital care at the end of life, we are driven to ask, "What can we do about dying?" And we must ask precisely because dying and personhood have become such entangled concepts in American society.

PART II

The Hospital System

Time and the Power of the Pathway

"You get to the hospital disheveled as hell from traveling all day. You're exhausted but there is no rest. You don't know what to do. You're in a hotel, a rented car, not your own space. You're dealing with your own thoughts about death that this experience provokes. Everything that happens keeps you off center. . . . The doctors are unreachable for conversation. There is constant change among the nurses, and you try to ingratiate yourself by bringing candy for them. You want to show that you know something, so you bring questions, an agenda. But there are control issues and you're made to feel that you shouldn't show that you know too much. You need to merge your knowledge of the person with the hospital knowledge. So the family manufactures 'the patient' on the spot.

"The hospital is like an airport, but it's not. It's like a supermarket you've never been to before. It's disordered. The space is disordered. Two in a room is disordered, especially when your relative is lying next to a dying person. Even the cleaning process is disordered—*this is crucial.* You're not supposed to hear certain conversations, or see bodily fluids. But there is nowhere not to. It is a place of smell, sound, space, and time disorientation. You see these tubes, bags, fluids, and overflowing wastebaskets, with unsettling debris, with blood. And it is *all over the place.* Swabs and waste are everywhere. And old food trays, waiting for someone to take them away. It's a boundaryless place. There is no classification, yet it is all about classification—charts, bureaucracy.

"There is a big contrast between the week and the weekend. On the weekend nothing happens. There is no staff. Holidays are time out of time out of time. Then Monday morning everything happens. Then scheduling is imposed and it's based on the bureaucracy, based on when things *must* happen.

"And the hospital space—the dining room is always in the basement. You descend past body parts, past radiology. And the cafeteria itself is disconcerting. The food is awful. But there is nothing to do except eat. And you need to talk, but you can't talk there. Then you need to get to a phone to call people. And where is the fucking phone? You can't find the phone. It's down the hall. . . .

"The family is under surveillance, even while trying to show solidarity with the patient. And everything takes place in public. You're put on your best behavior and must construct family obligations and general sociability. In this disorienting space the family has to make decisions. How can they? Decision-making doesn't happen in the hospital. It happens at home. Somehow you're there all the time, but decisions are still made when you're not there. But also, the family is already *not* making decisions. So, what's the role of children? Of a daughter-in-law?

"The patient is moved here, tested there. Social workers, case managers, have the script—which you don't know ahead of time. They know what the trajectory is. There are the operations, and waiting, and the doctor coming to talk. Where do you sit when the patient is not in the room, when the patient is in surgery? Whose room is it? The propriety of it. The problem of it. Do you sit in the room? Where? Where are the boundaries? Then the patient is moved to a new room and you have to reestablish relationships. Then there is the question of when it's excusable to leave. Maybe it is a gender thing. I would stay. My husband would want to leave. The doctor programs you, too—'If you're going to stay, stay.' Or, 'Go now.' Basically, the family has no control over any of it.

"Then a conference is finally scheduled. There are never enough chairs. There is nowhere to sit, no space to sit. The doctor wants to do enough, to give the patient a fighting chance for life, to be decent. Who is the doctor addressing—the patient? the children? The doctor of my mother-in-law was surprised that she died, even at age ninety-three. . . .

"Then you go into a funeral mode, another disorienting and new routine. And you don't know what to expect."

Daughter-in-law of a frequently hospitalized patient

TRANSFORMING TIME

From Deathwatch to Billable Treatments

Between the 1960s and the mid-1980s, the way American hospital culture understood *time*—its pressures, its value, its implications vis-à-vis
dying—changed dramatically. That change helped fuel the problem of
death, which cannot be described or understood without bearing in
mind the role time now plays in perpetuating it. Until the second half of
the nineteenth century, death arrived in its own time, and people simply
waited for it. It was beyond anyone's command to stop it, and the doctor, if he was present at all, was a marginal figure. By the 1960s, when
sociologists Glaser and Strauss and Sudnow studied the organization of
work and the management of death, *waiting for death* had moved, in
large part, into the hospital. Nonetheless, well into the mid–twentieth
century, *waiting* in the hospital was still structured by a medical science
that could do far less to stave off death than it can today and by a hospital culture that still allowed dying an unlimited amount of time to
occur. Once determined by processes taking place within the body, waiting is now determined by procedures and is structured by contemporary bureaucracy. It has become an entirely new phenomenon.

Throughout the 1960s intensive care units were still new and their
purpose was not always entirely clear to hospital personnel. Kidney
dialysis procedures, the cardiac monitor, and the defibrillator were available in ICUs, but those technologies were sometimes available on the

medical wards as well. Intensive care units were distinguished from other hospital wards not by their lifesaving machinery, but by the continuous presence of nurses.[1] Mechanical ventilators were just coming on the scene; few hospitals had them, and they were primarily used to ensure recovery for surgical patients.[2] The morphine drip did not yet exist. Intravenous medication of any kind was unusual on medical wards, and there were no mechanical pumps through which patients could self-administer pain medication. It was not assumed that patients could or should be in charge of their pain and its reduction. Pain medication and sedatives were given by pills or by injection only when medical staff thought it was necessary.

Patients stayed in hospitals for weeks and months. There was no institutional imperative to move them out as quickly as possible. Gradual signs of diminishing life were watched for and expected. Hospital staff routinely waited for death—a passive but necessary activity—and they watched it approach without concern for how long it took. Their waiting was not structured by hospital payment mechanisms and was rarely defined by the availability of medical treatments. Unlike today, waiting was not organized around subspecialty consultations, lab reports, diagnostic tests, family opinion, utilization review, or orders to forgo resuscitation or withdraw treatments. Instead, staff watched and waited for signs of physiological stabilization or instability and decline, not to interrupt the decline and stabilize bodily systems, but to make the patient as comfortable as possible *for the unknown duration of waiting.* Comfort was provided by responding appropriately to the visible symptoms of bodily disintegration that staff knew would occur—pain, choking, labored breathing, yelling, thrashing, or seizures.[3] Anxiety-reducing medication and other drugs that can today reduce or mask the "death rattle," the thrashing, and other physical signs of corporeal disintegration were not yet routinely available. Nurses gave back rubs and bed baths.[4]

Most important, that fee-for-service era had no technological imperative to deliberately stave off death. Patients who took a long time to die were described as "lingering," a state that was subjectively assessed by health professionals through their understanding of one patient's medical condition relative to that of others. A "lingering trajectory" was acceptable on the medical wards[5] and was tied to hospital economics. The hospitals of the 1960s were not financed as they are today. Then, health insurance was entirely in the private sector, physicians did a great deal of charity work, and hospitals, other than academic medical centers, were community supported. One nurse, reflecting on that era, told me, "Morbidity was a source of funds then." Medicare did not exist until 1965. When it did arrive, "the floodgates opened," that nurse recalled. Medicare generated a new stream of older and sicker patients and reinforced patterns of care already in place by assuring those patients that their hospital stays, regardless of length, would be paid for by the federal government. If they took weeks or months to die, Medicare would cover the costs.

A major change in the financing of hospital care, and thus the organization of death, took place in 1983. That year the Medicare Diagnostic Related Groups (DRGs) became law. This federal prospective payment scheme significantly modified Medicare reimbursement by assigning specific price tags to specific diagnoses. In an effort to curb hospital expenditures, this legislation restricted hospital reimbursement and made treatment a crucial component of any hospital stay. Reimbursement was linked to the provision of approved treatment. Most importantly for death, the DRG system would not allow *waiting* without specific, listed diagnoses and treatments. It disallowed a dying of unknown duration. "Lingering," which is not a specific medical condition listed in the prospective payment system codes, could not be reimbursed. Several young doctors told me, "Dying is not billable. You can't treat it." Patients are no longer permitted simply to stay in the hospital.[6]

During the 1960s, impending death was less obscured by administratively generated routines than it is today. That is because hospitals then were not yet financed by reimbursable diagnostic and treatment procedures, and all hospital activity was not guided by the pressure to employ those procedures. Hospital staff often knew, weeks and months in advance, that a patient would die during *this* hospitalization, regardless of how long it took. One experienced nurse recalled a patient she cared for during 1971, the first year she worked on the medical floors. That young woman, dying of cancer, stayed in the hospital several months receiving what would now be considered "comfort care"—turning, washing, toileting, and occasional pain medication injections. The patient had a husband and three young children, and no one expected her family to be able to care for her at home. She died in the hospital.

Sudnow noted in 1967 that *dying* was a predictive characterization, that when a nurse said a patient "is dying," she meant that the patient would die within a certain period of time, not that specific biological events that indicated dying were necessarily discernible either by direct observation or in laboratory reports. "The medical, or biological, or physiochemical basis for regarding a person as 'dying' are not entirely clear," Sudnow observed in 1967. "Noticing 'dying' seems to be a quite different order of conceptual activity from noticing bleeding, or fibrillating, or employing a disease category to organize some set of symptoms and findings."[7] Dying was a temporal, rather than a descriptive, specification, and it organized ward activities in certain ways. Dying, said Sudnow, places "a frame of interpretation around a person."[8] Forty years ago that frame was *waiting*.

It can be debated whether dying is medically clearer now than it was then. Dying is still a predictive enterprise, but two things have changed about the basis of those predictions. First, they are more dependent on "the numbers" generated by laboratory and quantitative analyses of blood components and organ function than they are on holistic observation of the patient. Indeed, *watching the numbers* is common medical jargon for interpreting laboratory reports that delimit the pathological state of the body's different systems. This is not to say that nurses' and doctors' direct observations and intuitive assessments do not take place and are not considered important—they do and are. (Those assessments are now categorized as part of "the art" of medicine.) But for billing or placement purposes, they are less official than quantitative data, and quantitative data are what inform hospital staff that a patient is dying.

Second, conditions that are considered life-threatening (so defined primarily through laboratory analyses of blood chemistry and organ system function) are treated until they become known as "no longer responsive to treatment." Only then are they considered fatal.[9] Both measurement and intervention have become more sophisticated in their powers to discern and alter pathological processes, and this has pushed the line between "life-threatening but treatable" and "fatal" closer to the time of death. And so now lab reports signify dying—in the sense that staff activity turns toward allowing or promoting death— only a few hours or at most a few days before death. I rarely saw dying declared by anyone—doctor, patient, or family member—more than seventy-two hours before it happened. More often dying was named much closer to death's actual arrival—within forty-eight hours, and often within twenty-four hours. Dying does not become institutionally recognized or named, and thus is not really happening, until medical staff interpret discrete measurements as irreversible and fatal.

Today, a frame of interpretation is still placed around "the dying patient," but now it is the knowledge that no more procedures are available to stop the pathological processes leading to death. There can be no *waiting for death*, in the 1960s sense, because that expectant sensibility has been replaced by the necessity for specific diagnoses, by the ability to discern and measure discrete pathology (and to continue taking those measurements until death), and by the mandate for treatments that attempt to halt physiological decline.

What particularly struck me when reading the 1960s studies were references to the word *deathwatch*, a term used mostly by nurses to characterize the vigil during which they kept a close watch on patients known to be dying.[10] A deathwatch could be initiated either by physicians or by nurses, and once it began, nurses on a ward organized among themselves to keep constant (or close to constant) surveillance of the patient's physical condition in order to attend to symptoms or behaviors that needed immediate attention, to assure that a patient was not alone, and to control family comings and goings. By sharing the work of the deathwatch among themselves, nurses could also manage patients' families—both to reduce family interference with staff routines and to "protect" them from seeing the final moments of dying. Families were rarely present at the patient's bedside at the moment of death.[11]

Waiting for death—without an institutionally imposed concern for how long it takes—was necessary and time-consuming in the 1960s. It comprised a set of staff (mostly nurse) activities that had to be coordinated with all the other aspects of hospital work. It was definitely a staff (and not a family) obligation. Today, as we shall see in the two chapters that follow, all that has changed. "The deathwatch has given way," said one thoughtful ICU nurse, "to saving a life or offering the best palliative care possible, to heading full bore into strategies and techniques for mastering death by staving it off or by choosing the time for it." Death today is mostly *decided*, not waited for. The disappearance of the staff-maintained deathwatch has considerably shortened the *time for dying*.

In all, one can summarize the differences between hospital deaths forty years ago and hospital deaths now around specific themes. The first is the new need and desire to bring about a particular conception of the "good death," that is, to plan death proactively, to express and then experience what one wants regarding it, and above all, to "control" it.[12] More often than not, in the 1960s and earlier the fact of death was not openly discussed between physicians and patients at all, let alone planned.[13] Second, there were no institutional limits on how long a patient could remain hospitalized, whether dying or not. Lingering, though it required more coordination of work activities among nurses to maintain a sustained and comprehensive deathwatch, was accepted as one of the ways in which people died.[14] Third, the time of *waiting for death* that Glaser and Strauss characterized as "empty," a time *"when nothing is happening to the patient,"*[15] has changed dramatically. It has become either the time for palliative care routines, when much is done to and for the patient, or the time to control the bodily processes of dying through the careful, timed withdrawal of life-support technologies. There can be no empty time today, as a patient must be receiving some kind of treatment to remain hospitalized. Finally, in the 1960s, although a patient known to be dying was described by medical personnel as being in an unstable physiological condition and a transitory state (often visibly indicated by a coma), that state was not sustained or imposed by technology and did not cause moral consternation. Hospital personnel knew that the transitory state would unequivocally end in death, so it did not generate discussion about ethical behavior. It did not trigger "decision-making" with the goal of moving the patient out of the zone of indistinction.

Overall, the expectation that they would be *waiting for death* structured health professionals' responses to the end of life during the 1960s. That expectation has disappeared—to be replaced by waiting for procedures and for decisions about what to do next. The necessary though burdensome attention to waiting that allowed death to come in its own time has been confined to the few days before death at most, if it is allowed at all. The result is that for families, death often comes as a surprise, even if the patient hovers at the threshold of death during a lengthy hospitalization. And aside from that now-constricted time set aside for watchful waiting, the deathwatch has been remade by bureaucracy and technique, transformed through the complex interplay of payment schemes, increased diagnostic precision and therapeutic choice, and the assumption that pain and suffering can be brought under control.

MOVING THINGS ALONG

"Now that so much has been written about the physiology of death, we can go on to the more interesting questions. How we die is, in fact, the least of it. Why we die, the question from which religion springs, we will never understand, and so we leave that matter in the capable hands of the philosophers. But when we die—this is a powerful business, and it is here that, at last, we are beginning to discover our heady dominion."

Andrew Solomon
"A Death of One's Own"

Understanding how the hospital works at the end of life, how it organizes time and moves things along, how it controls the meaning of time and the meaning of dying, is part of the story about how death occurs there. We begin with how and why things move and are moved along set pathways at the end of life and how hospital staff guide patients and families through the system.

The technologies available in contemporary hospital medicine, especially in the United States, shape dying. That is an accepted fact. Less often acknowledged is how hospital procedures and the bureaucratic mandates of the health care system produce the conditions for death. Many complain that the hospital dehumanizes patients by silencing their voices and stripping them of their biographies. Less visible but more insidious are the ways in which hospital structure itself organizes and routinizes dying and life-prolongation. Individuals can only act within systems of classification that already exist, which became apparent to me after I had followed many patients and families and watched them respond to institutional directives, many of which were uncoordinated. Neither those who work in the hospital nor those who travel through it control the classifying systems or define the frameworks through which medical problems and their solutions are understood. Each player can only make choices—can do anything at all—within the parameters of the structure that is already in place.

That structure is the health care system, of which the hospital is a vital, but not independent, component. One of the hospital's primary tasks within the system is to *move things along.* I heard that phrase often from social workers, case managers, nurses, and discharge planners during my observations of very ill patients, and it soon became clear why those staff members, who serve as cogs in the wheel of institutional care and efficiency, use that kind of language. Policies, care plans, and medical algorithms are all designed to move the patient on routinized tracks of diagnoses and treatments that categorize, ameliorate, and manage disease. For many patients the tracks lead to cure and to the saving of lives. For others who are near death, the tracks move, almost inexorably, from one hospital unit to another and one treatment to another.

Unlike other hospital staff, doctors never use the phrase *moving things along.* But they both do and do not identify their clinical work with the smooth functioning of the hospital bureaucracy. On the one hand, physicians try to resist the institutional pressures that weigh on them to follow the basic rules of hospital reimbursement. The mandates to use the least expensive procedure and level of care and quickly discharge patients go against their medical instincts to give every patient the most appropriate care possible. On the other hand, all doctors learn in their residencies how to accommodate bureaucratic health care delivery by getting patients discharged as quickly as possible, and what they learn stays with them. The ongoing opposition of doctors to the time constraints imposed by managed care creates a palpable tension in hospitals. Their resistance is often the subject of hospital committee meetings wherein administrators attempt to align physician practices with the financial demands imposed by managed care contracts.[1]

It is well known, and deplored by many, that the economic priorities of managed care now control the movement of patients (some insured, some not) through the hospital as rapidly and cost-efficiently as possible. What is less apparent, especially to those who stand outside the system, is how the movement of patients who are near death is also controlled, both in and out of the hospital and within it.

The kinds of *moving along* that occur in the hospital show us a great deal about the culture of death and especially about the power of hospital practices to define when and how dying occurs. Doctors and other hospital staff learn to see treatment and care in terms of *where patients are going in the system* as well as in terms of payment schemes, institutional regulations, and treatment logics, all of which enable patients to pass through that system in a manner considered timely by hospital staff. What is the rationale for moves within the hospital and how and why do persons near the end of life come into that system in the first place? If, as some surveys suggest, most people claim they want to die at home without invasive medical treatments, why are they getting aggressive medical treatment in the hospital just before they die?[2]

The treatment pathways on which patients are placed during their hospital stay were conceived separately from managed care, but now operate within its strictures. What to do (and what not to do) when new patients arrive with a specific condition (e.g., stroke, shortness of breath, heart attack) is initially obvious to trained medical personnel, whose goal it is to save life. What to do continues to remain relatively clear during a patient's entire hospitalization, so long as there is no ambiguity about whether the patient is thought to be dying. It is hard to know how many hospital deaths occur in which there is consensus, from early in the stay, that the patient is dying—perhaps half, perhaps more than half. When there is consensus among staff and family, and when death is allowed to occur without life-prolonging interventions, it is considered, in the terms of the popular discourse, to be unproblematic.[3] But, for many other patients, the imperative that they be moved along institutionally created tracks dramatically contributes to the troubled dying that has become such a national obsession.

The Logic of the Pathways to Death

Two common pathways stood out in my observations, two well-traveled roads on which very ill and very old patients are often placed. One utilizes heroic intervention, to use the well-worn phrase that conjures up aggressive, high-technology life-sustaining medical measures.

The other, revolving door pathway describes patients who are repeatedly admitted and discharged for recurring chronic ailments that cannot be cured. These illustrate the ubiquity of movement in the hospital and the typical forms that movement takes. Both roads act like magnets, powerfully drawing everyone into the field of their logic, which dictates how the patient is characterized, how symptoms are managed, how patients and families are processed, how families come to understand their relative's condition, and which things need to be done next. No one is actively aware of these two alternatives. Patient and family have no tools to analyze them. Staff, on the other hand, accept them and the movement imperative itself as unacknowledged background, as "natural" as air. They do not see them as powerful agents that determine staff activity as well as what happens to the patients they treat. For everyone, escape from the pathway's unseen logic is nearly impossible.

The heroic intervention alternative is without doubt the main topic of the widespread conversation about the problem of death. It is the primary source of the public's angst and desire "to take personal control of dying"—whether via health care organization reform, legislation to legalize euthanasia, recipes for and guidebooks to suicide or assisted dying, or, most radically, Dr. Kevorkian's machinery. The heroic pathway frequently looks like this: Mrs. Smith has trouble breathing or stops breathing. She may be at home or in a nursing home. A family member or other caretaker dials 911 and the paramedics arrive, or the caretaker puts her in the car and drives to the hospital. In the emergency department Mrs. Smith is intubated (a plastic tube connected to a mechanical ventilator or "breathing machine" is placed in her mouth and down her windpipe), if that was not already done in the ambulance or at home, and she is taken to the intensive care unit. (A variant is that Mrs. Smith loses or almost loses consciousness or has other symptoms of serious disease and is taken to the hospital. Once there, her condition deteriorates and she is taken to the ICU and intubated.) Diagnostic tests are performed, and treatments, including surgery, are started for diagnosed or suspected conditions.

If the patient's condition does not improve in a few days and she is not removed from the ventilator because she would die immediately or shortly thereafter, she enters the zone of indistinction—biologically alive, though only because she is sustained by biomedical technology, and without signs of unique, purposeful life. After a while, physicians, nurses, and other hospital staff may become uncomfortable observing the patient in that complex zone. Families are often confused and deeply troubled by it. In some cases, though death will eventually occur anyway, even on life support and without planned intervention, medical staff do not want to wait for that moment—which they never can predict with accuracy because it could take days or weeks to arrive. Many consider that those days of waiting only prolong suffering for patients and their families, and in addition, an uncontrolled death is thought to be more physically uncomfortable for the patient than a death in which respiratory support is withdrawn carefully and narcotics or sedatives are administered to reduce pain, anxiety, seizures, or other signs of physiological breakdown. So, it is felt, death must be facilitated through specific choices and deliberate actions.

Planned or orchestrated death occurs when there is agreement among family and medical staff that the patient *would not want to continue existing in this condition* or when the medical team decides that *it is time* to withdraw life-sustaining treatment. Both of those assessments have become ways of categorizing what is happening to very ill persons, and both are primary strategies for inducing movement when patients get stuck along the pathway. *The patient would not want* and *it is time* provide a way of thinking about life and about treatment that enables medical staff to move the patient out of the zone of indistinction and into the category of *dying*—for patients in the acute care hospital cannot be kept in that zone indefinitely. Yet I observed many patients in the intensive care unit who were stuck on the heroic intervention pathway and maintained at the zone between life and death for two to four weeks before death was facilitated.[4]

The revolving door pathway is not as dramatic to observe as the heroic pathway and is, therefore, not usually the subject of television or newspaper attention. It is, however, equally if not more common and is sometimes more agonizing and drawn out for everyone involved: Mr. Clark, elderly, with a serious chronic medical condition such as heart or lung disease, is taken to the hospital because he is short of breath or experiencing acute pain or other symptoms and either he or family members became frightened and sought medical relief. He is admitted to the medical floor, where he is seen by specialists, and diagnostic procedures and symptom-relieving treatments are initiated. He may be moved to the intensive care unit for a time if his condition indicates that more aggressive procedures are needed to control his symptoms or save his life. (At this point, he may be switched to the heroic intervention pathway.) Mr. Clark's own doctor, if he has one, may or may not be involved in the hospital's diagnostic assessment and treatment procedures. Once symptoms abate somewhat, Mr. Clark is discharged from the hospital—only to return eventually with recurring symptoms. Typically, this scenario happens perhaps three to six times in a year. While everyone involved may feel or know that the person is in decline and that death is imminent or probable, no one quite knows how to open a space in the hospital routines for sitting with the close of life. Neither the family nor the medical team is able to leave the revolving door pathway, which usually first moves toward aggressive treatment to sustain a precarious condition— even though the patient is in decline and is approaching the end of life.

Both pathways bring to mind an airport moving walkway—with high sides. Once a patient and a family are placed on one, its logic is more powerful, at least initially, than any individual voice, lay or medical. Everyone is stuck there—doctors, patients, and families. Though patients themselves may, and often do, express their wish to die and their desire to discontinue medical treatments, families are often highly ambivalent about this. They are ambivalent first about removing the patient, and thus themselves, from the technological lifelines connecting them to hope, and, second, about choosing among the available medical options that could lead them to think they are the cause—even remotely—of death. Any alternative that prolongs decline is viewed by many hospital nurses as the "facilitation of suffering" and is deplored in the popular discourse about problematic dying. But things are entirely different on the ground, when a patient cannot breathe or is in acute pain and the distressed family says, "Do something." Under those circumstances, the pathway becomes the source of hope at the same time as it distances the family from being implicated in perpetrating death. Defiance of the compelling trajectories of those choices is not typical and requires a strong sense of conviction, a clarity about what should be done.

In *Patrimony*, a memoir of his father's life, physical decline, and death, Philip Roth describes how, in anguish and doubt, he managed to resist approving heroic intervention for his father. Herman Roth, age eighty-six, had a nonmalignant tumor that had begun on a facial nerve but grew to push against the brain stem. He declined to have the recommended thirteen- or fourteen-hour surgery in "tricky terrain," as one surgeon characterized it. The tumor would not shrink with radiation therapy. Roth describes his father as becoming more and more debilitated, "little more than a shrunken thing with a crushed face, wearing a black eye patch and sitting completely inert, almost unrecognizable now, even to me."[5]

Early on the morning of his death, when I arrived at the hospital emergency room to which he had been rushed from his bedroom at home, I was confronted by an attending physician prepared to take "extraordinary measures" and to put him on a breathing machine. Without it there was no hope, though, needless to say—the doctor added—the machine wasn't going to reverse the process of the tumor, which appeared to have begun to attack his respiratory function. The doctor also informed me that, by law, once my father had been hooked up to the machine he would not be disconnected, unless he could once again sustain breathing on his own. A decision had to be made immediately and, since my brother was still en route by plane from Chicago, by me alone.

And I, who had explained to my father the provisions of the living will and got him to sign it, didn't know what to do. How could I say no to the machine if it meant that he needn't continue to endure this agonizing battle to breathe? How could I take it on myself to decide that my father should be finished with life, life which is ours to know just once? Far from invoking the living will, I was nearly on the verge of ignoring it and saying, "Anything! Anything!"

I asked the doctor to leave me alone with my father, or as alone as he and I could be in the middle of the emergency room bustle. As I sat there and watched his struggle to go on living, I tried to focus on what the tumor had done with him already. This wasn't difficult, given that he looked on that stretcher as though by then he'd been through one hundred rounds with Joe Louis. I thought about the misery that was sure to come, provided he could even be kept alive on a respirator. I saw it all, all, and yet I had to sit there for a very long time before I leaned as close to him as I could and, with my lips to his sunken, ruined face, found it in me finally to whisper, "Dad, I'm going to have to let you go." He'd been unconscious for several hours and couldn't hear me, but, shocked, amazed, and weeping, I repeated it to him again and then again, until I believed it myself.[6]

Most families cannot exert that kind of will at such a wrenching moment. Such defiance of the power of the heroic pathway is not often present among bewildered and overwhelmed patients and family members, who usually have no understanding of the course of end-stage disease, no knowledge of its symptoms, no idea of what to expect. Nor are physicians trained to speak to patients or families in ways that would divert them from being caught up in the procedures that are so publicly criticized and that the physicians themselves, in many instances, are working hard to limit.[7] And while many physicians in recent years, especially younger ones, tell patients and families in no uncertain terms when the end of life is approaching, they present that information within the hospital environment, a place where many assume miracles can be worked. The message is mixed: "You (or your relative) are dying." That is the fact. "But let's do this procedure." That is the hope. Each pathway is a potent magnet that attracts patients, families, and health professionals to its assumptions. In many cases the heroic pathway does lead to "saving life" and the revolving door leads to longer life (by temporarily stabilizing the medical condition). When wanted life is thus attained, the health care delivery system works. And it works often.

It is important to note that these pathways are constantly evolving. Though the heroic intervention and revolving door alternatives are common, they are not all-pervasive. The call for "palliative care" or "comfort care" at the end of life is a recent response specifically to the heroic intervention pathway. When innovative physicians and nurses introduce palliative care measures, they frequently have to challenge standard practices or negotiate with their hospital administrations to implement them. Frequently, the hurdle is the lack of Medicare reimbursement for such care,[8] even though it prepares for death and makes the end of life as comfortable for the patient as possible. Palliative care is not (yet) a standard aspect of hospital system bureaucracy. Not "natural" to the system, it is still an add-on, a glaring contrast to the way things ordinarily work.[9]

The Power of the Pathways and the Ideology of Choice

Relatively healthy people, when asked, often say they do not want intensive care treatments that will prolong dying. In contrast, very sick persons, both in and out of the hospital, and their families frequently cling to life. They want to preserve it as long as possible, even for a few days or weeks, regardless of the means and pain necessary to do so.[10] For very sick hospital patients and their families, personal opinions are complicated by severity of disease, course of treatment, details of medical care, gender, education, and religion. Studies have shown the complexity of asking a question about what one thinks one wants—and what one wants for another person—in a hypothetical future. In one such study, family members reported that their sick relatives wanted "comfort" rather than "aggressive" interventions near the end of life, while the sick persons themselves reported wanting more treatment, even if it caused pain.[11] Another study reported that 70 percent of hospital patients over the age of eighty preferred comfort to life-sustaining care.[12] Ninety percent of patients in one hospital study said they would want life-support technologies if their health could be restored. That big "if" is always the hope when use of supportive technology begins.[13] Another study found that 60 percent of questioned hospitalized patients in their eighties and nineties wanted to live as long as possible, regardless of pain or poor health, yet those patients' family members did not understand their relatives' wishes to prolong life.[14] Several studies found significant differences between what terminally ill persons want for themselves regarding life-sustaining treatments and what their families think they want.[15] Finally, elderly persons or hospitalized patients may change their minds over time about preferences for life-sustaining technologies.[16]

Despite differences and even contradictions among specific research findings, the personal impact of critical illness unquestionably changes one's perception of the relative importance of invasive, aggressive medical treatments. It also changes one's ideas about the value and quality of life itself. In the widespread quest for "better dying," the debates center on how much treatment is too much and when aggressive interventions should be stopped. But what kind of care counts as too aggressive or too lengthy, and how can anyone know that in the midst of trying to stabilize a critically ill person? Why should a spouse, child, parent, or doctor reject a treatment or procedure that has the potential to add days, weeks, or months to the precious life that each person has? The public, medical, and ethical debates about "good" versus "bad" deaths tend to emphasize and rationalize self-conscious decision-making during the illness, as if *free* choice—unencumbered by fear, grief, guilt, confusion, fatigue, lack of knowledge about medicine, the hospital, and the body, and the power of the pathway itself—were possible, given the task at hand. As if rationally, objectively weighing one discrete option against another were possible. Rational decision-making may or may not play a part in patient and family experiences in the hospital, and the debates fail most of the time to capture the urgency and disorientation that families experience as they are carried along a pathway.

The same debates also fail to acknowledge that families may and do want to remain passive, simply traveling along a road others have created, without taking responsibility for the fate of a life.

Much of the struggle over the intensity and kind of treatment near the end of life is about whether death comes at the *right time*. Often, it is only after medical staff and families acknowledge that the patient has reached the end of a pathway, that medicine has tried all its relevant tools, that death's time is finally recognized as having come. Only at that moment of new understanding can steps be taken so that death, or dying, can be called "dignified." Then the family, by giving permission to withdraw medical treatment, can participate with the medical staff in creating a decent, if not a "good," death.

I. THE HEROIC INTERVENTION PATHWAY

The following two stories illustrate the inevitability of moving things along. They are the first of many that form the backbone of the rest of this book. The accounts are common examples of hospital death, and they illustrate what is troubling about the way hospital deaths occur. My research addressed the sources and paradoxes of the widespread complaints about hospital death, and in making my observations, I concentrated on the patients and the scenarios that were difficult for doctors, nurses, and families. There were many. I wanted to learn how all the players—doctors, nurses, patients, families, technologies, and bureaucracy—are implicated in creating those deaths.

The work of the hospital, and the necessary adaptations everyone must make to it, generate all kinds of reactions, all kinds of tales about patients, treatments, and rules. Staff work within hospital walls and assumptions and see something different from what patients and families, who enter the hospital as strangers in moments of crisis and fear, see. Thus multiple, conflicting stories emerge from the place—stories about what must be done and why, what can be done and how. Stories about being stuck and stymied, about the importance of timeliness, about the characteristics of the person-in-the-patient and death-in-life, about the presence of suffering, and about the overarching question "What shall we do now?"

Because patients in the ICU often cannot speak, families are extremely important to staff for moving things along. Families, too, are being moved (or more accurately, prodded and manipulated) when doctors, nurses, and social workers ask them to make specific choices. The timing of their responses, as well as what they say they want for the patient, are important for staff because the timeliness of movement from procedure to procedure is so important. At stake in their decision-making are the family's future memories about what they did for their relative, whether they fought for life, and whether they saw themselves as implicated in the patient's death. Families are coping with potential and imminent loss at the same time as they must engage hospital-mandated "decision-making." Often, families are simply not up to the task, or they are not up to it in what hospital staff consider a timely way. This is because the demands placed on them are new and strange and because the focus of their attention and emotional energy is the person they know who hovers near death, and because, above all, they hope that that person will not die. In contrast, at stake for health professionals is a sense of appropriate medical practice—both to do no physical or psychic harm and to allocate human and financial resources prudently. These are divergent sensibilities, divergent moral responsibilities.

"We Don't Want Her on Life Support": Dorothy Mason

Day 1: I am tagging along on morning rounds in the intensive care unit. At 8 A.M. on weekday mornings, one of the critical care physicians (also known now as intensivists) goes from bed to bed, accompanied by that day's charge nurse and by the staff members who comprise the "health care team"—a respiratory therapist, a social worker, and a hospital chaplain. At each bedside the nurse describes the patient's medical status and latest test results, the procedures the patient is scheduled to have that day, her assessment of family members' understanding of the severity of the illness, and the features of the patient's condition that need attention by the team. The team members discuss, as fully and quickly as possible, the immediate plans, the less immediate therapeutic goals, and each of their concerns about treatment and about communication with the patient (if awake and alert) and family.

We arrive at Mrs. Dorothy Mason's bed, and the doctor tells me she arrived last night from a nursing home with "bad pneumonia, bad COPD,[17] and Alzheimer's disease." "I don't know how she got here," he says, "but her son was with her. He wants everything done." The nurse assigned to her tells me, "If this were my mother, I'd let her go. I don't know why the son is doing this—guilt? need? If she doesn't get better, the doctors will begin to talk to the son about taking her off the vent[18] and letting go, but not until she doesn't start to get better." Another nurse says, "She came from the nursing home extremely malnourished, weighs seventy-five pounds, and looks like she arrived from Auschwitz." All I can see is the head of a frail old woman who is connected to a breathing machine and to several intravenous lines for fluids and medications. In her medical chart, under admitting diagnosis, it says, "acute pulmonary edema, pneumonia, respiratory failure." Mrs. Mason is seventy-nine years old. Someone at the nursing home—that person is not specified— called paramedics when Mrs. Mason was observed to be in respiratory distress; she was brought by ambulance, with high-flow oxygen, to the hospital emergency room and intubated there.

Day 2: The lens through which all patients are viewed is colored by the imperative to move them along the pathway. By her bedside, several nurses sketch a socio-medical portrait of Mrs. Mason for me. "She's a No Code,[19] but still on the vent and getting nutrition and care. We just won't do CPR," I am told. Another nurse says, "She was made a No Code at 10 P.M. last night. Up to then the son wanted everything done. The doctor talked to the son earlier, then at nine o'clock last night he went to him again, explained the situation again, and asked him, 'Would you really want us to pound on her chest and crack her ribs?' That's when the son reluctantly agreed it was okay to make his mother a No Code." Later, the nurse on the evening shift says, "The son made the decision to continue full-out antibiotics for twenty-four hours. If there is no improvement by tomorrow, he'll consider withdrawing care. He has moved a lot, from thinking she was a viable hospital patient to acknowl- edging that she might die. He's come far."

Day 3: There is no improvement. Mrs. Mason is not responsive, though her eyes open sometimes and she seems to look around the room, but nurses tell me that she cannot purposefully move her eyes; there is no intent behind the look, no person behind the stare. That clin- ical judgment—that the patient is not fully, really alive—often contradicts the opinion of family members, who tend to see purposefulness in small movements and to think that the conscious person they knew before the crisis is still there, hidden within a sick body. To someone entirely inexperienced in evaluating conditions of minimal consciousness, there is no way to tell if "the person" is there, no way to assess how "alive" the patient is.

Mrs. Mason's son wants to continue antibiotics for an additional twenty-four hours to "see what happens" and then consider withdrawing supportive care. The patient's nurse for today confides to me, "She should never have been put on a ventilator in the emergency room. She should have had a nasal cannula, and then she would have eventually died, peacefully. . . . She has had Alzheimer's disease for a long time and has been incontinent for a long time. She came in with bilobar pneumonia [pneumonia in both lobes of the lungs]. In the nursing home they weren't treating it, which was wise on their part, but she wasn't supposed to die, because she wasn't made a No Code." The nurse goes on to say that generally, adult children have misperceptions about the "strength" of their hospitalized mothers. "It takes a lot for people to see that they are dealing with vulnerable old ladies," she says. It is difficult for Mrs. Mason's son to see anything other than a strong mother who has bounced back before. This is because, according to the nurse, "she had been sort of moving along, incontinent, demented, getting more frail, with lousy nutrition, but not that sick. This is the first time he's seen her really sick, maybe going to die. So he can't accept it at first."

Day 4: At her bedside I speak with Mrs. Mason's son for the first time. He is a businessman and has been coming to the hospital daily during his lunch hour and then again after work. He is sitting close to his mother's bed and looking at her tenderly, talking to her and holding her hand. She is unresponsive. He tells me, "She had a living will done about eight years ago, and in it she was clear that she didn't want her dying prolonged. Now it's tough in the hospital because she couldn't have predicted this sort of a situation, and I don't know if this is prolonging her life." He notes, "She's stable, not any worse than two days ago, but she's hardly responsive." He had been with her in the nursing home when the nurses there said she wasn't doing well and they called 911. He had come to the hospital with her. The doctors in the emergency room needed to know immediately if they should intubate her because without mechanical ventilation she would have died. With tears in his eyes her son reports that he said, "Yes, go ahead," because he wanted her to live, was hopeful she would stabilize, and could not accept being singled out to be responsible for her death at that moment. Although he made that decision quickly, he agonized over it. "It isn't her time yet," he says, and tells me she had been hospitalized a year before and had "come back" from other crises. "She is tough." But he would not want her to live indefinitely on a ventilator and neither would she. He only wants her to have the opportunity to get better, to get off the ventilator.

"You're not seeing the really tough decision points," he tells me. "They happened earlier. My toughest decision was moving her from home to assisted living in the first place eighteen months ago." She had covered up her Alzheimer's disease well. "She was social and she had a good sense of humor." He knew things were changing, but he didn't know how bad things were until about a year ago when he moved her to the nursing home and she was diagnosed with advanced Alzheimer's. Regarding the hospital requirement for a code status decision, he volunteers that he made his mother a No Code. He says to me, "Some families might think making a No Code decision is participating in killing the patient, but I don't think so." (He does not mention that he had had to be talked into making that decision.)

Day 8: The nurse calls me to the bedside, dramatically pulls the sheet off Mrs. Mason, and says, "Look at this." She has been trying to turn Mrs. Mason and is having a great deal of difficulty. Mrs. Mason's limbs are so contracted, her legs so tightly wrapped around one another, that the nurse cannot disentangle them. Mrs. Mason is not responding to the nurse's maneuvers or to our conversation. I am looking at emaciated legs with the skin hanging directly on bones that look brittle, as if they would shatter if they were touched. I have never been this close to such frailty.

Day 10: Mrs. Mason's son continues to want "aggressive" care, that is, continued mechanical ventilation, nasogastric tube feeding (a thin tube inserted through the nose that delivers nutritional liquid to the stomach), and antibiotics for the recalcitrant pneumonia. The medical staff are trying a different antibiotic. I go to Mrs. Mason's bedside with a technician who is going to draw her blood. He speaks to her in a loud but caring voice, close to her face, telling her what he is going to do, and she turns her head to stare at him. I reintroduce myself, and she turns to me and stares. But she does not respond in any other way or even blink.

Later I speak with Mrs. Mason's family doctor of three years. When I ask how he would handle this situation, he replies that he would never have put her on a ventilator in the first place. He would have "let her go initially. But once it's in place, it's very hard to remove." He has turned her care over to the hospital specialists. He is not making any of the decisions now but just observing the situation. He says that because she is so frail, she will eventually get an infection and die on the ventilator, but if she does manage to recover from this episode, her dementia will be worse.

At the bedside I speak again with Mrs. Mason's son and also with a second son who has just arrived from another state. Mrs. Mason is looking at her children; that is, her eyes seem to focus on them, but I cannot be sure. It is impossible to tell if she is hearing and then comprehending our conversation because she is so unresponsive. The nurse comes in to draw her blood. Mrs. Mason's sons both repeat to me that they do not want their mother to be on life support. I am not sure if they realize that their mother is, indeed, on life support.

I realize that I am of two minds. I want the family to allow their mother's death. I want them to tell the doctor to stop life-sustaining treatments because they are not really sustaining her life. She is so sick and so frail I cannot imagine her recovery. The treatments appear to be ineffective. She may be in extreme pain. This is a terrible way to die. Yet I am aware that Mrs. Mason is not my own mother. I am sure that I, too, would want to give the tools of medicine a chance to work, a long chance, even if the treatments looked painful. I have no idea how I would feel if I stood in the shoes of Mrs. Mason's children, if someone I cared about were in this condition.

Day 12: The intensive care doctor mentions to me that Mrs. Mason's kidneys and other organs are beginning to fail. Her family doctor discusses her failing condition with her children for some time and urges them "to withdraw ventilator support and let her die." They agree. She dies shortly after the ventilator is withdrawn, with her children, the family doctor, and the intensive care specialist at her bedside. When I see Mrs. Mason's family doctor in the hospital corridor a week later, he tells me that Mrs. Mason's son would not leave the bedside for one and a half hours after she stopped breathing. The doctor said he was amazed that "it took the son so long to let her die."

Of the 370 patients age fifty or over who died that year in the same hospital as Mrs. Mason, 22 percent (80 patients) followed the same pathway. They were rushed to the hospital in distress, placed on a mechanical ventilator in the emergency room so they could breathe and thus continue to live, and were then taken to the intensive care unit. After days or weeks of treatment they died in the ICU.[20] Mrs. Mason died following twelve days on the heroic pathway. The average length of hospital stay for the eighty patients cited above was eight days (the range was from less than twenty-four hours to sixty-three days). For the seventy-one of those patients who died in the ICU while still connected to ventilator support, the average length of stay was twelve days.[21]

"Trouble with God's Will and Medical Technology": Patrick Brown

Admission to day 9: The social worker assigned to the intensive care unit invites me to attend a medical team conference with Mrs. Brown, whose husband, age eighty-nine, has been in the ICU for nine days. He arrived from a nursing home with a diagnosis of "acute chest pain/prob-ably myocardial infarction and aspiration pneumonia." According to the nurses, he was designated DNR when he arrived—he did not want to be resuscitated should his heart stop beating. He was intubated (and would not have survived had he not been) in the emergency room, where, I learned later, the treating physician convinced his wife to change his code status to Full Code. (I never learned the reason for this change.) In the event of cardiac arrest, resuscitation would be attempted.

The medical staff are attempting "to wean" Mr. Patrick Brown from the ventilator.[22] The staff cannot predict what will happen when the life-sustaining breathing apparatus is removed, and they are concerned about potential events along the pathway. Will he have the respiratory strength to breathe on his own? They are unsure how to proceed if he needs to be re-intubated sometime later to survive. The pathway requires a decision about possible re-intubation. Would the patient want to be re-intubated? Does the wife know his wishes? The team wants to meet with Mrs. Brown to ascertain the patient's view about life prolongation.

Two physicians, a social worker, a chaplain, and I move into an all-purpose conference room near the ICU. Mrs. Brown arrives promptly. She looks to me to be in her mid-to-late eighties, somewhat frail, slim, and well-dressed. She is smiling, but her eyes are red; she has not slept much. She, rather than one of the hospital staff, opens the conversation, saying that the women in the house next door played drums all night. Mrs. Brown seems to me to be slightly off in this setting, slightly eccentric: "I'm a worrier, Doctor. I took a sleeping pill last night; it made my throat green. That's why I need water." The critical care physician smiles and replies, "You're in good company." "You're a worrier, too?" she asks, and the Doctor says yes. Mrs. Brown continues, "He needs a haircut. Can he have one?" and the doctor responds, "Yes, our nurses are good barbers." She continues to chat, apparently unaware that physicians are used to setting the tone and style of the conversation in these sorts of get-togethers.

We learn that she has been married fifty-six years, that she had supported Mr. Brown's career, that he worked on the Manhattan Project during the Second World War, and that she has cared for him since his stroke thirty years before. "He's the only thing I have and I want to hold on to him as long as I can," she says. "The last thing he said to me was, 'I want to live.'" She talks further about how particular he is with his clothes and his food. He wants things "just so." The social worker asks if there are other family members and if she has help at home. The physician asks what illness sent him to the nursing home. Mrs. Brown replies that it was simply because she could not lift him and care for him any longer. She adds, "The last thing he said to me in the nursing home was that he wants a haircut. Please, that was his last request. Do I pay [the nurse] for it?" His haircut request is a sign of his character and fastidiousness.

A second physician finally comes to the point of this meeting: "We have a little bit of a dilemma. He's not an optimal candidate to completely remove the tube right now. Sometimes it's hard to decide when to pull the tube out, but he could die if we do it. We're close to the time to do it, though, and we need to know what to do." The social worker and intensive care doctor both ask, "Would he want to die if he can't breathe on his own?" Mrs. Brown replies (as do many other family members), "I'll leave it to God's will. I want to keep him going as long as I can. I'm going day by day." She continues, "He's Irish, and strong. He's been here a week. When he first came in, I was told he'd only live four hours. I'll leave it to God's will." The social worker responds, "We have some trouble now with God's will and medical technology. Medical technology can prolong life long past the time when the person would die on his own." Mrs. Brown simply says, "I don't think he knows anything right now. I want to keep him going as long as we can." The physicians rise to leave and Mrs. Brown thanks everyone for saving her husband's life, reiterates her request for a haircut, and again asks, "Do I pay for it?" She smiles and says without irony or self-consciousness, "We had fifty-six years of marriage; fifty-six years of fighting. He's Irish. I'm Italian. I miss the fighting. We fought every day." All the staff smile and the intensive care physician says, "I appreciate your candor."

I am perplexed about how the medical staff are going to interpret Mrs. Brown's comments, given their need for a clear statement about re-intubation, and I am not sure at all what her reference to "God's will" means. I meet up with the physicians and social worker later, and each tells me he or she is not sure what Mrs. Brown "wanted" either. Nonetheless one doctor writes in the medical chart, "Wife inclined to re-intubate if necessary per family conference today."

Day 10: The intensive care physician waits for Mrs. Brown to arrive before removing her husband's ventilator tube. He wants to make sure Mr. Brown has the opportunity to talk to his wife and to answer, in her presence, the question that looms so large for hospital staff. The physician asks the nurse to notify him when Mrs. Brown arrives. Mrs. Brown comes in; she and the physician shake hands warmly. She has been down the hall, speaking with the hospital chaplain. A respiratory therapist assists the physician with the extubation. Mrs. Brown moves away from the bedside. The moment the respiratory therapist removes the tube from the patient's throat, the physician asks Mr. Brown if he is feeling better. He replies that he is. Then the physician immediately asks, "If your breathing goes bad again, would you want us to put the tube back in?" Mr. Brown does not answer with a nod or a verbal response. Instead he starts coughing hard, and the physician and respiratory therapist suction the fluids from his mouth and throat. At that moment Mrs. Brown walks over to the side of the bed. She holds his hand, reassures him that he is going to be all right because everyone is taking such good care of him, and playfully tells him that he must get better and come home to her. "Don't you want to come home and fight with me?" "You bet," he replies. She does not respond to the physician's question about re-intubation. She stays at the bedside about two minutes and then leaves.

I follow Mrs. Brown out of the ICU to accompany her downstairs. She is disoriented and does not know how to find the elevator or locate the main hospital entrance. When I ask, "How does he look to you?" she replies that she doesn't know anything. She goes to call a cab. I return to the ICU, where one of the physicians and the social worker are expressing their concern about what will happen to Mrs. Brown when her husband dies. They fear she will not cope well. The physician is certain Mr. Brown will die within a few weeks. They have not discussed this with Mrs. Brown. The physician who removed the breathing tube informs me that he was able to get a clear response from Mr. Brown shortly after his wife left. He does not want to be re-intubated, if that becomes necessary, to survive. Meanwhile, Mr. Brown is stable, breathing on his own without mechanical assistance.

Day 18, a week after the extubation: The hospital discharge planner is trying to find a new nursing home for Mr. Brown because he requires too much physical care to return to the institution he had been in before. But he is not yet well enough to be discharged, even to a highly skilled long-term-care facility. A physician writes in the medical chart, "Progress stalled by multiple factors. Intrinsic: age, old stroke, general weakness; Extrinsic: infection, fluid excess. Likelihood of recovery in question as time evolves." Mr. Brown is moved out of the intensive care unit and onto a medical ward because he does not require a ventilator.

Day 30: Mr. Brown has a new, different strain of pneumonia. He is only minimally responsive. He breathes with difficulty through a nasal cannula.[23] The chart note reads, "Condition is even worse now and any measures[24] are not going to alter outcome. Recommend comfort measures only." The staff's fears about Mrs. Brown have materialized. One physician tells me she had "decompensated completely, had a psychotic break, had a nervous breakdown." She is now in the hospital, on the psychiatric unit, and apparently thinks her husband has already died. The physician is attempting to locate a distant relative so that he can discuss with a family member the possible withdrawal of antibiotics, nutrition delivered by a tube into the stomach, and nasal cannula oxygen that Mr. Brown is receiving. When I ask, he tells me that withdrawing those things will hasten the patient's death "somewhat." I ask if he needs family members' permission to withdraw antibiotics and tube-delivered nutrition and to stop diagnostic and therapeutic procedures. He tells me he is not sure about that and adds that he is thinking about what to do regardless of family input, since Mr. Brown's closest relative, his wife, cannot speak for him or form her own, rational opinion.[25] He also reports that he had favored no intubation when the patient arrived and says that if Mr. Brown had not been placed on a ventilator, he would have died shortly after admission. He would not have had to go through "this entire month" in the hospital. But, this physician says, another doctor insisted on intubation and took Mr. Brown to the ICU.

Aftermath: A niece does arrive, locates Mr. Brown's papers, and finds a document stating that Mr. Brown did not want to be intubated and did not want his life prolonged by technological means. As soon as the medical staff are notified about that written document, they discontinue lab work, diagnostic work, and treatments. Mr. Brown dies several days later, while his wife is still hospitalized.[26]

Resisting and Organizing the Time for Death

Mrs. Mason's pneumonia was left untreated in the nursing home, an act that seemed to ensure her death there. Some ICU staff members thought she should have died there. Yet when in respiratory distress, she was rushed to the hospital and placed on the heroic intervention pathway in the emergency room. Mrs. Mason's son thought his mother could be cured of pneumonia and returned to her previous level of function, which he did not view as precarious. He did not see her extreme frailty, did not acknowledge pneumonia as her final illness, and certainly did not "prepare" for her death. He pressed for continued treatment and struggled deeply with the fact that she would not, could not, be saved if she had a cardiac arrest. The hospital policy of clarifying the patient's code status created an existential crisis for Mrs. Mason's son as he grappled with what Do Not Resuscitate meant for him. The health care team faced the problem of how to treat such a frail woman who would not recover. They wanted to withdraw all technological support as soon as she arrived in intensive care, but they could not reshape the heroic intervention pathway. That pathway is built on nursing homes' responses to respiratory distress and their liability concerns, on emergency department medicine that focuses on saving lives, on intensive care treatments, and on family hopes.

There is societal discomfort, expressed in the public discourse about problematic dying, with "prolonged" intensive care just before death. This reflects a recent preoccupation with the timing of death that was born, at least in part, from the attempts of those at end stages of AIDS and cancer to control their dying by reducing the duration of the pain, suffering, and humiliation that often accompany the terminal phase of disease. But proactively shortening a life is a complicated matter. Who is to say whether twelve days is too long, just right, or too short a time for someone to be in the ICU prior to death? Personal accounts in the media would suggest that those days of unnecessary suffering are also an affront to the dignity of the patient. No one wants "to be connected to tubes" for days or weeks before death. But when we enter the existential space of Mrs. Mason's son and look at the details of how the heroic pathway proceeds, we can begin to understand why so many people face similar circumstances. Mrs. Mason's son could not, would not, quickly authorize his mother's death in the emergency department, for that, from his point of view, was what he was being asked to do. Why should he authorize death when emergency medicine saves lives? He hoped for her recovery and worked toward ensuring it by requesting treatments.

When I presented the story of Mrs. Mason to members of a hospital ethics committee, only two persons, the two who were not health professionals, were outraged that medical staff pressured the son "to allow" his mother to die as soon as she arrived in the ICU. They were angry that hospital staff could assume the patient was suffering and angry also that staff could view "prolonging her dying" as inappropriate medical care. Why, they asked, should medicine "shorten" her life, decide that she should die *before* twelve days had passed? After all, Mrs. Mason might also have recovered in that time. They felt strongly that families should be "allowed the time they need" to consider death's approach, to make a transition from hope for recovery to acceptance that their relative will die. Their shared view, which was unencumbered by the pressures of institutional time on health professional practice, contrasts with what is *normal* for clinicians—the need to facilitate death when the medical staff are certain that death is inevitable regardless of treatments.

ICU staff talk a great deal about how families "need time to adjust" to the fact that a relative is probably dying. Staff members note that only after a few days of watching a person hover near death can families "choose" to withdraw all treatments. Nurses (and sometimes doctors) told me that they try to give families the time and support they need to "accept" a death.[27] But length of time is important here, and if families do not "choose" death after a few days, staff become exasperated. Only when Mrs. Mason's family physician named death as real, told her two sons that their mother was clearly dying and would die no matter what, did her son assent to the withdrawal of medical treatment.

Mrs. Brown attempted to advocate for her husband as best she could while he was in the ICU by visiting him almost daily and trying to ensure that his prehospitalization requests to her were met. But she could not articulate for hospital staff what they needed to know—the patient's wishes regarding re-intubation. She did not comprehend the subject of extubation and potential re-intubation as a pressing medical (and legal) concern. She was oblivious, initially, to the primary question facing the ICU team, and later, to the question of withdrawing treatments on the medical ward. Mr. Brown's medical decline plunged his wife into a deep personal crisis. The doctors, carefully following institutional norms, felt they should try to get another family member's assent for the withdrawal of treatments to facilitate what they considered the most humane and least-prolonged death under the circumstances.[28] Though most family members do not require psychiatric treatment following the ICU hospitalization of a relative, they are, like Mrs. Brown, unprepared for the kinds of questions that require immediate and straightforward answers. Those questions, based on how technology is used, how the body works, and how the hospital is run, are outside most families' realms of experience and cause a great deal of consternation when they are posed by medical staff. And those questions arise because the press of time and the power of the pathways are ubiquitous.

II. THE PARADOX OF RESUSCITATION: APPROACH/AVOIDANCE ON THE HEROIC PATHWAY

"I had to see my mother die twice, once on Saturday night, and that was peaceful, and now, for the second time. This is the medical miracle. This is where medicine was able to bring her after resuscitating her. This is how she was brought back. This is the level; we're not going to get any more. . . . But I'll stay with her now for this second death."

Daughter of a patient who collapsed at home, was resuscitated by paramedics, and remained in a coma for nine days in the hospital until family members agreed to allow hospital staff to withdraw life-sustaining measures

The potential for cardiopulmonary resuscitation hovers over the heroic intervention pathway as a perhaps lifesaving, always dreaded procedure. It may restore patients to *some kind of life* following a cardiac or respiratory arrest, but alternatively, it may be the most violent, "undignified" activity prior to death. In 1965 CPR was reclassified from an exclusively medical procedure, used only in certain kinds of cases, to a universal emergency procedure that anyone could perform. By implication, anyone, anywhere, could benefit from CPR.[29] After that reclassification (by the American Heart Association, American Red Cross, Industrial Medical Association, and U.S. Public Health Service), the default policy and practice at almost all hospitals in the United States became to initiate a resuscitation attempt for any patient, regardless of medical condition or age, in the event of cardiac arrest. Doctors and nurses who worked in hospitals from the mid-1960s through the mid-1970s recall that all patients who had a cardiac arrest were "coded," regardless of their condition or the physician's judgment about whether the procedure was appropriate.[30] Fear of prosecution, coupled with the ethos of that era that doctors should try to prevent death, ensured the perpetuation of the practice.

Though some efforts to limit hospital resuscitation attempts were under way in the early 1970s, not until after the case of Karen Quinlan had gained wide publicity did individual hospitals begin to issue guidelines for preventing the indiscriminate use of emergency CPR.[31] The formal DNR order came into being in 1974.[32] Yet consent for emergency resuscitation was, and thirty years later still is, presumed. In 1990, the *New York Times* ran a front-page story stating, "Cardiac resuscitation is being widely misapplied and overused, doctors say, leading to costly and sometimes painful efforts on patients who are unlikely to benefit."[33] By the early 1990s hundreds of thousands of people were estimated to have been on the receiving end of resuscitation procedures (no national statistics are kept), yet for most of them, the attempt did not succeed.

Studies have found that, depending on the patient's age, type of cardiac problem, number and type of other medical conditions, the physiological details of the arrest, and how soon the procedure was initiated after the person stopped breathing, 8 to 15 percent of hospitalized patients survive CPR to be discharged from the hospital.[34] But patients with metastatic cancer, AIDS, renal failure, sepsis, or pneumonia have less than a 5 percent chance of survival to discharge.[35] In one study of CPR in an intensive care unit, only 3 percent of ICU patients survived the procedure.[36] Actual numbers of people with heart disease or multiple medical conditions who are able to live functional lives following a resuscitative procedure are extremely small, and the quality of those lives, measured by any standard, is not well documented.

Nor is the fact well publicized that, in a certain percentage of cases, the recipient of the resuscitation attempt survives but is in worse condition, neurologically, than before CPR.[37] If a patient's circulation is not reestablished within a few minutes, neurological function declines sharply.[38] There are almost no studies about what post-CPR "survival" means. Sociologist Stefan Timmermans notes, "Survival rates hide the Russian roulette aspect of resuscitative efforts. The term *survival rate* highlights lifesaving while it glosses over the possibility—indeed, the likelihood—that these same interventions create neurological impairment. Because different vital organs can be restored after varying time spans, hearts and lungs will inevitably be restored while brains will not. With CPR, we save lives, but we produce people with a range of disabilities. The two outcomes are inevitably intertwined. Only one of them, however, is used to evaluate resuscitation. Even if we focus on the most promoted side of resuscitative efforts—the 1 to 3 percent of all people discharged alive—we still do not know much about the meaning of a resuscitative event in the life course of survivors. . . . If better techniques can save more patients, even more people will be left in a permanent vegetative state."[39]

I observed scores of patients who had undergone CPR, either prior to hospitalization or while in the hospital. For ten of them, the procedure restored heartbeat, pulse, and some degree of biological activity in the brain. It returned the body to some threshold of *aliveness.* But it did not restore *life,* that is, it did not bring a person back to a state of identifiable awareness or even the most minimally discernible functional or expressive ability. It brought the CPR recipient to some kind of betwixt-and-between comatose state instead. That CPR may induce the zone of indistinction, but not restore a person to *life,* is not well-known or appreciated. On television, CPR often brings people back to their previous lives. It is broadly thought to be one of the miracles of modern medicine.[40] But it also is one of the technologies that may bring death into life.

Knowledge gleaned from the many studies of poor CPR outcomes has not changed the tenacity of the practice.[41] The ineffectiveness of hospital resuscitation attempts on the very old and frail, the terminally ill, and those with metastatic or multisystem disease is widely acknowledged. Health professionals are well aware of it, and what to do about it has been debated in the media and in the medical and bioethics literatures.[42] But more powerful than individual medical opinion is the movement of the heroic pathway toward the use of CPR—propelled by hospital culture in which resuscitation attempts occur unless someone explicitly says stop and by public expectations that CPR can stave off death.

CPR is viewed both as a medical responsibility—though frequently an unwanted one—and as every patient's right. Death without an attempted resuscitation is often conceived of as "not doing everything possible." This reasoning makes it understandable how families can resist Do Not Resuscitate orders while *at the same time* claiming to want "dignified" dying, that is, death without violent or "unnatural" medical intervention.

Hospital policy regarding who can designate a Do Not Resuscitate order is not always spelled out for every possible situation and is under continual or periodic discussion. The ethics committee at one hospital I observed reviews its policy regularly in an attempt to offer a clear guideline for physician action. I listened to it discuss a number of murky circumstances. For example, what should be done about a very old or frail patient who has requested DNR but who then elects to undergo surgery? Standard procedure in the operating room is to resuscitate in the event of cardiac arrest. Does standard procedure in that environment override previously stated and written patient wishes? That question was debated for months without resolution. Despite painstaking discussion among health professionals about the appropriate use of resuscitation procedures, a clear family decision regarding code status almost always trumps physician opinion (regardless of whether the family decision expresses "what the patient would want"). It was not always clear to me or to physicians with whom I spoke whether hospital administrations would support physician action—for CPR *or* DNR—that opposed family desires.

Following resuscitation efforts, when brain activity of some sort is observed through diagnostic tests but the person is not responsive (or is only minimally responsive), one question dominates discussion: "How long should life-sustaining procedures go on?" Following an unsuccessful resuscitation attempt, the direction of the pathway finally shifts toward death. Families that do not understand the power or direction of that shift have an especially hard time understanding this sad and not unusual conclusion to heroic intervention. At this juncture of the pathway, when the *time* to withdraw life support becomes the dominant concern of the hospital staff, families truly feel the pressure of responsibility either "to give life a chance" and "to go for life," or instead "to put things in God's hands," "let nature take its course," and "let the patient die." At that point family "decision-making" is guided by the effects of procedure.

In the days following a resuscitation attempt that cannot be categorized as successful, time is the most serious concern for hospital staff. And time, conceived through the rules of the institution, is always gauged against a bureaucratically framed sense of the *normal* unfolding of events.

The next two stories reflect the impact of resuscitation on patients' conditions, on hospital staff's concerns with moving things along and with orchestrating what they consider to be the best possible death under the circumstances, and on the family's feelings of hope, disbelief, and responsibility toward the continuity of a patient's life. The stories reflect, too, different staff approaches to the control over time. In the first story, hospital staff are focused on family "decision-making" to move the patient along to what they consider a timely death. Yet the family members are allowed, in their own time, to reach agreement among themselves about what should be done. Nothing moves until they are comfortable in their consensus. In the second story, the doctors take firm control of movement toward death and announce when it is time for death to occur. Both kinds of scenario are normal, ordinary occurrences.

Allowing Time for Family Consensus: Faith Walker

Admission to Day 4: Faith Walker, age forty-eight, collapsed on the street and a passerby called 911. She was brought to the emergency room without any pulse, resuscitated, and then attached, by means of a tube inserted into her trachea, to a mechanical ventilator. She was taken to the ICU. The medical staff determined that she had probably had a respiratory arrest caused by her severe asthma. She required ventilator support to breathe and vasopressor medications, the drugs that maintain or increase blood pressure, to return her blood pressure to a viable range.

By the fourth day, Mrs. Walker remains, as she has since admission, unresponsive to painful stimuli—the sign of a deep coma. The physician in charge of her treatment shows me a list of fifteen or twenty family members he has drawn up, all of whom want to be involved in deciding about her care and her future. Mrs. Walker has four children and many siblings, cousins, nieces, and nephews. The doctor has been speaking daily with Mrs. Walker's husband and several other family members since she arrived in the ICU. He wants to meet this afternoon with whoever shows up to talk about withdrawing life-sustaining care. With families this large, he says, it is always difficult to get everyone to agree; usually one person says he or she does not want to withdraw treatment, even if everyone else agrees. He tells me (as do other physicians) that large families take longer to make decisions. Both the nurse caring for Mrs. Walker today and the doctor inform me that the pathway could unfold in two possible ways. Either the family will not allow medical staff to withdraw ventilator support, and Mrs. Walker will become a long-term ventilator-dependent, comatose patient, or the family could assent to the medical team's withdrawal of life support, and then Mrs. Walker would soon die. The doctor remarks that by now either he or a neurologist should have spoken with the family about a No Code order. But they haven't even done that much.

Family members have been visiting Mrs. Walker for brief periods, and the nurses and doctors have already met many of them. Mrs. Walker's husband does not want "the decision" about withdrawing care to be entirely on his shoulders. Several family members do not want life-sustaining support stopped—yet. There will be a family conference with the intensive care physician, and then the family "will take a vote" about what to do.

Doctors and nurses tell me repeatedly that it is absurd for family members to be put in a position in which they feel they have to take a vote, as though they were deciding whether a sentient, responsive *person* should live or die, or as though they were given the chance and the choice to end a life. For families, the "decision" to withdraw life-sustaining technology is viewed as a move against hope, against imagining potential recovery, and it is no wonder they hesitate or refuse to make that kind of decision. While doctors and nurses say they want families to make these kinds of decisions, medical staff would often prefer to withdraw life support on their own initiative—either when they assume the comatose condition to be irreversible or when they know the patient will die soon anyway.[43]

Day 5: A family conference that has been scheduled for five o'clock this evening takes place in the auditorium, the only hospital space large enough to accommodate everyone. When I walk in along with two ICU nurses, eighteen people are already assembled: siblings of Mrs. Walker, aunts, cousins, a daughter, and the minister from her church. This African-American family, like others I observed, relies on its religious community for emotional support and difficult decision-making.

A physician leads the discussion. He explains Mrs. Walker's medical condition: "Her higher brain cells are not functioning; her brain stem reflexes are gone." He stresses that five physicians have come to that conclusion and that there is evidence from the EEG and the neurological exam that she has severe brain damage. But she still has some reflex activity, which shows that the brain isn't dead. And she does make an effort to breathe on her own. In addition, she may have had a heart attack, as she has some damage to the heart and the surrounding vessels. The blood vessels in her foot are narrowed due to diabetes and hypertension. One foot has no pulses and is cold. But the main problem, he emphasizes, is that she is not responsive.

The physician turns to the course of medical treatment. "Even if we do everything we can to keep her alive, it's possible that her heart will stop. If we continue to treat her, we'll have to do three things: amputate her foot; put in a tracheostomy tube because she can't be kept on a ventilator forever; and put in a stomach tube to feed her. All of these things would only keep her alive. We're very good at keeping people alive at all costs. But the neurologists and everyone on the staff who has seen her suggest that we don't do that. We recommend that with someone who has little or no chance of recovery, that we withdraw the things we're doing, and put it in God's hands—let God decide. We recommend that we let nature take its course, and withdraw care. She may breathe on her own for a while, but I don't think for long. We think it's best that we withdraw care and let her die, because she is not going to have a meaningful life." The question that hangs in the air after this speech is whether Mrs. Walker would have some other kind of life *if she were kept alive* by technological means, one that did not resemble her life before her collapse, but one that she or the family could acknowledge or appreciate or desire for her nonetheless.

The language used, "let nature take its course," "let God decide," is highly formalized and is regularly used in situations in which medical staff try to impress on families that their relative will never return to the state he or she was in before the resuscitation attempt, that the patient is close to death, and that death is inevitable despite continued treatments. At this juncture of the pathway, the coupling of religion with medicine—of faith in God (who will do the right thing) with medical knowledge about physiological decline and medical use of life-prolonging technologies—appears often in hospital staff talk. Doctors, nurses, and social workers invoke religion through the use of certain stock phrases because, for families with little or no knowledge about the limits of medical technology and the processes of disease and decline, it works to move things along the pathway. This manipulative tactic often softens the sadness of the inevitability of death.

Though the doctor repeats throughout his twenty-minute presentation that Mrs. Walker has no brain function, his language waffles (as is often the case). He says that she'll "never" regain brain function but also that it's "unlikely" that she'll do so. Doctors who have seen unexpected emergence from deep and prolonged comatose states—"miracles," in common speech—are hesitant to speak unequivocally about medical outcomes. This physician tells me later that doctors always try to err on the side of giving more treatment, in case a patient can make a recovery. He and other physicians he knows have seen cases of "somewhat miraculous recovery." He recounts a story of a twenty-year-old man who had recently been in a coma for four weeks. The family hung on, wanting treatment to continue, and to the staff's surprise "the young man walked out of here. Once you have that kind of experience," he said, "you want to hang on and continue treating the patient." Although physicians are wary of speaking with absolute certainty about the future of comatose patients, they and other health professionals are nonetheless trying to move things along, and their waffling (both "never" and "unlikely") confuses family members about prognosis. Hospital staff may prefer to wait for a family decision about the withdrawal of machines and medications, but family members are hanging on the physician's words about the unlikelihood—which they interpret as the possibility—of recovery.

The physician pauses after his remarks and questions from the group begin.

Family member: Is she in pain?
Physician: No.
Family member: Can she hear?

Physician: Probably not. She only has the most primitive reflexes left.

Family member: We need to have a few days to make a decision. . . .

Physician: I agree. That's why I'm here, to answer questions and explain the situation and give you time to decide. . . . Mr. Walker wants family input. But at some point, we have to make a decision, and after five days, there is no chance that she'll wake up. [He explains the different types of comatose conditions.] With the type of coma Mrs. Walker has, that results from a period of no oxygen to the brain, people don't wake up. If she were to have a heart attack right now, we'd resuscitate her, but if it were me, I wouldn't want that indignity. [A family member asks the doctor to explain what a heart attack is. He does so.]

Family member: If she were to wake up, would she recognize us?

Physician: Virtually no one with this kind of brain damage recovers. What we are doing now is not natural. These things have only become possible in the last fifteen to twenty years. Did Mrs. Walker say anything about her wishes, about advance directives, what she would want?

Sibling: She said she wouldn't want life support.

Physician: This is something very important for the family to consider, what she wanted. Did she put anything in writing?

Family members: No.

Minister: Is she able to do anything on her own?

Physician: No, everything is assisted. The way she is living now is not natural. [Family members ask more questions about how the machines work, the patient's ability to breathe, her volition.] She's one step away from brain death. I'm asking for God's help to decide what to do. She's not going to recover.

Family member: Is she suffering?

Physician: She's not in pain and she doesn't feel anything.

Family member: Have you ever had a case where someone in a condition like this woke up?

Physician: No. [He repeats information on the different kinds of coma.]

Family member: The family needs time to make a decision.

Physician: Yes, I'm not saying you need to make a decision now, today.

Family members: She didn't have a stroke?

Physician: No. [He explains what a stroke is and how it differs from the brain damage that Mrs. Walker suffered.]

Family member: The logic part of her brain is gone. And her foot, it has to be amputated. And who is going to take care of her?

Family member: She doesn't want anyone to take care of her. She said that to me several times.

Family member: I say we leave it in God's hands.

Family member: One thing we need to keep in mind is if she were to come out of this, it wouldn't be the same Faith we know. The Faith we know doesn't exist. [The physician leaves the room to answer a call on his pager.]

RN: We want to emphasize that you don't have to make a decision now. That you can just think about the facts we've told you and think about what she would want.

Minister: And another thing, would she want to be resuscitated if her heart stops?

Family member (addressing the physician, who has just returned to the room): Where are the fevers from?

Physician: Probably from the brain damage. She's on antibiotics, but we haven't found an infection. But the foot will be a source of infection.

Minister: So there can be complications?

Physician: Yes. The lung can collapse, the heart can have problems. The foot will have to come off at some point. Her kidneys are fine. We're very good at keeping the body going. It's the brain that is damaged.

Minister: The main thing is—would she want to live like this?

Physician: Yes. Would she want to live like this—for months?

The physician stands up to leave the auditorium and tells the group that they are welcome to stay and talk among themselves. The nurse stands up and also invites people to stay in the auditorium. She repeats that they don't have to make a decision immediately.

Day 7: The family has still not reached any decision about either code status or removing the ventilator and allowing the patient to die. I am at the patient's bedside when three of Mrs. Walker's relatives arrive and ask the nurse if she will get any better, if she will be able to come home. Mrs. Walker looks peacefully asleep to me, not dead or even near-dead. The nurse explains that this is as good as it is going to get. "She's going to die. If I disconnect the ventilator, she'll stop breathing. Problems will come up. She'll need a tracheostomy and need to have her foot amputated."

After the family leaves the bedside, the nurse says (as do many other nurses during my research) that regardless of how often they are given information about the medical condition, it usually takes several days for families "to get it," to realize that their relative is not going to get better. Both she and another nurse who are caring for Mrs. Walker in her last days tell me that legally it is the family's decision, not the doctor's, to call an end to life-sustaining treatments. One of the nurses adds, "But why should families have to suffer and have the responsibility of making these kinds of decisions in the hospital? It's better if the doctor says, 'We're going to discontinue the ventilator now.' For the family to take a vote? To need to take a vote? That is ridiculous."

The physician in charge of Mrs. Walker's care tells me that when he does not know a patient, as in this instance, he defers completely to the family. His approach is common, I found in my observations, regardless of individual hospital policies. He has learned from extensive talks with Mrs. Walker's husband that he will not make a decision about withdrawing his wife's life support without broad family consensus. The minister who came to the meeting could have brought the family to a decision to withdraw the treatments sooner, the physician thinks, and seemed to be on the brink of doing just that. And if an African-American physician had been at the meeting in the auditorium, he, too, this doctor thinks, would probably have been able to bring this African-American family to a decision sooner. It would not have been productive to give a deadline to that assembled group, the physician continues, because "they would have focused on the deadline, rather than on the task at hand, which was to absorb the medical facts about the patient's condition and realize she wouldn't want to live like this."

Later that day Mrs. Walker's husband tells the physician that he is ready "to stop everything" and so are most family members. He informs the medical staff that the family wants to gather around the bedside at eight o'clock the following evening to say their good-byes and let her die. On the basis of that conversation, the doctor in charge of Mrs. Walker's care writes "No Code" in her medical chart. She will not be resuscitated *for a second time* should her heart stop beating.

Day 8: Staff move Mrs. Walker to a larger alcove in the intensive care unit so the family will have a place to gather. After a short service at the bedside, the ventilator tube is pulled out of Mrs. Walker's body, and she dies within the hour.

Physician Control over the Time for Death: Jim Stevens

Admission to day 5: Mr. Jim Stevens, age eighty-four, has lung disease. He was hospitalized several months earlier for shortness of breath and his symptoms were treated, but his condition continued to deteriorate. When he called his doctor five days ago, he was advised to come to the emergency department and was admitted to the medical ward. But by the next day his condition had worsened, and he was moved to the intensive care unit, where he was placed on a ventilator. The doctors thought he had a lung infection and perhaps tuberculosis in addition to his underlying lung disease and treated him with a variety of drugs. He continued to get worse and became unresponsive. Today, his fifth day in intensive care, Mr. Stevens stopped breathing. If the medical team had done nothing, he would have died. But he was resuscitated and has returned to the precarious, unresponsive condition he was in just before he had the respiratory arrest.

Mr. Stevens is an unusual patient in at least three respects. First, he has a personal physician of many years' standing who is compassionately involved in his hospital care and has discussed possible end-of-life scenarios with Mr. Stevens before this hospitalization. That physician has written in the medical chart, "Mr. Stevens wants to continue treatment so long as there is some reasonable chance of benefit." Mr. Stevens has also known the intensive care specialist for three years and has spoken with him over the years about wanting aggressive medical treatment if necessary, so long as he was responding to that treatment and getting better. Second, Mr. Stevens has a written document, a durable power of attorney for health care, in his medical chart that authorizes the use of life-sustaining measures unless his condition is terminal or he is in a permanently comatose state. Third, at the time he was taken to the intensive care unit, Mr. Stevens told the intensive care specialist that he wanted to be intubated and placed on a ventilator; that he wanted aggressive treatment so long as he had a chance of returning to his active life. There is no dilemma here. The patient's voice is clear and it has been heard. The physicians are in agreement with the patient and with each other.

I learn other things about Mr. Stevens from his personal physician. He is an active bachelor with a terrific sense of humor. He lives in an apartment complex for seniors. He goes ballroom dancing regularly. "Don't tell the Olympic Committee I'm taking steroids," he had jokingly remarked a few weeks before he was hospitalized. He is a poet. He has many friends. For at least half of every medical visit, his physician says, they used to talk about many things besides his health.

Day 12, morning: Seven days after the resuscitation, Mr. Stevens is not getting better; in fact, his condition continues to worsen. The medical team is unsure of the exact nature of his lung infection, which is not responding to the drugs. His lungs are "stiff," the doctors say, and cannot inflate to get the oxygen they need, even though he is receiving the maximum amount of oxygen the ventilator can deliver, administered at high pressure. The physicians think he will die within the week, either from the infection itself or from oxygen toxicity. They worry also that a lung might rupture from the high pressure required to ventilate him. They decide that *it is time* for Mr. Stevens to die before these further assaults on his body can occur.

The intensive care specialist and the personal physician go together to the bedside, examine Mr. Stevens, and discuss how best to approach the family members when they meet with them later today. Mr. Stevens's brother, sister-in-law, and niece all arrived from out of town a week ago, shortly after the patient was moved to the intensive care unit. They have been coming to the hospital daily, waiting for his condition to change. They are in an emotional limbo, don't know which way he will turn, and are trying to retain a glimmer of hope. They have been to his apartment and found his will and his written instructions about which mortuary to call in the event of his death. In one sense, they are quite aware that he could die. Yet, as with most deaths, there is simply no emotional or practical preparation for the shock of the end to a life. They are hoping he will simply recover and go home, as he has before.

Day 12, afternoon: The physicians usher the family into an empty patient room just outside the intensive care unit and bring in extra chairs. The doctors lean against the bed and the family members sit or stand. There is tension, a sense of expectation, as the family waits for the doctors to speak. Mr. Stevens's personal physician speaks first. He tells the family that Mr. Stevens is not going to get better, that he cannot come off the ventilator. "It's time to let him go," he says. The patient's sister-in-law asks what will happen if the ventilator is removed. Both physicians explain that he is getting 100 percent oxygen, but that is not enough for him. The intensive care specialist goes on to say that Mr. Stevens came into the hospital this time with a compromised respiratory condition. He is fighting some infection, and they don't know what it is. He is receiving ten different kinds of medications. Four of them are for tuberculosis. It would be possible to keep him alive on the ventilator, perhaps for another week at most, but then something would happen to cause his death anyway, perhaps a lung rupture or the infection itself. Mr. Stevens had wanted everything to be done, the specialist says, if there was hope that he could recover, but he didn't want to be kept alive if the situation was hopeless. Now they have reached the hopeless point, the specialist says—the medications are not curing the infections and there is nothing left that the machines can do.

Mr. Stevens's personal physician continues, "If you are all in agreement, then it's time." The patient's brother and niece seem to absorb that directive without too much difficulty. Mr. Stevens's sister-in-law, however, begins to cry. In the hallway before this meeting, she told me that she thought he looked a bit better today. Now, her face reveals that this news is a huge blow for her. She looks as though she has been hit with a sledgehammer and asks the doctors how long it will take for her brother-in-law to die. The physicians reply that it will not be long, and we all stand up and the doctors guide the family to Mr. Stevens's bedside.

Neither doctor asks the family if they want to be at the bedside or if they want to witness the patient's death. It is assumed that they want to be there. The value of openness and confrontation that the widespread conversation espouses—in talking about death, in choosing death over artificial life-prolongation, and in wanting to facilitate and witness a "good" death—is taken for granted. Many do wish to be at a relative's side when the moment of death, medically speaking, arrives. Others prefer not to. Such preferences are not always easily known or predicted. Mr. Stevens's sister-in-law bristles with discomfort as she is ushered into the ICU.

The specialist leaves the bedside. Mr. Stevens's personal physician draws the curtains around the bed while he explains that the nurses are going to disconnect all the tubes and that the respiratory therapist will suction out Mr. Stevens's throat so he does not make gurgling noises. He says he will be standing by to augment the morphine Mr. Stevens is getting from the morphine drip—he takes several syringes from his pocket to show to the group—if he thinks Mr. Stevens will need it for pain or discomfort. He doesn't think it will be necessary. The family is not asked if they would prefer to leave the scene; they are never given explicit permission to leave the now curtained-off and fully enclosed space. I sense that Mr. Stevens's sister-in-law still does not want to be here.

Two respiratory therapists and a nurse enter the cocoonlike area. With a great deal of activity they disconnect the tubes and move the poles holding the intravenous medication and the other machines away from the bedside. The nurse asks the family if they would like chairs to be brought in, but they prefer to stand at the bedside, holding the patient's hands and stroking his face. I stand at the foot of the bed. Five minutes after the ventilator is turned off, Mr. Stevens dies. First, his breathing slows for a few minutes, then it simply stops and his sister-in-law looks at the physician and whispers, "I think he's stopped breathing." The physician slowly moves to the bed, places his stethoscope on Mr. Stevens's chest, and says quietly, "Technically, death occurs when there is no more heartbeat, but the life force—how long that takes to leave the body—I don't know."

For quite a while afterward, Mr. Stevens looks as if he were sleeping. It takes about thirty minutes for the color of life to drain from his face. His sister-in-law bends over and kisses his forehead, saying, "Good-bye." Then she walks a few steps away from the bed and sighs, "That's over." The doctor says to the family, "You can stay as long as you'd like, as long as you need to," again assuming they want to stay near the corpse and implying that the right thing is to stay. For the next fifteen minutes or so the family and doctor stay within the curtained area and talk, with increasing ease as the minutes go by, about Mr. Stevens's wonderful sense of humor, whether to conduct an autopsy on his lungs to determine the cause of infection, and how to proceed with funeral arrangements.

When Mr. Stevens's sister-in-law and I walk out into the bustling world of the ICU, she says to me, "I'm numb now. I didn't expect this to happen today, or that things would happen so fast. I'm glad we had this week. A few days ago, we sat down and talked about what would happen if he died, and I'm so glad we had that conversation. We went to his messy bachelor apartment [here she smiles] and went through piles and piles of his papers. And I'm so glad we did." She says she feels relieved that they have done what he wanted—disconnected him from life support when there was no hope for recovery. "You know," she says, "he treated this hospitalization like the others. So we did, too. He said, 'It's nothing. They'll fix me up and I'll be out of here.'"

Control of Time and the Best Possible Death

A few days later, the intensive care specialist contrasts the stories of Faith Walker and Jim Stevens for me. The two patients had been hospitalized at about the same time. The most important difference in the way their deaths occurred, the physician says, was determined by his own knowledge of each patient and "what the patient wanted" with regard to being supported in a comatose condition. He had not known Mrs. Walker at all before she arrived in the ICU and thus could not assume anything about her wishes for life support. He had known Mr. Stevens for three years and had felt comfortable saying to the family that he knew the patient would not want to continue receiving ineffective treatments that could actually cause further discomfort. He felt certain that withdrawing Mr. Stevens's ventilator was the right thing to do. He characterizes the conferences with the two families as two ends of a continuum depicting how physicians' knowledge of the patient affects who controls time. In the case of Mrs. Walker, the doctor needed to let the family realize her condition *in their own time.* But with Mr. Stevens he felt he could assume more control over the situation and tell the family that *it's time* for the patient to die. Once physicians and nurses have a clear sense that death is imminent, they want to facilitate it, not prolong it, and they want to make it happen in as "natural" a way as possible. For that reason, they prefer to take patients off ventilator support before they die. Many doctors consider a death on a ventilator to be unpleasant for the patient and emotionally difficult for families to observe. It also takes longer to die when on a ventilator.

Resuscitation, when it ends in the zone of indistinction, sets up a dance with time—a negotiation with or a directive to families about the imperative of time—and creates pressure on everyone to make the choice between death now or the continued support of a person for whom death has been brought into life. That choice is created by technology, but its urgency and necessity at a certain juncture on the heroic pathway are determined by bureaucracy. As do most hospital staff, the intensive care specialist attributed cause and effect, the making of a certain kind of death, to his knowledge of the patient and to desires articulated by the patient and the family, rather than to the power and effects of the heroic pathway itself.

III. THE REVOLVING DOOR PATHWAY

No one factor is solely responsible for creating revolving door scenarios, scenarios in which patients with chronic conditions who are declining toward death have recurring hospitalizations to stabilize their conditions in the weeks and months before they die. This pathway is characterized by repeated trips from home or nursing home to hospital and back again. Many factors comingle to foster the revolving door—the diffuse fears of sick people, the specific panic caused by insufficient breath, families' lack of knowledge about what to do for their ailing relatives, doctors who do not act as guides to the end of life because they cannot prognosticate well and do not want to discuss death, Medicare and Medicaid reimbursement rules, and nursing home and hospital discharge routines. But Medicare and Medicaid payment policies bear the brunt of responsibility for shaping this pathway in the first place and for placing patients on it. Few people are aware of this. The next two stories reflect the ways in which reimbursement policies serve as the guiding framework for rationalizing and organizing when and why patients must be moved along to enter or exit the hospital. That framework is mostly invisible to patients and their families, and though it is acknowledged and often deplored by health professionals, it determines what they can do.

Within that structural apparatus, the kinds of medical conditions that characterize the end of life in American society, coupled with physicians' responses to those conditions, compound the difficulty of stopping a revolving door scenario. A study of Medicare patients at the end of life has delineated three distinct kinds of medical conditions that typify older patients in the United States. Only one type of condition, characterizing 22 percent of Medicare patients and exemplified by cancer, is considered "terminal." That is the only condition in which death is regularly anticipated by patients or by health professionals and then, perhaps, prepared for by hospital staff.[44] The other kinds of conditions, which together afflict more than half of Medicare patients at the end of life, do not, because of their symptoms and clinical course, give clues that death is near or that this hospitalization is the final one. One of those groups is characterized by congestive heart failure and chronic lung disease, conditions for which prognostication, and thus end-of-life planning, is known to be difficult because those patients can be stable for long periods and any exacerbations of symptoms usually abate with appropriate medical intervention.[45] The largest group of all (47 percent of Medicare patients) is characterized by extreme frailty, including dementia. Most people in those groups, even when they are hospitalized with life-threatening symptoms, are not necessarily assumed to be near death.

Dora Parker's story, below, specifically highlights federal reimburse-ment policies as the determinant of the Kafkaesque ways in which things move along. Ida Krieger's story, which follows Parker's, points to common, unintended family complicity with those policies through their bringing patients to the hospital in the first place. It points to physician complicity as well, both in their focus on symptom relief rather than "the big picture" and in their silence surrounding either the likelihood or the physical facts of death.

When the System Keeps the Door Revolving: Dora Parker

Admission to day 9: Martha is one of the no-nonsense, goal-oriented case managers I periodically follow around. She is petite, with black hair and black eyes, and she has a great deal of energy. Her job is to move patients through the hospital system as efficiently as possible. She is expertly trained both to manage the patient's disease and to save the hos-pital money. I am impressed by her range of knowledge and her compas-sion. She is a smart nurse who also understands the many details about institutional regulations and how, she says, they work to the detriment of her patients' care. This morning she is going to see Mrs. Dora Parker, "who has been here a lot. She's nice, alert, even with O$_2$ sats in the seven-ties.[46] Three years ago I sent her home to die. The doctors said she had about two months—but she's still here." Mrs. Parker was at Pine Care nursing home before coming to the hospital—"a horrible place," accord-ing to Martha. "They just house people and don't do a very good job at that, and she doesn't want to go back there. She hated it." Martha is work-ing this morning on trying to discharge Mrs. Parker to a different nurs-ing home, but she wishes Mrs. Parker would die here in the hospital and not be forced to endure another move and another institution. She has met with Mrs. Parker and one of her children many times, most recently during the patient's last hospital admission exactly three months ago.

I glance at the medical chart. Mrs. Parker, who is seventy-six, had been admitted eight days ago with a diagnosis of respiratory failure. She has several other serious chronic conditions. Her "chief complaint" is shortness of breath, which, she told Martha, "is getting worse each day." Mrs. Parker is getting a small amount of morphine, by mouth, every five or six hours to relieve her shortness of breath. I ask Martha if she can be discharged with morphine. "Yes," Martha tells me, and adds, "Her treat-ment plan is well established. She doesn't meet acute criteria."[47] The hospitalist (a physician who cares only for hospitalized patients) in charge of Mrs. Parker's care "doesn't like morphine drips," Martha continues, "but I want her to have that. It's better in a nursing home because otherwise they won't give the morphine. It's for her dyspnea.[48] It can go either way with the morphine. She can get it by drip or by mouth, whichever the facility wants to do." (Some facilities prefer to give it one way, some another.)

One of Martha's tasks today is to find out which nursing homes are available for this patient's condition and medication requirements and then report her findings to the family. The family will decide, she tells me, but she can be influential and state her preferences. She tries to reach the family by phone but is unsuccessful, so she says, "Let's go in and see the patient and talk about discharge."

We enter an ordinary room on the medical floor to find Mrs. Parker asleep. She looks ill to me—so small, drawn, and pale. She has a nasal cannula for oxygen, but still her breathing is labored. She is buried by the bedcovers. Only the contour of her chest is visible, slightly protruding from the blankets and making a little rise with each breath she takes. I am amazed that the shape of her legs is not at all apparent through the blankets. I stare at the place where her legs should be for a few moments, trying to discern them. Standing at the foot of the bed, Martha says quietly, "She's so sick. It looks like she could go in a few days." She mentions how cruel and how hard it would be to move her now.

When we leave the room, Martha fills in the story. Two or three years ago she had long discussions with Mrs. Parker and her family about end-of-life care. The family moved her to a nursing home, Cedar Acres, to die. But instead, she got a little bit better and her condition stabilized. That nursing home would not keep her long because she was not a candidate for rehabilitation services. Because she was not and would not be "recovering" any further, the facility would not be sufficiently reimbursed by Medicare to consider her care worth it. So, she was forced to move to Pine Care, where she developed pneumonia. "They should have made her comfortable," Martha told me, "and they could have done so with oral morphine and let her die. Of course she's going to get pneumonia. Stopping the pneumonia won't stop the dying.

"But they admit her here," Martha continues, "and she went from the emergency room to the ICU for three days, where they cured the pneumonia, and then they brought her down here [to the medical ward] to

let her die. They were that close [she holds two fingers together] from
intubating her. And she's a No Code. It's in the chart, but they didn't pay
attention. I need to talk with the family to see what they want." Martha
calls a family member again and leaves a message saying she wants to
talk about discharging Mrs. Parker to yet another nursing home in the
area, Walnut Grove. When she hangs up the phone, I remark that I
thought she wanted to talk to the family about letting Mrs. Parker die
here. "I can't," she replies. "Once she's stabilized, she can't die here. She
has to be moved out. They could have admitted her to die, but instead
they cured the pneumonia. Even after her ICU stay," she continues with
frustration, "they could have given her morphine and let her die. But
now she's stable and they can't let her die here." There is no longer a
treatment plan, and you can't keep a person in the hospital without a
treatment plan.[49]

Martha says, "I've got to go talk with her," and we walk back to Mrs.
Parker's room. Martha wakes her up gently and asks how she feels. "Not
so well," Mrs. Parker replies. She is uncomfortable and Martha adjusts
the pillows under her legs, raises the top portion of the bed, and gently
strokes some hair out of her face. Mrs. Parker wipes her face and pulls a
bit at the nasal cannula. Martha introduces me, and Mrs. Parker looks at
me and smiles wanly, saying she felt better yesterday. Martha says she
wants to talk to her about Walnut Grove. Mrs. Parker does not respond.
Then Martha tells her she tried to reach her daughter on the phone but
could not and wondered if she was working today. Again, no response.
It looks to me as though Mrs. Parker is struggling simply to hold on and
is concentrating so hard on her breathing that she cannot focus on other
things. Martha says, "I'm going to come back later. You need to rest."

We leave the room for the second time, and Martha mentions that
the hospitalist physician doesn't believe in intravenous morphine drips,
which are commonly used with dying hospitalized patients. He feels
that drips are all too close to assisted suicide, so as a personal policy he
just doesn't use them, ordering only morphine by mouth, every four
hours, or as requested by the patient. As a result, Martha tells me, the
patient is not really made comfortable, in her opinion, though the "edge
is taken off" the shortness of breath.

There are numerous approaches among doctors to the use of morphine for pain control, shortness of breath, and dying.[50] This particular
physician's stance is conservative but not unique among the doctors I

observed. Many use morphine more liberally in its intravenous form and give nurses a great deal of discretion in "turning it up" to relieve symptoms of discomfort, whether those symptoms are actually observed or are imputed. I was told by doctors and nurses that morphine is also used "to treat the family." That is, it is administered to patients whose deaths are known to be near so families will be comforted that their relative did not die in pain. Some physicians will use morphine not only to relieve pain and what they interpret to be suffering but also to hasten death, especially at the request of the family. In addition to the range of individual practices I observed, I was told by doctors and nurses who have worked elsewhere that regions of the United States vary in the use of morphine near the end of life. California is generally considered more liberal. Each physician decides—in the context of local practices and his or her own values—how close the use of morphine, by intravenous drip, comes to assisting death.[51]

Martha goes off to contact someone at Walnut Grove and have them hold a bed. She hopes that one of Mrs. Parker's children will call back before the end of the day so she can talk about the discharge plan. She would not, she says, initiate a conversation about death with the family right now, though she has in the past.

Mrs. Parker's written medical record, like all medical charts, tells a story of specialist treatment and physician commitment to or resistance against heroic intervention. The medical assessment of Mrs. Parker's condition and the treatment plan recorded in the chart on the day she was admitted bear no resemblance to the story of frustrated dying that Martha has told me. Instead, the chart reveals a tale of straightforward disease diagnosis and what will be done about it. The treatment plan does not voice the possibility of death. It is uninformed of Mrs. Parker's frailty and her recent moves from nursing home to nursing home. It does acknowledge her No Code status and notes:

> The patient has severe respiratory decompensation, complicating her chronic respiratory insufficiency, and this is probably secondary to a left lower lobe pneumonia. The patient will be managed by the intensivist in the intensive care unit, will receive supplemental oxygen and empiric antibiotics. She will also be followed by the cardiologist . . . and [the hospitalist service] will pick the patient up upon discharge from the intensive care unit.

Another specialist wrote,

> At this time I would recommend sputum Gram's stain and culture,
> initiation of antibiotic therapy with intravenous ceftriaxone, and pro-
> vision of supplemental oxygen with a nonrebreather mask. Depending
> upon the patient's degree of dyspnea and its relief or lack thereof with
> the nonrebreather mask, consideration can be given to using the BiPap
> apparatus.[52] As noted above, she has previously expressed wishes not
> to be placed on mechanical ventilator or to be provided with car-
> diopulmonary resuscitative efforts.

Although an oxygen mask and nasogastric tube feedings (her only
source of nutrition, since she is not taking any food by mouth) have
been recommended to Mrs. Parker by one of the specialists as measures
that will sustain and prolong her life, she has refused both. She has also
refused antibiotics for the pneumonia. She has made it clear to her
family and the medical staff that she is nearing death and does not want
her dying prolonged. She does want medication to control her anxiety
and a small amount of morphine to relieve her breathing difficulties.
But she has told the medical staff that she does not want to be over-
medicated with narcotics. She wants to be able to think clearly. Her
medical chart reports part of her conversation with the hospital chaplain as well. "I just want to go," she is said to have told him. Mrs. Parker
is among a minority of frail patients I observed who had a clear opinion
about specific medical treatments and were able to voice their opinion.
Mrs. Parker's straightforward refusal of life-sustaining therapies is
unusual.

On her ninth day in the hospital, the day I meet her, Mrs. Parker's
hospitalist has written this note in her medical record:

> Visited patient for lengthy time, greater than 30 minutes, and spoke
> with daughter about prognosis. Patient less conversant today, more
> confused. . . . We spoke about how she's feeling. She's concerned about
> being confused. Explained terminal nature of situation to daughter,
> and use of morphine and Ativan to alleviate symptoms of shortness of
> breath and anxiety. Daughter in agreement with this. Does not want
> further invasive treatments for her mother. Case manager and I will
> discuss transfer issues [to the nursing home] with daughter now.

Day 10: Martha tells me that she met with Mrs. Parker's daughter at 7 P.M. last evening. The daughter was crying at her mother's bedside and said she wished her mother had died here over the weekend so she would not have to move her again to a new institution. Martha, at that moment, felt that the patient was so frail and in so much distress that it was best not to try to move her. She decides to leave the patient here for a couple more days. Mrs. Parker tells her that she does not want to go to a place that is dirty and smells of urine. Martha is worried that in a nursing home the orders will be to give her morphine by mouth only, which means that it will probably not be given at all and that Mrs. Parker will be in pain and will really suffer. Martha hopes that a space will become available in the best nursing home she can find so that Mrs. Parker has a better chance to actually receive the morphine she needs to minimize her shortness of breath. Martha phones Mrs. Parker's managed care insurance company to get their permission to keep the patient in the hospital two more days. When I ask for clarification, she smiles and says she knows what to say, how to persuade them and get the approval she needs. She has to speak with a nurse and the medical director of the insurance company, then must receive permission as well from the administration at the hospital. She tells me that Mrs. Parker is better today, more alert, more stable. Yesterday there had been a mistake. She had received ten milligrams of morphine instead of one milligram. That's why she was so lethargic yesterday.

Martha reflects on the inappropriateness of Mrs. Parker's movement through the system: "The family suffered. It was torturous for the daughter. The daughter looks worse than the patient because we got the patient off-track and put her in the ICU when she was comfort care, DNR, preparing to die. That ICU stay should not have happened. It gave the children false hope that their mother was recovering." She goes on, "You can always treat something, but you've got to ask, will that treatment change the big picture? All the ICU stay did was to confuse the family." Mrs. Parker's hospitalist does not think the short-of-breath patient suffers, Martha remarks. But to the family, it looks as if the patient is suffering.

Day 11: Mrs. Parker is discharged from the hospital to Walnut Grove. Her condition is described in the medical chart as "guarded, terminal." That is the first written comment about the nearness of death.

A few days later: Mrs. Parker dies at Walnut Grove.

When the Family Helps the Door Revolve: Ida Krieger

Admission, day 1: "What can be done for her in the hospital?" Martha asks, both directly and rhetorically of the other staff at hospitalist morning rounds. She is referring to Ida Krieger, ninety-one years old, who has just been admitted. "She's been bouncing back and forth between here and home at least three or four times this year." She also moves between her daughter's home and a nursing home. "Every time she's in here, she says she's ready to die, ready to go. She has end-stage heart disease. All they can do is tinker with the drugs. They never really do relieve the shortness of breath. Maybe she's ready for hospice." Martha wants to look at her chart and "find out what's going on" with the patient. She says she wants to talk with the daughter and make a plan.

That afternoon: I see Mrs. Krieger's family doctor in the hospital hallway. He, too, says that "she keeps bouncing back between here and her home." He tells me she will probably go to a nursing home after this hospitalization and then be able to return home. "Every time she gets short of breath, her daughter panics and brings her in here." He reports that the daughter can't give her twenty-four-hour-a-day care and that the patient needs to be in a good nursing home where she is carefully watched. But will the family do that? He doesn't know. I ask what his role is, what can he do? Can he intervene to break this cycle that seems to frustrate everyone? He doesn't know. I ask what is being done for her in the hospital. He says, "They fix her up a bit," but then at home she gets short of breath.

Day 2: I arrive at the scheduled time for the staff meeting with Mrs. Krieger and her daughter. Martha is standing at the nurses' station reading the patient's medical chart. The hospitalist has decided that Mrs. Krieger needs a cardiology follow-up and has ordered some procedures. Martha picks up the phone to schedule one of the procedures, thoracentesis, for that afternoon. She explains to me that fluid is collecting outside Mrs. Krieger's lungs (pleural effusion), and the procedure will draw off the fluid and make her more comfortable, able to breathe easier.

Martha locates a wheelchair and finds an unlocked room nearby that is used for conferences. We go to Mrs. Krieger's room and Martha introduces me to the patient and her daughter. Mrs. Krieger is small, frail, alert. She is wearing her own pale blue bathrobe. Her daughter is probably in her late fifties. I explain why I am there and ask permission to sit in on their discussion. Martha wheels Mrs. Krieger down the hall, and her daughter and I walk with them to the small, airless, windowless room. The nurses store their lunches and coats here. A large bulletin board is covered with notices about the emergency protocol for the building, hospital employee benefit news, and snapshots of nurses' children. Diagrams of steps to follow when making a care plan are taped to the walls. The hospitalist arrives a minute or so later. Martha finds some juice and crackers for Mrs. Krieger. We all sit down at the table.

Martha: I want to review everything and talk about our options.

Physician (speaking directly to both the patient and her daughter): I talked with [the family doctor]. He's out of town today and the rest of the week, unfortunately, so I'm taking over for him. He can't be here. I know you've been bouncing back and forth between Redwood Shores and here and home and that you'd like that to stop. Let's talk about what we can do. What we can understand and accept. *(To the daughter)* She has cardiomyopathy—her heart muscle is very weakened. It is not pumping very effectively despite the medications she's been given. [Mrs. Krieger is alert, sipping juice through a straw and munching a cracker. She is paying close attention.] We need to have a more coordinated approach and plan. To back up a step first, it's worthwhile to get a cardiology evaluation. It's been a couple of years since she had one. . . . But basically, this is a ninety-one-year-old heart.

Mrs. Krieger's daughter: She's done very well, but then her water started building up again. The change of pills concerned me. But, when she had the cardiology workup a couple of years ago, should she have had a pacemaker at that time? Would that have helped? [The physician says that a pacemaker would not have worked. He talks for a few minutes about how a pacemaker controls heartbeats but not the strength of the beats.] But then in September she started coughing and choking. We've had different diagnoses: bronchitis from Redwood Shores, pneumonia from the hospital. I feel no one knows the diagnosis. I appreciate everything people have been doing, but I know she's going downhill now.

Physician: We need to find out if anything else still can be done; if not, if this is a heart in decline, we need to deal with it. [He continues to talk about how the cardiology exam will probably confirm what he thinks—that this heart is in decline and that nothing else can be done.]

Daughter: This is the first doctor who has tried to explain things. [She thanks him and Martha.] It's all been air before.

Martha: So as a family, you can make plans, discuss the quality of life you want. And then I can make that happen for you. [Mrs. Krieger's daughter asks her mother if she has been following the conversation.]

Mrs. Krieger: I have been following. I don't know what to do. [This is said in a shaky voice, teary, but with no visible tears. She seems so woeful.]

Martha: Let's take this one step at a time. We'll get the cardiologist to do the procedure first. Then we'll see where we are. You don't have to make a decision today.

Mrs. Krieger: I don't want to live. [Her daughter tells her repeatedly to calm down, to relax. The daughter stands up and puts one arm around her mother's shoulders; her other hand strokes her mother's cheek. They both start crying. The daughter apologizes to the hospital staff for crying. She tells her mother not to get upset: "You're making me upset. Just relax, you're going to be fine." I am acutely aware that Mrs. Krieger is not fine. She is short of breath, visibly anxious, and aware that she is approaching the end of her life. Both mother and daughter are trying to act courageously and with civility in this airless room.] But I can't make up my mind what I want.

Daughter: Nature just has to take its course, that's all.

Martha (repeating her refrain that they don't have to make any decisions today): We can plan how you want to spend your last days.

Mrs. Krieger: I don't want to go anywhere, not to a nursing home, any of them. I want to go home and die in my own bed.

Martha: Hospice is wonderful for that. Agencies can help, and there are medications given to deal with shortness of breath. A nursing home can be a last resort. You can visit while you're able to and choose one as a backup. And no decision is set in stone. You can be at home, but if it gets too much for the family, you can go somewhere else. No decision is set in stone. It sounds like what you want to do is go home and not have shortness of breath.

Daughter (who has repeatedly been telling her mother to relax): And then she can see her grandkids and great-grandkids.

Mrs. Krieger (to and about the hospital staff): I know they're nice, I just don't want to live.

Martha: After we know where we stand, I'll meet with you again at the
  bedside, with a social worker, and we'll get things organized. So
  you can enjoy the rest of your life. [They have a discussion about
  ordering a bed, a wheelchair, and other supplies for the home.]
Physician: The cardiology procedure will be this afternoon. We'll know
  the results almost immediately and have some final assessments by
  tomorrow. Maybe we'll be able to move on with all the current
  information by then.
Martha: Let's get everything [regarding equipment for the home]
  arranged today.
Mrs. Krieger to physician: I thank you for what you are doing.

The meeting ends, having lasted about fifteen minutes. Martha wheels
Mrs. Krieger back to her room and returns to the nurses' station, where
she says to me, "Yesterday, I went around with Dr. X—Dr. Death and his
sidekick. We did about four of these conferences, one after another. And
we shouldn't have to do any of them. They call this managed care. It's not
managed care. It's different tasks, everyone doing something different,
nothing is coordinated. Death and the end of life are not planned for at
all. Nobody wants to talk about it. So, as a result, there is no quality of life,
the patient and family are left in the dark. They get more anxious, more
depressed, and when they are told things repeatedly, they get to a point
where they can't hear what they are told." In Mrs. Krieger's case, she continues, these past hospitalizations shouldn't have happened at all, didn't
need to happen. All of these concerns could have been, should have been,
handled at home. According to Martha, Mrs. Krieger's doctor should
have talked about end of life and shortness of breath. He should have
made provisions both for the daughter and the patient, with morphine,
so they would not get upset with the shortness of breath that comes at the
end of life. The doctor could have called hospice and said, "We are at the
end of life now, how do you want to handle it?" In addition, all the cardiology workups could have been done on an outpatient basis. But, Martha
concludes, doctors don't want to talk about it.

Day 4: The hospitalist informs me that Mrs. Krieger did have the
medical procedure and the cardiology workup. She is having some of
her medications changed, and they are all waiting to see if the medication changes make her feel any better. "If they do, she'll go home. If not,
we need to talk to the daughter and say, 'This is it.'" He reflects, "We're

used to seeing shortness of breath, but for families, it's the first time. They don't know what dying looks like. And they freak out."

Aftermath: Mrs. Krieger does feel better and is discharged to a nursing home a few days later. One month later she returns to live at her daughter's home, but after only three days there, she returns to the hospital emergency department with shortness of breath and is admitted. The emergency department note in the medical chart reads, "According to the daughter, who is at the bedside, the patient has had a great deal of trouble breathing the last two nights and no one in the family has been able to get any sleep because of dealing with the patient's shortness of breath." Mrs. Krieger is started on intravenous fluids. The hospital staff respect her request for no invasive diagnostic or therapeutic procedures of any kind. On the morning of her third hospital day, she takes a turn for the worse and dies within the hour.

Medicare Logic, Family and Physician Complicity: The Revolving Door's Invisible Frame

Mrs. Parker did not die at the first nursing home she was sent to, Cedar Acres, although she was expected to by health professionals. That nursing home would not keep her longer than a few weeks because Medicare does not cover open-ended "custodial" care. According to the logic of Medicare, Mrs. Parker was taking too much time to die, and so she had to be moved to another facility that was certified differently. At the second institution, Pine Care, she developed pneumonia. She was not allowed by the Pine Care staff to die, but she was not treated for the pneumonia there either. She was sent instead to the hospital. Hospital physicians placed Mrs. Parker in the ICU, as is common, to treat her as effectively as they could. Very sick, extremely frail, but not imminently dying, she was displaced once more. She finally died in the third nursing home.

The American system of "long-term care" is more than fragmented; it is absurd. Few people, other than some health professionals, have any idea how federal payment schemes guide and determine treatment practices—and thus the patient's experience—near death. And the vast majority of families do not know anything about actual Medicare coverage when their relative enters a nursing home. Most patients and families assume that Medicare will cover their long-term institutional care needs, but Medicare only covers a limited amount, and a certain kind, of nursing home care. At this writing, in theory Medicare allows one hundred days of care in a nursing home. Some families are aware of that number, which they read in literature describing Medicare benefits. However, the actual length of stay fully paid by Medicare is twenty days, at the very most.[53] Beginning on the twenty-first day the family must make copayments.[54] Moreover, Medicare will not pay for just any patient but only for those who meet stringent eligibility criteria: They must be recovering from a condition. They must be able to benefit from rehabilitation and nursing services (despite the fact that most nursing homes do not have many registered nurses). And they must come to the nursing home from a three-day (or more) Medicare-qualified hospital stay.[55] As patients become more frail, and as they approach death, they become less eligible for Medicare nursing home coverage. Unless patients have private long-term-care insurance (which most do not) or are poor and eligible for Medicaid, they must pay for their own care.

Medicare and Medicaid both stipulate criteria for length of stay in nursing homes. Depending on how they are certified, some nursing homes will take only private-pay and Medicare patients; some will take a combination of Medicare and Medicaid patients; some will take only Medicaid patients. Medicaid in California (MediCal) has a flat reimbursement rate, which encourages nursing homes to select patients who are not very sick. Nursing homes that take all or some Medicaid patients do not want to keep those who take too long to die or need a great deal of nursing care because they tend not to have adequate nursing staff. Those nursing homes have cut back on staff to stay under the reimbursement rate and still make a profit, and they tend to look for any excuse to send a patient to a hospital (unless they have a particularly low occupancy rate and really need the patient).

Hospitals, on the other hand, will not keep dying patients unless they are able to meet the Medicare criteria for hospitalization, and so they send patients back to nursing homes as soon as they can. Hospitals prefer not to keep Medicaid patients for long stays because the reimbursement rate is low. There is no stipulated limit to how long a Medicaid patient can remain in a nursing home, but Medicaid nursing homes do not want patients who are dying. In addition, it may take months for patients and families to "spend down"[56] and proceed through the federal bureaucracy to become eligible for Medicaid.[57]

Families, without being aware of it, are complicit with Medicare and

Medicaid regulations in fostering revolving door scenarios. When relatives become acutely ill in nursing homes, families tend to want hospitalization for them. With each transfer, the number of days of Medicare reimbursement begins anew. Thus, repeatedly moving frail patients from nursing home to hospital and back again benefits institutions and the bank accounts of families, but not patients. Without a plan that acknowledges and prepares for death, as Martha noted, the events that unfold for many elderly patients and the pathways they travel before they die are dictated primarily by Medicare and Medicaid payment policies. *No one knows this.*[58]

Ida Krieger circled in and out of the system. Her shortness of breath was temporarily relieved each time she was hospitalized, but she was not moving along. She was asked to be part of the team, "to make decisions" about "what she wanted" in the way of specific treatments, location of her last days, and "quality of life," but she did not know how to die and no one was assisting her. Mrs. Krieger said she wanted to go home and die in her own bed. That was not the right answer to staff questions because she had not been designated as a hospice patient by any of the physicians who treated her. Thus her symptoms were not managed for death and she returned repeatedly to the hospital for relief of respiratory distress.

If Mrs. Krieger had been designated "a hospice patient," perhaps she could have been given enough morphine to overcome her shortness of breath. Then perhaps she would have died, without the anxiety so apparent in the conference room, either in a nursing home or in her daughter's home.[59] *If*, as Martha suggested, Mrs. Krieger could "discuss the quality of life" she wanted as death approached, they could, together, make plans. Yet few seriously ill hospitalized persons can conceive of or articulate all that the institution demands from them in terms of planning how to live when death approaches. *If* Mrs. Krieger and her daughter had known "what dying looks like," as the hospitalist remarked, perhaps they both would not fear death so much and would not have returned Mrs. Krieger to the hospital each time her symptoms reappeared. But who takes responsibility for allaying those fears through the explanation of specific bodily symptoms of decline and the promise of medication to make physical dying less fearful? These are three very big ifs, and nothing in the current system of hospital medical treatment ensures that they will be enacted.

Hospitalization at the end of life is not synonymous with the broadly understood psychological and social conceptualization of the "dying process." There frequently is no dying process per se in the hospital, which makes some deaths disquieting for families and for medical staff. The stories in this chapter underline an important point: the crucial shift in everyone's understanding, which "moves things along" from trying to stabilize or improve a patient's condition to acknowledging his or her "dying," often takes place only shortly before death. The timing of that shift is one reason for the widespread critique of inhumane hospital deaths. That dying is not the anticipated and planned process many people claim to want is also one reason why discussions about code status take place so close to the time of death and why DNR orders most often are not written in patients' medical charts until two days (or fewer) before death.[60] Bureaucratic time constrains the way in which death is understood by everyone in the system.

WAITING

"My sister went in for surgery last week and didn't make it off the ventilator. She's been fighting for her life for a long time, and in the past two years she has had more and more respiratory problems, more pneumonia. The doctors did isolate an organism and started treating it last night. In cases like this, where there is no prognosis, families go through—What if she dies? What if she gets better? What will her quality of life be? Where do I draw the line? Then there are the questions: Should you hang out at the hospital? Does it matter? Are you annoying the nurses? Do you want to let the nurses know there is a person there? Do the nurses know how much we care? And *not* being able to talk to doctors. I talked with the social worker today about what's needed if she goes home. They don't give you much time to make plans about the care she'll need. When they're ready to discharge her, they'll just say, 'Come and pick her up today.' I'm in limbo. I'm sick and tired of being on hold. I've faced the issue of turning off her ventilator. It terrifies me more than anything else. The hardest thing is feeling so helpless."

Sister of ICU patient

Hospital deaths that fuel public dissatisfaction are those in which the choices that must be made are inconceivable. For health professionals, choosing for or against this life-prolonging procedure or that one, choosing death now or death later, is the normal, routine way to move things along. For families and patients it is glaringly clear that these choices are simply impossible. Yet most accept that they or the hospital staff will make choices, and they muddle through them as best they can. Because staff want families to decide and families see choices as impossible, *waiting* also becomes partly a choice. An important dimension of hospital death is how waiting happens, how it is experienced, and how it is both integral to and disruptive of the pathways. Here we shift focus from how and why things move along and the ways in which hospital personnel guide patients and families through the system to a consideration of what waiting entails for the different players. What strategies do health professionals employ to end the kind of waiting that does not serve the pathway? What are the characteristics of *life* that patients and families consider while they wait for medical stabilization, improvement, or death?

The Faces of Waiting

Everyone in the hospital waits, and *waiting* has two faces. Paradoxically, the first kind of waiting enables things to move along. Waiting is the product of hospital bureaucracy, and it shapes and is given shape by all the small and large activities of hospital life. Waiting is essential to movement along the pathways. From the first moment of a patient's admission to the last moment before discharge or death, waiting—for information, procedures, consultations, results, decisions, a change in condition—punctuates hospital work. But the qualities and purposes of waiting are entirely different for patients and families than they are for health professionals.

For the former, waiting is distinguished by a feeling of anticipation mingled with hope and dread. The anticipation is born of incomplete understanding on a journey of uncertainty. Patients and families wait for doctors to arrive, to tell them good or bad news, to reassure and inform them. They wait for doctors to tell them what to do, which choices are best. They wait for diagnostic procedures and test results, which doctors must interpret for them. They wait to be treated and for treatments to work. They wait for stabilization or recovery, and they always hope while they wait. They wait for nurses to come to the bedside and make them more comfortable. They wait for pain medication and bedpans. They wait for friends and relatives to arrive from out of town. They wait to be discharged.

Waiting, for patients and families, is accompanied by an open, vague, and mostly uninformed expectation about the future. This emotional state is anchored in ignorance about medical facts and hospital rules and about what (specific to hospital pathways) to want. Waiting pervades patient and family experience in and of the hospital and identifies patients and families as outsiders to a system in which only staff know the possible scenarios. In this sense, waiting separates patients and families from those who give treatments or assist the treatment-givers and keep the work of the institution moving along.

Importantly, patients and families do this waiting outside the rhythm of their own lives. That feature alone is destabilizing. Also, the moments after waiting—when something has been revealed or resolved—are emotionally different from the moments of waiting. Then anticipation is replaced, usually briefly, with a sense of settlement—until the next round of waiting begins. In addition, patients and families sometimes wait for death. But that kind of waiting, as we shall see, is not routine.

Doctors, nurses, social workers, and others who work in the hospital also wait, but their waiting is entirely routine. It serves as necessary background to the action that characterizes their work, and it is understood through the rules of the place. Staff wait for lab reports and test results and DNR orders, for specialist and subspecialist consultations, for a patient's condition to stabilize so procedures can be done or for a patient's precarious condition to "declare itself"—hospital language for the physiological signs (usually "seen" in laboratory test results) of recovery or decline toward death. They wait for Medicaid forms to be processed, for discharge planning and discharge decisions, for families or patients to authorize the withdrawal of life-sustaining treatments and to acknowledge death, for patients to be moved along. Their waiting is understood through the pragmatic lens of giving the best possible care and the most relevant information in a timely and perhaps even cost-effective manner within the routine and rationale of the system. It is purposeful. Their waiting is formed by the bureaucratic and political realities of their professional roles and organizational worlds. Yet physicians, nurses, social workers, therapists, and other hospital staff, too, may wait with anxiety and sadness about losing a patient.

The second face of waiting thwarts movement through the system. It, too, is routine. It is created also by the structures of the hospital world, yet it is the source of many end-of-life dilemmas. When health professionals experience frustration over events that are not unfolding with bureaucratically defined timeliness, they employ specific strategies to foster movement. Those strategies are not necessarily effective. Sometimes patients and families respond to staff directives not by making the proactive choices that will move things along, but with feelings of anxiety and apprehension; they dig in their heels. This kind of waiting creates stasis, blocks movement along the pathway. It happens especially when patients, or more often families, sense that the outcome of treatment, or the outcome of a life that they think hangs in the balance, will not be determined by disease but by the actions of health professionals. At this point they hold back from any "decision-making" at all. The agony felt by Dorothy Mason's son, who continued to request treatments for her well after the staff wanted him to stop doing so, the awareness of Faith Walker's family that withdrawing the ventilator would "cause" her death, the inability of Carol Jones's family to "make a decision about withholding CPR" during their conference with medical staff—these are all common family reactions to staff directives to move things along. In this sense, *waiting* is the opposite of *moving along*.

An ongoing tension between these two faces of waiting is triggered by the way hospital treatment is organized and can be seen in the contradictory directives given by health professionals: families "need to make a decision" to withdraw life-sustaining treatments, yet they also "need time," need to take their time, to acknowledge the arrival of death. Waiting, in its second, obstructive sense, is unwanted by staff and thought to be perpetrated by families. Yet the public perception of dying would have it that *obstructive waiting* is caused by the demands and desires of doctors and by the technological imperative, not by patients and families. Nobody wants to be maintained on machines, waiting "unnaturally" for a drawn-out and "inhumane" death, many prospective hospital patients say. Most of the public comments about "terrible" or "unwanted" kinds of deaths claim that it is doctors, or "the system," or inadequate communication that puts patients and families in the untenable situation of waiting for a death that has been prolonged by unstoppable hospital routines.

Physician rhetoric itself fosters waiting. As we saw in the case of Faith Walker, physicians sometimes use the term *unlikely* or *one in a million* when responding to family questions about whether the patient will recover from a comatose or terminal condition. Mrs. Walker's physician was one of several who told me that they rarely say the word *never* when asked if the patient will get better. This is because in their experience or the experience of colleagues, someone, somewhere, did recover unexpectedly (though the *extent* of recovery is not mentioned) from the medically maintained threshold of life. Doctors try to be both precise and scrupulously honest in their choice of words (and also to be mindful of potential liability concerns should the patient start to show medical signs of "life"). Nevertheless, they are heard by families as being equivocal. *Rarely, unlikely,* and *barely alive* when spoken by medical staff mean "maybe" to families. That unintended ambivalence, which families interpret as admitting a sliver of hope, is a significant source of waiting in the hospital, and it is at the crux of the tension between waiting and moving along.

Waiting was an underlying theme in everyone's stories about the need to move along, about death. For patients and families, waiting captures the personal agony of being caught up in the power of the pathways. For health professionals, waiting signifies the frustration that so often accompanies the requirement to move patients along. For everyone, waiting fosters quandaries about the *quality of life,* a notion first brought to bedside discussions in the 1970s by theologians who debated the conditions of forgoing life support[1] and that now circulates widely in American society. Near the end of life, talk of quality of life implies deliberation about the proper time for a life to end. While those deliberations are routine now, patients, families, and hospital staff all understand the life in question differently from one another. How long should families and physicians wait for the patient's condition to improve? Who decides the appropriate moment for waiting to end and by what criteria?

When "life" and "death" are treated as equally weighted abstract concepts, quality of life becomes a fundamental criterion of choice in American thinking about severe illness. The term is often used now in debates about abortion, euthanasia, and "disability rights," for example, to justify one's personal values or religious principles and to juxtapose the autonomy of the individual against interests mandated by the state. In the hospital, when "control over dying" is under consideration, quality of life is mentioned by nurses and physicians as the pivotal factor in choosing either to go ahead with a potentially life-sustaining procedure or to stop aggressive medical care. It is invoked as if patients were able to imagine a state of illness more severe than their current condition and then were able to choose, rationally and unequivocally, between living in that imagined state and deliberately ending their lives. Yet for the patient at the threshold, the choice is perceived, and is made, on the basis of what is at stake for them at that very moment.

I. OBSTRUCTING THE ORDER OF THINGS

Patients stop *moving along* a pathway when they no longer respond to medical treatment but are not obviously dying or are not dying quickly enough. A specific medical condition *along with* hospital treatments and medical decisions put some patients in the zone of indistinction. When that happens, patients, or their families, are told that they must move in one direction or another, toward more treatments or toward the cessation of treatments and toward death, and that they must choose. Patients or their families are sometimes urged to choose movement toward death. Those individuals I observed who were asked by health professionals—either directly or obliquely—to choose death were the most difficult to watch because they had to confront the extreme fragility of their lives and imagine their nearness to death, a difficult, painful proposition.

The widespread appeal to take control of one's own dying (or to advocate for a "controlled" dying for another) can only be realized when the patient assumes herself to be dying, or family members assume that their relative is dying. One can only plan or implement a certain kind of *dying process* when one acknowledges—in tandem with medical staff—that death is on its way. That does not always happen. In the hospital, doctors most often become aware that death is imminent before families do. That difference, so apparent in the examples in these chapters, is part of the reason waiting occurs.

When the responsibility staff members place on patients and families to "choose" death is not accepted in a *timely way*, or is not taken up at all, the frustration of waiting becomes apparent to everyone. In the first of the stories in this chapter, staff members want the patient to acknowledge her dying, and they want her to move toward death according to the needs of the system. Yet they admit that their efforts to move her along are ineffective—it takes too long for a physician to broach the subject of the patient's terminal condition, and when he does finally suggest that the patient choose death by refusing treatment, she firmly rejects that "option." She frustrates the staff because she believes she will live, refuses to choose death, and takes too long to die. In the next story, the physician places responsibility for choosing death squarely on the patient, who opts for potentially life-sustaining treatment instead. In that case the medical staff hope, along with the patient, that potential treatments will enable him to leave the hospital alive. And in the final story, all members of the health care team want the family to choose death for the patient, but the family refuses to do so and stalls all decision-making.

These three stories reflect the ironic demands that both the heroic intervention and revolving door pathways place on everyone in the hospital: life-sustaining treatments are promoted until *it is time* to stop; then the pathways shift course and promote, or even dictate, the acceptance and facilitation of death. Patients and families are expected to conform to both these directives and to switch in a smooth and timely way from making life-prolonging moves to making preparation-for-death moves. Unsurprisingly, patients and their families often balk at having to make the switch.

Waiting, Not Dying: Cynthia Graf

Admission through month one: A nurse on the oncology unit introduces me to the *problem* of Cynthia Graf this way: Ms. Graf had thought that, as with her previous hospital stay, she would again get fixed up and be sent home. But this admission has been lengthy, and it doesn't look as if she'll leave. Ms. Graf's doctor hasn't yet discussed with her that she is dying. Ms. Graf does not want to go to a nursing home, but she can't return home because she requires too much nursing care. The staff hope she will soon die, but Ms. Graf is not ready to die. She wants to get better and go home. "What's so hard in oncology," this experienced nurse explained, "is if you stop treating, it's the sign that the patient is dying and that there is no more hope. With oncology patients, the last thing you want to do is have the patient give up hope." A physician has expressed a similar sentiment: "This is the hard part of a case, the change of course. You're pouring all these resources in them. All treatments are failing and you need to tell them you want to do less. And they want more."

Cynthia Graf's dying is a problem because it and she are both out of time and out of place. The staff know she is dying. Ms. Graf knows she is very ill, but she is waiting, in fact living, for her condition to stabilize.

She has organized every act, every thought, in the service of getting better. She does not consider that she is or might be close to her death, nor is she waiting to die.

Because she will be hospitalized for such a long time, I have time to hear various opinions about what is happening to Ms. Graf, what she needs, what she wants, and what people think is best for her. I also have time to hear Ms. Graf's own voice and how it comes up against the requirements of the system.

More than most other diseases, terminal cancer carries with it strong expectations in the United States and Great Britain for a death that is characterized as *good*. A "good death" allows the patient ample time to talk about it and also fosters the quest for "personal growth." A good death presupposes that the patient has acknowledged and accepted the process and is working toward bringing "closure" to her life. Deaths from cancer, when the patient has weeks, months, or years to get used to the idea of confronting death, are not really perceived as good deaths unless they display these elements. Cancer is perhaps the only disease that is routinely understood, in the hospital setting, to have a *dying process*. When a patient's condition is acknowledged by all to be terminal, then conscientious end-of-life care can be implemented. Deaths on a terminal pathway, through which a dying process is enacted, are usually termed good and unproblematic. They are not supposed to be comprised of contradictory treatments and bureaucratic confusion.

Ms. Graf is forty-one years old. She was diagnosed with an uncommon cancer four years ago and has had repeated hospitalizations throughout the preceding years for surgery and a variety of treatments. When I meet her one month into this hospital stay, the cancer has metastasized throughout her intestinal tract and pelvic region. She has had most of her gut surgically removed and has pain everywhere, especially in her legs. She needs a great deal of nursing care for wounds related to her disease, for infections, and for pain management.

The treatment regimen for Ms. Graf's day-to-day wound care, pain, fevers, and comfort is clear to the nursing staff and not difficult for them to implement, and her physician is sure of the way in which her condition will worsen and lead to her death. Nevertheless, staff are quite uneasy regarding how *to be* with this patient and how to plan for her death. Yet planning for her death is something that most of the health professionals involved in Ms. Graf's care feel they ought to do.

Ms. Graf and her illness are problematic for the hospital staff, who are uncomfortable with the moral demand Ms. Graf places on them. In their view, she is not allowing them to put into operation their responsibility toward her, a patient whom they view as inappropriately wanting life-sustaining treatments when they want to work with her toward implementing her death. Staff members agree about what they want to do—withhold nutrition and antibiotics. Those strategies would bring about the smoothest, least painful, most rapid death and would enable the nurses, doctors, and social workers to feel that they are doing the most appropriate thing, given the circumstances. But Ms. Graf thwarts those strategies at every turn.

On the practical front, staff have no plan for moving Ms. Graf along to death; *and* she has been stuck in the hospital too long. This troubles everyone involved in her care and treatment. First, the slowness of her dying is a source of extreme discomfort for many. Neither imminently dying nor getting well enough to be discharged, she is in a holding pattern that is always a problem for hospital bureaucracy. Her heart and lungs are relatively strong and unimpaired. It is unlikely she will have a cardiac arrest. The discharge planner periodically raises the issue of the cost of her care and the possibility of either moving her to another unit in the hospital where the costs would be lower (but there would not be as much oncology nursing expertise) or moving her out to a skilled nursing facility.

In addition, Ms. Graf is not activating her own *dying process* in the way the hospital staff, especially the oncology nurses and social workers, have come to expect. According to some of the social workers and nurses, Ms. Graf is not actively preparing, in ways that are visible to them, for a good death. She is not acknowledging or discussing the end of her life with them or indicating her "emotional needs" while accepting and even embracing her finitude. She is not asking for a quick release or a gradual but painless fading away through specific medical techniques. Indeed, she is not making any requests at all regarding how she "wants" to die. She doesn't ask to be sent home with hospice care or suggest stopping antibiotics or tube feeding.

The medical team is not working to put the patient on the road to a good death either, according to one doctor with whom I speak. "No one in medicine has addressed her death with her," he tells me. "No one has said, 'Look, this is what we need to do in the next week—say good-bye to your kid, go home with music and flowers, and die.'" He thinks it is inappropriate from a medical and ethical standpoint to let her "hang on, to keep her alive like this." He also thinks it is not good for her daughter to see her this way, "in this limbo, for months." All of the nurses I speak with share his view. But nursing is obstructed by medicine; the nurses cannot take the lead in guiding the patient along the terminal pathway, for the system does not usually permit them to take that kind of initiative.

Month two: The nursing and social work staff are increasingly troubled that Ms. Graf is not moving along. She has not identified herself as *dying,* and so a good death continues to be thwarted. At least one social worker wanted to talk with Ms. Graf's family about helping her plan for death by "giving permission for her to die." Another has tried for weeks to get Ms. Graf to accept her death by having her family members meet with the physicians so that together they can help the patient plan for the withdrawal of antibiotics and food.

A nurse wants someone, perhaps me, to "facilitate" the patient in writing a journal that would chronicle her experience of the illness, her thoughts in general, and her awareness of approaching death. "That is something we can do for her [eleven-year-old] daughter," she tells me. The journal never materializes. "She's in denial," I am often told. That psychiatric label is used liberally in the hospital to describe family members' as well as patients' lack of acknowledgment about their *dying transition* when that transition seems so obvious to hospital staff. "Denial" is most often a way to explain that the patient is not moving along as she is expected to do. That Ms. Graf is still not about to die in the next few days or perhaps weeks makes the nurses anxious about how to define and set care goals. They know how to change dressings and administer pain medication, but they have lost a sense of purposefulness about why, in the long run, they are performing those tasks. They agree to divide Ms. Graf's care equally among them, for she has become too much of an emotional burden for any nurse to handle on her own.

As time passes, being out of place and out of time become more and more central to how Cynthia Graf is identified as a patient, and her stay becomes more ethically troubling for the nurses. One way a good death can occur, according to the nurses and social workers with whom I spoke, is if she accepts her dying according to the Kübler-Ross and hospice scripts and makes choices—*within a medical idiom and on time*—about stopping treatments. Ms. Graf's example showed me which concerns hospital staff focus on when their ideas about how and when death should be implemented cannot be realized. In Ms. Graf's case, hospital staff use negatives to understand and define *dignity* in death. A dignified death would not go on for too long, would not be dominated by seemingly goal-less medical procedures, and would not be stuck because of denial.

The end of month two: I speak personally with Ms. Graf for the first time today. A nurse introduced us in the morning, and I return to her bedside later in the day, as she requested. Propped up by many pillows, she is visiting with a friend who is just leaving as I walk in. Ms. Graf wears a hospital gown, is nearly bald from chemotherapy, and has deep, dark circles under her eyes. Her bright red fingernails are long, perfectly manicured, and beautifully shaped. They are the only hint of the personality of this woman whose personal life has been stripped from her by the hospital and by the ravages of a terrible disease. I think her face is nice-looking. She puts on glasses and reads completely the consent-to-participate-in-research form I hand her. She asks a few questions, and I tell her I am interested in decision-making. She immediately replies, "Decision-making is the hard part. Some decisions are made for you and that's easy. But the ones that aren't, those are very hard." Hidden in these words is the knowledge that she can, and perhaps will, eventually say no to treatment and basic sustenance, thus ushering in her own death.

I ask what brought her to the hospital this time. She says her pump[2] became infected and she had meningitis. The second day she was here she had surgery to remove the pump and she was placed on antibiotics. Tests were done, including a lumbar puncture. The second week she developed a fistula.[3] "A big problem as far as the doctor was concerned," she said. "He talked to me sincerely, honestly, said this fistula really took the wind out of his sails. He can't offer anything for me. Dr. X, a surgical consultant, said a skilled plastic surgeon might be able to do something, but not till I've been on the TPN[4] for two months. My doctor feels you can always find someone to do surgery, but says I could come out of the surgery with two or three new fistulas and that I'd be much worse off after surgery than I am now. I have nothing left inside. This leaves me with a difficult decision. I definitely have all my faculties. Even though I can't eat or move, have no mobility, I can see my kid grow. But then, how long can I do that? Should I wait for surgery and the possibility that things will get worse? Or, I can let go of the TPN and the antibiotics and let things go. . . ."

Her voice trails off. Having raised the idea of purposefully bringing about her own death, she starts crying quietly. I sit by her side without speaking. A few moments later our conversation shifts to other topics: her family members and the extent to which she discusses her condition with each of them (not too much with her father, who has a heart condition; a great deal with her aunt); the fact that her daughter knows she "can't be cured" and that "the doctors are looking for a way to prolong my life and make me comfortable." She has talked with her daughter, she tells me, "about what will happen when something happens to me and she has to go and live with someone." She turns to gaze through the large window at the terrace, a lovely scene, full of greenery and flowers. She says she is in awe of the natural world and loves learning about animals and watching nature programs on television. She tries not to get depressed because she knows that although things are bad with her, others are worse off.

A week later: Ms. Graf's physician, very aware of the nurses' and social workers' discomfort with this case, makes an announcement at oncology staff rounds. He, also, is deeply troubled by her too long stay. "Graf stays here until she has an event that takes her life—unless someone has a better idea." He speaks softly, but the line of authority is absolutely clear. The room falls silent. He looks at the nurses and social workers. "Anyone have a better idea?" No one responds. He follows his directive with a summary of her condition and past treatment. This is his way of explaining why she has been here so long and why she will remain here. He gives details of her multiple surgeries, her active pelvic tumor and his efforts to treat it. At first there was progress—she knew she would die of cancer, but she could now walk, could go home. She had almost two months at home before the catheter became infected, she got meningitis and was admitted again. "We brought her to the hospital, stopped chemo. Got the meningitis under control. But the tumor went out of control. There were several tumors. Now she's in lots of pain and requires sedation. She requires blood. She can't move out of bed. Once she developed meningitis, I told her there was nothing more I could do. She'll survive a long time because there's no vital-organ involvement. I've offered hastening the process—stopping TPN and fluids—but she won't. We did make her a No Code. That was a feat."

Someone in the room asks about sending her home. The physician says she can't go home because she needs four nurses and her house would have to be turned into an ICU. It's impossible. Someone else asks about moving her to a nursing home. He answers that that would make his life a nightmare, with staff calling him six or seven times a day because they don't know how to care for her properly. One of the nurses says there isn't enough nursing care in a skilled nursing facility anyway for the level of care she needs.

Ten days later: Ms. Graf has a new infection and a new fever. One of her doctors opines to her that it is not good for her or her family to buy a day or two here and there, that this is not "quality of life."[5] Wouldn't it be better, he asks her, to stop everything and just go to sleep? She says yes, it would be better that way, but she does not take any action in that direction. Nurses report that another physician has asked her if she wants to be treated at all for these newest medical problems, implying in the asking itself that not treating the infection will assure and hasten her death, that she can and perhaps should choose this. According to the nurses who tell me about this incident, Ms. Graf looked her doctor in the eye and said with no uncertainty, "Treat me."

The nurses agree that Ms. Graf's physical condition is deteriorating steadily. I am told her body is already decaying, which is another source of anxiety for the nurses. Ms. Graf's aunt, whom she describes as her confidante and who visits weekly, has told me, "I think she feels she can get reevaluated for surgery and get a little better and go home. I think she's holding out for that. I think she wants and expects to go home. Her mind is strong, but her body isn't there." Indeed, a week after that conversation, Ms. Graf said when I came to her room, "I can't talk now. I have to call the nurse and get my pain medication. I'm going out soon with the physical therapist to get some fresh air [on the terrace] and do some strengthening exercises. I have to get stronger, get built up, in preparation for going home."

According to a study of terminally ill cancer patients, many choose to undergo aggressive therapies that are not beneficial and increase suffering because they do not understand the prognosis for their condition.[6] Patients in that study overestimated their chances of living another six months and were inclined to want anticancer treatments; physician estimates of how long those patients would survive were more accurate.[7] The study highlights the (often) discrepant perspectives of physicians and patients about the future course of disease. One important source of patient requests for more treatment, researchers found, was that doctors did not give them either enough information about their condition or the kind of information that would lead them to choose palliative care over aggressive intervention. Though many doctors tell patients "the truth" about terminal illness, they do so in a variety of ways that do not necessarily disclose that death is imminent. They often "tell the truth" in terms that patients cannot understand, for instance, by talking about potential responses to prospective therapies, which patients tend to assume will lead to a cure or at least to stabilization of their condition.[8] That study and others emphasize that careful communication by physicians is an important solution to reducing nonbeneficial treatments that only prolong suffering and dying, but the studies do not consider what "choice" means for some patients. "Choosing" to stop aggressive therapy can mean, as it did for Cynthia Graf, actively "deciding" to die. Some patients do make that decision when they say stop to chemotherapy or other treatments. Many others, including Ms. Graf, do not. Despite advanced disease, continuous pain, and extreme debility, the desire to live is extremely powerful. If I were in Cynthia Graf's place, I might make the same choices she has made.

The end of month three: Staff by now refer to Ms. Graf as "an outlier" because her stay has been so atypically long. That alone is troublesome. She simply does not move along. At oncology rounds at the end of her third month, doctors and nurses again raise the question "What is the treatment goal?" Someone responds, "There is no goal, except to keep her here until she dies. Some days she gets a little stronger, and when something comes up, she wants to be treated." Someone else says, "She's calling the shots." Some of the doctors and nurses are increasingly frustrated because they cannot manage her disease or facilitate what they consider to be a good death.[9]

After rounds, I visit with Ms. Graf once again. She is propped up on pillows in her bed. When I ask, "How are you?" she replies, "You know, I have a lot of fears, a lot of fears. But my family comes every day and that's good. And I sleep a lot, and that's good." Her hair has grown in just a bit since I saw her two weeks ago. She is still and does not make any unnecessary movement. She has an in-the-body quiet that I've seen before in people who are near death and projects a tranquil, centered self. It is as if all the meaning in the world were contained in her body, in her being, in that moment. She seems to have retreated from corporeal engagement with the world beyond her skin.

Two weeks later: Ms. Graf's aunt, paying careful attention to the patient's deteriorating physical condition and that she floats in and out of conscious awareness, makes a proactive decision to discontinue all intravenous nutrition, fluids, and antibiotics. Because Ms. Graf needs larger and larger doses of pain medications, she is no longer awake or mentally alert most of the time. She cannot carry on a conversation, even for a few minutes. The nurses and physicians reiterate that because her vital organs are not diseased, her death will be slow, even without life-sustaining treatments. Pain is the biggest concern for staff and family, and a pain consultant is called in to see if it can be better controlled.

Two weeks later: Ms. Graf continues to float in and out of consciousness during these last days of her life. The family is clear that they want Ms. Graf to be unconscious when she dies, and they ask the nurses to make sure of it. About twelve hours before her death, the staff give Ms. Graf medications to ease any pain she might be experiencing and to ensure that she is unconscious. Her family is at the bedside when she dies.

The Doctors Tread Water: Jack Carter

Admission to day 10: Jack Carter, age eighty-four, has congestive heart failure.[10] He had a heart attack and was rushed to the intensive care unit. Medications delivered intravenously restored his blood pressure and are keeping his condition stable. They not only saved his life,[11] they are, for him, life support, and he would immediately die without them. He also needs oxygen. Mr. Carter's cardiologist tells me that most patients with congestive heart failure get better with treatments in two or three days. Mr. Carter has been in the ICU for ten days and is too sick to leave his bed. He is not getting better and is in fact looking worse. "He's got a dead heart," the intensive care specialist says, and he tells the cardiologist, "He's circling around, not getting better. Where are we going with him? He can't live in here forever." The cardiologist wants to do a diagnostic angiogram[12] to see if an angioplasty[13] is called for. "I'd hate to see him die and then on autopsy discover that we could have fixed one cardiac vessel," he tells me. "Maybe there is a twenty-five percent chance that we can really do something to make him better." On the other hand, he is not sure the angiogram will find anything that a medical procedure could fix. The intensive care specialist does not think the angiogram is a good idea because the contrast dye used to see the condition of the arteries could also cause kidney failure. Mr. Carter's heart is so bad, both doctors agree, that he could not tolerate the dialysis that would be required if his kidneys were damaged.

The cardiologist knows Mr. Carter well and has been treating him for the past eight years. Mr. Carter looks "much younger than his heart," I am told, and has led an active life. The cardiologist has discussed the issue of life-prolonging treatments with Mr. Carter in the past. He said then that he would accept intubation with a ventilator and would want to undergo CPR if he had a reversible medical problem. He would not want life-sustaining treatment if his condition would not improve. As in most situations, those general and hypothetical wishes do not help the doctors with the current impasse. "We're between a rock and a hard place," the cardiologist comments. "We want him to recover, we're rooting for him, but we can't get him off the drips."

Day 10: I am present when the cardiologist explains the situation to his patient, telling him he's not getting better and can't go home like this. He explains about the angioplasty, the risk of kidney damage, and the uncertainty of their finding something they can fix. "I can't promise that this procedure is without some risk. It could make you worse. You could have a heart attack or a stroke. We have to weigh the risks against the benefits. It sort of depends on you and how much active living you have to do. It's like basketball and you're going overtime. What are your thoughts on this?"

Mr. Carter asks what the doctor would do in his shoes, and the cardiologist replies that he does not know. "I'm not eighty-four. I don't know what I'd do. Some guys at eighty-four would say they've had enough. Others would say they want to keep going." Mr. Carter tells him he is willing to take the risks and have the procedure in the hope that he'll get better. His wife agrees.

The patient has reached a crossroads on the heroic intervention pathway, and now he is stuck there. If the doctor does nothing, the patient will soon die. If the procedure causes kidney damage, the patient will also die. On the other hand, if the medical team finds one clogged vessel and opens it up, Mr. Carter will be able to go home and "live," even if he has to spend most of his time sitting in a chair.

The cardiologist speaks with the nurse about fine-tuning Mr. Carter's drugs—lowering the doses of the various vasopressors slightly, discontinuing some drugs, keeping others. The doctor wants to make Mr. Carter's condition as stable as possible before the angiogram and possible angioplasty, which is scheduled for the next morning. He reads Mr. Carter's medical chart carefully, looking for clues about how to proceed. If he considered the situation futile, he says, he would not have suggested the procedure to the patient. But because he's seen, repeatedly, that "even fixing one vessel enables a patient to go home and live his life," he wants to try.

Mr. Carter's nurse on the day shift explains to me, as have other nurses, that patients like this come in for a "heart tune-up." Patients receive medications that keep heart failure at bay for a while. They go home but then return to the hospital weeks or months later. "It takes several hospitalizations," she says, assuming the revolving door pathway to be the norm, "before people are really ready to face their deaths. They need to be hospitalized several times and not really be getting better. They need to return each time sicker than the last. Only then do they say enough is enough." Only then do they somehow "decide" that it is time to die. She does not think Mr. Carter is ready. Nurses repeatedly reported as fact that patients accept death after a *certain amount of time*. With debilitating medical conditions such as congestive heart failure, *death must actively be chosen*. I never heard physicians use this kind of language.

Mr. Carter had had an active life before the heart attack brought him to the hospital. He hiked, played volleyball, did a great deal of volunteer work. He hasn't been sick for long enough, this nurse thinks, to be ready to die. When I ask what she would choose if she were the patient or the patient's wife, she replies that she does not know, that it all depends on what kind of life the patient "wants," what he considers "a quality life," and whether he thinks an extremely disabled life (sitting in a chair, not being able to walk, needing supplementary oxygen all the time) is "worth" living.

After the cardiologist leaves, I speak with Mr. Carter for a few minutes. He has a clear plastic oxygen mask over his nose and mouth. He is connected by intravenous lines to the many medications hanging in bags on a pole at the side of his bed, and he is also connected to a cardiac monitor that beeps intermittently. He does indeed look much younger than his chronological age and is alert and animated. He has friendly, bright blue eyes and talks easily, not about the choice the nurse felt he needs to make in order to move along, but instead about how medicine can't do everything, how he feels he has weighed the risks and is willing to go ahead with the angiogram. After all, he points out, he can't do anything at all right now. He tells me he has thought a great deal about facing death, both after a heart attack twenty years before and after this one.

Several hours later, at three in the afternoon, the hospital chaplain visits Mr. Carter and, I learn later, hears a different story. Mr. Carter thinks he might die during or immediately after the procedure. He is afraid for his family. His wife and children have assembled in the waiting room outside the ICU, equally worried he may not live through the procedure. They are all crying.

At four o'clock the nurse on the evening shift calls the cardiologist because Mr. Carter's blood pressure has dropped. She is surprised this patient has "decided" to have the procedure. She remarks, as did the day-shift nurse, that, like many other patients she has cared for, he could have chosen to die instead. She, too, notes that he is not ready to make that choice, that he hasn't been sick enough, long enough. The cardiologist arrives and briefly examines Mr. Carter. He tells the nurse he is not sure Mr. Carter will live through the night.

At about five o'clock Mr. Carter's condition worsens. The cardiologist performs an electric shock procedure called cardioversion to stop a dangerous heart rhythm and jolt Mr. Carter's heart back into a normal rhythm.[14] It does not correct the problem, and shortly after the procedure Mr. Carter's heart stops beating. The medical team performs CPR in an attempt to resuscitate him. For nearly two hours, they do chest compressions, apply electric shock, and give blood pressure medications intravenously, hoping to restore his heartbeat and blood pressure. "He wanted aggressive treatment," the cardiologist explains afterward. Mr. Carter dies at 6:45 P.M.

Aftermath: The next day, Mr. Carter's day-shift nurse expresses her surprise about his death with tears in her eyes. In her view, he died before he had the chance to deliberately choose death over life. "Maybe he just didn't want to face that procedure," she reasons, wanting to see him in the role of an active agent in bringing about his death. Several days later, the intensive care specialist also mulls over the events. "In retrospect," he remarks, "we needed to do aggressive care earlier. We were treading water in a bad place for too long. We spent too much time only sort of being aggressive."

The doctors stalled movement along the heroic pathway. Mr. Carter remained in the ICU for ten days, then died there after an emergency resuscitation attempt—a not uncommon hospital scenario. When at a crossroads on the pathway, the doctors had pondered the two available alternatives: proceed with the angiogram—the only thing left to do medically and the obvious continuation of the heroic pathway—or ask the patient if "he wants" to step off the pathway and end his life.

When he asked Mr. Carter what his thoughts were about "how much active living" he had left to do, Jack Carter's physician placed responsibility for deciding about death squarely on his patient. Though Mr. Carter replied that he was willing to go ahead with the procedure, he also waffled and turned the question back on the doctor by asking him what he "would do in my shoes," i.e., lying in an ICU bed tethered to life-sustaining medications. His question was not unusual. Patients seek the advice of physicians about whether they are dying. Mr. Carter was well aware that clinicians know the biological truth about the body's decline, and he wanted his physician to speak that truth. Though the doctor gave an answer ("I'm not eighty-four. I don't know what I'd do . . ."), it was the *wrong* answer to the *wrong* question, in the sense that the question made the patient responsible for choosing or not choosing death, and the answer, according to the needs of the system, did not move things along or offer clear guidance for the patient so that he could "control" his own dying. In addition, the physician's answer did not remove the patient's responsibility for any "decision" made. Like families, physicians want to avoid the guilt and the personal responsibility of authorizing death or being seen as the "cause" of death. If, as the nurses suggested, Mr. Carter "was not ready to choose death," he was also not prompted or given permission or guided by his doctor to choose death. The doctor decided to prepare for the procedure.

Many would claim that Mr. Carter did not have a "humane" or "dignified" death because he died during (or immediately after) the violence of CPR, following a prolonged ICU stay, connected to tubes and machines. This view, in its abstract form, would have the patient conscientiously chart the course (and preferably in a straight and quick line, as though that were possible) to death. It would have the doctor comply with the patient's wishes. But like many patients who find themselves in the hospital, very sick, and on the heroic intervention pathway, Mr. Carter was willing to stay on it, whatever its outcome. A different interpretation of Mr. Carter's trajectory might instead suggest that the doctor did act "humanely" precisely because he did *not* guide Mr. Carter to select death, did *not* suggest that he end his life now. It could be argued that the doctor acted appropriately (within the American idiom of autonomous decision-making) by offering a choice and by leaving the final decision to the patient.

Though the doctor was well aware that the chances for stabilization or recovery were exceedingly slim, he offered and then decided to proceed with one last potentially stabilizing medical procedure. But before that could happen, Mr. Carter had a cardiac arrest and CPR was initiated, the last procedure available on the heroic pathway prior to death. Mr. Carter had said earlier that he was willing to undergo CPR if his condition were thought to be reversible. He had chosen to undergo the angiogram with possible angioplasty rather than withdraw treatments. The call for emergency resuscitation merely followed directives already in place. Performing CPR, despite its being considered by everyone as the most undignified way to die, was the logical outcome, within the hospital system, of the doctor's *and* the patient's considered choice to try to avoid death. CPR was the only alternative, at that moment, to "selecting" death.

The Family Stalls: Nhu Vinh

Background: Mrs. Nhu Vinh's medical condition was not unusual, nor was the response to it of her daughter, Mrs. Tran. Mrs. Vinh, age eighty-four, had been diagnosed with Parkinson's disease six years before her current hospitalization, though in retrospect, Mrs. Tran tells me, she had had symptoms long before the diagnosis. Shortly after her diagnosis, she needed round-the-clock care at home, which Mrs. Tran arranged with attendants. But, Mrs. Tran says, her mother still had "quality of life." She could go out to family functions and enjoy herself. The last two years, however, became much more difficult as the disease progressed. Mrs. Tran tells me the story while we sit together in her mother's hospital room. She has just washed Mrs. Vinh's long gray hair and is spreading it out against the pillow as her mother lies sleeping. It is a warm day and Mrs. Tran has turned on a fan to help dry her mother's hair. Mrs. Vinh is breathing through a nasal cannula. Her hands, visible above the sheets, are extremely contracted.

In the months before her hospitalization, Mrs. Vinh could not walk. It took three or four hours to feed her each meal. The attendants, whose work Mrs. Tran supervised closely, would spoon pureed food into her mother's mouth and watch carefully that she swallowed each mouthful. Mrs. Vinh had become incontinent, and her physical condition and mental state were deteriorating. But she could still interact with her daughter. Six weeks before I met the patient and her daughter in the hospital, the home attendants, doctors, nurses, and speech therapist who were caring for Mrs. Vinh all agreed without debate that Mrs. Vinh wasn't getting enough nutrition and needed a feeding tube inserted into her stomach.[15]

Mrs. Vinh had the common, low-risk, and low-tech procedure to insert what is known as a g-tube. But since that time, Mrs. Tran tells me, her mother has had nothing but problems, especially recurring reflux and fevers.[16] Mrs. Tran says with pride that in the two years prior to the insertion of the tube, her mother was not hospitalized and nothing had ever gone wrong.

Admission to day 7: After six weeks of problems following the placement of the feeding tube, Mrs. Tran admitted her mother to the hospital. Mrs. Vinh had pneumonia from aspirating her own secretions, and in addition the g-tube had accidentally moved (*migrated,* in medical language). Upon admission to the hospital, physicians treated the pneumonia and suggested replacing the g-tube with a tube inserted into the jejunum (j-tube), the small bowel, to avoid the regurgitation and possible aspiration of food into the lungs.

The procedure would require general anesthesia, and Mrs. Tran debated, along with her large extended family, whether the surgery was the right thing to do. They finally decided to go ahead with it. "This was a very, very hard decision because we knew she was a high-risk surgical patient," Mrs. Tran tells me. She is adept at quickly translating her way of knowing into language that American health care providers can easily understand, and she explains that as Buddhists, as Asians, their decision was not based on quality-of-life considerations—"My mother hasn't had any quality of life for two years." The family simply wanted to prolong Mrs. Vinh's life. On the other hand, they did not want to do anything that would create pain and suffering. They had previously decided that Mrs. Vinh would not be put on ventilator support if she could no longer breathe on her own, and she would not be subjected to CPR if her heart stopped beating. Other than that, her life should be maintained. Mrs. Tran explains these decisions and adds other things she

wants me to know about her: Her father had been a well-regarded Buddhist practitioner. She had come to the United States from Vietnam
thirty-five years ago. Her very young grandchildren, she says proudly,
speak Vietnamese. She has a disabled cousin whose care she supervised
for many years. She herself works in a health profession and has taken a
leave to care for her mother. She is spending most of her time, day and
night, at her mother's bedside.

Day 7: The surgery, the day after Mrs. Vinh was admitted to the hospital, was not complicated, but Mrs. Vinh has not been doing well since
then. She has not regained her previous physical condition and mental
state as the medical team and the family had hoped. The doctors treating
her have written in her medical chart, "end-stage care," "dementia and
chronic vegetative state," and "continues to deteriorate." The physicians
tell Mrs. Tran that her mother's condition is deteriorating, that she will
not survive the pneumonia. She was still aspirating, despite the j-tube, so
she could not be fed through it, and Mrs. Vinh is now receiving antibiotics, nourishment, and morphine through an intravenous line, and
that cannot go on indefinitely.

Mrs. Tran is exhausted. When she is not at the hospital, she arranges
for the attendants who cared for Mrs. Vinh at home to come and sit at
her bedside. She tells me, expressing both her convictions and her
ambivalence, "My mother is a fighter. She wants to live. I know this
about her very deeply. All of this talk about quality of life is not relevant.
She wants to live, even in this condition, that is why she struggles to
breathe so much, that is why they gave her the morphine, to make her
breathing easier. But, I don't know. Maybe they just should give her
more morphine till she stops breathing. . . . I want her to live, but I want
her to be comfortable." Mrs. Tran's brother is on his way to the hospital
from his home in another city. Mrs. Tran says that her mother is waiting
to die—waiting for her son to come and see her.

Now, six days after the surgery, the medical team wants to stop giving
Mrs. Vinh infection-fighting medications and move her along to her
death. They assume she is not conscious but know she is at the end stage
of her disease. They see no reason to prolong her dying and perhaps
cause her to suffer. They want to create a comfortable death. The hospital social worker tells Mrs. Tran that the staff want to meet with the
family as soon as her brother arrives. Mrs. Tran, quite familiar with predictable (and desired) hospital pathways, asks rhetorically, "Why do they

want to have a meeting? We've already made her DNR and no intubation. I am ready to take her home if she can be discharged. I can handle
it. I am set up for it with new caregivers. My mother didn't have oxygen
at home before, but we'd get it this time, and I'd learn how to do it. This
is not a problem. We've discussed everything already. There is no need
for a meeting. Why do they want a meeting? It's because they want to tell
me that if they take off the oxygen mask, she'll die more quickly. That
leaving on the mask is prolonging her life. It's just like the ventilator. If
you remove the mask, she'll live maybe a few hours, or a few days or a
few weeks, but she'll die sooner. That's why they want to have the meeting," she says matter-of-factly. Mrs. Tran is quite aware that the medical
team view her as the obstruction to a quicker death.

Implicit hospital policy mostly lets the family chart the course, even
if they obstruct the flow of things. (Hospitals also have explicit guidelines, though there are no laws, for the withdrawal of life-sustaining
treatments.) Families and health care providers do a delicate dance in
which hospital staff allow families to speak for very sick patients, letting
their voices be heard and their wishes for treatment be enacted, while at
the same time guiding the families along what staff consider to be the
appropriate course.

The Vinh family conference was scheduled to take place as soon as
the son, a businessman, arrived. I am standing outside Mrs. Vinh's room
with the case manager and the patient's son and daughter when the
social worker arrives to tell us she has to find a room for the conference
and a key to unlock it. A few minutes later she returns and guides us to
a small, windowless room, devoid of any decoration whatsoever, near
the nurses' station. There are not enough chairs and the social worker
and case manager go to find some. They return with the chairs just as
the doctor arrives. There is a moment's hesitation as everyone decides
where to sit, and Mrs. Tran points to a chair next to her and asks me to
sit there. "For support," she says. An adversarial tone between the staff
and the family has already been established. I sit with Mrs. Tran and her
brother on one side of the table. The doctor, social worker, and case
manager sit on the other side.

The conference follows the standard format for medical staff communication with families: medicine speaks what it understands to be
the truth about the patient and outlines the proper course of events, and
the family is expected to understand, to agree, and "to get with the pro-

gram." The doctor, an immigrant from China, speaks first and begins by reviewing the patient's medical condition. He is thoughtful and describes her condition as best he can.

> *Physician:* We removed the g-tube but now your mother is having prob-
> lems with the j-tube. We're treating her with antibiotics. She was in
> the ICU for a day or two, intubated. She still has pneumonia. That is
> not going away. She still has off-and-on fevers. Her breathing is more
> labored, more fast and shallow, because she doesn't have enough
> oxygen in her lungs. Basically, I'm sorry to say, she's not doing well,
> and I want to give you a true picture. This situation is difficult for
> everyone and for the medical profession as well. I'm afraid she's
> going to die very soon. She almost died already a couple of times. We
> have no way to treat her condition. I'm afraid she's going to keep
> aspirating because of her secretions, even if they suctioned her
> around the clock. Regarding her nutrition, we are hoping the j-tube
> will work. But meanwhile we're giving her IV feedings—it is life sup-
> port. We can do this short-term but not long-term. To me this is not
> in her best interest. She's not communicative. We can keep her alive
> a little while, though even with the best management, she can die
> anytime. There's really no good treatment for her difficulties. My
> recommendation is that we should keep her comfortable, keep her
> mouth from getting dry. I recommend that we cut down on the oxy-
> gen. She's getting fourteen liters at the moment—that's a lot. And
> stop the antibiotics and let her go to sleep. Let nature take its course.
> I'm very sorry. She's lived a full life. She's very near the end of her life
> at this time. There's no more quality of life. Most people in her con-
> dition would have died by now.
>
> *Mrs. Vinh's son:* Quality of life?
>
> *Physician:* She's not aware of her environment. She doesn't demon-
> strate anything. She cannot respond in any meaningful way.
>
> *Mrs. Tran:* Sometimes, in rare moments, when she opens her eyes, when
> she hears me talking, she turns her eyes toward me. So we can't say
> that she's totally unconscious. I believe she recognizes my voice.
>
> *Son:* If you don't stop any treatments, how long will she live?
>
> *Physician:* I don't know. Days, hours, months. Maybe you're keeping
> her body going, but her GI tract is not working. She can't absorb
> nutrients. Antibiotics are not keeping the fever under control.

Son: Is she suffering? She's not conscious, as you say.

Physician: She's not getting pain medications or sedatives.

Social worker: Are you worried about her comfort level?

Son: I'm basically wanting to know if she is alive. Is she conscious? Is she suffering?

Physician: Well, her body is alive, you're keeping it alive. Her consciousness is minimal—it's a persistent vegetative state.[17] There are gradations of this, of consciousness.

Mrs. Tran: But she's been like this for years.

Physician: As far as suffering, I don't think she's in pain, but I can't know for sure. Even if we do everything, I don't know how long she'll live. Most families won't keep someone alive on tube feeding.

Son: What is your recommendation?

Physician: Let nature take its course.

Son: What does that mean?

Physician: Stop the feeding and antibiotics. Give her a little oxygen for comfort only. Give a little morphine for pain. But let nature take its course. Even with the current treatments, I don't think she'll live more than a few days.

Son: We have some family members missing. We want to meet as a family.

Physician: She's in limbo land, between life and death. Regardless of our interventions, she'll die.

Son: It's very important that she has all the comfort. [The doctor leaves the room to respond to a call on his beeper.]

Case manager: Absolutely, that's what we want to do.

Mrs. Tran: So we can't talk about discharge?

Social worker: The doctor's job was to give you the medical picture and his recommendations.

Mrs. Tran: Does she have to be hospitalized?

Social worker: That's a hard call. The fever is an issue. Could we set this up at home? You'd have to be trained.

Mrs. Tran: We're talking about a short time until she dies, regardless of what we do, that's what he said. Right?

Social worker: Yes. If you withdraw some of these things, we can predict more closely, maybe. But if you keep all the interventions, we cannot predict. Whatever you decide, we'll accommodate.

Mrs. Tran: Are you in a hurry? Is there pressure? She still has family.

(Looks to her brother) Can you make a decision now? If we withdraw everything, she'll die—correct? She still has living brothers
and sisters. Maybe they'll feel that isn't right. That's a big decision.

Social worker: How much time do you need?

Son: Two or three days at most.

Mrs. Tran: One sister is in France. A brother is in New York. You have
to realize this is a difficult decision. This is a life-and-death decision. He's saying if we leave everything, she'll die slower. If we
remove everything, she'll die faster.

Social worker: Legally the children are the next of kin and can decide.

Mrs. Tran: I am the legal guardian. But still it's a decision of life and
death.

*Social worker (working hard to show respect for the way the family per-
ceives the situation):* I know, culturally, your family needs to come
to a decision.

Mrs. Tran: Not even culturally—this is life and death.

Social worker: It's also an option to take her home with everything she
has here if you need more time to make a decision.

Mrs. Tran: But even if you trained me, I'm not at the level of a doctor
or nurse.

Social worker: What most people do is go to another institution, and I
know that you don't want to put her in another institution.

Mrs. Tran: I really feel pressure from you.

Social worker: I sense that. But in a few days we need to know.

Mrs. Tran: I am ultimately the one who has to make a decision. [The
social worker brings the meeting to a close by reviewing the patient's
medical condition and again posing the question of whether to continue with medical support, and whether the family wants to take
her home or put her in an institution.]

Mrs. Tran: We want her home.

Social worker: It's not meant to put you under pressure, but we need as
much time as possible to help you set up at home, if that's what you
want.

For everyone in the room, the pressure on Mrs. Tran to "decide" to
withdraw life-sustaining treatments from her mother is palpable. Once
medical personnel are convinced that death is imminent or inevitable
(even though the time of death cannot be predicted with accuracy), the

haste with which the dying transition is initiated is important to the system. Mrs. Tran is obstructing the proper flow of events along the pathway by refusing to "decide" to withdraw treatments.

The conference ends and everyone stands up to leave. Mrs. Tran tells me she is going to leave the hospital for a while. She is not sure what the staff are going to do, but she is going to let her mind rest and not think about this—at least until she comes back in the evening. The social worker says that someone always takes the heat about putting pressure on families, and this time it was her turn, but she didn't mind. The nurse case manager goes to see Mrs. Vinh, who has obviously taken a turn for the worse. The case manager thinks the patient will die quite soon.

Two hours later Mrs. Tran leaves me a telephone message. She is crying as she says, "My mother just passed away at 7:30 P.M., and she had the elegance to pass away without her children making any decision."

For the doctor, Mrs. Vinh was not *alive* in any meaningful sense (she lacked any expressive capability), and that "truth" was indicated by all her bodily signs, including her apparent lack of consciousness. For him, Mrs. Vinh's general condition—very near death—trumped the vagaries of consciousness. For the patient's daughter, Mrs. Vinh was very much alive—she even died *elegantly*. The patient's son wanted to know the operational definitions of "quality of life" and "let nature take its course" vis-à-vis his mother's condition, since the doctor introduced those concepts. He needed to learn whether her condition could be classified as *life*. Any attribution of suffering would flow from that designation, as would any decision on his part about terminating life. The doctor made the ambiguous point that though the *life* of the patient is questionable, the family is keeping the patient (or at least her body) *alive*, and that is an *unnatural* (and perhaps pain-causing) thing to do. The patient's son remarked to the assembled group that if staff was going to place the responsibility for actively terminating his mother's life on the family, then they needed to meet as a family to gather support for such a profound choice. Such talk between hospital staff and the family about the patient's condition and the need to move things along is a standard part of the movement imperative. This particular meeting, like many I observed, ended with the typical doublespeak that is born when the movement imperative is coupled with hospital liability concerns: "Please (we ask you) move along smoothly, but we will (only because we must) accommodate your choice to remain recalcitrant."

The Burden of Being Near Death

Cynthia Graf was asked to choose, though belatedly, according to some of the staff, and then to prepare for her own dying. Jack Carter was indirectly queried about his desire to stop all life-sustaining treatments. Is authorizing one's own death in the hospital—according to the timing requirements of the movement imperative—suicide? Is it something akin to suicide? Do institutional pressures to withdraw lifesaving treatments in the hospital have a different moral quality and different moral outcome than the proactive decisions made by terminally ill persons who are at home, supposedly remote from institutional pressures to choose death "on time"? Regardless of where they reside when they are near death, most people do not want to or cannot deliberately choose to end their own life. Pain and awareness that death is close do not alter that fact. Both Ms. Graf and Mr. Carter were brought near to that point of choice by the pressure hospital staff felt to move them along, and both said no to it. Neither could take the step across the threshold to death (nor could Mrs. Vinh's daughter take it for her mother). Indeed, the nursing, social work, and medical staff all felt an obligation to help Cynthia Graf "prepare" for death, yet none of them succeeded.

What must it be like for a person who knows, who embodies, who *lives*, the fact that the buffer between life and death is terribly fragile and can be removed quickly and easily at the whim of others and at any moment? Only intravenous antibiotics and nutrition delivered through a tube sustained Cynthia Graf. Her body could not maintain its own *life* without those aids. Her vulnerability to the decisions and authority of others was extreme. She knew she was being kept alive, that that state was precarious, and that she had to speak in a clear, authoritative voice if she wanted to remain alive. She could not take for granted her life or her desire to continue living. Her awareness of being kept alive did not, however, indicate to her, the way it did to staff, the nearness of death. And why should it? That her life was medically supported was not a reason for her to "prepare" for death, to "choose" to die.[18] For as long as she remained conscious enough to do so, she resented and resisted, with all her strength, all staff suggestions and overtures that she activate her own dying. She was not waiting for death as they were. She only wanted to get well enough to go home. Everyone waited around her.

The specter of euthanasia accompanies that of suicide and hovers around families when they think "life" and "death" hang in a delicate balance. Where is the line to be drawn between giving permission to stop life-sustaining treatments and aiding the death of another? Most families I encountered strongly resisted moving their relative out of the zone of indistinction and into a clearly recognizable dying phase. Families, hopeful (and sometimes sure) that medical technology and expertise will save life, are reluctant to learn that often it fails to do so. Even though families are told that technological support is only maintaining the bodily functions, not the *life,* of the patient, unless and until they are convinced that it is certain that death will result from a medical condition, the pressure to withdraw medical support can appear to be the same as or akin to outright murder. Much waiting is the result of the connection families make between killing and withdrawing treatments. Faith Walker's large family resisted the pressure to withdraw treatments until enough time had passed that they were more certain than not that she would never regain *her life.* Dorothy Mason's son resisted that pressure until he was told by more than one staff person that his mother was really dying now.[19] Mrs. Vinh's daughter fought the time-has-come rationale until her mother's death—anticipated, yet not immediately expected—intervened.

What is spoken by medical staff and what is heard by patients and families are not the same thing, as we have seen in family interpretations of *unlikely* and *never* to mean "maybe." In addition, clinicians speak the language of biology, disease, and the body, and the words they choose are steeped in the institutional obligation to move things along. Patients and families frequently do not speak at all, and when they do, it is often of suffering, pain, hope, and fear. They do not always speak in ways hospital staff can hear or can integrate with the demands of disease, treatment, and the imperative of movement. Patients and families look to doctors for direction, yet doctors do not usually know how to speak to them about death. On the other hand, doctors look to patients and families to learn what they are ready to hear and to know, but what patients and families express is not always helpful for what medical staff want, and feel they need, to do.

The twin difficulties of speaking and being heard are perhaps most poignant around the issue I call doublespeak—the contradictory directives and explanations that physicians offer, however unwittingly.[20] Doublespeak takes two forms that I observed, and both were apparent in conferences and meetings involving staff, patients, and families. The first form embodies the movement imperative and can schematically be illustrated as follows, "Take your time, but make a decision (hopefully the one that moves things along) now." The family of Carol Jones was pressed by one doctor to decide right away whether to withdraw life-sustaining treatments and by another to authorize DNR should she have a cardiac arrest. When the first physician saw how anxious the family became when faced with those tasks, he backtracked and told them they did not have to make those decisions immediately. Doctors and nurses together, in several conversations, eventually persuaded Dorothy Mason's son to authorize the DNR order that would prevent his emaciated, demented, and very ill mother from having to undergo a resuscitation attempt. But first he had to ponder the relationship of authorizing the DNR order to murder. The pressure on Mrs. Tran to allow, as quickly as possible, the removal of Mrs. Vinh's life-supporting measures was among the most extreme that I encountered. But the staff felt they had to respect Mrs. Tran's reluctance, and if Mrs. Vinh had continued to hover at the threshold of death instead of dying shortly after the conference with the family, the health care team would have helped set up life-sustaining care for her at home. In any case, *waiting* occurs when the movement imperative is blocked or stalled by what families say they want.

The second form of doublespeak, evident in the Nhu Vinh and Faith Walker family conferences, revolves around the mystery of life, the difficulty of easily defining life's end point, and the fuzzy characterization of the relationship between the two notions. This second form emerges in the language physicians use to explain physiological decline, the absence of beneficial treatments, and the nearness to death. It takes the following shape: "Your mother is not actually (or completely) dead, or dead yet, but neither is she alive." Or, "She's not really alive, but we can keep her alive a bit longer." Or, "He has no meaningful life, but we can continue to take care of him." Though I never heard a physician utter any of those exact sentences, families often hear similarly contradictory and ambiguous phrases.

When combined with the conditions imposed by the machinery of life support, such talk by physicians contributes to the creation of the zone of indistinction. Practically speaking, *life* and *death* merge in this second form of doublespeak. Life is present, but to the physician, the condition of that life indicates the nearness or the transition to death. Families see unresponsive or machine- and tube-dependent patients, listen to medical equivocation about the patient's condition, and have no idea what to make of this zone. So they prefer not to acknowledge it. They are asked to make decisions, but they have too many doubts about the *life of the person* whom they can see with their own eyes. They cannot follow staff directives without substantial anxiety about what they are being asked to do. This stalls movement and makes everyone wait.

II. "LET'S WAIT AND SEE": THE INDETERMINATE CONDITION OF OLD AGE

Though, in bureaucratic terms, no one dies of old age today, families must still confront the meeting of old age and disease, and the complicated relation between them, when an elderly relative is hospitalized. They must imagine *either* impending death due to some combination of age and disease *or* treatable medical conditions regardless of age. And then they must choose. Sometimes, however, choosing gets stalled, and for a period that may seem to drag on and on to families, a patient's condition does not indicate either survival or death and hovers in the zone of indistinction instead. Neither staff nor family know what to do next, so neither strongly pushes for, or resists, a particular course of action. Yet even when they are perplexed about the course to take, medical staff always want to err on the side of life-prolonging strategies, and they move in the direction of stabilizing treatments, and, if possible, of further diagnosis as well. I never saw a family obstruct that move, and indeed, in that moment of not knowing, I can think of no one who would say no to that approach. It is only later, when staff and family review events, that they think about alternative choices they could have made to remove the patient earlier from the troubling gray zone.

The problem of choosing treatments for those in decline in late life and of determining what kinds of treatments are too much when death may be near or welcome rests on the legacy of confusion and debate about the indeterminate condition of old age itself. When a person is old and frail, medicine's ability to manage illness and stave off death always confronts inexorable decline, yet it does so within a hospital culture where, paradoxically, "no one dies of old age." Dorothy Mason, malnourished and with severe pneumonia and advanced dementia, suffered respiratory distress and was rushed to the hospital, where she died after twelve days on a ventilator in the ICU. Her children thought she could recover from the pneumonia despite her extreme frailty (in her case due to the combination of age, dementia, and undernourishment), and they advocated for aggressive treatments that the nurses considered inappropriate. Dora Parker, weakened by respiratory failure, was sent to the ICU in order to stave off death for a time, but the treatments she received there served only to keep her near death while she was shuttled from nursing home to hospital and back again because of Medicare payment schemes. She was not allowed to die, but she was too frail to recover. Nhu Vinh, with advanced Parkinson's disease and dementia, was in the last stage of her illness and at the very end of her life when her daughter brought her to the hospital. Knowing her mother was near death, she nonetheless struggled to keep her alive with a feeding tube. In an earlier era, these three women would not have been hospitalized, though specific diseases may have been attached to their conditions.

Highlighted in the following two stories are the ways in which families and physicians face the indeterminate condition of old age and its relationship to disease and also what waiting looks like when it is due to that ambiguous condition (especially when the voice of the patient is equivocal or silent). Whether decline is caused by disease alone or by disease and advanced age in tandem—and whether either possibility indicates death—is not known at the beginning of a hospitalization, as we have already seen. That lack of foresight adds a dimension of moral angst to waiting: Is the life of the patient ending appropriately, "naturally"? Has the right moment for death arrived? Or, should we fight for continued life, regardless of the patient's condition? In the first story, the family and the doctor are not sure in which direction to move—to find disease and feed the patient or to help the patient die. After four weeks of treating the patient, they remove the feeding tube; the patient dies two weeks later. In the second story, though the physician thinks that inserting a feeding tube—thus sustaining life—is the appropriate thing to do, the family agonizes over whether placing the tube, and later deliberately removing it, are ethical. In this particular case, the patient lives, in the zone of indistinction, after the tube is removed. In both stories, family distress over waiting is related to the patient's age, and thus their waiting is characterized by their profound ambivalence and deliberation over life-extending procedures in late life or the facilitation of death.

Stymied by Failure to Thrive: Greta Adler

Background: While her son was out of town, Greta Adler, age eighty-five, was admitted to the hospital for malnutrition and "failure to thrive." *Failure to thrive* is a descriptive category in clinical medicine, not a diagnosis, and it stands between normal old age and disease, functioning both to label and to respond to the ambiguous causes of decline in late life. In the elderly, for whom there is no standard rate of decline, it usually means any cluster of the following: weak, tired, poor appetite, malnourished, depressed, socially isolated, physically impaired, cognitively impaired, and, in general, not doing well. It can be a sign to the physician to look for organic disease. But although failure to thrive can be due to undiagnosed disease, it can also appear in advanced age, close to death, without specifically diagnosed disease—the result of metabolic, endocrine, or other processes of aging. It can accompany normal (though difficult to define) aging.[21]

Admission: The hospitalist physician in charge of Mrs. Adler's care tells me Mrs. Adler is a "high-functioning" person who has been "declining." She has spinal stenosis[22] and lower-extremity weakness. She is not walking. She is not eating. She is taking antidepressant medication both for depression and to stimulate her appetite. She is in great pain. Simply, she is not doing well. Her nurse at home felt she was deciding to die. The hospital medical team put her on a morphine drip to reduce her severe pain, and the medication has made her sleepy. Now she needs to be awake so the staff can "get her nutrition up," a common medical response to failure to thrive. The physician also tells me that the family is in a "transitional moment," facing the end of Mrs. Adler's life. From the start the physician has been of two minds—find the disease and treat it so the patient can live, or assist the patient and family with her dying. That unremitting tension characterizes Mrs. Adler's hospitalization and is common in the case of old and frail patients.

Day 2: I meet Mrs. Adler's son, a middle-aged professional man. We talk at great length about his mother's life, her illnesses, his own involvement in her care and deep concern for her well-being, and the strain and guilt he has felt in his attempt to give her adequate care while also working and raising four young children. I ask what led to his mother's hospitalization, and he replies that this was one of a series of setbacks, part of an illness and decline that has been going on for a few years. To start with this hospitalization, he says, would be coming in on the middle of the story. A stroke four years ago is "what really began this physical decline, but that brought out the most extraordinary reserves of strength and resilience and determination in her. She had to learn to speak again and all of that." She was in and out of the hospital several times, and since then, she has gotten weaker and responded less well following each hospitalization. And, he notes, she has many, many chronic medical conditions.

At home Mrs. Adler had not been eating and was becoming more and more dehydrated, weaker, less alert, less oriented. Her condition frightened the paid caregivers, who were not able to make her eat, and they called her doctor. Mrs. Adler's doctor felt she needed to be hospitalized and admitted her. Mrs. Adler's son tells me that during her last few hospitalizations the doctors tried to persuade him not to take his mother home but to send her to a nursing home instead. He refused each time, saying nursing home routines and conversation would not, he felt, be stimulating enough to keep her involved in life. "She has a group of musicians who come every week. . . . And we gave her an eighty-fifth birthday party and she played the piano. She still has that." He noted that the doctors did not see that side of her, for in their presence everything in his mother "went limp. . . . She wanted someone to fix it. Her doctor would say, 'Are you in pain?' And she would say, 'Yes, all over, everything but my eyelashes.' And they would have something that was very difficult to work with. . . . She was feeling a kind of physical, biological depression. . . . That's what the doctor saw and it certainly was true."

As we talk, Mr. Adler tries to determine whether his mother's undernourishment was a decision on her part, "even if it's kind of a passive decision, to stop living. . . . If she's had it, and in many ways she has, she's said so." But he is not sure and feels that her inability to eat is perhaps the result of physical problems. "It's quite possible that it is the result of her not being able to digest protein. If that's causing her not to be able to eat and then she gets progressively weaker and then she can't swallow and all the things that come from that, well, then that's not a decision at all, it's something that is happening to her. If we could help that, then maybe she could have more time. But every time she loses something, it's a little death."

His dilemma is what to do, what treatments, if any, to start. He explains it this way: "The doctor offered as one possibility a feeding tube. To try to give her enough strength. That's one alternative. The other is doing nothing. It seemed to me that a feeding tube for her in her particularly sensitized, everything-hurts-state would be a real violation.

And since we don't even know what she wants, I just didn't want to do that. But also I'm not willing to say, 'Don't do anything,' because I really don't know what's going on. She and I have talked about what to do, what kinds of extraordinary measures to take, and still, I don't have enough information. It's a horrible decision to have to think about anyway, but I don't have enough information to even consider *not* helping her. So what the doctor and I decided this morning was to take a middle alternative, to try to stimulate her appetite, to see if she could start eating so she could get some strength back. Maybe then she will be able to talk about what she's feeling and how much she wants."

Several days later: Diagnostic tests reveal an infection, which the medical team, Mrs. Adler, and her son agree to treat. Mrs. Adler's hospital physician tells me, "She's in pain. They did blood cultures, which came back positive. She has endocarditis.[23] It's being treated with antibiotics. So she also has a temporary nasogastric feeding tube because you can't treat with antibiotics and not feed. She needs food to improve. You either have to treat fully or decide not to treat at all. The patient agreed to treatment, but passively." Then the physician looks at me and asks rhetorically, "What are we doing? She's just going to stop eating when this treatment is over. She wants to die. When I asked how she was, she said, 'The only thing I want is to visualize myself at my own funeral.'" The doctor writes in the medical chart that Mrs. Adler is willing to accept antibiotics and tube feeding.

I have visited briefly with Mrs. Adler twice. She was cordial, extremely frail, and woozy from the medications. She attempted to engage me in conversation but drifted off to sleep after a few minutes. She did not have the energy for even a short social exchange.

Day 28: Mrs. Adler is to be discharged to a nursing home tomorrow. She has been on intravenous antibiotic therapy and nasogastric tube feeding for four weeks. Oral pain medication has replaced the intravenous morphine. She is still very frail, extremely lethargic, and not aware of her surroundings or able to converse.

The social worker informs me that during the past four weeks she, one of the hospitalists, Mrs. Adler's son, and other family members had four conferences to discuss Mrs. Adler's course and how to proceed. The social worker says she found all the conferences troubling because each was with a different hospitalist, each of whom approached the question "Is this the end of her life?" somewhat differently. One doctor was supportive about taking out the feeding tube and "letting nature take its course," she reports. The other doctors did not support that choice. Two of the hospitalists raised the topic of a permanent feeding tube in the abdomen to replace the nasogastric tube, a temporary measure. By the fourth conference Mrs. Adler's son was sure that he did not want a permanent feeding tube placed in his mother. One of the physicians later told me that the patient did not want a permanent tube either.

Day 29: Mrs. Adler is discharged to a nursing home without a feeding tube of any kind, though her son is aware that she will die if she does not eat.

Two weeks later: Mrs. Adler dies in the nursing home. After her death I speak with the hospitalist who cared for Mrs. Adler the most and ask him to reflect on what happened. He says, "When I first saw her, I literally could not examine this woman. She would not give me a history. She was in so much pain, she was just crying, crying, 'Don't touch me, don't turn me, I can't be turned, I hurt too much, let me alone.' " It was apparent to him that Mrs. Adler did not have adequate pain control. After learning from her that she would not want to be resuscitated if her heart stopped, the doctor put her on a morphine drip. "For that kind of patient who doesn't have cancer, you know, a lot of doctors won't cross that line. She was going to die if we didn't do anything. I felt the thing the patient needed was to be in control and to feel like she could trust someone. So I made a contract with her that I would give her continuous morphine so she wouldn't have to beg for it, and that we'd get her out of pain and we'd reassess." He says he discussed that strategy with the patient's son. "I wanted him to know that I was giving her continuous IV morphine. And that one of the possibilities was that she might die, and that I was going to titrate it to a dose that was going to keep her out of pain and alive, as much as I could." He goes on, "I have no problem with what I did. I do feel that the system would question me on a patient who does not have a terminal disease."[24]

The physician recalls that over the next few days he tried to talk to Mrs. Adler about eating and drinking. Because she had a fever, the doctor decided to do some medical tests, and the blood cultures came back positive. "She in fact had a strep infection that was probably very subacute and kind of slowly growing, and this may have been the cause of her body pain and her giving up and her not being able to eat and all that. Quite literally, I was shocked. As a physician, you always think, 'Well, at least I did the right thing by triggering these tests,' but I really didn't think that was what was going on. She really had endocarditis. I thought she was going to die, from giving up, just giving up, with a little help, a little morphine. It was not my intent for her to die, but when I saw her and I felt how much she'd given up and how much heart pain she had, I thought she could pull the trigger herself internally. So I was surprised to find out after I had been away a few days that she was alive and that she had a medical illness, endocarditis, that deserved IV antibiotics."

The physician addresses the irony of putting a feeding tube in someone who has been refusing to eat, who has been asking to die, by noting that if you are going to treat an infection with antibiotics, you must proceed with full treatment. In the case of someone who has been protein-starved and malnourished, full treatment includes tube feeding. He said, "Dropping an NG [nasogastric] feeding tube into a woman who doesn't want to eat seems really barbaric. Had she said, 'Do not treat this infection. I won't take the feeding tube,' that would have been a pretty clear message about what she wants." But, he says, the patient was agreeable to the antibiotic therapy and the nasogastric tube.

In the end, Mrs. Adler had twenty-eight days of treatment. When I remind the physician that Mrs. Adler died two weeks after hospital discharge, he remarks, "What did we gain?" But he cannot answer his own question. Toward the end of our conversation I again ask, "So why did you admit her to the hospital?" Reflecting, he says, "To help her die . . . subconsciously, maybe I was bringing her in because she needed some help in how to die. Failure to thrive."

Doomed to Death in Life: Evelyn Barker

Hospitalization, admission to discharge: Evelyn Barker, age eighty-seven, is admitted to the hospital because of a stroke. After six days on the medical floor she is moved to the rehabilitation ward, where she is not getting better. She needs total physical care and cannot speak or swallow. It is not clear to her family or the medical staff whether she understands anything they say or if she can communicate at all. The big question for the family is her quality of life. Is this what she wants now? Her family has been questioning whether Mrs. Barker wants to live like this—bed-bound and unable to communicate. She had been a professional woman, a writer, held in high regard nationally, and had told her family that she never wanted to be a burden to them. Her daughter and son are asking themselves whether they should withdraw nutritional support, and if so, "How to let her die with dignity? How to end her suffering?" They are having conversations with hospital staff about whether, and how, they could ethically assist her death by not prolonging her treatment in the hospital with a feeding tube. If they decide to take her home, how will they provide care while letting her die? The social worker has had several conversations with them about the role and practicalities of hospice care.

A social worker emphasizes to me that Mrs. Barker does not have a terminal illness. Her doctor does not want to withdraw nutritional support—she is not dying. But the doctor is making every effort to learn what Mrs. Barker wants to do about further rehabilitation and artificial feeding. This physician documents her attempt to assess what Mrs. Barker wants in the progress notes she writes in the medical chart during the period when it begins to be clear to the medical team and family that the patient is not progressing in rehabilitation:

Day 21) Medicine: Quite alert at this moment. Asked her if we should give up—she shook head no. Asked her if we should keep fighting to regain as much function as possible. She nodded yes. I related this to her daughter, who wonders if she really understands. Urged daughter to ask same questions.

Day 22) Medicine: Alert. Tolerated nasogastric tube feedings. Wt. about 105. No edema. No change in her condition. I await family's decision about the PEG.[25]

Day 23) Medicine: Up in chair. Tries to talk. Makes sounds today. I get the impression she does Not want to continue tube feeding.

Day 23) Chaplaincy services: Visited with patient's daughter after family conference. We discussed the ethics of withdrawing her mother's feeding tube. She will pursue this with physician. She will speak with social worker about discharge planning options for her mother. I will continue to follow.

Day 24) Medicine: Above noted. I believe her husband will have to make the decision, as the legal next of kin. I still cannot tell for sure what the patient wants. Sometimes it is yes, sometimes it is no.

Nursing home, end of month one: Following her monthlong hospitalization, Mrs. Barker is discharged to a nursing home, where she remains one month later, when I have a conversation with her daughter and son. The daughter begins by informing me that her mother's decline began approximately three years ago. A spry and active woman well into her eighties, she had become "more tottery, more prone to falls," had given up driving and begun to use a cane. It took her a long time to do things. She stopped going to the grocery store. She could not climb stairs easily or sit in the theater because of her swollen ankles. She had atrial fibrillation and high blood pressure. Summing up Mrs. Barker's condition prior to the hospitalization, the daughter says, "She was in ways kind of losing ground, and unhappy about it, but mentally she was still quite with it." And then she had the stroke. To describe the stroke's impact on Mrs. Barker's life, the family details her outstanding and pathbreaking career for a woman of her era and how she was an intellectual resource for her family and community. Her daughter says, "So when the stroke robbed her of everything that had to do with language, it robbed her of her very being."

I ask about the hospitalization, and Mrs. Barker's daughter begins with the nasogastric feeding tube, which was put in on the third or fourth day. "The doctor said we should put a nose tube down, and I said, 'Okay, I'll discuss it with my father.' And my father said, 'That is a heroic measure,' or, 'Is that a heroic measure?' And I'd never been faced with anything like that, never even had to think about that kind of thing, and I had a lot of problems trying to figure that whole thing out." She remarks that this was not a dilemma for the doctor. "What she said to me was, 'You want to do this because you don't know what will happen, you can't tell how much she'll recover, and you will feel guilty if you don't.' Which was probably true." Mrs. Barker's son adds, "But there was no discussion of alternatives. . . . What we should have said was, 'Wait a second. Let's think about it. Do we have a choice not to? What are the pros and cons of that?'" The daughter talks at length about how Mrs. Barker had no written advance directives in general or about artificial feedings in particular. But the daughter states unequivocally, "The last thing she wanted was what has happened to her."

The conference with members of the medical team on Mrs. Barker's twenty-third day in the hospital stands out for her daughter as a memorably awful moment: "So there we were. I had said to the doctor, 'What do you predict out of all this, what do you see?' And she said, 'I think she may learn to swallow, but she'll always be at risk for aspiration. I think that she will be able to communicate some way, but not fluently. I think that she'll be able to go from bed to chair'—but she was not clear if that was with help or not. When I told that to the rehab group, they said that they thought it was an optimistic statement. And part of my asking this was because there was constant pressure to put a stomach tube in—I felt pressured by the nurses who said, 'This is uncomfortable. You really want to get that nose tube out of there because it's so uncomfortable for her, so much more comfortable to put it in the abdomen.'"

Mrs. Barker's daughter and son speak, in retrospect, about her good hospital care. But, they emphasize that they were alone in making decisions because they were the ones who had to consider their mother's existential condition. They decided, along with their father, that under no circumstances would they authorize the stomach tube, regardless of the pressure they perceived, and in fact they wanted to remove the nasogastric tube and not replace it with anything. They spoke with the chaplain, still wondering if their wish to remove nutritional support was "the ethical thing to do." When they received support from the chaplain to stop the tube feeding, they informed the doctor. The daughter goes on, "And then we went about trying to figure out what we were going to do. My idea had been to bring her—we couldn't take her to my father's house—to bring her to my house to get round-the-clock care, get hospice, and let her go. All of us agreed to that." Mrs. Barker's son adds, "And the doctor said it would probably take about a month, about four weeks. She came round to our way of thinking and was very supportive."

"I started calling people," the patient's daughter goes on, "and started to line up round-the-clock care and all of that, that was Friday morning. Friday afternoon I got a phone message from the speech therapist saying, 'Wonderful news, she can swallow.'" The son chimes in, "And we looked at each other, wonderful news? We were prepared to have the hospice gang come in, and four weeks and her suffering will be over." The daughter adds, "And there you are in this horrible situation where you're thinking, 'How can you be a good person and not rejoice that she's improved enough to swallow?' And yet, what's it all mean?" She says, "One of the staff said, 'Now, I want you to find a time when we can meet and I can show you how to feed your mother'—we were still at risk for aspiration—like this was to be my greatest pleasure. And I don't want to feed my mother. We felt two-faced, going to the hospital, looking at the nurses and rehab staff and trying to let them revel in their joy and then thinking, 'That is just prolonging a horrible situation for her, and for how many months or years?' I went away and said, 'She's doomed. She's doomed to what she doesn't want.' So there we were, with everybody dancing in the hallways, except for us."

During the month she has resided at the nursing home, Mrs. Barker has learned to swallow, so she is no longer at risk for aspirating food into her lungs. But she is not talking, is still paralyzed on one side, and expresses extreme distress when she is out of bed, according to her daughter. Mrs. Barker cannot respond verbally, and the family is not sure how good her hearing and vision are. Mrs. Barker's son says, "She's depressed . . . given up . . . she's cognitively less there than she was . . . less animated."

Mrs. Barker's daughter tells me that, in hindsight, if they had known they could have withdrawn the nasogastric tube or never had it inserted in the first place, they would probably have made that choice. "Our whole thought along the way was, 'We're new to this, let's give it the best chance we can,' " she reflects, as do many other families. No one wants to choose death if they think there is hope for life. Dealing with the after-math of that choice—whether for life or death—raises the question, for families, of whether they did the right thing. Mrs. Barker's daughter says, "But I'm not sure that's the right thing [to give it the 'best chance'], looking back. Maybe it's just time to end. I think that no one looks at it in terms of the risk of having to live a nonlife versus put the nose tube in and maybe there's a chance of improvement." Mrs. Barker's daughter concludes our conversation by telling me, "People ask, 'How is your mother?' I've come to the point where I say, 'She seems to be comfort-able, she's not in a medical crisis, and as far as her mind, it's totally gone.' Is my mother there? No. I lost my mother the day she had the stroke."

The Feeding Tube and the Zone of Indistinction

Failure to thrive can describe a form of life at the zone of indistinction, and the feeding tube, like the mechanical ventilator, can sustain people in that zone for prolonged periods. Just as the mechanical ventilator serves as a stabilizing, lifesaving treatment for patients who cannot breathe, the feeding tube, which can be inserted through the nose, the abdomen, or the intestine, serves as another kind of treatment, this one for patients who enter the gray zone because they are weak, undernourished, declining toward death, or have, in some indeterminate way, lost the spark of life.[26] The feeding tube is low-tech and simple. In the United States today it is the pragmatic medical response to the need to "do something" about decline in advanced age. It has become a common treatment for frailty—whether that frailty is due to a diagnosed disease, the inability or lack of desire to eat, or the natural bodily signs that precede death. In 1995, 121,000 elderly people in the United States (about 30 percent of them with dementia[27]) had gastrostomy tubes inserted, and that number continues to increase. Europeans I have spoken with find use of the feeding tube as a treatment for decline in old age to be odd indeed—an "unnatural" way of avoiding death and a cause of suffering. That specific use of the tube is a decidedly American phenomenon.

Debate about whether artificial nutrition for frail, demented, or severely disabled elderly people constitutes appropriate medical care, humane care, futile treatment, or irresponsible allocation of resources has been both lively and unresolved in the medical community for more than a decade.[28] And many American families will face the decision about whether to place a feeding tube in a frail parent or other relative. Some, like Mrs. Vinh's daughter, view tube feeding not as a treatment or a negotiable procedure but as a basic activity of nurturance and of life itself. Others, like the medical staff attending Mrs. Adler and Mrs. Barker, view it as a necessary component of an overall treatment plan. Still others, like Dora Parker's and Mrs. Barker's family, think of the feeding tube as an unnatural act of heroic medicine and a technological means of denying death. Then there are family members similar to Mrs. Adler's son—they do not firmly categorize tube feeding as either basic sustenance or obligatory treatment and cannot decide whether tube feeding is the best or the worst thing to do to their relative. Some analysts of health care delivery practices emphasize the growing costs of keeping more and more elderly persons alive in this manner, claiming that the costs of housing people connected to feeding tubes outweigh any "quality of life" benefits. Recent medical analyses show that feeding tubes are inappropriate for people with advanced dementia.[29] Yet families and physicians continue to request and condone their use.

Stories occasioned by feeding tubes raise the question of where responsibility lies. Patients themselves are frequently incapable of making decisions about tube use. In fact many, if not most, recipients of gastric feeding tubes are unaware when the procedure takes place, are not cognizant of a tube permanently placed in the stomach, and do not resist or give permission for such intervention. Family members, once they learn the procedure exists, do not want to feel guilty for "choosing" to let a relative die because he or she cannot or will not eat. Physicians feel compelled to inform families of the options available to them. And gastroenterology specialists respond to calls from colleagues to insert the tubes. The *need* for feeding tubes is created by the technological imperative and the political and economic forces that drive health care delivery. Their use reflects the organization of medical practice together with the power of one moral claim over another.

Neither Mrs. Adler's son nor Mrs. Barker's daughter, like many family members I spoke with, knew what kinds of treatments their parent wanted, even though they did know how their parent wanted to live. Broadly conceived advance directives of "no heroic measures" simply did not apply to pressing questions about whether, and for how long, to fight infection, feed through a tube, or pursue rehabilitative measures. Mrs. Adler's son struggled deeply to understand whether his mother's lack of appetite was volitional or the result of a disease. That knowledge, he hoped, would help him decide how to act as her advocate. He agreed to proceed with tube feeding as a temporary measure while his mother's infection was being treated, but he did not view it as a permanent solution to her slow decline, and he had the tube taken away before his mother was discharged from the hospital.

The doctor's retrospective account of Mrs. Adler's hospitalization attests to the murkiness of the physician's role when faced with failure to thrive and a lack of clear and sustained directives from the patient. Should he treat infection, which would include nutritional support, or help the patient die? Mrs. Adler's doctor treated the pain, knowing that morphine could inadvertently end her life (and perhaps that was what she wanted), and he also treated the infection, with the goal of prolonging Mrs. Adler's life.

Mrs. Barker's daughter and doctor tried to understand "what she wanted" while she was hospitalized. But nasogastric tube feeding was instituted early in the patient's hospitalization, regardless of their ability to discern an answer from her, because the physician did not know what the future would hold and was responsible for ensuring that the stroke patient, who was not dying, lived long enough to make some sort of recovery. Yet the question "Why are we artificially feeding her, considering her poor quality of life now and in the future?" became central for the family when Mrs. Barker's condition stabilized, without improvement, in the zone of indistinction. Through the diligent efforts of the rehabilitation team, Mrs. Barker could swallow and thus eat and so would *live*. But, her daughter anguished, what kind of death-in-life would her mother have, and how long would it go on?

III. AGREEMENT AND ANTICIPATION: WATCHFUL WAITING

I observed scores of examples of those two forms of waiting—first, the obstruction of movement, and, second, the inability of patient, family, and staff alike to choose a path with conviction because the patient's condition was indeterminate. But in addition, there is another, equally common form of hospital waiting, one that comes closer to the waiting of an earlier era. In this third form, doctors announce death's inevitability at the same moment that the patient or family conceive it to be finally necessary—an appropriate relief to the suffering of irreversible or catastrophic illness. Then *waiting for death,* as a mindful, completely absorbing activity, takes place. Then death is not a problem.

One of the most easily accepted deaths I witnessed was the vigil of a young man who took me to his ninety-seven-year-old grandmother's room on the hospital's general medical floor. Though she was unconscious, he introduced me to her. He wanted me to meet her. It looked as if she were sleeping peacefully. He told me she would soon die and he would stay at her bedside until she did. He wouldn't have it any other way; she had raised him after his mother had died, and he would honor her by staying with her. She had been living in her own home until, five days earlier, she had called him and asked for help. He drove her to the emergency room, where a nurse told him she had had a heart attack and that he should not expect her to live. Unlike Dorothy Mason, the young man's grandmother had not been intubated, though she was sent to the intensive care unit for two days so that her cardiac condition could be monitored. Once she was stabilized, the staff moved her to the medical ward to die. She was receiving no life-prolonging treatments, only morphine by injection. Her grandson sat at her bedside for three days, patiently awaiting her anticipated death.[30]

The following four examples show ways of anticipating death. In each of these stories, the patient moves relatively easily toward death because no one in the system acts to stave it off. In the first story, the patient deliberately gets off the heroic pathway to await his death. Everyone around him agrees with and supports his decision. The second patient and those around him wait, for weeks, for death. In the third and fourth stories, the timing of death is manipulated according to staff and family rationales.

Courageous Waiting: Edward Harris

Occasionally a patient declares that it is time for his own death, and everyone in the hospital organizes things to respond. Edward Harris has decided the time has come to die. Sixty years old and suffering from a progressive, degenerative disease, he has been hospitalized twelve times in the previous twelve months for medical crises related to his condition. Each time he came home from the hospital, his daughter says, he was worse off, able to function less adequately. He also has end-stage renal disease and his life has been sustained by kidney dialysis three days a week at an outpatient clinic. A divorced farmer who had always been physically active, Mr. Harris realized he was headed for a nursing home, where he would be maintained on dialysis and would become more and more incapacitated. A few months ago, he had to be resuscitated on the way to the hospital, and he said then that he had had enough.

Admission to day 4: Mr. Harris is admitted from the emergency room to the intensive care unit and, four days later, decides to stop dialysis, thereby ensuring his death. His doctor informs him that the toxins will build up in his body until he becomes comatose and dies in his sleep. ("Not a bad way to go," several hospital staff tell me.) Everyone—his daughter, the ICU nurses, and his doctors—respects his decision. He asks his doctor to help him end his life quickly, but the doctor says he cannot do that, though he can make sure that Mr. Harris will die without pain. The medical staff expect him to die within two weeks; one nurse says it may take only a few days. The staff move him to a quiet room on the general medical floor where his daughter and many friends can visit without restrictions. I first visit him there the day of his move, and he tells me without emotion that he does not want a slow decline with more illness and disability. He is getting his financial affairs in order, preparing for his death. He is afraid.

Day 4: His nurse on the general medical floor tells me that Mr. Harris is not a No Code. Knowing that he had been made No Code in the intensive care unit, I flip through his medical chart and show her where the doctor had written "DNR" in the progress notes. She informs me that, on her unit, there has to be a specific order on a yellow sheet placed in the front of the chart, or Mr. Harris will undergo a resuscitation attempt should he have a cardiac arrest. She goes to a cabinet and takes out a yellow form, places it at the front of the chart, and says she will find the doctor and have him sign it. (I am amazed at the complexity of hospital bureaucracy.)

The unit social worker specifically asks Mr. Harris's daughter if she understands the implication of her father's decision, and she says she does. She has been driving to the hospital twice a day, from a great distance, to be with her father. They do not talk much. The social worker speaks with her about funeral arrangements.

Day 5: At the health care team's weekly rounds of the unit, where the care and discharge of each patient are discussed, a nurse raises a question about where Mr. Harris will die. Someone asks if he wants to die at home and if there is anyone to care for him there. After rounds, the social worker asks Mr. Harris where he prefers to spend his last few days. He says he prefers the hospital because he wants the nursing care. (His daughter tells me she prefers that he remain hospitalized as well.) The social worker asks if he wants to talk about anything, and he says, "No, but I am afraid." Later that day, the social worker tells me they might start a morphine drip so he can remain in the hospital. He has to be receiving treatment that is reimbursable to stay there, but, she quickly adds, "we need to take into consideration his pain and comfort, too."

I learn from the nurse caring for Mr. Harris that he is getting an injection of a small amount of morphine every eight hours. He is not in pain, she says, but he "has to be on something to stay here." She has asked him if he agreed to the injections and he said he did. I go into his room and he greets me cordially, gripping my hand tightly, as a young child does, and looking directly at me. We chat briefly, and I release my hand and leave the room a few moments after he closes his eyes. I mention to the nurse that I don't know how she does what she does. She says she feels lucky that many deaths occur when she is not there and then remarks, "I'm a tour guide. I make the journey a good one for them. I make sure the red carpet is laid out and that they have a hand to hold and can talk if they want." I ask what she thinks will happen in Mr. Harris's case. She says he may be started on a morphine drip when he loses consciousness and may never be in any pain at all. It's harder for cancer patients, she says, who sometimes fight and don't want to give in to narcotics, who don't want to let go. But with Mr. Harris, he will get toxic. He will get sleepy and slip into a coma. He could live a week or two, not longer, because he isn't eating anything.

Day 12: Edward Harris dies eight days after deciding to discontinue dialysis. No one thought he would die today. The nurse tells me he asked for his morphine injection a bit early and she gave it to him. She thought it did make him more comfortable and relaxed. He asked to see a chaplain, who came and chatted with him and sang songs with him. Six hours after his last morphine injection, two hours after his visit with the chaplain, he died. The nurse says, "He simply went to sleep and didn't wake up. It was beautiful. . . . His blood pressure dropped, and he died within the hour." The social worker is impressed, astounded by the patient's waiting, and remarks, "How he could have such courage to sit in his room and wait for death, just waiting."

"When's It Going to End?": Albert Dressler

When I meet Albert Dressler in his hospital room, he has already been in the hospital three weeks. He has gastric cancer and introduces himself by saying he is terminally ill but feels pretty good today. He is finished with chemotherapy and surgery, will not be leaving the hospital, and does not want to leave the hospital. The important thing now, he says, is preparing others for his death and not knowing when it will come. Mr. Dressler is seventy-two and recently retired. He is sitting up in bed, alert, and focusing his attention and his piercing gray eyes on me. He has a nasogastric feeding tube, which irritates his throat and makes it difficult for him to speak, and he sucks on a Popsicle to ease the irritation. Despite the tubes, the Popsicle, and the hospital gown, I sense immediately that he had been a formidable personality before his illness.

Day 22: I return to visit Mr. Dressler, who says he has lost forty pounds over the last five months and does not have much energy. After we chat for a while, I ask him what three things are important to him now. He replies without hesitation—his family, his health and future, and his work and volunteer activities. He had been a high school math teacher and retired early to become the president of a private foundation. I learn later from his family that he was loved by generations of students and by his entire community. He says he wants to have a good talk with his son and daughter and feels he needs to give them support now. "After all," he says, "they are going to go through a shock in a short time. Health is a cumbersome project right at the moment. Because I'm hanging in there. That's the best way to describe it. And it's important because I need to be hanging in there." Then he points to the plastic bag of nutritional supplement hanging from the pole near his bed and says, "There, I need that, that white stuff. Cut that off and I starve to death." The overarching question always on his horizon is how much longer he will live. He is concerned that he not be in pain as he dies. Most of his conversations with his family doctor are about "what the future brings on me."

A week later: Mr. Dressler is considering whether to go home. "I realized I wasn't going to croak in the next six weeks," he says. A home care nurse comes by to explain hospice and how all the intravenous lines, feeding tubes, and machinery will work at home. He is worried that the buzzers on the machines will drive his wife crazy and that his care will be too much for her. He can't make up his mind. Standing in the hallway outside his room, his wife, Rose, tells me, "Whatever he wants, so long as his mind is clear. It's his decision, even if he wants to discontinue the feeding." She is facing his death head-on, it seems, and calmly. His brother and brother-in-law are also there, discussing whether to have a large memorial service.

Six and a half weeks postadmission: Mr. Dressler has decided to remain in the hospital. One of his nurses says, "It looks like it will only be a couple of weeks." The case managers and discharge planners have been attempting to calculate whether it would be more cost-effective for both the hospital and the family if he was sent home with hospice care. After assessing the costs of equipment, medicines, and nursing care he would need at home, they unanimously decide the cost would be about the same, or even less, for him to stay in the hospital another two weeks or so. He has begun getting morphine injections every six hours for pain. I am chatting with him when his wife and family doctor come in. They invite me to stay, for though Mr. Dressler is drowsy, he is enjoying the company and conversation. The doctor asks him about pain. Mr. Dressler replies in a voice that is now only a whisper that it had been "seven" on a scale of one to ten but now it is about "six." The doctor says maybe they can control the pain better with a morphine patch—sometimes that works, sometimes it doesn't. Or, he could try continuous morphine in an IV, a small amount. Mr. Dressler says, "I'll think about it." The doctor asks him how much he weighs. He answers, "One hundred and fifty-one pounds." The doctor asks him how much he used to weigh, and Mr. Dressler says, "One ninety-five, and I'm never going back there again." He sighs and looks at his wife, who looks sadly back at him.

The following day: Mr. Dressler tells me he is getting weaker every day. He doesn't talk much, and rarely in complete sentences. He says he doesn't want much stimulus now and isn't reading or watching TV. He dozes frequently.

The next day: Mr. Dressler is sitting up in bed, looking out the window, when I come to visit. I tell him he looks peaceful and he says yes, he is. I ask if he feels death is near, and he replies without hesitation, "No." He cracks a joke when the nurse comes to give him his morphine injection. He has asked his doctor to reduce the amount of morphine because the pain has subsided. (His nurse tells me that pain in terminal cancer patients is highly variable, and there is not necessarily more pain as death approaches. It can wax and wane.) His wife and children spend a great deal of time at his side now, and many friends and relatives come by to see him. I ask him if visitors were good, bad, or neutral, and he says, "Neutral."

When I speak with Mr. Dressler's family doctor later in the hospital corridor, he tells me he can never predict when death will occur, but thinks Mr. Dressler might not live through the weekend. There is cancer throughout his abdomen; he may get pneumonia because he is so inactive, and his immune system is gone. "He's going down. His family is coming this weekend, and he may wait and say what he has to say to them, or he may not have the energy to hold out." I go back to see Mr. Dressler, and the doctor comes in a few minutes later, pulls up a chair beside the bed, takes Mr. Dressler's hand, and says in a rather loud voice, "Mr. Dressler, can you wake up to talk to me? Are you sleeping?" Mr. Dressler opens his eyes and says, "Yes."

Physician: Are you in pain?
Mr. Dressler: No.
Physician: Do you need more or less morphine?
Mr. Dressler: Less.
Physician: Okay, I'll cut back from three to one and a half or two milligrams. [Mr. Dressler nods his head.]

Physician: What are you thinking?

Mr. Dressler: When's it going to end?

Physician: I don't know. There are some things we can do. I'm not a prognosticator. We can stop the TPN, the food you're getting in the tube. If we stop that, it will hasten your death. Do you want me to stop it?

Mr. Dressler: Yes.

Physician: You're also getting antibiotics to keep the pneumonia and other things at bay. We can stop that, too. [Mr. Dressler nods and the doctor begins to cry quietly. He tries to hold back his tears, but they come anyway.]

Physician: I'm going to miss you. *(After a few moments of silence)* Where's Rose?

Mr. Dressler: She's around.

Physician: Okay, I'll call her and coordinate with her to get the family here. Do you want to die at home or in the hospital?

Mr. Dressler: In the hospital.

Physician: Do you want your family to be here?

Mr. Dressler: Yes.

Physician: We can stop your feeding now or wait till the family gets here. [Mr. Dressler nods and the doctor strokes his head and hand fondly.] Okay, I'll find Rose.

The doctor leaves the room and I approach the bed and ask tentatively if there is anything Mr. Dressler wants to talk about—stopping the nutrition and the antibiotics? He says, "It seems like the right thing," and gives me a big smile and puts out his hand. I hold it for a few minutes and he drifts off to sleep. When I move to release my grasp, he says, "Too tight?" I am touched that he wants me to stay and say, "No, it's perfect." A few minutes later, his brother and son walk in, and I let go of his hand, saying, "I'm going to let you visit with your family." Soon his brother comes out to stand with me in the hall. He is crying and says this is the first day he feels that death is imminent.

Three days later, in the seventh week after admission: At five o'clock on a Sunday morning, Mr. Dressler dies while still receiving the nasogastric tube feedings and morphine injections every six hours. The antibiotics had been stopped the previous Friday. The case manager tells me that his length of stay was unusual. Patients don't often stay that long in the hospital before they die. "We thought he'd be here maybe seven or ten days. We were going to get him ready to go home," she says. She had no idea that he would stay in the hospital for so many weeks. "We're in a difficult position," she continues, "to be advocates for the patient and to give the best possible care, but to do it within the constraints of the system. Sometimes it's really hard, but this is my job and this is what I have to do." She says that if she won the lottery, she would build a hospice unit attached to the hospital and would even work in it as a volunteer. Patients like Mr. Dressler would be moved from the hospital straight to the hospice unit. Such patients would not have to imagine how their families would cope with them at home, or imagine whether dying in the hospital or at home would be better for themselves and their families, and then decide.

Treating the Family: Peter Rossetti

Waiting for death does not always happen with the passive anticipation exhibited by Albert Dressler and those around him. Death, when it is going to occur within hours or days, can be facilitated deliberately or can (at least for a while) be postponed. The demand for "control over dying" and "death with dignity" is, in effect, a demand to manipulate when a person dies, a demand that is one expression of the life-planning and life-management strategies that characterize contemporary medicine and modern (perhaps especially American) society. In the space of *waiting for death*, families, doctors, and nurses sometimes work together to orchestrate the timing of death—to speed it up or slow it down.

Some families who come to the bedside specifically to wait for death want the waiting to end as quickly as possible once death has been declared imminent. They want *dying* to be speeded up. They ask doctors and nurses to hasten physiological dying because they equate that transition with existential suffering and physical pain. In addition, their own waiting seems unbearable. In such circumstances, physicians and nurses speak of "treating the family" as an important part of their end-of-life work. Some health professionals want the family's experience of a patient's death to be as anxiety-free, as guilt-free, as "good," as possible. Those who hold that view may administer morphine and other drugs, not necessarily to hasten dying, but to serve as a sign to families that they are conscientious health professionals and are doing everything they can to diminish pain and suffering. Physicians and nurses told me that they can never actually know if a nonresponsive patient is "suffering," but those who treat the family say that families have to "live with" their end-of-life experience for a long time, and so one responsibility of health professionals is to ease their emotional discomfort. Just as there is a range of physician comfort and behavior regarding the administration of morphine to patients who are near death, there is also a range of physician and nurse practices regarding treating the family.

Admission, day 1: I meet the family of Peter Rossetti, age eighty-three, in the ICU. "The family is basically holding a death vigil," one of the intensive care physicians has told me. Mr. Rossetti had a mild stroke three weeks ago, was briefly hospitalized, and then went to a rehabilitation facility. Yesterday he was supposed to have returned home, but as he was getting ready, he had a second, this time massive stroke. He was sent back to the acute care hospital in a coma. Mr. Rossetti's family physician, who was shocked to learn of the second stroke, has informed the family that the patient has severe brain damage and there is no possibility for recovery. Attached to a cardiac monitor, Mr. Rossetti is receiving oxygen through a nasal cannula and a small amount of intravenous morphine. His wife of sixty years, son, and two young-adult granddaughters are at his bedside, also shocked, they tell me, by what had happened. "This was so sudden," his wife says. "He was very healthy. There was no indication that anything like this would happen. He was not a candidate for a stroke. We don't want to prolong anything," she adds. "I wish this were over. It is so hard to watch him like this, so hard to watch him suffering." One granddaughter, who has arrived from out of town, is crying as she says, "You don't know what to do, where to be. It's hell to see him like this, but I wouldn't want to be anywhere else."

I learned from the nurse this morning that the night-shift nurse had demanded of one of the doctors that he leave an "open" morphine order, so that she could administer what she considered to be an adequate dose to relieve the patient's discomfort. The existing order, two to five milligrams, was insufficient for pain relief in her opinion. The doctor increased the order, but only up to eight milligrams every few hours. The morning nurse I spoke with said that some doctors are not comfortable leaving orders for large doses of morphine. "You can tell when you need to make the patient more comfortable," she said. She wished she could give a large dose, basically to "kill" the patient, to quickly end the "suffering" of both the patient and the family.[31]

I sit with Mr. Rossetti's family for several hours the morning of his first full day in the ICU. They do not want to leave the room. They all agree they want the morphine drip "turned up" to hasten death. They take turns sitting close to Mr. Rossetti, stroking his hair and face, holding his hand. Off and on someone cries. The son remarks, "I know with hospice they can be more creative with the morphine," implying that in another context morphine could and would be used to hasten death. In the early afternoon, one of the doctors tells the nurse caring for Mr. Rossetti that the morphine can be "turned up now." The nurse comes to the bedside and asks the family how Mr. Rossetti is doing. When they ask if she can "turn the morphine up," she does so. The nurse notes that his rate of breathing has slowed and he has periods as long as ten seconds without breathing. This could continue through the next shift, however, and he may not die for twelve or twenty hours. When I leave the bedside to speak with her, she tells me the family needs a break. They want to be there when he dies, but they need to get out; they've been at the hospital since six-thirty this morning. She thinks it's not good for them if he goes on for hours and says staff are trying to get a private room out of the ICU for him, to accommodate the family, but one isn't available now. "We're not doing anything," she adds, "just turning him and keeping him comfortable."

The family's priest arrives, prays at the bedside, and speaks with the family for a few minutes. He does not stay long. After he leaves, one of Mr. Rossetti's granddaughters says, "That was nice. You feel like you are doing something." The patient's son says he is glad they have a faith. The granddaughter counters, "But fishing was always more important to him than Mass."

Later that afternoon Mr. Rossetti's wife says, "I can't believe I'm doing this. Two days ago he was fine." She strokes her husband's forehead and repeats, "Just go to sleep, go to sleep." To me she says, "I'm so glad the family is with him." Mr. Rossetti's son tells me, "We've turned off the monitors. We couldn't stand looking at them." The family sits at the bedside expectantly, hardly taking their eyes off Mr. Rossetti, thinking that each breath could be his last. When I stand up to leave toward the late afternoon, Mr. Rossetti's wife says to me, "We will get through this."

Mr. Rossetti dies during the night. When I contact one of his granddaughters a month later, she mulls over her experience of her grandfather's hospitalization. She recalls that the nurses were extraordinarily caring and did everything they could to make her grandfather, and the family, comfortable. "But," she says, "the waiting period was frustrating, emotionally draining for all of us. We wanted to get it over with, so he wouldn't have to suffer anymore." Staff say that families impute "suffering" in a dying person when it is they, the family members, who "suffer" while they watch someone they love die.

Slowed and Hastened Dying: Daphne Stradakis

Sometimes treating the family means staving off death so family members can come to the hospital while the patient is still "alive" in order to "say good-bye." In such instances physicians use the tools at their disposal to temporarily postpone death until after the family has gathered at the bedside, then they change tactics to facilitate, or at least to allow, the patient's dying.

Week four, Wednesday: I meet two members of Daphne Stradakis's family and her oncologist. Mrs. Stradakis has just taken a turn for the worse and is "going downhill fast," the oncologist tells me. He has known her a long time and had treated her for cancer a decade earlier. He has just met with her husband and sister-in-law and learned that Mrs. Stradakis's brother, son, and daughter will arrive from out of town on Friday. The oncologist is planning to keep the patient alive by administering blood transfusions and medications until they all have time to visit with her. Mr. Stradakis tells me that this is his wife's third bout with cancer. She has been in the hospital over three weeks while the doctors worked to stabilize her condition. "We've had time to think, to breathe," he says, "and that is good." The patient's sister-in-law says, "She's gone downhill fast. She's physically suffering. The doctor is going to try and keep her going until Friday. Then they'll stop the treatments." Mrs. Stradakis is sixty-five years old.

Yesterday the social worker on the oncology unit wrote a note in Mrs. Stradakis's medical chart: "Husband and sister-in-law stated today that they expect patient to die here. She is still a full code. May we have clarification of code status?" That note was the social worker's way of asking the oncologist to write a Do Not Resuscitate order in the chart right away. Nurses and social workers often communicate with doctors through their notes in the medical chart.[32] Today, after meeting with Mrs. Stradakis's family, the oncologist writes "No Code" in the chart. The nurses on the unit are relieved.[33]

Week four, Friday: Mrs. Stradakis, who now drifts in and out of conscious awareness, is moved to a private room down the hall. Her family has arrived and is gathered at her bedside to await her death, which they want to have occur as quickly as possible now that they are all present. The physician has been able to ensure that the patient *lived* until her family arrived. Now, well aware of the family's desires, he writes in the medical chart, "Family requests pain be relieved as quickly as possible. Request regular increase in morphine to accomplish this. Family feels she is slipping quickly and wants comfort a priority."

Saturday through Tuesday: Mrs. Stradakis's husband repeatedly tells the doctor that he thinks his wife looks as if she is in pain, and he wants the doctor to increase the pain medication. The oncologist continues to be responsive to family sensibilities, and though he may or may not be able to assess the patient's pain, he writes in the medical chart on Saturday, "Still in pain. Family expects her to pass away soon and wishes comfort measures increased." For three more days, he slowly increases the morphine dosage while the family watches, wishing "it would be over." The family members take turns keeping a watch at the bedside. None of them wants to be away from the hospital for long. On Tuesday the physician stops the intravenous fluids and discontinues all laboratory work.[34] Mrs. Stradakis dies that night, with her entire family at her bedside.

Though both the obstructive and the indeterminate forms of waiting are common, hospitals are full, also, of bedside vigils such as these last four examples. Only when death is named and expected, when a space for *waiting for death* has been created, can families characterize the death of their relative as "good" later on.

Waiting is part of hospital necessity and is specified by the bureaucracy, and waiting is also created by patients, families, and occasionally physicians who do not make "decisions" and thus thwart movement along the pathways. Waiting can result from several things: obstruction of and resistance to institutionally mandated movement; the indeterminate condition of old age itself; and an untroubled, watchful anticipation. The public discourse focuses its attention relatively narrowly—on ways in which patients and families are caught up in a system that is determined by physicians' orders and the use of "unwanted" technologies, and on how patients and families must struggle to obstruct the logic that promotes aggressive treatments. This perspective usually does not acknowledge the other important sources of waiting described here—first, the "need" for families and patients to make timely decisions about death; second, the ambiguous and sometimes waffling language surrounding the inevitability of death; and third, the historically tangled relationship of old age and disease. Each of these features of hospital culture is perpetuated in daily practice and contributes to waiting. Together, they support the kinds of dying that are considered problematic by so many.

PART III

The Politics and Rhetoric of the Patient's Condition

"Suffering," "Dignity," and the "Quality of Life"

"In November and December of my first year there, many died in the ICU. In one week, I participated in 'bagging and tagging' five bodies, turning their cold bodies, washing off the feces and blood, taping them into white plastic shrouds, listening to their bodies hit the metal morgue cart with a muted 'thunk.' Imagine lifting a wet cloth with a pencil; this is what dead or dying flesh looks like hanging on their bones. Sometimes I would be involved in resuscitation efforts lasting an hour or more, fruitless and desperate battles with the grim reaper, who hovered over the beds, almost palpable. Bodies mercilessly desecrated in hopes of a rare, miraculous victory. Occasionally people would be truly dead by the time we arrived, and the [resuscitation] efforts of the team would be merely routine, part of a bureaucracy: you would exchange knowing glances but continue so the proper forms could be filled out.

"I began to believe we were doing patients and loved ones a disservice by keeping the horrid details from them. Euphemisms for the resuscitation were lame at best; asking a family member if they 'wanted everything done' was a leading, loaded question—a trick question. Of course they want everything done! But if you were to explain precisely what could happen . . . In cases where there was no next of kin, the patient's treatment was often more humane. When it became futile to continue medical treatment, the physician alone would make the decision to cease aggressive treatment. . . . All the medications and most treatment would continue; we were simply going to skip the application of defibrillator paddles, the broken ribs, the forcing down the throat of a breathing tube. When death came calling, we'd know it was time and allow a gentle transition between this world and the next.

"These are things no one wants to talk about. It is not good manners to discuss these ugly things. So I spoke only with colleagues, who were themselves in the same battered spiritual condition. Some seasoned nurses offered advice: do not bring it home with you; focus on the clinical aspects; the rest has to be ignored or left to the families to deal with. Advice was offered by an oncology nurse with over twenty years of experience with death and dying: 'Do not cry in front of the patients or their families; there are enough tears already being shed without adding yours. The family does not need you to cry, they need you to provide physical care and comfort. Let them do the crying; hand them a Kleenex and get on with your work.' I used this advice almost daily in my practice.

"I learned that most doctors do as much as they can for their patients, not for billing but to hedge their bets against death and judgment. Judgment from family members who know little to nothing about medicine, but who understand quite well the power of threatening litigation. Some physicians had a deeply rooted moral sense and acted with kindness and wisdom in all cases. Others were like corks on the tide of a family's emotions and whims, letting them be the decision-makers in everything. Sometimes there were disturbing family dynamics, which should have cast enormous suspicion on their right to make life-and-death decisions for the patient. They would insist blindly that Everything Be Done in order to ease a guilty conscience about their past relationship with this now mute patient.

"Shift after shift, month after month, I lived and breathed the suffering, life, and death that permeated the air and the walls in the unit.

Some of the suffering was necessary and understandable, as young mothers and energetic souls valiantly struggled to stay alive and continue to raise families, go to college, see the sunset at the beach just one more time. Yet much suffering seemed so incredibly unnecessary, like octogenarians with living wills discovered after the fact, or aggressive surgeries on debilitated and/or chronically ill people who had not a fighting chance of surviving these insults to their bodies and souls.

"For two years this went on, until one rainy February when my husband and I checked into an inn by the sea. I thought I was relaxed and happy, but that night I dreamt of all those patients I had seen die, whose bodies I had cleaned and bagged. One by one I looked at each of their faces, recognizing their souls, letting each of them go, floating out over the ocean. I awoke with a detailed memory of my dream, feeling truly at peace with my soul. The advice to not become involved and to form a tough, repellent barrier against my patients had backfired. What I learned that day was to enable me to know and demonstrate true compassion in my work. To be truly human you must experience life bravely, and facing issues of death and dying takes courage. When a human being dies, everyone present is affected, whether they want to be or not. I now let their spirits come in and through me, recognizing their passing, then consciously letting them go."

Written by an ICU nurse in preparation for an interview with the author, 1997

6

DEATH BY DESIGN

Through the lens of bureaucratic time we have examined hospital path-ways and how they make dying happen in particular ways. Through the lens of waiting we have explored the vulnerabilities of those who are dying and seen how they can confound and slow the process. We have seen both that death is impossible to imagine and choose and that it can be anticipated without being considered a problem at all. We turn now to the debates that are waged about the patient's condition and to the rhetoric that serves as the foundation for those debates. Talk of dignity, suffering, and quality of life circulates widely in American society in general, and it permeates hospital culture, organizing the ways staff and families think about patients and what should be done. Interpreting those three terms in reference to any given patient is a matter of negoti-ation; and in that negotiation the terms themselves become the lens through which decisions about control over dying are viewed before those decisions are taken and enacted.[1] The locus of responsibility for the patient's future shifts during these transactions, and the ways in which it shifts, and onto whom, are all part of the negotiation.

This chapter depicts the interactions of the medical team and family, as together they bargain over a precise time for death for Angela Stone, a patient in the ICU. As is often the case, this patient's quality of life emerges as the crux of the matter. One critical care physician has succinctly described the negotiations over who can authorize an end to life-sustaining treatments as "political rather than ethical."[2] Indeed, they are political in a double sense. First, physicians must be responsive to family desires and to their equivocations as well as to institutional pressures to move things along—they are caught between those two imperatives. Because patient self-determination and its extension to family members is now a normalized fact, and because of the possibility (no matter how remote) of litigation, families are allowed and are asked to speak for patients whose own voices are silenced by illness—whether or not they know "what the patient wants."

Working within the politics of family influence, doctors, when it is clear to them that death is imminent, face deciding between "death now" (by controlled removal of drugs and machines) and "death later" (by cardiac arrest or multiple-system organ failure, even on life support). The stories of Carol Jones, Dorothy Mason, Faith Walker, and Nhu Vinh all illustrate the tensions that emerge between doctors and families in that decision-making scenario. In those cases we saw that physicians are not making the "life-and-death decisions" that families sometimes think they are. That is, they are not weighing whether to authorize the death of a *biologically viable person* against whether to restore that person to self-sustainability through medical technique.[3] Rather, doctors may decide to stop life support, then try to persuade the family to let the patient die, when they feel certain that the treatments and machinery are maintaining (but only temporarily) a body that could not *live* otherwise. Thus the physician becomes the arbiter for deciding when *life*—which is by then considered *not life*—"should" end. In about half the cases I observed in which this kind of decision took place, the family had to be persuaded.

The second sense in which such negotiations are political has to do with assessing whether quality of life is present or absent and how much of it there will be in the future, and how dignity can be achieved through the orchestration of a particular kind of dying. Together, family and staff must interpret both quality of life and dignity in dying for the patient and arrive at a consensus about "what the patient wants," even when they cannot be sure. And then, through their entirely different sensibilities about the critically ill person and the demands of the hospital system, family and staff must come to an agreement about the time for death. As we saw in the stories of Jack Carter and Nhu Vinh, the rhetoric of quality of life and its use to interpret the patient's condition are often brought into play in debates about whether to continue or forgo life-sustaining treatments. Mr. Carter's physician and nurse wanted him to imagine what quality of life he wanted, so that he could "decide" whether to proceed with a risky (but potentially life-extending) procedure or "choose" death. Mrs. Vinh's daughter was frustrated by staff talk about quality of life and considered it irrelevant to her mother's comatose state. She wanted her mother to live, regardless of how quality of life was imputed to her condition. Yet she did not want her mother to "suffer." Sometimes, as in the story that follows, one of the three terms seems to predominate in bedside talk and in negotiations about the time for death. For Angela Stone, *quality of life*, specifically, becomes the rhetorical vehicle through which death is designed and accomplished. (For the patients on *life support*, whose stories are told in chapter 7, *dignity* and *suffering* are most often the operative terms.) As we shall see, in a two-stage process over two weeks, Ms. Stone's physicians shift responsibility for decision-making about her death from the patient to the family and back again. Both shifts are accomplished through the use of rhetoric about Ms. Stone's dignity and quality of life. That rhetoric has become so common, so natural, that neither the doctor, the medical team, nor the family and friends question its use or power to shape the timing of death.

Language constructs and promotes meaning. Physicians use the phrase *quality of life*, along with the equally loaded notions *death with dignity* and *enough suffering*, deliberately and at specific moments to affect the ways in which families (and also other members of the medical team) understand the patient's experience and to justify action. These phrases circulate widely as clichés in the hospital and in society, where shared knowledge about what they mean is assumed. One physician suggested to me that though doctors use the term *quality of life* deliberately, they may not use it thoughtfully. He noted that both *quality of life* and *death with dignity*, especially, are shorthand for complex feelings that doctors find difficult to consider or express. Both terms came into widespread use through the influence on medical practice of bioethics, where their meanings have been debated, via the disciplines of theology and philosophy, for close to forty years.[4] Physicians invoke the phrase *quality of life* to rationalize bringing to an end either a conscious life that is close to death (even if on life support, as in the case of Jack Carter), or a life that may be self-sustaining but is without consciousness (as in the case of Nhu Vinh). *No quality of life* may also—I was told by the same physician—express doctors' own terror at being in a condition without apparent consciousness or self-sustainability, at being *alive* like that.

Then physicians use the phrase to mean that they would refuse (at least hypothetically) similar treatments for themselves. Their use of the phrase *no quality of life* is also a rationalization that they want patients' families to adopt in order to move things along.

Quality of life is impossible to pin down, define, or evaluate. It has no empirical basis. In one study of physicians' consideration of patients' quality of life and how such consideration determines medical decision-making, researchers presented a specific patient management problem to 205 physicians.[5] The patient was a sixty-nine-year-old man who had an "acute exacerbation" of his chronic lung disease. He had never voiced his opinion about the use of life-support therapies or about his own quality of life to his doctors, and his doctors had never asked him about these topics. There was no plan, in advance, for dealing with a situation that would require mechanical ventilation and other supportive treatments to ensure life. When the patient's condition deteriorated, physicians were forced to decide between emergency intubation, thus sustaining him with machines and drugs, and no intubation, thus allowing him to die. Nearly half of the physicians chose to not intubate, citing quality of life as critical to their decision; they considered the quality of the man's life sufficiently poor to withhold further "heroic" treatment. In contrast, nearly one-third of the physicians preferred to intubate the patient, and they, too, mentioned quality of life considerations as a rationale for their choice. That group considered the patient's quality of life to be good enough to justify prolonging it. Quality of life, the researchers note, refers to a vague and variable set of attributes based on different perceptions, and it "has come to serve as a criterion for the utility of intervention in many clinical situations, including life and death."[6]

Some bioethicists and physicians have proposed that quality of life refers to the patient's subjective satisfaction with life.[7] Others maintain that quality of life is an evaluation made by others looking at a patient's condition and thinking about it in the context of the patient's life.[8] In either sense it is still an ambiguous notion. One philosopher thoughtfully suggests that the concept must be judged by how it is used. He examines its use with reference to a property or characteristic of the individual; a goal of caring for another person; a state of interaction between a person and his environment; and the moral worth of a person and his life (a use that the writer considers ethically troublesome).[9]

Quality of life, as a concept, is also troubled by another well-worn phrase and tenacious idea, *sanctity* of life—a term that some commentators have used to mean that human life is, in itself, holy or sacred or godlike in some way. In this light, life, regardless of its condition, should be considered with the greatest possible respect and reverence. It can never be understood fully through biology or any other scientific framework, for its sacredness will always be beyond rational investigation and utilitarian judgment.[10] At least since the 1960s, with the rise of academic bioethics, sanctity of life has been reconceptualized in secular terms as well, and it now refers to the value of respect for the individual, and autonomous, human being.[11] Yet *sanctity* is just as ambiguous as *quality*. Sanctity may express the stance that life, because of its inherent preciousness, should be protected at all costs.[12] Alternatively, it may be used to argue that human life should not be degraded (for example, by the indefinite use of life-support technologies) or that some conditions degrade life to the point that it is not worth living.[13]

Shifting Responsibility for Choosing Death: Angela Stone's Quality of Life

Suffering from severe asthma, fifty-four-year-old Angela Stone was in the ICU for a full month. As her stay there wore on, what was seen as the *contents* of Angela Stone's quality of life and the way her quality of life was understood changed. I first heard it discussed among the medical team, family, and friends during their initial meeting, twelve days into her hospital stay. Her extraordinarily poor and continually diminishing quality of life was established at that meeting, where, interestingly, no explicit judgment was made about it. The features that comprised it were added up and it was simply stated as fact. Little could be attributed to Ms. Stone's own subjective evaluation—only a comment from a friend that Angela had said, months earlier in a nursing home, that her life had "no dignity." Otherwise, the quality of her existence had to be pieced together by others, and it was. Her life, they felt, was "a struggle." "She's gone down, down, down," they said, "try as she might." Her list of serious and irreversible medical problems was enormous. By the twenty-eighth day of her hospitalization, a judgment was added to the shared knowledge about Ms. Stone's life. The staff agreed that her lack of quality of life, her "lousy" quality of life, was reason to allow her to die. Death, they felt, would be more humane than continued existence with all of her problems.

Admission to day 11: I learn of Angela Stone one morning during rounds in the ICU. She has asthma so severe that she had to quit her secretarial job. Her lungs are seriously impaired. She cannot think clearly or concentrate. She has not been paying her bills or taking care of her affairs for at least two years. In the months before this hospitalization she had to move out of her apartment and into a nursing home, where she became progressively more disabled until, finally, she was unable to get out of bed without help. She was depressed and was losing her will to live. Then one day she had a cardiac arrest following an asthma attack. She was resuscitated at the nursing home, brought to the hospital, and placed on a mechanical ventilator. The cardiopulmonary resuscitation restored her heartbeat, but led to a severe worsening of her brain function.

Angela Stone also has medical problems resulting from her long use of powerful steroids and from lack of oxygen during her cardiac arrest. She has toxic shock syndrome.[14] She does not respond when nurses and doctors talk to her. One of the physicians tells me that a patient's neurological status is the key element in "making goals," and Ms. Stone's unresponsive condition has not changed for several days. Her parents have arrived from out of town. In their mid-eighties, they have not seen their daughter for several years.

Day 12: Ms. Stone's primary physician, an internist who has been caring for her for several years, calls for a conference with the patient's parents and the friends who have been coming daily to visit. The conference is called because the patient is stuck, not getting worse, but not getting better either. She hovers in an unconscious limbo. The internist in charge of the patient's hospital care has the most at stake in trying to move things along (thereby playing by hospital rules) because he is ultimately responsible not just for her care but for selecting a pathway that everyone can accept. He has to orchestrate a conclusion to the story of this hospitalization that is acceptable to the family and the medical team, and he has to do it in a timely way. In these kinds of cases, the physician has a three-part goal that is marked by inherent tension: to honor the patient's "autonomy" about choices under conditions of critical illness; to defer to family (if possible) when the patient's "choice" cannot be discerned so that the family can express the patient's wishes (if known); and to select a hospital pathway that will, in the end, be "chosen" by everyone concerned with this patient. That elusive goal is the reason, most often, that members of the medical team call for meetings such as this where they will walk a thin line of respect and control, deference and manipulation.

The First Meeting. Step #1: If the Patient Has No Voice, the Family Becomes Responsible

Five P.M., day 12: In addition to Ms. Stone's parents, her internist, and three of her friends, today's meeting includes the two hospital medical specialists most involved in Ms. Stone's care—a pulmonologist (lung specialist) and a neurologist—as well as a respiratory therapist, hospital social worker, psychiatrist, and Ms. Stone's case manager (a nurse by training who had coordinated some of her care before she was hospitalized). We gather in a small room away from the ICU and sit around a large table. The internist sets the agenda and the tone. During the hourlong meeting everyone is told something about the patient's medical condition, recent life history, and personality. The internist asks the family and friends to think about making decisions for Ms. Stone; her parents, especially, are becoming increasingly aware of how debilitated their daughter has become. The theme of the meeting is the possibility of recovery—and what kind of recovery—given the severity of Ms. Stone's condition.

> *Internist:* Angela has not filled out a Durable Power of Attorney for Health Care form so she can't tell us anything. What we do know is that she has massive problems: asthma; she can't walk; thin bone fractures. She's becoming weaker and weaker and is unable to care for herself and make decisions. She is having seizures resulting from a benign brain tumor. Angela was in a nursing home, trying to get stronger, trying to make decisions about life. But she was getting weaker and weaker. What happened? She had a cardiac arrest, toxic shock syndrome. She was resuscitated successfully and brought here.[15] Her blood pressure has improved. Her infections are being handled and she is off antibiotics. However, she is on the ventilator, sleeping most of the time, not responding. It's hard to separate her chronic problems from the new ones.
>
> *Pulmonologist:* Her kidneys got bad for about ten days. . . . As for her breathing, we're trying to turn down the vent to see if she can breathe on her own. She can't. There has been no progress in the last several days. I think she can get off the machine, but it will take

weeks to do it, at best, because of her asthma and her overall weakness. That's optimistic. The issue is the tube. We'll have to do
surgery for a trach [tracheostomy]. It's better and more comfortable for the patient. At the moment she's not awake enough to
talk.

Friend: Is the tube the way Angela would breathe forever?

Neurologist: I've known Angela for three years. She has a variety of neurological problems. She has a benign tumor on the brain, which led
to seizures and then complications. Some problems are chronic,
some were treated. She's not breathing well during sleep and her
sleep apnea makes her thinking worse. Now, she's not in a coma, but
it's almost a coma. This, plus she started with a compromised brain.
She's had a cardiac arrest. Her kidney function and seizures complicated her brain function. And now she has too many medications
that we can't get rid of. Two days ago she was more responsive than
she is now. She opened her eyes. Today is not good. This is coupled
with muscle weakness, which contributes to her not being able to
breathe well, so she can't get off the breathing machine. [At this
point the pulmonologist explains in greater detail why Ms. Stone is
so weak.]

Internist (to neurologist): How likely is it that she'll wake up?

Neurologist: It's hard to say, but two days ago her response was good.

Patient's mother: She opened her eyes. It depends on how she does
from here on.

Patient's father: When I was talking to her today, her eyes started to
open at the same time.

Friend of patient: Is the seizure medicine Dilantin? [The internist
and neurologist each talk about why they changed the seizure
medications.]

Internist: Angela has had more and more cognitive problems over the
years. These medications reduce her cognitive function.

Psychiatrist: I've known her about a year, seeing her for depression. It's
always worthwhile to treat, even though she has reasons to be
depressed. I tried several antidepressants to help with mood. I also
talked with the neurologist about strategies to get her more
involved in her own recovery.

Internist: As her depression has gotten worse, she has gotten more passive, and this has made her overall situation worse. We do want her

mood to improve. [Angela's father asks about therapies at the nursing home.]

Internist: She needs to want to participate with heart and soul, and she's refused. She hasn't wanted to participate in her own care.

Father: We haven't heard that before, that she refused therapy.

Social worker: On a positive note, she has a good support system. It may all come down to you all making decisions for her—if she won't.

Internist: There's the question of where can she live if she gets better. Her problem list is longer than most. But I don't think we're there. Critical decisions need to be made now. We need to ask, would she want to be on a ventilator for one or two months? If her heart stopped, would we want to start it? This is what we're faced with. Because she never gave us clear guidance. We need to hear if she expressed any wishes.

Neurologist: She talked on a number of occasions that she was tired—several times—and "How much more can I take?"

Friend: She said once, "This life has no dignity." [Angela's father asks questions about the ventilator. The pulmonologist answers them.]

Father: Is the machine still helping her breathe?

Pulmonologist: Yes, 80 to 90 percent of her breathing is done by the machine.

Mother: She's been gone so long, we don't know anything about her anymore.

Neurologist: There is no indication of whether she'll get better.

Case manager: I have talked with her many times about quality of life—living in an apartment versus living somewhere else. She never said anything to me about a ventilator. And we talked about the struggle her life had become, that she couldn't live in an apartment. Every minute required her energy just to survive. She never said she didn't want to struggle. *(Turning to the patient's parents)* You raised a heck of a daughter. She's independent and smart and very stubborn.

Father: We tried to call every week or sometimes twice a week. We could tell, week by week, that there was a deterioration, less of a drive in energy.

Case manager: I think that's something you need to think about. She's gone down, down, down. She hasn't been able, in the last two years, to come back up. Try as she might.

Internist: She's definitely gotten weaker in her lower extremities. She's had progressive weakness. And there are other problems. She has been on the newest special medicines for asthma, but these are causing problems. I don't hear from anyone that she wouldn't want to be like this. If we're going to go ahead, if we're going to take this route, we need to put in place a trach [tracheostomy] and a feeding tube.

Pulmonologist: Let's say she doesn't wake up any more than this. Is that what she would want?

Friend: I don't think so. She has never said so. But that's what I know about her.

Father: How is her insurance coverage?

Case manager: Her insurance has no limits, as long as she stays in the acute hospital. The social service department will need to talk to you about funding sources if she'll need chronic care. [Angela's parents and the social worker talk about Medicaid and SSI.[16] The social worker says she will start the paperwork.]

Internist: That can be done in the absence of her consent?

Social worker: I think so. [The social worker and the case manager talk further about the patient's insurance coverage.]

Internist (redirecting the discussion to the topic of moving things along by charting a particular pathway): I need to get back to where are we going between now and a month from now. I don't hear anyone saying, "It's time to stop."

Pulmonologist: I do this for a living. If her heart were to stop, and we were to restart it, her brain function would be nothing, and she wouldn't leave the hospital. [The neurologist agrees.]

Father (to internist): Do you concur?

Internist: Yes. I'd feel comfortable, if her heart stops, we leave it. If that decision is made, I want everyone to feel comfortable with that. Legally, as next of kin, you folks have authority, and that's what we're bound by in the absence of a decision by the patient.

Mother: I'd go along with that. [Angela's father does not agree. He asks questions about resuscitation.]

Friend: Do we know what her brain function will be like if she wakes up?

Neurologist: No. [Another friend asks questions about a tracheostomy.]

Internist: In this context, it's a plus, not a high risk. I want to lay out the worst-case scenario. What will, eventually, happen. She'll get complications: hospital-acquired pneumonia, she'll have a special IV, skin breakdown. There will be more technical things that she'll need.

Friend: Do you think recovery is possible?

Pulmonologist: I don't know that we can expect her to be better than she was at the nursing home. Maybe it will be six weeks till we get her off the ventilator. Then she still will be very weak. Still with neurological problems. Still with asthma, and she'll need six months of rehabilitation. I don't know if she'll ever be walking around. The rosy picture is months and months of remaining in a hospital or nursing home. She won't be better than she was at the nursing home.

Friend: Please describe her condition.

Internist: She was in bed in the nursing home. She couldn't come to the phone, even by the bed. She rarely went in a wheelchair to the dining area.

Pulmonologist: Because of the cloudiness in her thinking, she couldn't pick up the phone or the bell.

Mother: We're hearing things we didn't know.

Internist (checking his watch): We need to stop. You don't need to make a decision now about code status. Think about it. You need to make a decision about starting antibiotics. Maybe need to think over the weekend. [The pulmonologist and the neurologist discuss the patient's metabolic problems and whether they think she'll wake up.]

Father: I'm eighty-five. How many more trips can I make? We can only do so much to get here and get home.

Internist: I need to talk to Angela's parents about the code status issue tomorrow. We'll talk more next week about the trach.

Everyone stands up to leave. As I walk out of the room with Ms. Stone's father, he tells me this is the hardest thing he's ever had to face in his life.

The internist wanted to establish whether the patient has given any indication, either written or verbal, of what she would want the medical team to do given her current condition and, especially, whether she would want to be resuscitated again should she have another cardiac arrest. If the patient had clear wishes that the family could communicate to the health care team, those wishes would be followed, *so long as they moved things along,* and there would be no moral or practical dilemma. But Angela Stone has left no guidelines. So, the team members shifted their talk to describing the struggle her life had become, her medical problems, and the trajectory of her condition over the past few months, speculating about how things could unfold in the coming days. They discussed these things both to clarify aspects of her condition for one another and to gently guide the family and friends to choose a pathway for her. But some of their talk about her condition and its potential developments was murky. The neurologist reported that Ms. Stone was not in a coma, but it was "almost" a coma. He had no idea if she would wake up. The lung specialist thought she might be able to come off the ventilator, but perhaps not, and if so, it could take weeks or months of effort. Everyone questioned the patient's stamina to endure a long period of rehabilitative work and her desire to do so given her recent refusal or inability to actively engage in therapies at the nursing home. No one was sure about her will to struggle and live. Only one piece of prognostic truth emerged at the end of the meeting: the lung specialist assured the group that Ms. Stone would not be better, in any way, than she had been in the nursing home.

The possibility that, unless something is done to stop it, there will be another emergency resuscitation procedure looms large for the internist. In the middle of the meeting he decisively switches his point of reference from "what she would want" to "what we're faced with—would we want to start it?" to move responsibility from the patient (who cannot hold it) to the family, to urge them to consider allowing a Do Not Resuscitate order. The shift in the doctor's language from *she* to *we* marks the first critical moment in the reshaping of both medical responsibility regarding what to do about the patient's condition and the shared understanding about Ms. Stone's quality of life. The internist hopes to avoid another resuscitation attempt that he knows will, at best, only return Angela Stone to an unconscious state of dependency on machines. But Ms. Stone's father does not go along with the medical team's advice to make such a choice. He thwarts necessary decision-making. The physician responds by fashioning a priority list for Mr. and Mrs. Stone—the code status decision will have to be made tomorrow; the decision about antibiotics and a tracheostomy can wait until next week. The more for-midable topics—Ms. Stone's desire to live, her dignity, and her quality of life, all of which hinge on her degree of consciousness—are mentioned during this meeting, but they do not become the responsibility of others until later. For now, the internist seeks only to shift responsibility for cer-tain medical procedures.

Interlude: Learning Angela Stone

Day 16: Angela Stone has been in the ICU for over two weeks, and today I am spending some time at her bedside talking with her parents and trying to know her in some way. She is a small person, absolutely inert in the bed. She is connected to many tubes—for medications, blood, food, and to get rid of bodily waste. The largest tube is in her mouth, attached to the ventilator. She lies on her side and looks to be in a deep sleep. It is hard to imagine how anyone can sleep in this environ-ment. The intensive care cubicle is flooded with sunlight and noisy with beeps and whooshes from the machines and background chatter from people working on the unit. The door to Ms. Stone's cubicle is always open. Nurses regularly check her medications, intravenous lines, vital signs, and body position. Both her parents are sitting at her side, and they talk with the hospital staff who come and go on their rounds. Ms. Stone's mother shows me a photo taken four years ago, the last time her daughter came to visit them. It is a black-and-white, wallet-size photo of a smiling woman. I can see no resemblance between the animated image in the photo and the patient, who is almost grotesque in her absence of expression. Mrs. Stone tells me Angela has been sick since she returned home from that visit. Mr. Stone reports that he has just talked exten-sively with one of Angela's doctors, who told him she would not stay like this. In the next week she would get better or worse. He leans toward his daughter and, talking softly, tells her that he and her mother love her very much and April is her nurse today. He tells me when she last opened her eyes and that her latest medical development is a rash. Mrs. Stone says it disturbs her to see Angela shaking from the seizures. "She's suffered a lot in the last three years," she says.

Days 17 to 20: I often sit with Ms. Stone's parents at her bedside, chatting with them as they wait, and I note that they do not ask the staff about her condition. They do not ask any questions at all and only speak when someone speaks to them. They do not seem curious or anxious for medical knowledge or a prognosis. They do not assume their daughter is dying, nor do they assume she will recover. Mrs. Stone says, "We hope and pray every day." Mr. Stone tells me he is meeting with bankers and lawyers to settle Angela's affairs, which he is having a hard time sorting out. She did not have a legal power of attorney. He has been speaking with someone in the benefits office at the company where Angela worked. He relates all this to me with great patience and equanimity. He never expresses anger or frustration or sadness.

Day 20: Mrs. Stone reports that the doctor has just been in, but she has forgotten what he said. The nurses are with Angela "all the time, doing things, I don't know what." She asks me if "that bag of red stuff" hanging on a pole by the bed is blood, and I reply that it is. When her husband is not present, Mrs. Stone says to me that she doesn't want Angela to suffer, that she "wants it to be over—you know what I mean. Or we want her to get better. We can't sit here, waiting, forever."

In the hallway outside the ICU the social worker informs me that Ms. Stone's mother is "ready to let her go, but her father isn't." She has just had another meeting with both the patient's parents and a few of her friends, which she did not find satisfying because none of them talked about planning for death. They were not moving in the direction of terminating life support. Mr. Stone wants to wait, she says. He has no particular expectations, is not anticipating recovery or death. The social worker gave him the Medicaid forms to fill out in the event Ms. Stone needs long-term care. A pathway out of the hospital to a chronic care facility is still a possibility, and the discharge planning staff need to prepare for it. Filling out the paperwork is Mr. Stone's way of coping, the social worker says, and it has to be done anyway. There is no place for the patient to go from the acute care hospital unless she has Medicaid; only Medicaid-certified nursing homes will care indefinitely for severely chronically ill patients (unless a family is willing to pay privately). The social worker does not know if the nursing home where she resided would take Ms. Stone back as a Medicaid, rather than private insurance, patient.

Day 24: I arrive at Ms. Stone's bedside on a day when the respiratory therapist is there. One job of respiratory therapists in the ICU is to monitor how the patient is doing on the ventilator. Can the pressure and percentage of oxygen be turned down? Does the patient need more help from the machine to breathe? Can the patient be removed from the machine? The therapist tells me that Ms. Stone has been on ventilator support for nearly one month. She is now on full support—the ventilator is doing 100 percent of the work of breathing. Two weeks ago Ms. Stone had been doing some of the work herself. She needs a tracheostomy and long-term-care placement. But the humane thing would be to let her die, the therapist says. She did not have any quality of life in the nursing home, where she was bed-bound and struggled to breathe, and he questions whether she would ever be able to return to that level of functioning, low as it was. The medications are creating problems, he explains. The steroids are causing her skin to break down, causing bedsores. He leans over the patient so that he is a few inches from her face and calls her name softly. She opens her eyes and looks straight at him with an intense, penetrating gaze. It is her only response to the greeting. I am amazed that there seems to be in her gaze so much character, so much "quality" (in the sense that a unique, individual expression is revealed)—considering her physical condition. A person seems to look out from an absolutely inert body and it jars me. Ms. Stone has looked straight into the eyes of various bedside visitors during her hospitalization, and everyone who meets her gaze has pondered what volition or desire or thought could be behind it. Was that stare coming from Angela, the person? Was she there? Or was the stare a physical effect of her condition?

Mr. Stone comes in with a radio and says the doctor has suggested it, for stimulation. He places it on the small table closest to her head and turns on a classical music station. He tells me that he and his wife come to the hospital on alternate days now. They have to deal with their daughter's paperwork the other days.

The Second Meeting. Step #2: The Patient "Regains" Her Voice and "Reassumes" Responsibility

Day 28, Tuesday: Angela Stone has been in the ICU for a month. The medical team is convinced they can do nothing more for her, and her condition continues to deteriorate. Two weeks ago at the first meeting they were not absolutely convinced that there was nothing more to do or that she would not show some signs of improvement. But now the doctor knows it is up to him to pave the way to a smooth, or as smooth as possible, transition for Ms. Stone's parents so that they can face her death. He decides it is again time to meet formally with the family and "with as many people present as possible." He plans—unless there is strong protest from some quarter—to set the stage for her death, to let the family and the friends know, in no uncertain terms, that it is time to withdraw the ventilator, allowing Ms. Stone to die.

While arranging chairs in a circle in one of the empty ICU cubicles, Ms. Stone's nurse for the day comments that the hospital doesn't even have proper places for family conferences. Mr. Stone and I have arrived at the same time, and he greets me cordially. Mrs. Stone and two of her daughter's friends are already seated. All the women are teary. One of the friends mentions that they met with one of the doctors earlier today, and he told them that Angela is not going to get better, that "it is best to let her go." Otherwise she will be "like this" indefinitely. Mrs. Stone cries as the friend relates this information and says, "Yes, it is better to let her go." Though during our bedside chats Ms. Stone's parents have occasionally talked about her suffering, this is the first public statement that it has increased to some intolerable level, both for her and for them. It is seen to be worse now than death. The statement about what "is best" is also an acknowledgment by the patient's mother and friend that they can or should authorize the move toward death by allowing the termination of treatments. The nurse brings the parents juice in little paper cups as the social worker and internist enter and greet the group.

The internist is the first to speak once everyone is seated. He starts the meeting by noting that the neurologist cannot be here today, but that they are in agreement about Angela's condition.

> *Internist:* It's time to start with the question, where are we, where have we come in the last couple of weeks? Very little has changed. Angela's mental status hasn't changed. She'll open her eyes and squeeze a hand, but it's not purposeful. Has anyone seen anything different?
>
> *Father:* Occasionally, she'll open her eyes when I talk to her, that's an improvement. But, no appreciable change.
>
> *Internist:* She arouses to a voice more easily, but we don't know if she recognizes that voice. But she hasn't been able to follow a command. It isn't real consciousness—though she's not in a coma. Also, her lung function hasn't improved. We tried to wean her off the vent and were unable to. Both of the ICU lung specialists think

it is very hard to get her off the vent. They think it would be a months-long proposition, not just days. Her infections have been treated—she's no longer on antibiotics. She's not having seizures. Her sodium now is in the normal range. She's getting tube feedings, but her protein stores are poor. The other doctors think it would take months, with a tracheostomy and a feeding tube, before she could be making any progress. So we are at a decision point. I feel comfortable, and I know my partners feel comfortable— including the neurologist and the psychiatrist—that we have done as much as we could, that we have waited long enough. I'm comfortable enough to now let her go.

Mother: She'll never go back to an active life?

Internist: No.

Father: If I understand Dr. [pulmonologist] correctly, the asthma has caused irreversible lung damage. She can't support life. She can't outgrow this, right?

Internist: Right. Her asthma is severe. She had problems with her brain functioning as well. Seizures, CPR, all those things also hurt her brain. And her lungs are very damaged. There is complete unanimity among the doctors. All of us feel it is unlikely she'd recover.

Father: Another asthma attack could knock out other systems—like her kidneys?

Internist: That is what in fact happened with this last attack. And we put her on life support.

Father (to one of his daughter's friends): Do you have any comments?

Friend: I think we should let her go.

Second friend: I agree.

Father: What would K [another friend] say if she were here?

Friend: K feels she's gone already.

Mother: She'd say let her go *(begins to cry)*, and so do I. This isn't the Angela we know. Personally, I think it's time to let her go.

Father: "Let her go." What connotations do we mean?

Internist: In this setting, it means stopping the ventilator. She is on life support. She's been leaving for a long time, in terms of not doing things in many areas. I agree with her friends that she hasn't been here. She hasn't been making decisions. I suggest we don't do it today. We do it tomorrow. Dr. [X] will be here tomorrow; he can make her comfortable. If she starts to breathe rapidly, he can give her some medication. He'll be here. [The internist is referring to a particular critical care specialist who has experience removing ventilators from patients who are near death.]

Social worker: You have mentioned you want a spiritual service. [There is some discussion about a bedside service among the family and friends.] I'm happy to contact [hospital chaplain]. [She tells Mr. Stone he needs to decide who to invite to the bedside service and that Angela shouldn't be alone. Mr. Stone asks Angela's friends who would want to be here, who else should be contacted. Various people are named. One of the friends says she'll phone them.]

Father: How about Thursday? [Two days from now.]

Internist: Okay.

Mother (crying): It's hard. [She takes her husband's hand.]

Internist: I think by doing this we are doing what Angela wanted. I think it is helpful to think of it this way, that it is not your decision and not the doctors' decision. She wouldn't want to be on a ventilator for three months.

Father (cries for first time here): I couldn't go back on a plane home knowing she was going back to a nursing home.

Mother (also crying): I couldn't face the nursing home. When we were on the phone with her, there was a roommate screaming in the background. I couldn't go home knowing she was going to live like that.

Father: I couldn't leave her, knowing the nursing home would be her resting place, instead of a burial. Let's call [chaplain].

Internist: Okay.

Father: Dr. [neurologist] was so frank in our last meeting. I appreciated that.

Internist: I'm very comfortable that his feeling is in sync with mine. [He stands up and shakes the parents' hands, to signify that he is ending this meeting.] Thank you for coming. It is very hard to take this step, but this is what Angela wants.

Father: You've looked after her for many years. The doctor-patient relationship has never been more complete.

The internist gets tears in his eyes, as do I, and then he leaves the room. The rest of us sit there for twenty minutes or so. The nurse who arranged the chairs comes back in and offers more juice. Mr. Stone turns to me and asks, "Dr. Kaufman, what is your opinion?" I reply that I wish I had known Angela before she was hospitalized. Then Mr. Stone walks across the ICU to say good-bye to his daughter. When he comes back, he takes his wife's hand and says, "We will get through this." "Yes, we will," she responds.

After Mr. and Mrs. Stone leave the unit, I linger to speak with the social worker and Ms. Stone's nurse about the patient's impending death. The social worker asks the nurse how much time will elapse following the removal of the breathing tube (or turning off the ventilator) before Angela dies. The nurse says that sometimes people live, that is, continue to breathe, long after the ventilator is turned off, but she does not think that will happen in Angela's case. She hopes the tube is left in place, in the trachea. Then people can't say, "You prevented the patient from breathing." But, she says, when the tube remains in place after the ventilator is turned off, it's like breathing through a straw, "and you can imagine how that is. We give morphine to the patient so the family doesn't get upset watching the patient either gurgle without a tube or struggle for breath with the tube."

When I see Ms. Stone's primary doctor later in the day, he remarks, "We couldn't possibly have come to this place two weeks ago."

Mostly it is physicians, not families of very ill persons, who decide when "it is time" to withdraw life support. That decision is based on agreement among members of the medical team that nothing can be done to ensure even the most minimal recovery. Sometimes the decision comes when the patient's condition deteriorates dramatically, when "the numbers" signify a change for the worse. In Angela Stone's case, the team knows her condition will deteriorate, though nothing, specifically, has happened yet to signify decline toward death. At this second meeting, after weeks of stagnation on the pathway, Ms. Stone's primary physician transformed the question "Does anyone know what she wants?" into "This is what she wants." And when he said, "She's been leaving for a long time, in terms of not doing things in many areas," he suggested that she had been moving toward death anyway. After Ms. Stone had been in the ICU for a month, her doctor empowered her with responsibility, consciousness, decision-making capability, and intention. It becomes the job of the medical team, family, and friends to follow her lead, to assist her in going down the path she has "chosen" and is already taking.

This use of specific language conferring the patient's agency and desire for death marks the second critical moment in this story. The first moment—in which the doctor shifted the frame of understanding from "what she would want" to "what we're faced with"—was the physician's attempt to move responsibility for action from the patient to her family, in the hope that they would allow a Do Not Resuscitate order. In this second moment, the doctor shifts the location of responsibility again, this time back onto the patient. In both moves, his language illustrates how hospital staff (but usually doctors), at a point when things get stuck, reconceive the locus of responsibility, enabling them to change or withdraw treatments. The internist persuaded the family to accept his decision by using a multiple explanation: nothing more could be done; they have waited long enough and, most important, Angela "wouldn't want to be on a ventilator for three months"; and, in fact, she is now ready to die. When the doctor noted that Angela would not want to live on a ventilator, her parents broke down, cried, and admitted that a burial is indeed better than a return to the horrors of the nursing home and her excruciatingly ill condition.

At the moment a shift in locating responsibility has been made, a shift toward interpreting the patient's desires, it is not uncommon to hear physicians claim that "this is what the patient wants." That rationalization and that specific language serve two purposes. For the family, they soften the emotional blow and the reality of the shift from aggressively prolonging corporeal function to definitively terminating life. Second, the phrase signifies for everyone that responsibility for "choosing death" is removed from both the doctors and the family and placed back on the patient. In the hospital, the doctor is the only person allowed by social convention to be the active agent in technically managing death. In this case, Ms. Stone's doctor removed moral and legal responsibility from any of the staff physicians when he said, "This is what Angela wants." He granted authority to the critical care doctor to organize death, but portrayed him only *as a technician who would be carrying out Angela's wish.*

Mr. Stone's suggestion that Thursday be the day for death can be read either as agreement, finally, with the doctor and the need to move things along, or as resistance to the doctor's first choice, Wednesday. If resistance, his request for a specific date for death may have been his way of trying, in the only way that seemed possible at that moment, to assert some kind of control over his daughter's fate, to claim some shred of parental responsibility. In this kind of circumstance, the "choice" of a particular date for death is, on the one hand, entirely arbitrary, but on the other hand, it also emerged from the internist's practical considerations. He picked the first day that one of the critical care doctors could be present to control the signs of apparent suffering, to make dying appear to be peaceful and smooth, and to make sure the procedure was medically controlled so there could be no perception, on the part of other hospital staff, family, or friends, that death was hastened or dying prolonged by medical intervention. It must be clear that the patient is not made to suffer as a result of medical technique, and her death must be made as "natural" as possible. Putting Ms. Stone's death off by one more day made no difference to the internist or to anyone else on the medical team, and the doctor gave in to Mr. Stone on this point, avoiding an argument.

Organizing Death

Day 30: At morning ICU rounds I learn that Angela Stone's death is scheduled for one o'clock this afternoon. The Stones have told the social worker that they do not want to be present at the bedside at the moment of Angela's death. "We don't need to eyeball the doctor and watch what he's doing." But they do want a bedside prayer service prior to the removal of the ventilator. They asked if the service at the bedside would replace a funeral, and the social worker assured them that it would not, that they could go ahead and plan whatever funeral they wanted.

When the critical care physician who has been caring for Ms. Stone most during her hospital stay comes into the ICU for morning rounds, he tells the social worker he is too busy to be at the bedside at one o'clock. He has patients to see all afternoon. The respiratory therapist asks him if she can do anything, if the nurses can start a morphine drip. Perhaps, she suggests, he doesn't need to be there. He says no, he needs to be there to make sure Ms. Stone is comfortable, but he simply can't do it at one o'clock. He asks the social worker to speak with the patient's friends to see if they want to be present when he disconnects the ventilator. But he can't set a time right now. He has patients in his office until four o'clock in the afternoon. He needs a block of uninterrupted time with Angela, he says. So it will have to wait until later in the day. He needs to be practical and consider the amount of time he needs to facilitate the most appropriate death for the patient.

The critical care physician leaves the ICU, and the social worker tells me she wants to be at Ms. Stone's bedside when the machines are turned off—"for my own education, to demystify it for myself." She leaves to phone the patient's friends. Later in the day one of the case managers stops me in the corridor to ask about Ms. Stone and when her death will occur. I tell her what I know. She wonders if the doctor "knows how to do this." When I see the social worker after she has contacted the friends, she asks me how death in the intensive care unit is done. I begin to realize that, after eleven months of observations, a few of the nonmedical staff are starting to ask me about controlled deaths in the ICU. I am learning that even within the hospital, among people with a great deal of experience around critical illness and death, not everyone is cognizant of how death in the ICU is planned, managed, and carried out.

2:30 P.M.: I see Mr. and Mrs. Stone leaving the hospital cafeteria with one of Angela's friends. We stop to chat in the hallway. They all seem calm and relaxed, though Angela's friend looks sad. I ask if they had the prayer service, and they say yes, it was nice, and five or six friends attended. One of the hospital chaplains officiated and the social worker was there. The Stones mention that Angela was more alert today than she has been all month, and the friend agrees, remarking that she seemed to acknowledge people in the room. "She was quite present," she says. This feature of Angela's condition does not seem to disturb any of them; they just report it as one more of the many shifting facts about her medical state. Mr. and Mrs. Stone are on their way to make mortuary arrangements. I wish them well as they leave the hospital.

I go upstairs to the ICU and speak with the social worker, who is standing just outside Angela's cubicle. She tells me that the service itself was short, about twenty minutes. Mr. Stone had prepared some prayers, and the chaplain "was very good." Each person there spoke to Angela, including one friend who stood close to her and said, "You know, when we were going around the room, I wanted to pass, as I never have anything to say," and at that moment, Angela smiled. The social worker says she was shocked by such responsiveness. Angela seemed to everyone to be more alert and aware this afternoon than during the entire previous month; she had unequivocally responded to the voices around her. "I was thinking through the whole service," the social worker says, "what if they do a this-is-it service and she wakes up? Won't this disturb the parents?" But, she says, none of those things happened.

The chaplain arrives and we continue to talk about the apparent increase in Ms. Stone's level of consciousness during the prayer service. He says he came in this morning, before the family arrived for the service, just to see Angela, and he was disturbed by how alert she was. He even went into the hospital chapel, he says, to think about this alone. *What are we doing? Are we bringing on her death prematurely?* Then, he says, he "regrouped" and remembered that Angela had been so disabled in the nursing home that she had had no "quality of life" whatsoever, and that she could not even go back to that. Then he felt better about what they were going to do.

In that moment of presumed greater alertness, Angela Stone embodied the long-standing debates about the multiple meanings of both "quality of life" and "sanctity of life." A sign of her unique personality seemed to be visible, as was some transcendental feature of her "spirit." Those *qualities* seemed to her observers to stand out against (or within) her decaying body, which demanded the termination of medical treatment.

The nurse for the day is doing her usual routine, making the patient as comfortable as she can. She has not started a morphine drip. She says she has heard through the grapevine, but not from the doctor himself or through any other direct communication, that he will be up here about five o'clock to "do the death." Another nurse comments that the doctor who is going to withdraw the ventilator has cared for Angela during previous hospitalizations. He was devastated when she was admitted to the hospital this time. He's known her for about two years, she says, and this is the worst case of asthma he's ever seen.

When I run into Ms. Stone's internist at about four o'clock in the afternoon, I learn that he has already heard that she was more alert than ever during the prayer service. That information does not seem to disturb him.

Last Hours

Just after 5 P.M.: I arrive at the ICU's double doors at the same moment as the critical care doctor, and we walk into the unit together. He is in a good mood and says, "What a day, very busy, I've had no backup. I'm the fall guy." Only four patients are in the ICU. A nurse is caring for Angela Stone and another patient nearby. A second nurse is on the other side of the unit with two patients. It is quiet. The hospital employees who finish work at five o'clock have left. The door and curtains to Angela's cubicle are open.

Sitting at Angela's bedside is her old friend Sheryl, whom I met at the first meeting with the medical team. She greets me warmly by name. She introduces me to another of Angela's friends, Grace. As we chat at the bedside, a man enters, explaining that he has come to be "backup" for Sheryl. His name is Bruce, and he has not been to the hospital to visit Angela. While we talk, I notice that a morphine drip has been started.

The critical care doctor asks everyone to come away from the bedside and move over to the nurses' station, where the social worker and chaplain are standing—though their workday is over. There, the doctor explains to everyone what he is going to do. He is not in a hurry, and he speaks slowly and carefully. He will give Angela some medicines first and let them work for a few minutes. Then he will "turn the ventilator down" (reduce the pressure and amount of oxygen) and see how Angela responds. If she gets restless or looks uncomfortable, he will give more medication and "turn it right back up until the medications work." Then he will turn the ventilator off. He will put a "t-piece" in her mouth so she can breathe room air through a tube. This device works similarly to a room humidifier and will make her breathing easier. The doctor says that with the t-piece in place, her airway remains open, it's easier on her, and one won't hear any gurgling. He will stay long enough to make sure she is comfortable. He asks if anyone has questions. Sheryl asks for more information about the t-piece. The social worker asks how the doctor will know if she's uncomfortable. The doctor replies that any grimacing or movement would be a sign of discomfort. He also mentions that since Angela has a history of seizures, he will give her medication to prevent them. When close to death, however, she may have a seizure anyway, and that could be hard for everyone to watch. But he will try to prevent it. He asks again if there are questions. Grace is quiet during this exchange.

The doctor goes on to talk about Angela's "lousy quality of life" in the nursing home. He also notes that Angela's parents do not want to be here at the moment of death and that he agrees with them "philosophically and practically." He says he wouldn't want to be at the hospital bedside for any death in his own family. He would want to remember the person as he had lived. He says, both lightly and seriously, that he has no intention of dying in the hospital. Everyone laughs.

There is more talk among Angela's friends. Sheryl mentions how sick Angela has been. There is a great deal of joking commentary about what a mess her house is, how she never was a good housekeeper, how they had offered to clean the house but she always refused, how she put things in bags to go through "later," how she had no energy whatsoever, the last couple of years, to clean up. The respiratory therapist, whom the doctor had called when he arrived at the ICU, comes in and stands at Angela's bedside, waiting for the doctor's instruction to replace the ventilator with the t-piece.

5:30 P.M.: Following the doctor's lead, we return to Angela's bedside. Grace, who has been completely quiet, stands back from the bed a bit, and I stand at its foot with the chaplain and social worker. Sheryl is on one side of Angela, holding her hand. The doctor is at her other side, very close to her face. He says in a pleasant tone, "Angela, I'm going to give you some medicine now. It will make you sleepy. You'll be okay." Angela's eyes are open and she looks straight at him. Again, what is behind her gaze is unknowable. Is she sentient? Can she understand or feel or intuit what is about to happen? It seems to me to be an open question. The doctor touches her shoulder, stands close to her, and says again softly, "It will be okay." He is seeking to reassure her, letting her know she can trust him. Angela closes her eyes. It is impossible to know if she understands. Her state of consciousness is unfathomable.

The respiratory therapist moves some of the medical equipment away from the bed and gets the t-piece ready. Angela turns her head to the other side, opens her eyes, and seems to look at Sheryl, who continues to hold her hand. I notice that Angela still has a feeding tube in place. It has not been disconnected.

5:40 P.M: The nurse gives Angela an injection of morphine and Valium. She tells us what she is doing. The doctor explains that the Valium will keep Angela calm and prevent seizures, repeating that seizures are scary for people to watch. It grows quiet in the patient's cubicle, calm. Everyone is watching Angela. When anyone speaks, it is in a hushed voice. I move to stand beside the doctor and ask, "Is this hard for you?" He replies, "Is what hard?" "Is it harder for you when the patient's eyes are open and she's looking at you?" He answers, "No, not really. It's equally hard when eyes are closed. It's always hard. Nobody wants this job." He explains to the chaplain and social worker, who have left the foot of the bed to stand closer to him, that he "is not hastening the process. That's not my job. My job is to make her comfortable. I don't know how long it will take." If he were Dr. Kevorkian, he says, he could cause death with an injection. He has no idea how long it will take for her to stop breathing. Some people go on for days, he says. He thinks that in her case it will not be long, but he cannot predict.

5:45 P.M.: The doctor turns the ventilator settings down and talks with Angela's friends. Sheryl puts oil or water from a little bottle on Angela's hands and face and neck. The doctor goes over to the ventilator and moves the controls, watching the computer screen while he turns off the machine. The mood in the room is relaxed and the whole unit remains quiet. The doctor and nurse together turn off a couple of other monitors so they will stop beeping. Sheryl is smiling.

5:50 P.M.: The doctor asks the respiratory therapist to push the ventilator machine out of the way and "put Angela on room air." The therapist inserts the t-piece in her mouth in seconds, and mist is visible coming out of one end. Sheryl puts her hand up to Angela's mouth to feel the mist. Angela is breathing on her own, with no assistance from the machine. It is noticeable immediately that her breathing is more shallow and uneven than when it was controlled by the machine. The nurse gives another injection of morphine, in addition to the steady drip coming from the intravenous tube. The doctor tells her, "We can turn that drip up to one hundred." The nurse turns the dial controlling the flow of morphine into the IV. Earlier today, at morning rounds, this doctor mentioned that he had to be present for Angela's death because some nurses are "uncomfortable turning up the morphine." This nurse shows no outward signs of having moral difficulty with the procedure, but I do wonder why the doctor does not turn the dial himself.[17]

5:55 P.M.: Angela moves a little bit. But only for a few seconds. The nurse gives her another injection. The morphine drip is now up to three hundred on the dial. I am not sure who turned it up again, the doctor or the nurse. I ask the doctor if Angela's breaths are getting slower, farther apart. He says they are about six seconds apart and ours are about four seconds apart. He says it just looks like there is a lot of space between breaths because we are sitting here and watching her. The social worker is at the bedside touching Angela's arm. The chaplain goes to stand just outside the cubicle. I am leaning against the wall at the foot of the bed, notebook in hand, and hear the doctor say to the social worker, "It won't be long." She asks, "How do you know?" He smiles and says, "That's my secret." Grace is sitting in a chair at the back of the cubicle, away from the bed, somewhat removed from the immediacy of this. Bruce stands at the foot of the bed. Sheryl is holding Angela's shoulder. The pink color is noticeably draining from Angela's face. The doctor goes to sit on a stool at the nurses' station. The social worker follows him, talking. Bruce pulls up a chair next to Grace.

6:07 P.M.: Angela's breaths are getting farther apart, more uneven. I leave the bedside to sit next to the doctor. Thinking about the societal preoccupation with hospital treatments prior to death that are deemed to go on "too long," I ask him if there is any way that Angela's stay in the ICU could have been shorter, if the decision to bring about her death by withdrawing the ventilator could have occurred earlier in her hospitalization. The doctor thinks for a minute, then says, "No, not really." Two weeks ago, he explains, he was not ready to do this. Maybe that was his optimism. "But that kind of decision is irreversible, you know." He goes on, "Theoretically, she's young. She has thirty years left. That's why they bust their asses to save the babies—they have a whole life ahead of them." Maybe last Friday he would have been ready. But not two weeks ago, and certainly not at the first meeting with the family on the twelfth day of her hospitalization. If the neurologist had said then that there was no hope for recovery, the doctor says he would have replied, "It's over, let's end this." But the neurologist didn't say anything like that. So the doctor didn't feel ready. He says, "The money has been spent already, and the emotional suffering . . . who can know? What's one or two weeks, really?" He says he isn't sure, but he thinks the tough part is "making the decision and saying good-bye." He thinks "a few more days or a week" didn't matter to the family. The doctor keeps an attentive eye on the patient throughout our conversation. He is not reading or making phone calls or doing anything else.

6:20 P.M.: One of Angela's friends phones the unit. Sheryl leaves the cubicle to take the call. People are moving in and out of the cubicle, talking with each other. The doctor walks over to a table to do some dictation, keeping his eye on Angela.

7 P.M.: I start to get ready to leave. I go to the bedside to say good-bye to Angela's friends, and Bruce invites me to sit down and tell him more about my research. I do so and we chat for a while.

7:15 P.M.: Angela's internist comes in and introduces himself to the two of Angela's friends he has not yet met. He looks at the cardiac monitor, which is still on, then repeats to the group a couple of times, "Angela seems very comfortable. She is very comfortable." He tells the assembled friends that Angela's heart is strong and that she is not going to die right away. It could be after midnight, or the middle of the night, and they can feel free to leave. They thank him, and I leave the unit. During the two hours I was present, Sheryl continued to stand beside Angela and hold her hand. Angela's other two friends also remained close by, standing or sitting at the bedside, walking in and out of the cubicle and going to the nurses' station to make phone calls or talk to each other. They never left the unit.

The next morning, 9 A.M.: I telephone the unit and the clerk tells me that Angela died about 11 P.M. The clerk remarks that the previous evening most everyone, including the doctor, left the unit shortly after I did, and she thinks it is sad that nobody was there when Angela died. Sheryl and Bruce had stayed until about ten or ten-thirty, and when they left, the clerk told them they could call anytime to inquire about Angela's condition. No one called. The unit clerk has called Angela's parents and told them of her death. She felt someone should call them and it might as well be she. Mr. Stone answered the phone. The TV was blaring in the background, and when she told him the time of Angela's death, he yelled to his wife, "Angela died." Then he hung up. The unit clerk is amazed that he did not ask a question, did not want to talk.

Several days later: I speak with the unit clerk again. She tells me that the critical care doctor was disturbed about Angela's death. He told her that it was hard to do this and he hopes he doesn't have to do it again. Later, I ask the nurse if it was hard for her to administer morphine and turn up the dial on the drip. "No," she says, "not at all, especially when the circumstances were like that. What is hard is the reverse, like going on and giving care when it is torturing the patient, like the case of Mrs. Smith [another patient in the ICU at the time]. That was really hard, and I went home and didn't feel good about what I had been doing all day."

In the weeks between the two meetings, the absence of any quality to Angela's life was asserted increasingly often. An evaluation was also added—she would be better off dead. The respiratory therapist noted that she had no quality of life. The humane thing would be to let her die, he said. The physicians, too, judged her condition as worse than death. It was better to die than to live like this indefinitely. By the time of the second meeting on day 28 of Angela's hospitalization, her friends and her mother had come to agree with the medical staff. They felt she should no longer be allowed to remain in a limbo of slow deterioration without foreseeable end. When Angela's primary doctor claimed, "We are doing what Angela wants," he established a consensus among the group that the quality of her life was no longer acceptable to her. We must accept, his language informed everyone during the second meeting, Angela's evaluation of her own condition, and most important, we must accede to her judgment regarding how to respond.

The perceived truth of these words depended on the *readiness* of everyone present to acknowledge that it was better for her to be dead— both because death was preferable to her quality of life on life support and because that is what she wanted. Timing was crucial. While the doctor in charge of the case had the responsibility for creating the language to move things along, the family, the friends, and the entire medical team had to cooperate by acknowledging that his claim was absolutely correct, that Angela was, in the end, the person responsible for choosing death. That claim was not made and could not be made until Angela had been in the ICU for a month. It took time to articulate and then agree to Angela's "life worse than death" and to shift responsibility first away from Angela (who had not expressed her opinions about life support) onto the family and then back to Angela. Her death could happen only when the pain of her life was apparent to everyone and both desire and responsibility for ending that life was assumed to be hers. Only then was the time right for death.

LIFE SUPPORT

"Things are delicate right now about the dialysis. I wouldn't want him on life support. I wouldn't want him to have CPR if his heart stops. But dialysis is God's decision. It's not my decision to stop that."

Wife of patient on third day of two-week hospitalization.
The patient, who had end-stage renal disease, died while still receiving dialysis.

Choices about the time for death are shaped by the enormous power of the movement imperative and, depending on the patient's condition, by the specific rhetoric that is used to interpret the patient's desire to live or die. That rhetoric, as we have seen, is a normal part of hospital practice, and it serves the logic of the bureaucratic system by enabling things to move along. Another feature of the story of how death is made consists of the events, players, and motivations that surround life support—who wants life support and why, when and how it continues or stops, whose voices are silenced and heard, and the impossibility of "choice," all in the context of the multiple understandings of life support itself. The complex practices of life support provide yet another explanation for why the "problem of death" is so widely perceived and why the popular goal of "death with dignity" is so elusive.

Life support is a central fact of critical illness in today's hospital world, a fact that both drives and rationalizes the power of the pathways that organize treatment, the faces of *waiting,* and the rhetoric through which death is deliberated and timed. *Life support* refers both to specific

medical procedures and to the various interpretations of those procedures. The term *life support* per se is never used in daily hospital practice, and health professionals do not use it at all.[1] Rather, it is a term that
circulates in public talk, especially to refer to what many people say they
do not want if it will only prolong dying.

Newspaper opinion pieces, popular books about personal control
over dying, and organizations that promote dialogue and change in end-
of-life medical care would have it that the technology-driven American
hospital system is the primary culprit in the problem of prolonging
dying unnecessarily because it promotes the use of "unwanted" life-
sustaining measures. Patient (and thus family) "suffering" is considered
by many, both within and outside of medicine, to be a direct result of
"overly aggressive" life support procedures. Yet physicians (who, even as
they struggle to work autonomously within hospital bureaucracies, are
very aware of the social criticism directed toward them) repeatedly gave
me a different perspective. On the contrary, they said, it is families who
do not want to and cannot "let go" of their relatives and want to keep
them on life support past (sometimes long past) the time when there is
a life to support.[2] Over time, I observed both groups to be right and both
to be culpable. In some instances, hospital staff and families, in about
equal proportion, wanted to pursue life-sustaining treatments in the
hope that the patient, the person, would be restored to some level of
function. In other instances, both groups intervened in equal numbers to
stop the domination of the heroic pathway.[3] And sometimes, ambivalence, silence, or evasion reigned and neither doctors nor families pressed
hard for life-supporting measures or their withdrawal. Regardless of *who*
tries to stop the course of life-sustaining, death-defying treatments,
which treatments are stopped or avoided, *when* treatments are stopped or
whether they are stopped at all, life support is a mutable phenomenon,
always linked to the politics and rhetoric of the patient's condition.

It took more than a year of observation in several hospital units
before I started to question the concept of life support vis-à-vis the discourse on problematic dying and to try to discern the whole range of
activities that actually constitute it. The mechanical ventilator and cardiopulmonary resuscitation—the obvious and most dreaded means of
sustaining life—are both so extraordinary, so engrossing to observe, that
for a long time I was content to let my gaze stop there. I was limited, too,
by the widespread conversation about the problem of death, which

focuses its critique largely on those two activities. As I learned more about other treatments provided to patients with precarious lives, I gradually became more confused about what life support actually entails. I tried to understand how the many lifesaving treatments contribute to sustaining life or to prolonging death. People who were not necessarily attached to mechanical ventilators and who had not been resuscitated were nonetheless being "supported" in the ICU. The support came from vasopressor medications, kidney dialysis treatments, or a combination of other things, including surgery, antibiotics, and tube-administered fluids and nutrition. All of those things could be life support.

The contingent nature of life support was first made evident to me when, eventually, I questioned an experienced critical care nurse about it. Our conversation began when I commented that the mechanical ventilator seemed to me to be the only obvious life support technology. She replied, "I think at some point in time the mechanical ventilator *can be* life support. I don't believe that all the time it is. But let me clarify that a little bit. The patient with pneumonia comes in. And that is the only thing he's got, pneumonia. But he's not breathing well from it and it's really compromising his respiratory status, so we intubate him. Is that ventilator at that point in time life support? In my opinion, no, that's an adjunct to his therapy to get him well. If pneumonia is the only thing that he's got, then we can treat it and get him out. But the course of the disease can continue, and he can end up on dopamine or any of the other vasoactive medications—again, depending on the course of the pneumonia. We may put him on that because we don't have his fluids up yet, or he's hypotensive and we just haven't gotten on top of the infection yet. Again, my feeling is that that's an adjunct to therapy that's helping him bridge that point. It's a treatable problem.

"At some point in time it *can* be life support if in fact the treatments we have tried aren't working for that patient. Then I believe that those things can be life support. It truly is a very murky area, one that I don't think anybody has ever tried to capture, because my opinion of where life support sort of starts for that person may be very different than where life support starts for someone else. All of those things can be life-supporting measures. There's no question. But I think you have to look at the therapy of the patient and what it is that we're doing for the treatment of that patient, and whether or not that is something that is helping or not. Or, if the patient is just continuing to either go downhill or maintain—and even maintenance can be okay for a while. But if the patient starts to go downhill, then you have to go back and reassess all those things and say, what are we doing any of this for, at this point? But I don't always believe that the ventilator is life support. It is a life-supportive therapy for some patients. For a number of patients it is a piece of the therapy that gets them through, to get them well. For other patients it's something that isn't going to help because their underlying disease process is so bad. Or, they are too compromised from that underlying disease process. And that's a very gray area. I mean, if you have somebody with metastatic cancer and you put him on a ventilator, is he going to get off that ventilator? Probably not. But if it's somebody with a pneumonia and you put him on a ventilator, is he going to get off? Probably."

Next I asked her about kidney dialysis. "Again, I think it's in a similar category with the vasoactive medications and the ventilator. I think that sometimes it's a therapy that can help. Hemodialysis, any kind of renal replacement therapy treatments for end-stage renal disease, can help, can turn around kidney function in some patients. Then at a certain point, depending on what else is going on with the patient, it can either become life support or not, depending on where the patient's disease process is going. If the patient's kidneys are turning around, if his kidney function is turning around, then it's an adjunctive therapy. If the patient is not doing well and the rest of his disease is not getting better, and all we're doing is keeping his electrolytes sort of in balance, but everything else is still the same or is crappin' out, then it becomes a life-supportive measure just like anything else. The difficult thing about dialysis is that in some cases everything else can turn around but the kidneys. And then you have the patient who is required to have dialysis three days a week. And then the question is, is that life support?

"It's somewhat subjective. I mean, I could say that for this patient on the ventilator it is life support because of these factors. And somebody else could come in and say, 'The guy is seventy-five years old, what makes you think that this ventilator is going to save his life, that this is life-supportive treatment?' So you'll get a very different picture. It's very subjective unless you have really specific, objective criteria. And I think that is very difficult because you will never get a group of people to agree."

This critical care nurse defined *life support* by interpreting the relationships among actual disease processes, medical procedures, and the body's response to the diseases and the procedures. She grounded it in the "subjective" judgments of clinical medicine about the patient's condition. In some sense, life support can be known as two things—either "support" of the body's systems or postponement of death. But that latter categorization is made only in retrospect.

Several kinds of indeterminacy surround life support. First, individuals who claim, when they are not seriously ill or facing death, that they do not want emergency life support procedures often change their minds when death seems near. Families, too, generally want to give their relative "a fighting chance," even when they know or assume that the patient "did not want to be on life support." In addition, seriously ill hospitalized patients whose bodily systems are being supported by various medical means often change their minds about *which kinds of life support* they would accept in the future. Some decide, contrary to their pre-illness claims, that ventilator support, if necessary for continued survival, would be acceptable given their present condition, though CPR would not be. Others draw the line differently, stating that dialysis is acceptable, or tube feeding, for example, but that mechanical ventilation is not. Families, too, may shift the line of acceptance when the condition of someone they care about is deteriorating. Second, life support is made indeterminate because hospital staff, patients, and families sometimes have difficulty interpreting whether any given procedure or cluster of procedures is life support or the kind of life support that is wanted. Dorothy Mason's son, Greta Adler's son, and Evelyn Barker's daughter agonized over how to categorize the kinds of treatment their mothers received. And finally, the use of life support is subject to negotiation, persuasion, and demand. Families can drive decisions about how many, and which, lifesaving procedures to employ, and they can say stop. Though families and patients have the least knowledge about medical matters and face impossible choices, and though physicians often attempt to control the timing of death when they know further treatments will not improve the patient's condition, families that express clear viewpoints about what they want for the patient are not often ignored.

In the five stories in this chapter, the politics and indeterminacy of life support provide another example of why it is so hard to stop sustaining a life even as it hovers near death, why *dignity* is in the eye of the beholder, and how *suffering* may or may not be considered essential in determining what to do. In the first three cases, families drive the decision about how much life support is enough; in the final two, focus shifts to the patient as decision-maker. In the first story, Earl Morrison's family is in conflict with the entire medical team and wants heroic treatment to continue to death. They tell the doctors that their position stems from their religious faith. In this case, "what the patient would want" is transformed into the expression of, and staff acquiescence to, family desire, and the family's religious faith obstructs the physicians' preferred actions (not a highly unusual scenario in urban hospitals). As we have seen, staff need and want family guidance about treatment choices, and awareness of the threat of litigation encourages deference to families to speak for "what the patient would want." Thus, hospital staff rarely act against a family member's specific request.[4] In the second story, Norman Cline's family's desire to sustain life is in conflict with the patient's wishes. The patient retains his voice but the family continues to "speak for" him. Then we see that the "pain" and "suffering" of the patient do not always play a significant role in the politics surrounding life support. In the third case, Constance Brady's family leads the medical team in stopping treatment, though there is never complete resolution about "what the patient wanted," which procedures were life support, and whether the right thing was done. In the fourth story, Walter Cole, the dying patient himself, shifts his position regarding which life-support procedures he will accept as his health deteriorates, and in the fifth example, the patient, Cathy Lewis, describes how and when she "went against" her own previously declared wishes and said yes to life support. Then she describes the consequences of that choice for the rest of her life.

Religious faith may play an active role in the ways patients and families decide what to want or in why they arrive at a certain position about life support. The influence of religious faith on decisions about life support is, in the end, highly variable, and it may not be brought to bear on what to do about hospital treatments at all. Well over half the patients and their families whose hospital course I followed did not bring up the subject of faith, religious observance, or God either in deliberations about what to want or in their activities at the bedside. On the other hand, many patients and families *are* guided by "God's will" or "God's decision" in desiring continued life-prolonging procedures. Earl Morrison's story illustrates one way in which families interpret God's intent throughout their relative's long hospitalization. The Morrisons are African-American and Catholic. The statement quoted at the opening of this chapter was made by a woman whose family is white and belongs to what the social worker described as a "nontraditional Christian sect." The woman said to me, "We live by the Bible," and she did not allow the doctors to stop providing the dialysis treatments, which continued up to the moment of her husband's death. But strong religious faith is not a predictor of family desire, and occasionally, as we saw in the case of Peter Rossetti, families with strong religious faith often want death "to be speeded up," rather than staved off, so that apparent suffering will not be prolonged. There is no question that a sense of faith affects what to want when death is near, but there are as many expressions of religious faith as there are individuals and families, and neither the presence nor absence of religious faith, in and of itself, can predict when or where patients or families will draw the line respecting particular forms of life support or can explain the reasons they change their minds.

Though the word *dignity*, as it has come to be used in the hospital near death, has its source in theology and bioethics,[5] it does not function either rhetorically or pragmatically as a clearly defined principle that is understood similarly by everyone who works in or passes through the hospital system. Rather, this open-ended construct circulates freely within the institution, deployed specifically, like the term *quality of life*, as a potential means to instrumental ends. When the patient's condition has silenced his voice, the onus of responsibility is on staff and family to decide what constitutes dignity, either in actual treatments or their withdrawal, and thus, how respect for the unique person can be shown. Together, clinicians' and families' decisions that foster or resist the heroic pathway, their desires to save life but also to facilitate the *least worst death*,[6] and the perceived and negotiated rights of families all shape the ways dignity is practiced vis-à-vis the patient who is being maintained at the threshold of death.

"We Want to Go for Life"—Dignity Is in the Eye of the Beholder: Earl Morrison

From the moment Earl Morrison is resuscitated in an outpatient dialysis clinic, it is obvious to everyone that the medical activities surrounding him constitute life support. Hospital staff are soon united in wanting to stop aggressive interventions before they reach the violent conclusion of an emergency resuscitation attempt. Choices are made and lines between staff and family are clearly drawn, but not in the way that is generally assumed. The medical team want to create what they consider a "dignified" death while there is still time to control it medically. The family, in contrast, claim the moral high ground in wanting to maintain Mr. Morrison's life using technology. Anything less, in their view, is murder. The medical team see dignity in withdrawing life-sustaining treatment. The family want to continue medical treatments that support Mr. Morrison's precious existence.

Admission: Earl Morrison, a man with end-stage renal disease who has been a hemodialysis patient for three years, suffered a cardiac arrest while on the dialysis machine at the outpatient center. He was "coded" (resuscitated) and brought to the emergency room, where, according to his doctor of many years, he "arrested again, at least one, probably two more times, and had to be shocked a total of three times. And wound up in the intensive care unit in a coma." Mr. Morrison was then attached to a mechanical ventilator and will not survive without it.

Day 4: The brief, introductory information I was given by the patient's long-term primary physician is reiterated today by several nurses when I see Mr. Morrison for the first time. He is lying still in the ICU bed with his eyes closed. He is fragile-looking and drained of life, but the words *near death* are not used by anyone to describe his condition. Nor are words to that effect written in his medical chart. The neurological consultant has written, "The patient was in the dialysis unit when he had a cardiac arrest. He was resuscitated promptly. However, it is unclear how long his downtime was." If Mr. Morrison had not been resuscitated, he would have died. He is "deeply comatose," according to several staff members. His primary physician tells me he has "gone into a vegetative state." The cardiologist treating him says, "He's brain-dead." Despite those discrepancies of diagnosis, his entire medical team, which by now includes the primary care physician, a cardiologist, a renal specialist, a neurologist, a pulmonologist, and a critical care specialist, all agree that he should no longer receive any life-sustaining treatments, that he should be allowed to die.

Mr. Morrison, age seventy-five, has a long medical history of serious illness: bad coronary artery disease, lung disease, hypertension, and diabetes. He has a large family: a wife, many children, many siblings with many children. All of them have rallied to his bedside. Mr. Morrison's primary physician assembles the family to tell them the bad news. Their relative is "deeply comatose." He is not responsive to anything, including deep pain. He has brain stem activity, his eyes wander, things are going on in his brain stem. He isn't brain-dead (a point that contradicts one previous diagnosis), but he is "unaware, as far as we could tell." The doctor says the family should think about what Mr. Morrison would want, then outlines the four steps of withdrawing life support that he wants to take: to write "Do Not Resuscitate" in the medical chart, thereby preventing a second resuscitation attempt should Mr. Morrison have another cardiac arrest; to stop dialysis treatments, thereby allowing kidney failure and death; to slowly reduce to nothing the oxygen support enabling Mr. Morrison to breathe; and to move Mr. Morrison to a private room, outside the ICU, where the family could gather and where the patient could die surrounded by as little medical paraphernalia as possible. The family say they will think over those suggestions, consult their Catholic priest, and decide among themselves by consensus.

Day 5: I accompany the medical team on morning ICU rounds. The intensive care specialist, the cardiologist, and the renal specialist voice their agreement that Mr. Morrison should not, in their shared opinion about what constitutes both appropriate and humane medical care, be receiving dialysis any longer. The consulting neurologist is perhaps more flexible about the timing of events, or perhaps he wants to be sure that the medical chart—a legal document as well as a medical one—contains detailed records. He writes in Mr. Morrison's chart, "I would recommend to continue following the patient over the next 24–48 hours in order to determine whether indeed his progress continues to be poor, and if so, suggest making recommendations to the family to discontinue support."

The primary care doctor says, "He'll probably code [undergo CPR procedures following another cardiac arrest], and it won't be successful, and he'll die."[7] The cardiologist replies, "But he could code tomorrow and he could code two years from now." The cardiologist confides to me that he does not know whether the hospital has a policy about what to do when medical staff are unanimous in wanting to stop treatment but family members want treatment to continue. Later in the day, another doctor clarifies the situation for me. If standard tests determine that the patient is brain-dead, hospital staff can withdraw support, regardless of what the family wants. (Yet in such cases medical staff sometimes wait until family members "accept" the death.) If, like Mr. Morrison, the patient is in a coma or persistent vegetative state, the hospital administration does not explicitly condone the withdrawal of life support unless the family (or a document previously written by the patient) gives permission to do so, and few physicians will withdraw life-sustaining treatments without family consent.

Several days later: Mr. Morrison's primary physician tells me how surprised he is that the family has declared that it is "unanimous in wanting to continue all life support, including CPR if he should arrest again. I actually thought that they were pretty much in agreement with me, that he probably wouldn't want to continue and that he would want life support stopped, and that's what we ought to do. I was actually very surprised after the long discussion we had about this. The family consulted their priest and want 'to go for life,' as the wife says." The physician says Mrs. Morrison, in particular, cannot fathom the idea of stopping any treatment—that, she thinks, would hasten his death. "And that's exactly the way she sees it—as tantamount to euthanasia," he adds. He tells me that Mr. Morrison's wife made a rational and consistent argument, one that is also "based on her religious beliefs—she says it's a Catholic thing. I think that is arguable. There are Catholics in this community who would say that this is not a Catholic position." The family, he says, is realistic about the prognosis. "There's only one relative who talks about miracles. . . . The wife understands that he is dying, knows that that may happen anytime, is not expecting miracles, but just cannot affirmatively take that step to end his life." He concludes, "We took opposite points of view about this letting go. . . . In the end, I could just say, 'I respect your position. I think it's your decision about what he would want, and I'll support it.'"

Other members of the hospital staff are not as generous about the family's stance. Most of them consider the decision to be misguided and feel that dialysis treatments and ventilator support should immediately be withdrawn. For them the meager signs of physical life that are sustained only through technological intervention are not enough *life*, and they know with medical certainty that Mr. Morrison's condition will not change for the better. "Some people [on the hospital staff] put it in moral terms," Mr. Morrison's primary doctor says, "that it is immoral what we are doing to him. Just like the moral terms the wife uses when she says it is immoral to stop." Though Mr. Morrison's wife accepts the physician's explanation that her husband no longer has enough *life* to exist without supportive technology, that condition is not a reason, as she sees it, for actively killing him.

Two weeks after admission: Mr. Morrison is still in the ICU. His primary care doctor brings together several members of the hospital ethics committee, some of the treating physicians, and several family members in the hope that an open discussion will resolve what is now regarded by hospital staff as an untenable medical situation and a problem of family recalcitrance. The physician's first hope is that the family can be persuaded to stop life-prolonging treatment. If that is not possible, he hopes the medical team can, through learning the family's perspective on the situation, feel more comfortable providing care to a permanently comatose patient. Neither of these hopes is realized. Following that meeting the primary physician writes in Mr. Morrison's chart, "All about the same. Ethics committee discussion with physicians, family, social worker, committee members—the meeting was to allow all parties a chance to express opinions/beliefs about continued treatment. All present agreed that the family has the right to make the decision, that they were doing so conscientiously/in good faith; although not all present agreed that the decision was the 'right' one. Plan is to continue all treatment. We will continue to revisit code status." While I learn from hospital staff that they consider Mr. Morrison's continued treatment unacceptable because it will in no sense enable recovery, I also learn that the hospital administration will not condone or legally support any physician action that opposes his family's desires.

Three weeks after admission: The primary care doctor tells me, "I vacillate between, on the one hand, appreciating the family's position, wanting to support them, and thinking that in fact it is their decision to make, and on the other hand, when I go to examine this person, this person who *was* a person, it's uncomfortable to see what we're doing, keeping him alive in this state. It doesn't quite feel right. My sense is that, you know, a lot of it is projection, that *I* wouldn't want to be kept alive in an intensive care unit like this, dialysis every other day, on a ventilator, unconscious."

The hospital social worker assigned to Mr. Morrison informs me that the primary care doctor had called in a gastroenterologist, who had refused to insert a feeding tube in the patient's stomach, saying it would not benefit the patient and would only prolong dying and that in good conscience he could not do it.[8] Another gastroenterologist has agreed to insert the tube, but not for another two weeks, as he wants to wait to see if the patient's condition changes for the better or worse. The social worker is perplexed about these developments and their implication for discharge of the patient. She ponders aloud whether the second GI specialist wants to wait to let the patient die. If the patient has a stomach tube inserted right away, she could discharge him to a facility that cares for long-term, comatose, ventilator-dependent patients. Without the feeding tube, "We are in a discharge limbo," she says.[9]

One month and four days after admission to the ICU: I learn from an ICU nurse that Mr. Morrison was having cardiac problems while on dialysis yesterday and treatment was thirty minutes shorter than usual because the renal specialist felt that further treatment was unwarranted. Early today Mr. Morrison had a cardiac arrest. The nurse caring for him at the time tells me, "He was coded for a very long time. They shocked him ten times . . . usually they shock a person maybe three times." The family was not at the bedside at the time and was called when the code was over. They came, sat by the bedside with the hospital chaplain, and prayed together, then left the hospital.

The primary care doctor gives me his version of the final moments: "Mr. Morrison died after a longish CPR—truly a 'full code.' Not a peaceful death. But clearly the death his loved ones chose for him by requiring that all efforts be made to keep him alive. Of all the procedures we put him through, this was the worst, something I wanted to prevent from happening. The family, particularly his wife, knew my wishes. She and they considered them, I think, but couldn't let go even that much—to have a DNR order written. I spoke with the wife just after she arrived in the ICU after Mr. Morrison died. She was tearful and appreciative of everything I, we, had done to help keep him alive. She knew we had tried our best. She and her family have to live with what happened, and it appears that giving 'life' our best shot is some consolation to them. Even though I wish his death could have been other than it was—more 'peaceful,' 'better'—I don't regret acceding to his family's wishes."

The way in which hospital rhetoric produces meaning about the patient's condition again became evident to me as I listened to various hospital staff describe what happened. As I was trying to understand the story of Mr. Morrison's hospitalization and treatment, I noted that the language used, first by the primary care doctor and later by the intensive care nurses, to describe the patient's condition was the medical language of diagnosis and physiologic emergency and the institutional language of appropriate-response strategy. Death was never mentioned. Speaking of the initial cardiac arrest for which Mr. Morrison was admitted, no one said "He almost died." The cardiac arrest was not framed as either cause or indication of his demise. If it had been framed as *the cause of death,* the month of ICU treatments and staff angst about those treatments would not have occurred. But in the out-patient dialysis clinic setting, *death* was only *possible death,* the catastrophic medical event that was the starting point for the first CPR procedure. After that procedure, the patient, perhaps alive but without *life,* was stabilized on mechanical ventilation. He was comatose and could potentially make some kind of recovery. At that point both the physicians and the family hoped that Mr. Morrison would recover.

The story did not end until a month later when, as the primary care doctor explained, Mr. Morrison "died after a longish CPR—truly a 'full code.'" The prolonged and unsuccessful resuscitation effort was viewed by doctors and family members alike as the actual passage point between life and death. Mr. Morrison was not considered dead until the resuscitation procedure ended. Indeed, the dramatic and extraordinary resuscitation effort sanctioned and legitimated Mr. Morrison's death,[10] demonstrating (graphically and violently) that death had been fought up to the last moment of life. That unusually prolonged effort demonstrated to the grateful family that medical staff were indeed honoring their request to "go for life."[11]

"Will You Help Me Die, Please?"—Unwanted Life Support in the Face of Suffering: Norman Cline

Norman Cline's family demands, as did Mr. Morrison's, that the patient's life be supported and maintained indefinitely. In this example, though, the patient's voice is not silenced by disease, and he has agreed to aggressive treatments to sustain his life. After weeks of those treatments, however, he declares that he wants to die. Neither the family nor the medical team will act on his wish. I have never seen as much tension between patient and family as that which develops following Mr. Cline's change of mind about life support. The medical team does not attempt, as it did in the case of Mr. Morrison, to convince the family "to let go" because not everyone on the team is convinced that continued treatments will not prove beneficial. Nor does the team try to resolve or intervene in the conflict over life and death between patient and family. The medical team and the family never discuss whether Mr. Cline's suffering can or should be ignored. Instead, the doctors leave control in the hands of the family.

Mr. Cline's suffering is acknowledged out loud by everyone except his primary physician, but it is considered by his children to be temporary. It
never influences what to do about life support.

Admission: From the very first day Norman Cline's hospitalization is
marked by his extremely precarious condition, the medical staff's growing conviction that he will not recover enough to return home, and his
family's insistence that he live. Mr. Cline has asthma and severe chronic
lung disease and was admitted following a bad asthma attack at midnight. His son and daughter rushed him to the hospital. When told he
needed to be put on a ventilator because he was in respiratory distress,
Mr. Cline, together with his children, made the decision to do so. Mr.
Cline is frail and has been using oxygen at home for months. His son and
daughter tell the nurses that this hospitalization is "a double whammy"
for them. Still reeling from their mother's death a year ago, they do not
want their father, age seventy-five, to die. The immediate goal, everyone
agrees, is to bring the asthma under control and treat the pneumonia that
was quickly diagnosed. The hope is to get him off the ventilator as quickly
as possible.

   Mr. Cline's doctor of many years sums up for me the patient's first
days in the hospital: "We didn't know at the outset whether or not he was
going to survive the acute illness. I mean, he was really very sick when he
was first admitted. And there was significant doubt in my mind and in
the minds of others who were caring for him whether he'd even survive
beyond the first several days of the hospitalization. Because his level of
overall functioning was satisfactory to him and he was able to enjoy a
reasonable family life with his children and grandchildren, we elected,
because he wanted to—and we were in agreement about this—to be
aggressive about his initial treatment, with the hope that we would be
able to return him to some point close to where he had been previously.
So that was the initial assessment and focus of his therapy. I recognized at
the outset that if we got him through the first few days of the illness and
it appeared that he would recover, that we would be in for a much more
difficult course thereafter. . . . Once he did, then it became a much different kind of problem. That's when it became much harder to deal with."

   Week one: The two nurses who care for Mr. Cline most during his first
week in the hospital predict that he will never be able to get off the venti-

lator because his lung disease is so severe. On the seventh day the doctors decide to perform a tracheostomy, knowing it will be more comfortable for Mr. Cline than the ventilator tube in his mouth. With special valves, some patients learn to talk despite the tracheostomy, and everyone hopes Mr. Cline will be able to communicate once his condition improves.

Week two: The medical team work hard to "wean" Mr. Cline from ventilator support by having him spend longer periods of time each day without it. His doctor's aim is to enable Mr. Cline to be without the ventilator entirely during the day so he can resume his life at home and then use a BiPap oxygen mask[12] at night. Soon, however, the staff realize that this initial goal for Mr. Cline is becoming more remote. One of the critical care physicians tells the ICU team during morning rounds, "He has less than no reserves. He has minus reserves. He's like a grenade with the pin off. He could go anytime. The family doesn't get this. They keep saying, 'You're going to get better, Dad.' " For the first time, one of the lung specialists writes in the patient's medical chart, "Poor prognosis, probably unweanable."[13]

End of week two: Mr. Cline's son asks the hospital chaplain to facilitate a discussion with the medical team. Highly educated and well informed about medical matters, the son and daughter both want advice and a sense of things from the staff. Mr. Cline's primary physician, a nurse, a social worker, and two respiratory therapists who have been treating Mr. Cline are present for the discussion, as is the chaplain. The chaplain tells me afterward that, in her view, Mr. Cline's children asked thoughtful questions but never received a straight answer. They asked if their father would ever be able to speak again in sentences. Staff replied that they did not know. They asked how long, if at all, it would take to wean their father off the ventilator. They were told it could take a couple of months, but then, it could take twelve months. They asked how long they should plan for their father to be in the hospital—another two or three months? The staff did not give them an answer. They asked the social worker if they should investigate long-term-care facilities. The social worker replied, "You don't need to do that till the time comes." They asked the doctor several hypothetical questions: What if their father needs surgery? What if he gets worse? The doctor never articulated a scenario of decline. According to the chaplain, death was never mentioned as an open possibility. The family got no indication from the hospital staff that they should begin to discuss the end of their father's life and no clues for beginning to think about death. They did hear from the doctor—the chaplain is certain about this—that their father was extremely compromised, without reserves, and that any small infection or new medical problem would be a tremendous setback for his recovery. (Later Mr. Cline's son will tell me that the medical staff did not give him any information that was useful.) The chaplain reflects, "If you go to a car mechanic and ask about a part that's breaking down, how long will it last, you wouldn't be satisfied with the answer 'We'll cross that bridge when we come to it.' If you wouldn't be satisfied with that answer about your car, you certainly wouldn't be satisfied with it about your father."

The next morning: The critical care doctor leading morning rounds (who was not present at yesterday's discussion with the family) says, "Mr. Cline is really end stage. I'm surprised he's lived through this. His outlook from here? He'll need to go to a nursing home or a long-term-care unit from here. I'll bet his lung function was twenty percent of normal before he came in here. He's dying. There's nothing to do, nothing to fix." The chaplain responds, "The family is trying to do noncrisis decision-making. They are responsible and that is what they are trying so hard to do." The critical care doctor replies, "I would encourage them to ask more questions. Sometimes doctors don't want to answer. They need to be specific and ask, what if this happens? what if that happens? They need to be told he won't live through a surgical procedure." The chaplain tells me later that Mr. Cline's children have told her they have trouble talking about "what-ifs," about a future that includes further complications or death. It makes them nervous, they said. The chaplain tells me that Mr. Cline's son and daughter think "they can fine-tune the technology to ward off death, to make him live."

I talk with Mr. Cline's nurse for the day, a young, thoughtful man. He says Mr. Cline was off the ventilator for nearly eight hours the day before. Today is not as good, and he has been off only for a few hours. In addition, his skin is so thin, so brittle, it is painful anytime he is touched. "His skin breaks if you look at him," the nurse says. "It's the result of long-term prednisone use. He needs the drug, but this is the bad, long-term side effect." Still, the nurse has put Mr. Cline in a chair facing the window so that he can look outside at the view, and he was gratified when Mr. Cline turned to him and broke into a big smile. "He was so happy to look at something pleasing, something other than the furniture and walls in his ICU room," the nurse says.

End of week three: There are complications. Mr. Cline begins to have gastrointestinal bleeding and requires several blood transfusions. Because he is bed-bound and has such fragile skin, he has developed a bedsore,[14] which grows larger and more painful as his hospitalization progresses, despite attentive wound care. His nurse tells me he has pain everywhere and it is becoming worse. His arms, the only part of him besides his head that is exposed above the sheets, are incredibly thin. Nevertheless, he uses what strength he has to bang on the guardrail of his bed to get the nurse's attention. He cannot move otherwise because of the pain. Some of the nurses mention that his pain is not well managed, and a pain consultant is called.

Week four: Mr. Cline has begun telling the nurses—mouthing the words because he cannot emit sounds through the tracheostomy—that he wants to die, that he never wants to go through this kind of pain or this kind of treatment again. One nurse says, "He called me over this morning and asked me to give him something to let him go. I said, 'Do you mean to die?' He said, 'Yes.' He wants to talk to the doctors about it."

Two days later, Mr. Cline expresses a similar sentiment to the social worker, mouthing the words, "Will you help me die, please?" She responds (without irony) that he is the one who is in control—control, that is, to express his wishes about treatment decisions—and he needs to tell his family and his doctor. When Mr. Cline repeats his wish to his son and daughter, they tell him he will get through this and call for a psychiatric evaluation. The children had convinced Mr. Cline to have psychotherapy following his wife's death, and they think it could be beneficial now. The psychiatrist writes in the medical chart, "Impression is that he is not clinically depressed but wants to die because he feels his lungs will not get significantly better and he does not want to ever go through his present ordeal again. He is very clear in communicating this. He is capable of making decisions about his health care." In another note a few days later, the psychiatrist writes, "At this time I am unable to say the patient is significantly depressed. It is my opinion that he does not have a psychiatric illness that is interfering with his ability to make decisions regarding his health care."

It is unusual for a patient's family to call for a psychiatric evaluation. Psychiatrists are most frequently called in by hospital medical teams who want them to assess whether patients are clinically depressed or have any psychiatric symptoms or illnesses, whether they are competent to make treatment decisions, and whether their distress due to illness, pain, and suffering has made them unable to make "rational" decisions, unable to weigh the risks and benefits of specific treatments. Staff want such clarification both so they can try to respect the patient's "autonomy" about treatment choice and so that any decisions on their part to continue or withdraw treatments have legal protection. Many clinical case studies in the past two decades describe patients who are depressed about their medical conditions and personal circumstances and request that life-sustaining treatment be terminated, allowing them to die.[15] Deliberation about patients who wish to stop life-sustaining treatments is framed first by the press for individual rights and second by the thirty-year legacy of concern for informed, autonomous decision-making. Thus psychiatric consultations focus primarily on whether patients have the capacity to make well-considered choices regarding the refusal of life-sustaining therapies.[16] *Suffering*—in this context, the patient's anguished, embodied experience of his condition and his life—gets transformed in hospital talk generally and in psychiatric evaluations specifically into evaluation of mental or psychological competence and rationality. And competence itself is always understood through the "legalistic prism"[17] that informs physician actions.

Week five: After much discussion over days among Mr. Cline, his children, and his doctor, Mr. Cline is now willing to try antidepressant medication, but only, he says, to please his children. The medication is started, but Mr. Cline continues to reiterate that he wants to die. The social worker writes in her chart notes, "Met with patient again. Patient again expressed desire to die. 'This is not living. Enough is enough. Please help me.' Patient appears to have full capacity. Patient frustrated. 'It's my body!' he says."

Later, Mr. Cline's doctor reflects, "So when he first started expressing some of these feelings, I wasn't quite sure what we were dealing with, you know, whether he was or wasn't saying that. But after a while it became apparent that he was, and he voiced it enough times so that we were able to satisfy ourselves that that was in fact what he was saying. . . . Once I was convinced that, yes, he really was expressing these things, I initially interpreted it as just enormous frustration over the protracted nature of the illness, his inability to communicate, his not wanting to continue to live like he was currently living, his lack of apparent improvement, and began to address those issues with him and with the family members. . . . But I also recognized that we were in a never-never land, so to speak. We'd gotten beyond the most acute phase of his illness and he'd recovered from that, and we were now in a phase where we were providing a lot of aggressive supportive care. But if we were to stop that supportive care, it wasn't where he was going to suddenly stop breathing and die. That wasn't what we were dealing with anymore. . . . He was reaching a point where he didn't want to function at or below that level and decided, 'I don't want this.' In this particular case, some of the decision-making may have been taken away from him in the latter parts of the illness by the family, who became his surrogates, really, and decided, 'Well, this isn't great, but at least we'll still have our father, even if it's at this level of functioning that he finds unsatisfactory.' I think if allowed to make the decision independently, he would probably not have wanted to go on as long and as vigorously as it did."

Week six: Mr. Cline's doctor and the hospital social worker begin making arrangements for Mr. Cline's transfer to a hospital that specializes in ventilator-dependent patients. Because he has so many acute medical problems that need constant attention, he still needs hospitalization. He has, however, been spending most of the day off the ventilator, and the staff hope that further independence from it is possible. A few days before his transfer, his nurse talks with me about his condition, his frustration, and his anger—Mr. Cline has had trouble communicating throughout his hospital stay; he is in excruciating pain much of the time; he has been bed-bound for weeks; and he has just mouthed to her the words, "I want a quick demise." One of the speech therapists who works with Mr. Cline says, "Sometimes he feels like a fighter, sometimes he wants to give up and die." But he has reluctantly agreed to move to the long-term institution and to have a permanent stomach-feeding tube inserted prior to the move. By now his doctor knows Mr. Cline will never be completely independent of the ventilator and will have to live in a facility that can handle his ventilator needs. "It really wasn't the kind of outcome that we were looking for when we began all of it," he tells me later.

Two weeks after his move to the new institution: Mr. Cline gets a new infection and dies.

If they draw a line at all, patients, families, and hospital staff may all draw the line differently about when, why, and how to stop life support.

And those differences are one manifestation of "the problem of death." Earl Morrison's medical team agreed that continued supportive treatments were inappropriate, but the family would not authorize what they considered to be unethical euthanasia—two straightforward points of view. Mr. Cline's situation was more complicated. He could speak for himself and did. He changed his mind about life support. And throughout his long hospital course it was not clear to everyone that aggressive procedures were useless to stabilize and even improve his condition.

Mr. Cline wanted to stop everything when, in the fourth week, he could no longer tolerate the pain and the invasive treatments themselves. His children remained optimistic about his future and saw his suffering as only temporary, and they refused to discontinue supportive therapies. The nurses and therapists saw and heard Mr. Cline's suffering but were not in a position of authority to do anything about it. The social worker could only tell Mr. Cline that he could express his right to patient self-determination. Mr. Cline's primary physician did not bring suffering to bear on the matter of what should be done. He focused his attention instead on Mr. Cline's being clinically stuck in a "never-never land," extremely frail and unable to exist without the ventilator, and on what, if anything, he could do to adjust treatments.

Perhaps if Mr. Cline's doctors had articulated clearly to the family a scenario of decline to death instead of answering their questions evasively, if the family could have imagined their father's death, if Mr. Cline himself could have been even more insistent that he wanted to die as his condition worsened, then perhaps the story would not have played out the way it did. But the family's commitment to prolong Mr. Cline's life prevailed.

"How Long Do You Do This?"—the Family Prompts an End to Suffering: Constance Brady

Constance Brady's family acknowledges that the patient is dying in the midst of procedures that the staff hope will be lifesaving. They have no qualms about interrupting the heroic pathway, and once life-sustaining measures cease, they calmly wait for death. Unlike the medical team, Mrs. Brady's family harbor no apparent ambivalence about death's approach and are most concerned to protect the end of her life by seeking to avoid the "pain and suffering" she has experienced in life.

The activities that comprise life support are never easily defined in

Mrs. Brady's case. In addition, the benefits of the procedures that save and temporarily sustain her life are evaluated differently by different players, for whom different things are at stake: doctors and nurses try to stabilize her condition in the thick of crisis; the patient's pre-illness wishes are paramount in the minds of her husband and daughter; and staff members variously consider the kind of life Mrs. Brady would have after life-sustaining treatments. Whether treatments are administered for too long or too short can only be evaluated after the fact.

Admission to day 2: Constance Brady, age eighty-four, is diagnosed with a ruptured bladder and gallstones when she arrives in severe pain at the emergency room. Her family is clear that she does not want to be resuscitated in a life-threatening emergency, so "Do Not Resuscitate" is written in her medical chart as soon as she is admitted. She immediately has surgery to repair the bladder. The following day she has a massive heart attack, and the DNR order is modified on the spot by the medical team without notifying the family, as frequently happens, so that lifesaving drugs can be administered. According to an ICU nurse, "Her DNR order was changed to a 'pharm code.' That means if her heart stops, they'll give her medications, they just won't do CPR or pound on her heart.[18] But they will treat a myocardial infarction. That's what you do." Shortly after the heart attack Mrs. Brady is moved from a medical ward to the intensive care unit.

Day 3: I arrive at the ICU to find a great deal of activity around Mrs. Brady. A physician, a nurse, and two respiratory therapists are furiously attending to the now unresponsive patient, giving her oxygen through a face mask and administering intravenous medications, all the while monitoring machinery and discussing among themselves her precarious condition and how best to treat it. But it is not clear to all the members of the health care team whether this is the kind of "life-threatening emergency" that Mrs. Brady or the family had meant when, before the heart attack occurred, they chose, in principle, "no resuscitation." Mrs. Brady required these treatments to survive. Taken together, they are not, technically, cardiopulmonary resuscitation—yet they are cardiopulmonary support that enables her to survive, and they include some of the drug treatments that accompany a resuscitation procedure. The medical team work to preserve Mrs. Brady's life without resorting to full-blown resuscitation. They are attempting "to save" her life at the same time as they are drawing a line between lifesaving procedures following a heart attack and unwanted resuscitation during or after a cardiac arrest.

After Mrs. Brady is stabilized, the notes that staff members write in her chart are the first indication of the difficulty in defining whether the specific treatments given were life support and in knowing, precisely, what the components of unwanted life support are in her case: "Acute respiratory and cardiac decompensation. Required intravenous volume, dopamine, assisted external ventilation. . . . Conservative treatment as per family and patient request."

Day 5: Mrs. Brady became comatose today, and the medical team agrees that her prognosis is poor. She has been moved to a bed on the medical floor and is receiving a routine morphine drip to ease her breathing and reduce discomfort in preparation for her death. The question of whether Mrs. Brady received wanted or unwanted, authorized or unauthorized life support two days ago is pondered differently by different people. Her family physician of thirty years tells me that she has had a living will for ten years. She does not want heroics. The document itself is at his office—he has neglected to put it in the medical chart. He describes her as a remarkable woman who stoically endured many years of terrible arthritic pain before this hospitalization. She did well for about twelve hours after the bladder surgery. Her myocardial infarction was treated aggressively. "It was her husband who said, 'Let's stop this,' and I agreed. Sometimes it's hard to resist everything that's offered here. I expected her to die forty-eight hours ago. I'm surprised that she's still breathing." He is glad the family said stop to the pursuit of life-sustaining measures, but as the family physician, an outsider to the lines of authority in the ICU, he stood clear of taking a stance about whether to proceed, and for how long, with heroic measures. A nurse who has been caring for Mrs. Brady gives me a different, simpler summary of events: "Her advance directives were ignored. She was treated aggressively for five days. That shouldn't happen." This outraged medical floor nurse is the only member of the medical team who is not ambivalent about the kinds and the extent of Mrs. Brady's treatment.

Day 6: I sit with Mrs. Brady's daughter at her mother's bedside. She is waiting for her mother to die. She speaks easily, though not about her mother's medical condition, her desire to forgo aggressive intervention, or whether her wishes were respected. "This is very hard. I expected her to die immediately after being moved from the ICU. But she's so strong, she hasn't died yet. This is perhaps the best medical care she has ever received. I wanted her to have something, the morphine. She's had so much pain, excruciating pain, for thirty years. I wanted her to be pain-free now. She isn't allowing herself to die because she doesn't think her husband can take care of himself. I've been talking to her, over and over, telling her that it's okay to let go, that I'll take good care of him now. Don't worry. You can let go now." Mrs. Brady's daughter sits at the bedside for eight hours, until her mother's breathing slows and finally stops. Her mother's death is inevitable and nonproblematic.

Four days later: The ICU nurse who was part of the team working furiously "to save" Mrs. Brady after the heart attack wants to review the events leading up to her death. She tells me that Mrs. Brady's husband and daughter wanted to stop all treatments and the daughter had asked her, "How long do you do this? How long do you continue to do this invasive care?" Taken aback by the questions, the nurse tells me she replied, "Sometimes we stop if we feel we can't do anything else. Sometimes we keep going and the patient gets better. Sometimes we keep going and the patient dies anyway." I learn that the intensive care specialist and the family physician were persuaded by the daughter, or agreed with her, that treatments should stop. The cardiologist, however, was extremely reluctant to halt the vasopressor medications because, he noted, the heart takes longer to recover. According to the nurse, he said, "We need to give the medications a couple of days to work." But under pressure from everyone else, he relented. The nurse turned off all the machines. But Mrs. Brady rallied and began to breathe on her own. She was moved out of the ICU Wednesday but didn't die until early Friday. The nurse continues, "I wonder, maybe if we had kept her on vasopressors longer, for another forty-eight hours, her brain would have perfused better,[19] and she would have woken up, gotten better. We were trying to avoid the situation of having her be a convalescent-home patient, which nobody wanted. She didn't want that. But it seemed at the time, the best thing to do was discontinue the medications."

Three weeks later the ICU nurse is still pondering the way events unfolded, and she is still unsettled, wondering if the team, if she, did the right thing. "I worked really hard that day when we were still doing everything to keep her alive. I went home and said, 'What I did was wrong. I, we, shouldn't have done all that.' But the next day, when we decided to stop everything, I felt that what I did that day was right, to discontinue all the tubes and everything." She reiterates that the cardiologist had not wanted to stop treatment. "But after the husband had said stop, and we talked about it, and he's made that decision already, we just can't go back and keep things going." She rationalizes the team decision, prompted by the family, to stop lifesaving treatment. But she remains troubled about their actions. When we speak again months later, she still wonders whether Mrs. Brady would have lived—and would have lived a life considered acceptable to herself and her family—if the team had persisted with their life-sustaining care.

When the Patient Is in Charge: Walter Cole

The story of Walter Cole provides a stark contrast to that of Norman Cline. *What Mr. Cole wanted* is consistently kept in view by family, friends, and the health care team and, importantly, remains central to deliberations about what to do. Everyone at Mr. Cole's bedside sees his will to live and then seeks out and is at pains to interpret his shifting positions about what forms of life support he will accept. His hospital course provides one example of how patients change their minds when an only-imagined future becomes the embodied condition.

Admission and week one: Walter Cole is forty-five years old and has advanced AIDS. He has been fighting the disease for a decade and has had many medical treatments for its recalcitrant opportunistic infections and terrible symptoms, but he has never before had a life-threatening infection. A friend brings him to the hospital when, after weeks of getting progressively weaker, he develops a high fever. He is diagnosed with dangerously low blood pressure, respiratory failure, pneumocystis, dehydration, and a variety of opportunistic infections. A friend says that in the months before this hospitalization, Mr. Cole has had a sense that "things might be terminal soon." He has been quite sick before, but now he feels different and is afraid he might be dying.

Mr. Cole wants aggressive medical care and will consent to being resuscitated if that is necessary to keep him alive and if there is reasonable hope it would restore him to his previous ability to function. He wants to live. He is an actor and a playwright, is active in his church, and is surrounded by many friends. His doctor of several years talks with him extensively the day he is hospitalized about whether he would want a breathing tube if necessary. He does. He is designated a Full Code and is being treated aggressively for all his acute medical problems, but his medical problems are not responding to the drugs, and he needs an oxygen mask to breathe. He speaks less and less frequently and with growing effort and cannot move from his bed.

Week two: When Mr. Cole imagines the future, he still considers mechanical ventilation and resuscitation as potentially useful interventions—if they would bring him back to a life he wanted. Several of his friends take shifts and stay with him night and day in the hospital. For the hospital staff, the friends' round-the-clock presence and commitment to caring for Mr. Cole shape his social persona and his will to live and extend the reach and power of his weakening voice. The friends work hard to interpret and then to express, exactly, what he wants in terms of continued treatments. Like many critically ill but conscious individuals, Walter Cole knows what he wants only up to a point, and so difficulties will arise when his life-threatening symptoms come up against specific treatment and pathway options. When it seems to those observing him that he does not know what to want, his friends are under pressure to interpret his wishes to the staff. One of Mr. Cole's friends tells me, "There was a turn for the worse and things got a little murky. One night he was having extreme difficulty breathing; he was very anxious. The nurse asked me, 'Does he want to be ventilated?' And I said, 'Well, I know he doesn't want to be kept alive by a ventilator. He would want to be put on a ventilator if there was a reasonable prognosis that he could then come off the ventilator. Not just be sustained by it.' He'd been saying, yes, he does. But then he said no when he was in such distress. So I wasn't comfortable saying absolutely yes or no."

Week three: Mr. Cole has told his nurse that he does not want the ventilator, but his condition is deteriorating rapidly and she is worried. Every time she tries to turn Mr. Cole, the oxygen in his blood desaturates to a dangerously low level. He is still a Full Code. If he can't get enough oxygen and stops breathing, she will have to call the team to perform emergency CPR and intubate him. She does not want that to happen because she knows it will be a violent way for him to die. She is positive he would not survive a resuscitation attempt. She calls the critical care doctor in an effort to change the patient's code status from Full Code to No Code. The critical care physician arrives immediately and goes to Mr. Cole's bedside.

"Squeeze my finger if you want to go on the ventilator." Mr. Cole does not squeeze. The doctor repeats his request and again there is no response. "What about CPR?" Mr. Cole shakes his head no. The doctor tells Mr. Cole that his blood pressure is dropping and he isn't getting the oxygen he needs. He asks him a few more questions to make sure he is alert. "Raise your right arm. . . . Good. Squeeze my finger. . . . Good." Then the doctor says, "We'll give you what you need to stay comfortable," and goes to the nurses' station, where he writes "Do Not Resuscitate" in the patient's chart. The nurse is visibly relieved. Mr. Cole has expressed a clear opinion, and the physician has acted on it. The nurse and doctor talk for a few minutes about increasing doses of medication for pain and anxiety. That afternoon I ask the nurse what she thinks would have happened, had Mr. Cole been intubated. "He would have survived," she says, "but then there would have been no end, because we wouldn't be able to get him off, and he isn't getting any better. It would have made things go on longer."

The medical team decides to replace his simple oxygen mask with a BiPap mask. Later, his primary doctor reflects on Mr. Cole's changing stance toward life support: "At that point, we began to see some ambivalence on his part around how aggressively to treat him. As he failed to improve despite multiple changes in his medications, adjustment in the medication for the pneumocystis, additional tests, a pulmonary consultant, the whole bit, he modified that decision for intubation because he realized he may very well die on a ventilator. And he chose not to go on a ventilator, and not to want CPR. And I was very supportive of those decisions because I think it would have been a torment to be on a ventilator. And so he was in this rather precarious position of maximum oxygen support, maximum pressure support [via BiPap], the equivalent of being on a ventilator, but not on a ventilator. But he was able to respond to people. He was able to nod, to talk a little bit, and he was able to mouth words."

The following morning at ICU rounds the physician on duty for the day says, "He's in a gray zone really. Still getting that drug for pneumocystis, still on BiPap. It's not really comfort care." One of the nurses agrees and tells me, "He's being treated actively for the pneumonia, but we won't do other aggressive things." Mr. Cole's primary doctor comes up to the ICU to talk with Mr. Cole's friends, who are becoming increasingly responsible for speaking for him as he gets progressively weaker. The doctor feels there is at most "a five percent chance" that Mr. Cole can get well enough to go home, and the doctor wants "to go for it." Mr. Cole's friends agree that she should treat the pneumonia aggressively. The doctor orders a new drug.

Week four: Almost one month into Mr. Cole's hospital stay, there is still no improvement in his overall condition, and he is growing weaker. One of the ICU nurses explains to me that he has "an incredible hurricane of oxygen going into him through the mask—thirty liters," but he still isn't getting enough air to maintain life. The doctor decides it is time to talk to Mr. Cole about stopping treatment, and she wants as many people as possible present at the bedside when she has that conversation.

I enter Mr. Cole's ICU cubicle with the doctor and the patient's brother and friends. It is the first time I have been near his bedside. I have never seen so many get-well cards, letters, and photos in a patient's room. One wall is completely covered with cards and notes; another wall is covered with the photos—most of them of Mr. Cole posing with different friends. His vitality and extensive social life tumble into the hospital room, complicating my knowledge of him only as a very sick man, clinging to life and connected to life support.

The doctor pulls a chair close to the bed and takes Mr. Cole's hand. Four of the friends who have been taking bedside shifts are there. The doctor begins by telling Mr. Cole that she has been switching medications in an attempt to treat his various problems, yet none of them are making him better. "So today I'm asking, where are we now? Should we continue being so aggressive or stop? It would be easier if I knew what you wanted. I think the chance of your getting better is getting smaller and smaller. I want to know from you, should I do less or keep doing what I'm doing? That's my question for you and for your friends. But I know you're here and you're the one in charge. I know other problems will come up, and should we be aggressive when they do?" She says these words softly and slowly, aware of their import. She pauses for a moment and then says, "I think I'll stop now. Did you understand what I said?" Mr. Cole, very softly, says, "Yes." The doctor has to put her ear right up to the oxygen mask to hear him. Then she asks, "If we have another problem, and if you need new transfusions, do you want me to treat that?" Mr. Cole does not respond. "Are you getting really tired now?" Mr. Cole remains silent. The doctor tries another tack: "Do you want me to slow the medicines down, slow the treatments down, and let you pass away very comfortably?" The room is silent except for the sounds of the machines. Mr. Cole does not respond in any way. "I don't think you know the answer, quite," the doctor concludes.

The doctor goes on, "Sometimes people come to an understanding that they've tried hard enough, and as much as they want to be alive, they don't want to suffer and struggle. And that's what I want to know, if you've come to that point, if you don't want to struggle anymore. It took you a long time to make a decision about the breathing machine, and you made a really good decision. I've reached a point where I know I've done everything I can medically, and there is no more I can do. I don't know where else to go. But I'm also willing to keep supporting you, just like we have been, to see if something happens." She is silent for a few moments, then puts her hands on Mr. Cole's shoulder. "All of us are okay with whatever you decide. We'll be there for you." After a few more moments of quiet, while everyone watches Mr. Cole, alert for the smallest sign of communication, the doctor says, "I want to let you know that most people know when they are ready to make that decision. I'm going to continue to support you. I want you to know that I can make you very comfortable, if you don't want to struggle, and you won't have any shortness of breath. I can make you very comfortable. And I'm sure that your friends will be here with you. I think that's what I wanted to talk about. I don't want to push a decision—until a decision is ready." The doctor stands and asks Mr. Cole one last question, "So, Walter, for now do you want us to keep doing what we've been doing?" Mr. Cole answers softly, "Yes." Everyone in the room hears him.

The physician walks away from the bedside and says, "I want to thank everyone. It was helpful to have you here. For everyone to hear the same thing. We'll certainly talk in another week, all around the bed like this, for an update." She leaves, and two of Mr. Cole's friends follow her to talk away from the bedside. They tell the doctor how great the entire medical staff has been during the past weeks and talk for a while about whether and how to modify Mr. Cole's anxiety medication. The physician repeats that Walter is in charge, and she is glad that he is. "It's easier," she says, "when the patient is responsive and understands the treatment and will make the decision. A decision will come when it's ready." Mr. Cole's friends express different understandings of his condition. One mentions that he knows Mr. Cole is near the end of his life. Another is not so sure about that and asks if the doctor can say anything hopeful about prognosis.

The day after the bedside conversation: The hospital chaplain assigned to the ICU has had several brief conversations with Mr. Cole, and he tells me, "Walter Cole is a deeply spiritual man, very involved in the church. He has been in treatment for AIDS for over a decade. He is serving God. His agreement is to live to serve God, so he would not make the decision to pass away yesterday. He feels that God will get him through this, not necessarily to health, but perhaps to death. He does not want to assist the process or take death in his own hands."

Week five: As promised, the doctor returns to the bedside for another conversation about ending life-sustaining treatments with Mr. Cole, two members of his family, and his closest friends. "This time," the physician recalls later as she summarizes the meeting for me, "he was a little less able to be there. I was able to be very clear to him that I thought things were futile. I was very convinced it was time to pull the plug. It was time to stop this and he was suffering too much. I was comfortable being clear about it in the room with his friends. I think that was the first time I was ever in a position to tell that to a patient who was so sick. Usually, the patient is unconscious and you are in the room telling the family and everyone else. He was able to say, 'It's time to be comfortable.' That was a real first for me, and I think it was remarkable for everyone. It was a tribute to everyone, his friends, the nurses, and the doctors, because everybody was really willing to help him, and not to drug him so he was unconscious. One of the parts of this that was so powerful, in terms of his end-of-life care, was the ability to be at the bedside with him, as sick as he was, and have him be involved in end-of-life decisions."

One of Mr. Cole's closest friends recalls that last meeting at the bedside this way: "All the doctors had felt that continued treatment was futile. His doctor had definitely earned my faith and trust at that point, and I trusted her and believed her when she said that. Walter was basically not able to really communicate at all, but I felt like he understood. After the doctor gave the synopsis and said that the best thing to do was make him comfortable, he did respond. I asked him, 'Do you want to be more comfortable?' And he said, 'Yes.' That was the one thing that was clear. He had written a durable power of attorney before he came to the hospital: 'If it's futile, I don't want to go on.' So he had said it before. The fact that he was present was so important. They made the decision to put him on a lighter mask so that he'd be more comfortable. And before they did that they upped the morphine. Everyone thought he would die quickly. So, from that point on he was not conscious. That was less than twelve hours before he died.

"He very much wanted to live," Mr. Cole's friend reflects. "He really, really did. And I feel even at the very end, at that last meeting we had, he didn't want to die. But he was ready to accept it. I think he'd come to that even earlier, when he decided he didn't want to be ventilated. When it got to the point where he thought, 'If I go on life support, that's all it is, the hope of recovery is almost nil. So if I go on life support, it's just gonna be keeping my heart pumping and keeping my lungs operating.' When you're healthy it's easy to say, yes, this is what I'd want. It's another thing to be faced with your own mortality and still have the clarity of thought and emotions, and the strength and courage, to say, when you're alone and you can't breathe, 'No, don't put the tube down my throat.' I really respect him for that. Very courageous. I don't think that was in any way a desire to die, or, you know, move things in that direction. He very much wanted to live. But he was ready to accept whatever came. Including death."

Evaluation of the length of Mr. Cole's hospitalization and perspectives on his treatment were mixed. A few days after Mr. Cole died, one of the ICU nurses told me, "They kept that man alive a week to ten days too long." Another nurse said, "It's confusing, a patient who wants DNR but full medical support. I don't think we see that too much. He hung out with sats[20] that were incompatible with life for a long time. But statistically, there was a chance he'd get out of here. That's why we continued treating him aggressively." A third nurse commented while crying, "I only hope there will be that many people around my bedside when I die."

Mr. Cole's doctor and friends worked hard to understand the kinds of life-supporting treatments he would accept. They straddled a line between procedures they deemed to be "tormenting" yet life-sustaining and care that simultaneously envisioned both future life and probable death. The remark by one of Mr. Cole's critical care physicians that "it's not really comfort care" reflected the method used to straddle that line devised by hospital staff together with Mr. Cole's friends. As long as Mr. Cole's voice remained strong enough to express his desire to battle for life, that desire was honored through carefully considered life-sustaining treatments. Respect for patient "autonomy" and "control" in this case meant that Walter Cole was made responsible by friends and doctors for deciding the time of his own death. Cynthia Graf and Jack Carter could not make that impossible choice. Norman Cline tried to take that responsibility but was thwarted and ignored. Walter Cole took the responsibility and expressed a choice, an exceptionally difficult thing to do. Given the value placed on patient self-determination in the American hospital, Mr. Cole's death—in the ICU after a month of life support—was as good as it gets.

A Bookshelf and a Lamp—Dignity as Life Support: Cathy Lewis

Of all the patients sustained by some form of life support whom I have come to know, Cathy Lewis has the most complicated relationship to the systems that support her life because she embodies the most independent form of life. She possesses too much life for the systems of care to handle without challenge. She is and is not near death. She is competent by any standard, is in charge of her affairs and makes decisions, not about treatment but about the conduct of her life. Cathy Lewis's ability to articulate her reasons for choosing life support as she hovers near death is unusual.

The first episode was during a medical crisis when she could not breathe. The second was during her later acute-care hospitalization, when she was medically stable but contemplated suicide as an alternative to continued profound debility and loss. But *life*, even in a very debilitated form and with deeply curtailed agency, won out. When I meet Ms. Lewis, she has once again been forced to the edge of life—not by critical illness but by the institution's safety and fire regulations. Her story embodies a different sort of vulnerability at death's threshold. She is not near death in a physiological sense, but she is aware that the rules of the institution can easily overwhelm her fragile will to live. The bureaucracy of the hospital—the only place that can sustain her life—can kill her by stripping away her sense of dignity. Her need to keep her identity viable has come up against hospital safety rules and she has to be her own advocate. Her voice is strong and it is heard, but she wonders whether it is strong enough to support a purposeful, dignified life.

Day 10: Looking back on her life from her bed in a specialized unit for long-term, mostly ventilator-dependent patients, Cathy Lewis muses on having been sick from the time she was three years old. Now in her fifties, she recounts to me a life of severe headaches, fatigue, all-over body pain, and occasional cognitive impairment, all of which doctors and alternative healers failed to understand. She spent years going from doctor to doctor and to acupuncturists, herbalists, and other kinds of practitioners trying to find a name and a cure for her condition. When she was in her twenties, she began to have difficulty functioning. Nevertheless, she went to college and professional school, lived on her own, and worked full-time as a public-school teacher. When she was about forty, she was diagnosed with lupus,[21] a connective-tissue disorder that can affect any and all organ systems. She tells me, "I have a very, very severe case of lupus. Nobody had expected me to live past maybe five years ago. Ten months ago, my doctor told me I had six months to live. I knew he was speaking the truth in some way, though I knew it wasn't literal. I think I paid attention very carefully to the message that I was in a terminal situation."

For the last eight or ten years, she continues, "it has been one thing after another, one hospitalization after another, walking, not walking, walking on crutches, and then, about four or five years ago, becoming really wheelchair-dependent and not being able to walk at all. Becoming less and less mobile in any way. Going through rehab several times, getting better, stronger, and losing it again. So the pattern became, about two months at home and several months in the hospital. I maintained my apartment," she says, "maintained living alone, which was very important to me, even with helpers. I had to stop working about four years ago and to struggle with Medicare and Social Security to get the money not to work. That's when I started regarding myself as totally disabled. . . . Then, a few months ago, I had the crisis which brought me here, and I knew I couldn't live alone anymore. I knew I needed twenty-four-hour care."

Ms. Lewis has had several previous medical crises, in which she was rushed to the hospital in respiratory distress from lung hemorrhages and placed on a ventilator to breathe and live. "I nearly died two or three times," she tells me. Those crises resolved relatively quickly, and she was always able to resume breathing on her own and return home. But she was becoming more and more disabled by osteoporosis, spinal fractures, and paralysis and numbness in the lower half of her body and was in need of more skilled in-home support. By the time of our first meeting, ten days after her admission, she cannot turn in bed or sit up without help from at least one person. She speaks in a forced whisper through a tracheostomy. For most of the day she needs the forced air of the mechanical ventilator in order to breathe. Her long course of lupus has affected all parts of her body, all of her organ systems. She has recurrent lung disease and serious respiratory infections. She is diabetic. Her kidneys, pancreas, and spleen are affected. Her bones break easily. She has bedsores. She is in pain. Medications for recurrent infections and for pain pour in through tubes in her chest. This and our subsequent meetings must be carefully scheduled during the one or two "good" hours each day when she has the energy to speak and is not being seen by doctors, respiratory therapists, nurses, the social worker, and other hospital staff.

Ms. Lewis's extreme physical dependence is countered by a very independent social demeanor. She sits in bed wearing her own clothes, not a hospital gown. Two tray tables in front of her are piled high with books, notepads, pencils. Her cell phone and datebook are at her side. Several large potted plants are on the floor. A CD player and other objects from home are on a bookshelf. She has created a home office and a homelike environment in this specialized hospital unit. I called two days in advance to set up this appointment with her.

Ms. Lewis's most recent medical crisis left her lungs more compromised than ever before, and her overall condition is extremely precarious. Her story of her most recent brush with death contradicts the assumption, widespread in the medical and the bioethics worlds and in the public discourse, that one can and should "decide what one wants" prior to a medical crisis and, importantly, that one will not change one's mind later. Her words reveal a phenomenology of dying that many analysts and observers of "the problem of death" fail to grasp.

"I had to make the decision, in the moment I was in, really, regardless of my living will, because I was conscious," Ms. Lewis explains. "I had to make the decision, did I want to be resuscitated? Did I want to be intubated or not? I was not able to breathe, but I remember very clearly I was conscious at that moment. The other times, I was not conscious and the doctor made the decision. But this time it was me. And that scared me tremendously. I knew what a big decision it was. I had already been talking with my doctors about this before that moment, weeks and months before. So it was very much on my mind. In the hospital, on the verge of not breathing at all, the doctor got my attention and he said, 'Do you want us to resuscitate?' And in that moment, I just kind of checked inside myself and asked, did I want to live under these circumstances, and probably worse, as time went on? This would be the time to speak up if I wanted to check out. And although I thought that's what I wanted to do, that isn't what I did. I went against my living will and said, 'I want to live. Resuscitate me.' That was a very deep-rooted decision. And I knew it was right at the time. I've had some doubts since then, but at that moment I knew it was the right thing. And then afterwards, I felt like a real coward.[22] I still do somewhat. So now I've been dealing with the implications of that." Nonetheless, she has chosen to remain Full Code. If resuscitation were necessary again and could restore her to a sentient existence, she would want it.

Week five: Ms. Lewis still feels she must justify her choice for self-preservation. She wants to create a life and a home within the medical institution. She knows that this specialized unit will be her last home, and she has struggled to make it reflect her ideas of home and self. She tells me a story about a bookshelf and a lamp that captures her struggle to define her existence. Life itself is at stake in a fight over furniture because Ms. Lewis knows she is in danger of giving up the will to live if her despair becomes too great. "I don't know how much you know about my doings, but I've been involved in some fights with the hospital about what kind of furniture I can have in my room," she says. "There were bookshelves over there [she points toward a now empty wall]. And though I submitted dimensions before I ever bought anything, and they were approved, once the shelves actually got here, they changed their minds and said that I couldn't have them, that they were a safety hazard. . . . I knew there were going to be struggles along those lines because I don't want to be here. I don't like being here. I'm here because I have to be. . . . My pervasive experience here," she emphasizes, "is that I have no choice about anything. And I try to scratch out the very barest mini-mum, like a bookshelf, or like a lamp.

"You can't believe the controversy over this lamp." She indicates a floor lamp within arm's reach of her bed. "People have commented that it makes the room look softer, homier. And I'm glad for that, but that's not why I got it. I got it because I wanted to have some control over when the light went on and off in my room. I thought that was a pretty bare minimum of autonomy, of quality of life. It's generating a lot of controversy, and it might be taken away at any moment. Right now we're kind of in a truce. So I'm trying to figure out if I can live with those kinds of strictures on my life. I don't know if I can. What can I summon up as an expression of myself that will be, at the very least, tolerated, if not appreciated?" She continues, "It matters what I need. What I think. I don't think I'm going to find anything of the medical level of care that I need that also allows me the kind of personal freedom that I want. . . . I remember the moment that occurred to me some years ago, that I never was going to have a private moment again. That I might have a few minutes in between my attendant and my nurse doing one thing or another, but I would never have any significant solitude because I needed help. I can't turn over in bed by myself. I can't sit up by myself. And that's not going to change."

The hospital unit social worker feels a different sort of despair. Caught between her advocacy of a patient's right to self-expression and the institution's rules, she feels impotent in the face of the bookshelf and lamp controversies. She tells me that when she met Cathy Lewis in the acute care hospital where she had been resuscitated, Ms. Lewis was considering having the ventilator and all medical support removed. She was pondering death as the best possible solution to her condition. The social worker wanted to offer Ms. Lewis an alternative in the form of a place where she could, perhaps, realize some sort of meaningful life while she inevitably declined. The social worker gave Ms. Lewis a vision of a future in which she could be herself and create a life for herself. After a short period of ambivalence, Ms. Lewis nervously accepted the offer. The social worker was pleased when Ms. Lewis agreed to try to "live" on her long-term hospital unit. But the safety rules trumped the social worker's ability to advocate on Ms. Lewis's behalf. "In retrospect," the social worker tells me, "I should have brought up all the safety issues before she moved in here. But then, if she knew up front that she couldn't have her personal things, she would have chosen to die instead."

Cathy Lewis has other stories about loss and life support. When she moved to this long-term-care institution, she had to relinquish her doctors of many years because they do not work in this city. "I had to give up all of my doctors after many years of putting together a team. People who could work together and people who I could work with. And now, overnight, they're gone. And I had no choice about it. It's been very upsetting that I had to change doctors in order to stay here. I had worked with those doctors for a long time, and they really knew me. To their credit. And now I have to do that all over again—if there's time. I don't know whether there will be or not."

Ms. Lewis is trying to live. "I don't know what the future is," she acknowledges. "The doctors tell me that I'm medically stable, but I don't feel stable. I feel that anything could happen at any moment. . . . I live with that every day. Or several times a day. It's the paradox of time that in one sense, I have all the time in the world. I don't have to get up and go to work. In another sense, my time could be up any minute. I can't count on living very long. But I don't exactly know what that means."

Eleven months later: Death has come for Cathy Lewis. The social worker tells me, "She fought so hard. She didn't want to let go for a long time. She talked with me, the chaplain, and other staff here about her fears about death. The activity therapist, especially, guided her on a journey through dream and art therapy. Finally, she felt she had arrived. That weekend she went into respiratory crisis, respiratory failure. We had to move her over to the acute care hospital to treat her. She never made a decision to give up support. She simply went into a respiratory crisis and died." One of the physicians who cared for her during her long stay says, "We gave her eleven months. Our goal was one year. We gave her the best possible life she could have."

Life support consists in the ways hospital treatments are interpreted and employed by those at the bedside, and it is linked, always, to how those players respond to the patient's condition. Families may drive the decision to continue life-prolonging measures, as the stories of Earl Morrison and Norman Cline illustrate, or families may call a halt to the heroic pathway, as did Constance Brady's family. Interpretations of the patient's *suffering, dignity,* and *quality of life* (or lack thereof) are foundational to understanding and then negotiating what to do. Sometimes those terms are used, by staff or family, to stop aggressive treatment; alternatively, they may be used to promote life-prolongation. I observed both kinds of scenarios. In addition, patients' own expressions of what they feel and want vis-à-vis life support may be heard but ignored (Norman Cline), may be sought and respected as a guideline for medical action (Walter Cole), or may reflect an insoluble struggle between the necessity of self-determination for survival and the reign of bureaucratic logic (Cathy Lewis). Finally, patients (or their families) may change their minds during a hospitalization about when to start and stop life-sustaining measures, or about which measures they will accept, for example, when their health deteriorates or when pain alters their desire to live. Life support is informed by the competing pressures of religious faith, self-determination, the power of the heroic pathway, and other characteristics of institutional logic that are brought to bear on the question of what to do, and it is enacted through the politics and rhetoric of the patient's condition. The ways in which it is negotiated are a significant determinant of how dying and the time for death are made. The mutable nature of life support, together with its deep cultural roots in both the promise of high-tech medicine to restore life and the pervasive assumption that death can be forestalled and probably should be, provides one more complex reason why hospital death is so troubled.

8

HIDDEN PLACES

The Zone of Indistinction as a Way of *Life*

> "'Life' is problematic today because new understandings and new
> technologies that are involved in giving it a form are producing
> results that escape the philosophical self-understanding provided
> by both the classical world and the Christian tradition. No new
> political or ethical vocabularies have adequately come to terms with
> it either."
>
> Paul Rabinow
> *French DNA*

Specialized hospital units, such as the one housing Cathy Lewis, are
designed primarily for the long-term maintenance of patients who
hover at the zone of indistinction. They provide a marked contrast to
the acute care hospital, yet they are, in some sense, a logical outcome of
the routine practices that take place in acute care institutions. The specialized places enable extremely impaired people to *live* via life-
prolonging/death-defying medical care for long periods. The striking
feature of these units is that, there, movement stops and bureaucratic
time neither guides health professionals' work nor constrains family
options. Time and its management are not important in the ways the
acute care hospital's bureaucracy demands. Waiting, too—as an activity
essential to movement or as an obstruction to movement—is irrele-

vant. These institutions are invisible to the general public and are one, perhaps inevitable, result of the way the contemporary acute care hospital is organized around the convergence of intensive care medicine, the mechanical ventilator, the feeding tube, the fact that something can always be done, and patient and family "choice." The units are the result of decisions to sustain life—decisions made, usually, while the patient is in the acute care hospital, most often in the ICU. When a patient has been stabilized, but cannot *live* without life-sustaining technologies, she is sent to one of these institutions. There, death is brought into life in a myriad of ways.

The long-term consequences of the stabilized condition, death-brought-into-life, are revealed in the day-to-day activities that characterize the work of health professionals in the unit and in the kinds of connections that unit staff and families forge with patients. The long-term stabilization of a person at the zone of indistinction elicits many kinds of responses, and watching the care of long-term, minimally responsive patients reveals anxieties, medical goals, health professional responsibilities, and familial relationships that are somewhat different from those that characterize acute care medicine and shorter hospital stays. The responses to long-term patients and the dilemmas their existence sometimes creates for those who care for them show an additional range of ways in which *life, death,* and *the person* are organized through medical routines. The *impossible choices* that families face in the acute care hospital are replaced in these units by *impossible conditions,* conditions that are simply the result of a decision to sustain life. Just as the hospital's impossible choices have become routine, so, too, have the units' impossible conditions.

In these settings of long-term maintenance, the terms *suffering, dignity,* and *quality of life* circulate, as they do in acute care, to describe and evaluate patients' conditions and to locate responsibility for patients' futures. Yet in the unit the rhetoric surrounding those terms is evoked far less frequently as a vehicle to propose and rationalize death. There, interpretation of those terms is framed not by the pressure to move things along, but by the fact that *the person* can be maintained at the zone of indistinction (seemingly) indefinitely. When ascribed to the patient's condition, *suffering, dignity,* and *quality of life* are evoked to control and arrange death only if someone wishes to change the routine.

I. THE SPECIALIZED UNIT:
ROUTINES WITHOUT PATHWAYS, *LIFE* WITH NO END

"My kind of thumbnail position is that the unit exists because, for the majority of patients, somebody either made no decision or made the wrong decision at some point in time during treatment. And so I have not seen any reasons, from the intellectual and fiscal end of things, for what we are doing. From the emotional end of things, I mean, I totally understand. I couldn't—just randomly—say, 'We're going to pull the plug on all these patients.'"

Nurse manager of a specialized hospital unit

The specialized hospital unit I observed is five blocks from a commercial center, and it houses scores of people in some form of long-term or permanent comatose condition. Patients there embody the shadow side of the demand for "death with dignity." They do not die, yet they cannot live without technological support. Many of the patients are without higher brain function, and most people consider them to be unaware of themselves and others. They are fed through tubes that can allow their bodies to thrive for years. Many are connected to mechanical ventilators that enable them to breathe; others have tracheostomies to ease their breathing and prevent choking. About one-third of these individuals are in what is called a persistent vegetative state (PVS), the result of trauma or degenerative disease, and many of them require respiratory support to survive.[1] The rest suffer from a variety of other medical conditions, mostly severe or end-stage metabolic and neurological disorders or acute injuries resulting in lack of sufficient oxygen to the brain. Not all patients on the unit are in a permanent coma or persistent vegetative state. Some are severely impaired or unconscious as a result of strokes or other neurological diseases. A few patients are conscious, cognitively intact, and can speak and use a wheelchair but need mechanical ventilation to breathe.

This particular hospital unit opened in the 1980s with three patients. By the mid-1990s, it reached its full capacity of thirty-two. In 1997, the year I conduct fieldwork there, the unit expands to care for almost sixty patients—whether chronically comatose or conscious but ventilator-dependent. California has about forty-five hospital units similar to this one. During my fieldwork, I learn that because the medical and nursing attention, along with the technology, are excellent, people in such units can "live" without higher consciousness, connected to breathing machines, tracheostomy tubes, and feeding tubes, for a long time. In 1997 the average stay for patients in a comatose condition on the unit I am observing is five and a half years, and two patients have been in a vegetative state for fifteen and seventeen years respectively. About once a year, I learn, a "wake-up" patient is able to leave the unit and go home after extensive rehabilitation. In the decade since this unit opened, only four families have decided to withdraw ventilator support from their comatose relative, thus allowing the patient to die.

Hospital units and freestanding institutions that house persons permanently tethered to life support are recent inventions. Medicare and Medicaid pay for them and consider them cost-effective. In 1983, when Medicare began to reimburse acute care hospitals based on each patient's diagnosis, rather than on the actual cost of care,[2] it became unprofitable for hospitals to keep patients on ventilators for more than a few weeks. Some long-term-care hospitals that focus on chronically ill patients were exempted from those Medicare rules, enabling the creation of hospitals specifically for ventilator-dependent, chronically ill patients, and the number of centers caring for such patients has grown over the past two decades. In California, MediCal (the state Medicaid) created specialized units for ventilator-dependent patients in 1987. The primary incentive was that such units were more cost-effective than intensive care units in acute care hospitals, and thus they provided an economically viable option for housing and treating persons whose biological lives had been "saved" by the mechanical ventilator in combination with other technologies but could not be sustained without the continued support of such mechanisms.[3]

Patients who do not die in acute care hospitals but do not recover enough to survive without the kind of technological support that only an institution can provide are eventually moved from an ICU to one of the specialized, long-term units. While no one deliberately keeps their existence a secret, and while the buildings that house them may be architecturally freestanding, the specialized units are entirely internal to the hospital system and thus remain hidden from general view. Generally, one is referred to such a unit from the acute care hospital; people infrequently enter them from home. Doctors and discharge planners inform families that these places exist and make arrangements for moving patients to them. Federal health care financing arrangements, along with a system of referrals internal to the hospital world, together with the culturally assumed *need* for this kind of care, all form an environment that sustains people at the zone of indistinction.

The mere existence of these specialized units creates a mandate for ensuring the maintenance of life. After all, these are *hospital* spaces, entrusted with the delivery of the best possible medical care. These units are places of order and routine: monitoring patients' vital signs and treating their diseases, making them comfortable (if that is possible and can be known), and providing them with sensory and occupational stimuli and social interaction. Yet these are also experimental spaces where medical knowledge is tried out on an unusual patient population. A great deal of time and energy goes into micromanaging comatose patients' bodies, which are no longer self-regulating. Metabolism and respiration do not automatically happen and cannot be taken for granted; normal physiological functions are both produced and regulated by virtue of detailed and ongoing staff surveillance. The comatose patient's voice is silent. Any patient resistance to institutionalization or to strategies of life-prolongation cannot be perceived by the medical staff or by families. Any distress those patients experience about their existential condition is unknown to others. All activities performed on them take place without their complete awareness or consent. Thus while great energy and attention are spent on knowing and normalizing the body and making it comfortable, the person's experience of being maintained in the zone of indistinction in the specialized unit is never revealed. Family or friends become the vehicle through which patient experience, past and present, is interpreted.

These units emerged from social and economic conditions in which respirator technology, the politics of health care financing, and conceptions of need, individual patient rights, autonomy, and choice all converged. The units, in turn, have created multiple effects. For example, knowledge about the relationship between normal physiology and disease is extended through clinical care practices. A new kind of patient population and new kinds of persons are produced on these units, both through the specialized care routines and through the kinds of questions that are asked about comatose and minimally responsive patients: Does the person have subjectivity (an awareness of himself as a human subject in relation to other subjects), agency (the ability to act reflexively, intentionally, and meaningfully in the world), and/or self-identity (a knowledge of who he is in the world, a sense of others, and the ability to distinguish between the two)? The relationship of subjectivity to agency, especially, is pondered in discussions about the end of life and quality of life. Debates about medical responsibility and patient and physician autonomy are further complicated by the day-to-day staff routines that allow *persons* in the zone of indistinction to thrive. The specialized units foster a new kind of medico-cultural inquiry because the diseased bodies in need of regulation are also vulnerable, dependent persons. Those bodies/persons elicit—at least among those for whom the existence and purpose of the units is seen as surprising—a reconsideration of the meanings of social and technological progress and of medical goals in the service of that progress.

Here, the zone of indistinction is laid bare. If both *death* and *life* can be prolonged indefinitely in the comatose body, thus collapsing death and life into one amorphous category, what is the framework for defining either? And if, as anthropologist Marilyn Strathern suggests,[4] the grounding function provided by facts about the cessation of life—e.g., the end of "natural" respiration—has been destabilized by use of biomedical technologies, how can activities that prolong life, or death-in-life, be construed as moral?

Living and Working on the Specialized Unit

The specialized unit feels to me like a cross between a hospital (because of the equipment and presence of medical staff) and a nursing home (because the patients are long-term and handmade blankets are on beds and personal photos and drawings are on the walls). Yet the ventilators' constant whooshing and intermittent beeping and the somewhat tangy smell of recirculating secretions that they produce both permeate the unit and mark it as utterly different from any health care institution I have ever visited. The combination of staff, too, does not resemble that of ordinary hospitals or nursing homes. Physicians are not ever-present and their voices do not dominate the day-to-day routine. Nurses—mostly licensed practical nurses and certified nursing assistants or patient-care aides—in particular take great pride in patient care. Many have worked here for years and like working here. Patients' fevers and infections are treated immediately. Bedsores rarely develop and are ameliorated rapidly when they do appear. Nutrition is adequately maintained by scrupulous surveillance of caloric intake and weight. Muscle tone and flexibility are monitored through exercise and movement regimens. The nurses' work is distinguished by the relentless jobs of washing the many unresponsive patients and adjusting the positions of their bodies, removing secretions from their tracheostomies and giving their medications through tubes. A recreation therapist works one-on-one with patients to provide sensory stimulation to those who are comatose and to engage alert patients in expressive or interactive projects. Respiratory therapists go from patient to patient, assessing their breathing capabilities and working with them to extend their hours off the breathing machines. "Quality of life" is mentioned more often than "dignity" or "suffering," but none of those ideas appear to guide the daily routine.

The specialized unit is a home for some, a place where nursing and medical routines combine with other aspects of living, whether or not the patient experiences, acknowledges, or appreciates them as such. For others the unit is the last stop, a place to reside or be housed (depending on your point of view) for the duration of the final decline or until the rare decision is made by family to remove ventilator support and let the patient die.

I am able to discern four types of patients here.[5] First, there are the elderly (both comatose and alert) with lung disease and multiple chronic conditions who would have died following an acute respiratory condition except that they were put on mechanical ventilation and medically stabilized. Now they can never be removed from the ventilator and could reside in the unit indefinitely. Second, there are younger patients in some state of unconsciousness or partial consciousness. A traumatic accident (usually a car crash) or brain injury has brought them to the unit, where they may reside for years. Third, there are patients with degenerative neurological diseases such as multiple sclerosis or ALS who are ventilator-dependent and in the final stage of their illness. Finally there are patients I would characterize as being in some sort of higher-level-of-awareness limbo. A trauma to the brain had plunged some of them into unconsciousness. Over months, they regained enough consciousness to be somewhat responsive and expressive, yet their functional capabilities are extremely limited (some cannot sit up by themselves) and their previous identity seems lost, destroyed, or questionable. Their engagement with the world seems a thing of the past, and they are dependent on the unit for their existence and for the hope of any further recovery.

One woman in her eighties with lung disease has lived on the unit for years, simply because no one is available at home to assist her with tracheostomy care. She comes in her wheelchair to holiday parties and other gatherings in the activity room, watches television in her own room, and is visited often by many small grandchildren. A man in his thirties, thrust into some kind of minimally conscious state by an automobile accident, is described by several staff as having a "good quality of life." Lying in bed, connected to a ventilator and a feeding tube, his face becomes animated whenever someone approaches and talks to him. He smiles broadly at jokes, enjoys closing his fingers around someone's hand, and is thought by all to have a "delightful" and "upbeat" personality. "He likes to flirt," the nurse assistants tell me. His parents dote on him, and his "health" is good—the nursing staff say he "is strong" and has never had an infection. He has been lying on his side, with closed eyes, for more than a decade. A homemade blanket covers him. The radio beside his bed is always tuned to soft rock music, and photographs of his family are on the wall. His half of the two-person hospital room is his personalized bedroom.

Between the completely alert elderly woman and the extremely neurologically impaired young man are patients with varying degrees of brain impairment. The sister of a patient who had been in a car crash the previous year comes about once a week to do physical therapy exercises with him to prevent his muscles from stiffening and limbs from contracting. She thinks her brother would recover enough to return to some sort of functional life if only he received more intensive therapies from the staff. He has been in this unit nearly a year by the time I meet him. A physician and a nurse both tell me that the sister simply does not understand, or believe, the permanence and severity of his condition and that he will never recover as much function as she hopes. At the time of my visits, this patient has both a tracheostomy tube and a feeding tube. He has to be moved by others from his bed into a chair because he cannot initiate, apparently, any gross body movement. When sitting upright, he opens his eyes, though he does not direct his gaze or respond when the nurses who come to do his daily care greet him and joke with him or ask him to do basic things such as straighten his legs or lift his head. To my astonishment, he is much more alert and animated when his sister visits. He looks straight at her and smiles broadly. When he sees her standing outside his doorway chatting with me, he beckons her with his index finger and has a playful look in his eyes. But he cannot speak or otherwise communicate, nor can he move his limbs at his sister's request. It is extremely difficult for me (and for others) to assess the extent of his ability to control his body and act with it in the world. It is impossible to learn the degree to which a sense of self is embodied in him. Yet a family member's presence triggers an expression of consciousness.

Staff also tell me about one young man with Down syndrome, cardiac disease, and a seizure disorder who "cheers up everyone on the unit" with his sunny personality. "He has so much love and he boosts the morale of the staff." His lungs are severely damaged, and he cannot come off the ventilator. Nevertheless he is alert, communicates actively, though in a simple way, with everyone who enters his room, feeds himself, and is able to move around the unit with his portable ventilator. His precarious health is sustained by repeated trips to the acute care hospital's ICU whenever he has an infection or cardiac problem that brings him close to death. His family has designated him Full Code. The medical staff have told the family more than once that a resuscitation attempt may "save" his life, but it would also further impair his heart and lungs and worsen his cognitive status. That prediction has not caused family members to change their minds.

Resuscitation would be attempted on most patients on the unit, should their condition become life-threatening. For these already severely neurologically impaired patients, a resuscitation attempt could restore the heartbeat, but it could also further diminish alertness. Only about one-fourth of these patients are designated No Code or No CPR by their families. I ask several nurses if they could pinpoint any feature of the patients or their families—age, religion, ethnicity, immigrant status— that in their opinion determined or influenced the decision to designate a patient No Code. They agree that no demographic or easily identifiable cultural features typify that group. Nor do any medical features point to a particular code status choice. The No Code designation, they tell me, is simply not predictable.

Because patients reside here for months and years, families that remain connected to them and provide physical care and emotional support develop routines that contribute to the character of the place. The son of an old and alert ventilator-dependent man sits at his bedside, suctioning his tracheostomy and reading a Chinese newspaper aloud while also humorously bantering with the Chinese-speaking staff. He has quit working at his family-owned restaurant to drive for an hour to the hospital twice a day to visit his father.

The middle-aged father of one patient had, at one point, attempted to care for his son at home in their rural community but could not manage. The patient, a man in his thirties who had a brain aneurysm several years ago, needs a great deal of nursing care and ventilator management. He might reside on the unit for the rest of his life. His father comes to the unit almost daily to do physical therapy exercises with him.

Spouses and parents of several patients are here daily, or at least frequently, making every effort to discern and then communicate to staff their patient's food choices or movie preferences, need for a better bed, for more sensory stimulation, for different medication, and the like. Some are very informed about infections or ongoing medical care problems and discuss possible solutions with the doctors, nurses, social workers, and respiratory therapists. Spouses and/or parents can be seen hovering by one or two of the bedsides, requesting that "everything be done" to keep their relative alive, including repeated resuscitation attempts and trips to the intensive care unit to stave off death. Other patients have relatives or friends who come to the unit to sit by their bedside briefly only once a week, once a month, once a year. At least a third of the patients never have visitors; yet even these patients' families make "choices" for them from afar. California state law requires that families choose whether their relative should receive a flu shot once a year (most say yes), and the institution sends an annual letter to relatives requesting them to review the patient's code status. A social worker tells me that when a family member decides against a flu shot, it is a sign to her that they may be starting on the long road toward terminating treatment. It may be a year or more, she tells me, between the passive choice of "no flu shot" and the proactive decision to remove the ventilator and let the patient die.

As in many other urban hospitals in California, many languages are spoken in the unit. In addition to English, the patients' native languages here include, Chinese, Portuguese, Spanish, Tagalog, Thai, and Vietnamese. Licensed practical nurses and patient-care aides are African-American, Filipino, Chinese-American, and Euro-American. Physicians, nutritionists, and therapists are fewer in number than nurses and are less ethnically diverse. Among the staff, philosophies about life-prolongation vary considerably, but among the nurses one theme seems to dominate:

"Leave these people alone. Let them live. They are not bothering anyone. Leave them here to live this way." One licensed practical nurse who has worked with comatose patients for several years tells me, "You have to have a very special heart to work here. It's so sad. Who are we to decide? It's for God to decide, for the family to decide. We don't like to talk about it." When I ask another nurse how she could work in this place so many years, she replies, "Yes, it is depressing to work here. But this is charity work. Somebody has to take care of these people. Someone has to do it." Other nursing staff think it is wrong, in an abstract moral sense, to keep comatose patients who require ventilator support alive. Yet they also feel there is a job to be done, and they are committed to caring for the patients. One nurse told me that, in her opinion, about a third of the patients here have "quality of life." They can converse at least to some extent, and they have expressed a desire to be kept alive on a ventilator.

Physicians who work on the unit express to me an entirely different view. They speak of their discomfort about participating in prolonging lives that, for the most part, to them, have "no quality." They tell me they would not make this kind of choice for themselves or for their family members. Yet one physician, who spends more time on the unit than the other doctors and thus knows individual patients better, points out to me that certain patients, especially those who are cognitively aware, do indeed have a "good quality of life." He cites routines tailored as much as possible to their level of awareness, relatives who visit often, and, for those whose attitude can be discerned, a feeling that the unit is "home."

Daily Maintenance

I accompany one of the nurses on her daily rounds as she medicates, suctions, washes, repositions patients. She chats and jokes with the patients the entire time. She has worked on the unit for several years and knows her patients as individuals. When she approaches each bed, she greets the patient, asks how he or she is today, and announces what she is going to do. When the patient moves—either engaging or recoiling from her touch—she responds verbally, calmly.

I watch as she moves one large though slim man from his bed to a chair, a complex activity and, I think, full of suspense. She positions his inert body in a sling by sliding its fabric under him, then moving and rocking him back and forth until he is properly positioned on it. With full concentration, she hoists him into the air with a pulley, then lowers him into a sitting position in the chair. This accomplished, I am relieved. The patient does not appear to be tense and seems to stare blankly across the room while being moved.

The nurse tells me something about each patient as we move from bed to bed and room to room. "Fred Jackson was in a car accident four or five years ago. He gets medication for muscle contractions. His room-mate was hospitalized because of a drug overdose. He gets Valium for seizure activity." She crushes some tablets and puts them with water in the stomach tube. She tells me, "I have to use my judgment about how much water to give. I'm going to give him a little extra today." At another patient's bed: "He understands what you say to him. Sometimes he puts out his hand or finger and tries to stop you. Sometimes he is in a bad mood." She asks the man how he is feeling and he responds by thrashing in the bed. "Are you in any pain, are you in any pain?" As she pours water in the gastric tube bag hanging from the IV pole, she says, "I'm going to give you some water, are you thirsty?"

When we approach the next bed, she says she is going to try to suc-tion this man quickly because he does not like it. "But who does?" she adds rhetorically. He is "light" to suction, she tells me. I watch as she inserts a slender, long tube into his throat at the tracheostomy site. It makes a slurping gurgle, similar to the sound of the little tube that suc-tions water from one's mouth when one is in the dentist's chair. But this is much louder. The entire task takes about one minute. When the suc-tioning device is in the patient's throat, his face contorts and turns red and his entire body stiffens. It is a hard procedure to watch. The nurse talks to the patient through the entire process, saying, "Good job, good job." White liquid, foaming with bubbles, comes out through the tube. The nurse repeats the procedure three times, rapidly. Then she thanks the man and tells him he did well. His face and body relax completely. Only when the procedure is over do I become aware of the sounds of a talk show coming from the bedside radio, of the large posters—scenes from parks—on the walls around the patient's bed.

Perpetuating the Zone of Indistinction: The Persistent Vegetative State

A physician who guides me to some of the patients' rooms explains that most in this section of the unit are in a persistent vegetative state. That means, he tells me, that they have periods of being "awake" and "asleep." Some of them can track with their eyes, but none of their move-ments is purposeful, and they do not actually respond to human contact. Then he describes other patients who, though not clearly aware of their surroundings, are "somewhat more alert and awake" than those in a "completely" vegetative state. There are also patients who "are locked in" or who "may be locked in," that is, they can comprehend their situation and can respond if they so choose, perhaps by moving a finger or their tongue, but they cannot move their body or talk.[6] There are also "gray areas," he tells me, mental and bodily states that medicine has not been able to categorize, areas that stand somewhere between complete uncon-sciousness and partial awareness. But the inability to neatly categorize those states using airtight definitions does not bother clinicians in their day-to-day work. They are more concerned with delivering optimal care and with understanding what the patient would want, if he or she could speak, than they are with precise diagnosis.

One nurse on the unit expresses others' views as well when she explains that patients have "a kind of spark. There is a response of some kind." They have a "glow," and they have "light." She tells me she tried to "scientifically categorize" the patients when she first began working on the unit, in an attempt to get to know them and their condition. "When I first started here, I had a little logbook, and I'd walk around and make rounds, and I had five categories of awareness, and I was trying to get the patients set in my mind, so I would give them a number—1 being no response and 5 being totally aware. And it kept fluctuating. Depending on the time of day that I went around. And the medical director asked me what I was doing and I told him, and he just kind of smiled. And after about a month of doing it I gave up because there was no rhyme or reason to it. It didn't seem like there was, or I could not put people into categories. Try as I might, I couldn't do that. And he [the medical direc-tor] saw that my book was gathering dust in the bookcase and he said, 'So, you gave up your categorizing the patients.' I said, 'Yeah, there's no way to do it.' He said, 'Well, I was going to tell you that the first day, but you need to learn some things on your own.' And that's just the way it is. Because you'll get a patient who, there's no movement, there's no reac-tion at all. And then you'll have to do something which is obnoxious, like start an IV or something. All of a sudden you'll get a response, you'll see something you didn't see before. Or, you speak their name and you get a little startle reflex that you didn't see before. There's definitely something. Every patient has something, no matter what the diagnosis. They all have some human quality."

In medical science the self is always identified with consciousness,[7] but how much consciousness is needed to be a person, to be alive? In the context of American society and medical practice, to invoke the idea of the person is to involve the notion of consciousness. Rooted in the modern Western philosophical tradition, the implication of consciousness in defining *the person* is unavoidable and fundamental. While contemporary medical science stays away from defining consciousness and personhood in any abstract or philosophical sense, it "locates" consciousness[8] in the neocortex, where, using the techniques of neuroanatomy and neurophysiology, we are able to identify the presence and absence of neural activity and neocortical function.[9] The Multi-Society Task Force on Persistent Vegetative State, a group of physicians from different medical specialty fields and organizations, published its definition of PVS in 1994, distinguishing among states of unconsciousness.[10] Since then, the idea of consciousness—whether it is present, to what degree, and how it can be located, observed, or known—has been debated for medical conditions that involve impaired brain function.

"Persistent vegetative state" has been described in the medical literature as a "clinical condition of complete unawareness of the self and the environment, accompanied by sleep-wake cycles with either complete or partial preservation of hypothalamic and brain-stem autonomic functions. . . . The distinguishing feature of the vegetative state is an irregular but cyclic state of circadian sleeping and waking unaccompanied by any behaviorally detectable expression of self-awareness, specific recognition of external stimuli, or consistent evidence of attention or intention or learned responses."[11] It is also further characterized by "the loss of all higher brain functions, including awareness, feelings, and the capacity to suffer. However, the brain-stem and hypothalamic activity necessary for prolonged survival continues, so that such patients may survive for years or even decades with artificial feeding and, when necessary, cardiopulmonary support."[12]

The Multi-Society Task Force on PVS clearly and neatly distinguishes that condition from "coma." It characterizes both conditions by unconsciousness, that is, by "global or total unawareness." However, patients "in a coma are unconscious because they lack wakefulness and awareness. Patients in a vegetative state are unconscious because, although they are wakeful, they lack awareness." In coma "the eyes remain closed, and the patient cannot be aroused."[13]

Yet things are not so simple. Both the straightforward description of PVS and its simple distinction from coma in these descriptive statements have been debated and challenged since they were published. The issues of consciousness, futility, and fear of "terminating life" are especially recalcitrant in those debates.[14] The diagnostic criteria of PVS and coma are said by clinicians to be problematic, and thus the fear of misdiagnosis is ever present. Studies have raised questions about prognosis and the length of time needed both to make an accurate diagnosis and to define a case as beyond recovery.[15] Ethicists, lawyers, and others criticize the definitions in the medical literature for their lack of coherence and their moral ambiguity.[16]

Patients characterized clinically as being in a gray area of awareness are also situated in a gray area of clinical and scientific understanding. A study of the attitudes of neurologists and medical directors of nursing homes regarding the care of patients in persistent vegetative state reveals disagreement about, first, whether patients in PVS retain awareness, and if so, how much awareness they have, and, second, whether they should be considered dead.[17] These study findings are unsettling because they reveal confusion about the nature of consciousness and ambivalence about what constitutes the *person*. Chosen because they were considered to be among the clinicians most experienced in the observation and treatment of unconscious or minimally conscious patients, the study subjects reported contradictory assessments of consciousness and personhood. Though persistent vegetative state is characterized in the medical definition by lack of subjective awareness, a substantial minority of the participating physicians believed that PVS patients experience pain, thirst, and hunger, that they have some awareness of self and environment, and that they can be made more comfortable by the administration of food and fluids. On the other hand, almost half of the physicians considered PVS patients to be dead.

Physician ambivalence about consciousness and about life itself was reflected in the attitudes expressed about treatment. One-third of the study subjects felt that patients in PVS who had infections, diabetes, hypertension, or other diseases should be treated for those conditions. Four-fifths of those surveyed thought it would be unethical to give PVS patients a lethal injection; yet most thought it would be ethical to use the PVS patients' organs for transplantation, even while they were still considered, by definitions established by medical science, to be alive.[18] The advances in clinical care that have enabled the prolonged existence of patients who are minimally conscious or nonresponsive have not addressed the questions of what constitutes consciousness or personhood.[19]

The role of the law in interpreting medical actions to produce legal definitions of states of being is only beginning to be explored regarding states of minimal consciousness. The authors of one report, "'Near PVS': A New Medico-Legal Syndrome?" review definitions and criteria for diagnosis of vegetative conditions and agree that there is no medical consensus about the criteria encompassing the PVS spectrum. Nor are there criteria to guide diagnosis in patients with minimal consciousness who fall outside PVS.[20] That lack of medical consensus has fostered a new *legal* recognition of an intermediate category between PVS and locked-in syndrome, known as *near persistent vegetative state,* or "minimal" cognitive capacity. In two court cases, two medically different patients—one *near* PVS with minimal cognition, the other with PVS and no cognition—were treated the same by the courts, and both were allowed to die through the withdrawal of life-sustaining treatments. The report authors show how medical categorization is subject to legal decision and conclude that "a new class of patient has emerged, and has been endorsed by the courts without any medical consensus from the medical community."[21]

Invoking the Person

In the specialized hospital unit, the weekly staff discussion of individual patients serves as a laboratory in which the careful scrutiny by staff creates and maintains a version of health for the patients. Each patient is discussed once a month. The medical goal on the unit is to keep the patients as healthy and stable as possible. This is done by using the skills of the entire health care team in the ongoing management and careful monitoring of patients' bodily systems and, to the extent feasible, of their consciousness, cognitive status, emotional well-being, and social life on the unit. In these weekly meetings, a given patient's body, mind, and self are all assessed, with the aim of reducing acute disease and creating and maintaining viable physiological function, emotional equilibrium, and a web of active, appropriate family concern. *Health,* always a relative and slippery term, becomes even more confounded in this setting. Without question, this place keeps people as "healthy" as they can possibly be, if health is understood to mean sustaining biological life and if health stands in opposition to death. If, however, health refers to a disease-free state, or the (relatively) unimpaired functioning of the body's organs and systems, or the ability to be entirely self-regulating, then many patients on this unit lack health.[22]

Yet, in a day-to-day practical sense, health *is* achieved here. To maintain physiological norms, a great deal of time and energy goes into the detailed management of the body's systems. Most bodies on the unit are no longer *natural,* that is, they are no longer self-regulating—metabolism and respiration do not happen automatically. Ordinary functions must be produced for patients by ongoing staff surveillance. Staff carefully monitor patients' cognitive and emotional states as well. They give anti-depressant and other mood-altering medications if they think such intervention might stabilize or improve a patient's mood or make the person less agitated or more calm. Feedback about those medications is difficult or impossible to discern, and staff sometimes question the worth of anti-depressants for mostly or entirely unresponsive individuals. Yet psychotropic medication is considered part of a complete therapeutic armamentarium that may help the patient's well-being.

As with staff/family interactions in acute care hospitals, staff who work in the specialized unit want to be kept informed about what continued treatment the patient and family want, especially in the case of patients who are declining toward death. When a patient's mental and physical conditions worsen, it is especially important for staff to monitor the family's level of knowledge about the decline in the attempt both to avoid what is considered to be futile treatment (and resulting potential litigation) and to facilitate timely and necessary conversation about how best to acknowledge and prepare for death. All patients' immediate family or close friends have an open invitation to attend staff meetings when their relative or friend is being discussed. Few come at all; some are there consistently.

At such meetings, staff and family queries range from the practical and immediate (Should the patient be given more or fewer calories through her feeding tube? Can the family bring in an acupuncturist? Would a different kind of bed be better? Must he be in a restraint to prevent pulling out a tube? Can you have her sitting up in a chair when I come to visit?) to the more difficult and long-term (recreation therapist to staff: "Can we put him on a portable ventilator so he can leave his room? He's so depressed. Should we try antidepressants?" Physician to family: "Your son can never come off the ventilator. If we need to resuscitate him, he'll have less brain function afterward. Have you thought about this?"). More complex assessments are taken up as well, occasionally in great detail—whether, for example, a patient at the end stage of a disease wants "to go on like that," or how to communicate with absent families about treatment, or how to stop what staff perceive to be requests for nonbeneficial treatment. At the end of the report on each patient, the nurse manager gives a brief summary plan for the next month.

In cases where consciousness seems remote or mostly absent, *the person* is invoked primarily through discussion of the body and its regulation. While some emotional trace, for example, a smile or a show of pain, is helpful in revealing something of the individual, it is not essential for the determination of personhood. That can be done through discussion of the largely passive body and the challenges of keeping physiological systems stable and free of infection. The health care team regulates and normalizes patients' bodily processes and systems *at the same time* as it creates persons. In this place, what is knowable and what is important to know about the health of the body, of the person-in-the-body, and of the person/patient in the family and in the hospital are discovered and made in the daily routine and in the shared forum of the team meetings.

Patient #1

Nurse: No changes.

Recreation therapist: No changes. He does have periods when he's calm, smiles, and doesn't resist. You just have to catch him; it's not any particular time of day.

Nutritionist: His weight is up a little high, since May, and he has ongoing constipation. Shall we give him more water? Or just watch it?

Nurse: Is he always constipated?

Second nurse: No, he sweats a lot.

Nurse: Yes.

Nutritionist: We'll try that first and see how it works.

Nurse: So, we'll monitor his weight and fluid intake . . .

Patient #2

Nurse: All vital signs stable.

Physical therapist: She has decreases in her left shoulder range, but this has fluctuated in the past couple of months. Occasionally she resists with that arm.

Pharmacist: Is she in pain?

Physical therapist: She doesn't indicate, but she would look at you.

Recreation therapist: She would indicate.

Physical therapist: She was really alert, up in the chair, smiling.

Recreation therapist: She is really aware that she's in a new room.

Nurse: They have these periods of sleep/wake. And we try to assess when. Sometimes they resist. Sometimes they're flaccid, depending on their sleep/wake cycle. [Discussion of the patient's "subluxed" thumb: whether to exercise it; whether to make a modified splint for it.]

Physical therapist: Her thumb is really contracted. You can only get the thumb out a little bit.

Nurse: To keep her hand really clean she needs a shower, but we can't do it daily. . . . She's stable as far as nutrition goes. We'll monitor skin, weight, thumb, and the skin around it.

Patient #3

Nurse: No significant changes.

Recreation therapist: Her eyes are open but she does not track. She has facial grimaces or sometimes she moves her hands toward her face. She continues to need sensory and social stimulation.

Chaplain: I've always sensed that she's frightened of me. I've never made contact. I stay back.

Nurse: I get that impression also.

Pharmacist: We start the folic acid this month.

Patient #4

Social worker: It seemed to me that he got more alert and was smiling more in his new surroundings [this patient was recently moved to a different room].

Nurse: He was really responsive to me for the first time in ten years. I asked him how he liked the room and he smiled and nodded.

Recreation therapist: Maybe he likes having a private room.

Nurse: I don't know if it's the paint or the newness or the light or how it's set up.

Second nurse: From his new room you can see activity, you can see people, and you're not so isolated.

Recreation therapist: I was just concerned that he was in a room by himself. I wanted to monitor that—is he at risk for social isolation? Maybe he doesn't like to be alone.

Chaplain: I get the opposite reaction. When I go into the room, he looks to the other side, and when I walk over to the other side, he looks the other way. [Everyone laughs.]

Physical therapist: There have been some increases. There is less resistance now and he is letting people work with him. I went in there right after he was moved in and I was so surprised. He was almost smiling.

Patient #5

Nurse: She's still kind of sick.

Physician: Do you know what her urine output is?

Nurse: [Goes to get papers]

Physician: It looks like she was going into multi-organ failure.

Nurse: [Reads some numbers]

Physician: She has a stone, positive blood culture. Dr. [X] talked with the family about making a decision not to transfer her to acute care. She has gram-negative sepsis, probably from the kidney. But as long as she's making urine . . .

Nurse: Her output is tea-colored. [She reads numbers from different nursing shifts.]

Social worker: The family is very attentive. They are very hands-on, sweet. Some come in the morning; some come after work. It's a devoted family.

Recreation therapist: She's not opening her eyes or responding. So whatever we had achieved, which was ever so slight, has decreased.

Nutritionist: She's generally tolerating her tube feeding pretty well despite all this.

Social worker (to physician): Should we or you have a discussion with the family? Are they clear on what's going on?

Physician: The family is clear about what's going on.

*   *   *

The weekly conference is an important event and process where existence of and potential for self-awareness and responsiveness are analyzed through pragmatic concerns. Bodily systems and functions are tinkered with so that life can be maintained whether or not one believes that *life* in such a condition can be lived at all.

Person, Illness, Progress:
The Unit's Most Malleable Categories

Beings who are comatose straddle and obscure the boundaries between living and dead, organic and technological, artificial and natural, challenging the way we think about person, illness, and progress. Those latter three notions are reworked, played with, and negotiated on the specialized unit through the knowledge made and the practices employed there. Permanently comatose individuals only leave that state through death—which is uncommonly sought and can be technologically and clinically avoided. Perhaps comatose beings on such units are works of what anthropologist Claude Levi-Strauss called bricolage.[23] He used the term to describe the ways in which myths are constructed in preliterate societies by the unsystematic pasting together of fragments brought together by chance. Anything available—ideas of the cosmos, knowledge of the environment and human behavior, historical events— is used to explain themselves and the world. On the specialized units, fragments—of technologies, health care financing arrangements, societal discourses, and kinds of bodily care—converge and are incorporated into daily routines in new ways. Health professionals and families take what they know about life, death, and the idea of *the person* and use that knowledge to explain a particular medico-cultural world to themselves and to cope existentially with what they are implicated in creating.

The activities surrounding permanently comatose beings are a cultural experiment in ways of knowing and defining what *a person* is. In a society where the individual is free to create and fashion the self and, in fact, where identity depends on reflexive self-fashioning,[24] *meaningful life* is powerfully linked to the ability to express, to tell to others, the important facts about oneself. George Herbert Mead, Michel Foucault, and others show us how the individual self in European and North American societies is understood as both object and subject to itself.[25]

Self-determination arises because the individual can distance itself from itself. Relationships, events, and social and historical processes are considered external to the self, which is seen to be freestanding and autonomous. The self is intentional and conscious and not identified with the physical body. It has the potential to disengage from society in order to be truly free. These qualities support what it means to be human.[26] These pervasive assumptions are forced into relief when we consider the condition of comatose beings. In the practices that enable and surround comatose patients, the ideal, freestanding self is juxtaposed against the permanently passive body for which autonomy, freedom, or expressive intentionality are not possible. This juxtaposition of older, tenacious ideas against new practices and life at the zone of indistinction confounds some and provokes comments such as the one by the nurse manager that opens section I of this chapter.

Nothing is resolved on the unit. That is, no new, acceptable image of self and person emerges to encompass both the distinct self of modern philosophy[27] and the tethered-to-technology and thus tethered-to-society being that is located in specialized hospital units. Only uneasiness about the disjuncture exists, yet that uneasiness infrequently raises pragmatic questions about medicine's goals on these units—for the view that medicine provides is that humans can overcome nature through the application of scientific discovery and through sheer perseverance.[28]

It is well known that chronic illnesses confound medical science and frustrate its practitioners because, in most chronic cases, action does not result in movement toward positive resolution and the features of sickness cannot be overcome. Yet perseverance is important both as a means to try to postpone or thwart further decline and as a symbol of hope for eventual medical progress. The permanent comatose condition is the chronic illness that most profoundly perplexes medicine. First, because perseverance has no actual or symbolic payoff, and, second, because the patient offers no possibility of insight and psychological development.[29] In a society where the self is dependent on its own constant creation, insight regarding one's condition, and the articulation of "self-knowledge" and "personal growth" gained as a result of the condition, are considered essential for "living with" illness. Yet unlike most persons with long-term chronic conditions, the comatose patient is not self-interpreting. He or she cannot work on the self and cannot objectify the self in order to participate in and react to treatment. The condition is not experienced phenomenologically, and thus comatose patients do not "live with" the illness. On the specialized unit, it is the social features of illness—such as concern, empathy, responsibility, and interpretation of *the person*—rather than any patient's autobiographical features that are underscored, and they determine the unfolding of events, including the time for death. Medical care persists, but it is both removed from its goals of cure and amelioration and severed from its role of contributing to the modern autonomous and reflexive self.

The notion of progress in medicine has been seriously challenged by the call for "death with dignity" and the rejection of technologies thought to interfere with "natural" death, cause pain and humiliation, or reduce "the quality of life" during its final days, weeks, or months. Comatose beings in specialized hospitals challenge the idea of progress as well, but for an entirely different reason. Technology is still desired; but although the most modern technologies and care practices are employed, *nothing happens.* There is no movement along a pathway and usually no change for the better.

To be sure, notions of scientific progress figure prominently in the hopes some families harbor—hopes they express in their commitment to a comatose patient, as we will see in the stories that follow. Yet for other families and for some health practitioners, as we shall also see, the use of technology is visibly and daily unhinged from progress. Although the technological imperative continues to guide action in the service of high-quality clinical care, that imperative no longer acts as a foundation for what is right.

This challenge to a historical and far-reaching assumption is one important source of the ethical dilemma surrounding keeping persons— bodies—suspended for years in a condition neither fully alive (that is, having subjectivity or agency) nor dead. Clinical staff members who are committed to high standards of care, especially the use of technology to solve problems, but who disapprove of their own participation in creating and maintaining beings in this gray zone, are extremely aware of the source of their own ethical quandaries. Clinicians on the unit act as bricoleurs: they employ the parts of the system they know well (technology, natural science, mechanistic explanation, and the management of systems) to shape a story with which they are familiar—the delivery of excellent medical care. Having done so, although the patients they treat may never improve, their own practices remain justifiable.

II. THE SHADOW SIDE OF "DEATH WITH DIGNITY"

"Death is not a thing or event existing independently of human consciousness; it is simply the word given to a certain threshold, inter-
face, space, or point of separation."

David Armstrong
"Silence and Truth in Death and Dying"

Each time I walk through the unit, learn something about the patients,
speak with staff and follow them on their routines, I receive a lesson
in how *persons* at the zone of indistinction are made, loved, and cared
for. And I see how the gray areas, which medical science cannot adequately articulate, become central to clinical, social, and moral practices
surrounding long-term comatose conditions. The following stories of
Sylvia Sato, Maureen Peterson, and Paul Lenczyk represent, by extension,
the stories of thousands of socially invisible people who hover in impossible conditions. They present a contradictory companion piece to the
demand for a straightforward patient- and family-controlled end to life
and end to suffering, a demand that exists, I found, mostly in abstract,
hypothetical conversation. The growth of hospital units to house and
technologically sustain such patients, along with the human energy
devoted to their care, are testaments to the power of this shadow world.
I learned from spending time on the unit that the discourse about "death
with dignity," though widespread, is not everywhere; nor does that discourse begin to capture the anguished sense of moral responsibility that
accompanies deciding, proactively, to end a life.

"This Is My Responsibility and My Obligation"—Faith in the Immutable *Person:* Sylvia Sato

Sylvia Sato, age sixty-five, has resided on the unit for five years. When
I first meet her and her husband, she has been in a vegetative state for
one year. Her husband's sense of duty guides his unending hands-on
care of his wife, and his unwavering hope for a positive outcome to her
condition—via medical discovery, compassionate treatment, or his own
participation in ensuring her survival—guides events and the ways in
which Mrs. Sato herself has become "known." "They should treat
patients with compassion, like human beings," Mr. Sato tells me.

My knowledge of Mrs. Sato comes from conversations with her husband, social worker, chaplain, and respiratory therapist, as well as from the medical chart and weekly staff conference. Taken together, those voices define Mrs. Sato for me, creating a biography-in-illness. They also articulate the fuzzy boundaries of *a person* and how ideas about the person guide pathways of care. Just as reproductive technologies have altered older kinds of knowledge about how and when life begins, who controls that process, and what a family is, so, too, has respirator technology, along with the clinical skills surrounding it, muddied notions about the *normal* cessation of life, *natural death,* and the meaning of personhood. What becomes clear to me on the unit is that everyday acts of treatment, care, and compassion are what illustrate, and thus define, both medicine's goals and family responsibility vis-à-vis *the person.*

Ten years before we met, Mrs. Sato was a healthy woman who worked full-time as a legal secretary and had a rich life with her husband, children and grandchildren, siblings, and their families. Overnight she became entirely paralyzed and was diagnosed with a "spontaneous cervical cord hemorrhage," according to the medical record. For the past decade, she has required institutional care to survive. For the five years she has been in this unit, her husband has come three days a week, twelve hours a day, to sit with her and assist the nurses with her care.

When Mrs. Sato first arrived, although she was quadriplegic and required respirator assistance through a tracheostomy tube to breathe, she was completely alert, had learned how to talk, and was able to communicate effectively. The year before we met, she suffered a "traumatic event," according to the hospital staff with whom I spoke, went into respiratory arrest, and a code was called. Paramedics found her "mottled and cyanotic[30] and unresponsive," her medical chart reveals. They stabilized her condition with drugs and then transported her to the acute care unit. Two days later, when she was awake and alert, she began to have seizures of unknown origin. When the seizures stopped, Mrs. Sato was unresponsive. The medical chart reads, "Her condition was consistent with a vegetative state. . . . Discussion with the patient's husband resulted in the decision for a No Code, but a decision about withdrawal of therapy was not made at this time. It was decided the patient would be returned to subacute care and she would have continuous supportive care but no resuscitation and no return to acute hospitalization. . . . There is no potential for rehabilitation." Mrs. Sato never regained consciousness. She has been physiologically stable but unresponsive ever since.

Mr. Sato's story of his wife's current condition is framed by the history of their strong marriage, their family life and work ethic, and his all-encompassing sense of duty and responsibility for her care and continued life. He tells me, "Well, since she had the seizure, I'm taking it that she might come back. I didn't lose my faith in her not coming back . . . I'm just hoping and praying that it'll just be a matter of time, that she'll come back and things might be a little bit normal again, to the way she was. But, no, I haven't given up any hope at all. . . . We've been married since 1957. That's a lot of years that you don't give up. And when you made your marriage vow, you said in sickness and health. That should mean something. That's the way I feel. So you can't give that up. It's hard for me to do things right now because we've always done everything together, even grocery shopping and window-shopping, just to be together, because both of us, we always worked too hard. . . . We never thought we would ever end up like this. We never made plans for life support, anything like that. The doctor told me right after she got the seizure, 'What are you going to do when we get to a certain point?' And it's hard to answer. I have to live with it. And that's a bigger burden than what I'm doing now, I think. I just couldn't give an answer. . . . I don't wish this on anybody, but I think it's all part of life. Some people have it good, some people have it hard. Some are in more tragic condition than I am, because I still have her."

It is impossible to pinpoint an essential motivation for the kind of "choice" Mr. Sato, or any other family member, makes when faced with a relative who cannot survive without life-supporting technologies. His response to his wife's condition emerges from his responsibility within his marriage as well as a lifetime of experience forged by particular historical and cultural circumstances. Mr. Sato was one of many children, raised on a farm. His family did not own the land, they rented, and Mr. Sato worked long hours as a child picking crops. His wife came from a farming community as well. For three years during the Second World War, he and his family were interned in a camp for Japanese-Americans in the Southwest, which he referred to as a "concentration camp." He described that experience without bitterness or strong emotion; it was simply part of his youth—he was thirteen years old when first interned. The camp was set up like army barracks, with latrines and bunks, he said,

and there was an "ordinary" American school. He didn't understand anything about the circumstances, he said, and he often had fun—for example, when he went to movies set up in an outdoor amphitheater. "You
know," he told me, "we were good Americans. We said the Pledge of Alle-
giance every day." His wife was interned at a different camp. They met
much later, after the war.

"I'm not very religious," Mr. Sato told me. "When we were young, we
used to go to the Buddhist church, though we never knew what the minister was saying, because it was in Japanese. We just followed along. Now
I go more toward Christianity, but I'm not baptized or anything. I just try
to be good, to do things right, not to follow a book or anything. Common
sense." His wife was raised Buddhist but was now Protestant, he said.[31]

At the time of the respiratory arrest, heroic intervention saved the life
of Mrs. Sato, who was conscious though severely disabled. When the
seizures two days later put her in a vegetative state, physicians discussed
with Mr. Sato "the option," as they put it, of withdrawing therapy and letting her die. But Mr. Sato would not make such a choice. The acute care
medical staff had broached the subject of termination because they considered her meaningful life to be over, her status as a living person gone.
In contrast, the clinical routine in the unit acknowledges life, though it is
a life that is without subjectivity and is maintained only through clinical
care, ongoing intervention, and medical surveillance. The nurses talk to
Mrs. Sato as if she were a conscious being. Their easy banter with her at
the bedside and their gentle and positive coaxing that she "wake up"
define her as a person, though one who happens to be in a coma. The
nurses' talk may mask a deeper realization about her as not sentient and
about her relative nearness to death, but their actions belie it.

Mr. Sato's unwavering hope and sense of duty define Mrs. Sato as a
valuable person with a potential future, a social being connected by love
and personal history to him and to family. As seen by him in the context
of her life history, pre-illness personality, their marriage, and their family,
she *lives*—a complete, though physically vulnerable, person. Though she
lies curled on her side in a hospital bed, unresponsive and unable to
move on her own, tethered to life support, her eyes opening and closing
seemingly randomly, Mrs. Sato is, to her husband and perhaps to the
nurses, a whole person—in a deep sleep—who may surprise everyone by
simply awakening one day. She is one example of the liminality, the shifting nature of the category "person," that is fostered in this hospital unit.

There is no moral quandary here for Mr. Sato. He feels responsible for his wife's care and acts accordingly through his long days of hands-on, physical assistance. His ongoing hope for some kind of meaningful recovery is rooted in knowledge of the healthy person she once was and, in his eyes, could potentially be again. Similarly, for the unit's staff there is no explicit moral quandary in terms of the day-to-day care for and approach to Mrs. Sato. Their current discussion of her at the weekly conference is perfunctory. Only minor changes in her physical condition, tangible problems in her nursing care, or the anticipation of either is discussed. Her course had been uneventful in the preceding month. The nurse manager describes her condition as "overall stable." The physical therapist reports, "She has a minimal decrease in right hip fluxion." All the other clinicians reported "no changes." The broader question about the focus and purpose of medicine's gaze lies beneath the surface of this daily practice, unacknowledged.

"It Is Time Now to Honor Her Written Wish"—the Mutability of Personhood: Maureen Peterson

Maureen Peterson was sentient, self-interpreting, and wanted to live when she arrived on the specialized unit. Now, nearing death, she is unresponsive. I note that now, even as the parameters of Mrs. Peterson's subjectivity, especially whether she suffers, are being debated, they are also being produced in a manner framed by medical knowledge, the norms of hospital language and practice, and staff and family interaction.[32] Knowledge about Maureen Peterson's "quality of life" and "suffering" has been transformed over her stay on the unit, as it was for Angela Stone, so that her death may be legitimated.

Four years before I meet Mrs. Peterson, she walked onto the unit with a progressive neurological disease, a nurse tells me. A highly educated professional woman in her sixties, she could talk through her tracheostomy and express herself, and she understood that she had a progressive disease that would eventually cause her death. At the time of her admission, she thoughtfully put in writing her wishes regarding the timing of her death. That document (her Durable Power of Attorney for Health Care) is prominently displayed in her medical chart:

"I do not want efforts made to prolong my life and I do not want life-sustaining treatment to be provided or continued: (1) if I am in an irreversible or persistent vegetative state; or (2) if I am terminally ill and the application of life-sustaining procedures would serve only to artificially delay the moment of my death; or (3) under other circumstances where the burdens of the treatment outweigh the expected benefits. I want my agent to consider the relief of suffering and the quality as well as the extent of the possible extension of my life in making decisions concerning life-sustaining treatment."

I learn from no fewer than five staff members, however, that although her written wishes indicate a desire to stop interventions that would only prolong dying, Mrs. Peterson has clearly and repeatedly expressed her potentially conflicting wish to continue life-prolonging measures, even though her condition is becoming worse. She has wanted the ventilator, wanted the tracheostomy, wanted to be kept alive through those measures. Now she is unable to communicate by blinking her eyes or any other actions, and staff are perplexed regarding her desire to continue living in this state of questionable responsiveness. Staff acknowledge that "she is not the same person she was four years ago."

Although Mrs. Peterson is close to death, discussion of her condition at the weekly conference does not anticipate her death but does attend to the need to prepare for it. Her progressive deterioration is described in terms of the irreversible breakdown in her physiological system, especially her inability to swallow, muscle decline, and increasing chest problems. The physician wonders aloud "how much longer she can go on in this state." Most important, Mrs. Peterson is described as "unresponsive" and having "declined" *as a person*. She rarely opens her eyes and seems to make no efforts to communicate with staff or family. Neither staff nor family can interpret what she wants now.

This will prove to be the last conference before Mrs. Peterson's death, but it is not the first time the idea of terminating Mrs. Peterson's life-sustaining treatment has been broached. Shortly after Mrs. Peterson arrived on the unit, one of her children wrote in a letter to one of the staff, "The quality of Mom's life? I've always said that if Mom could not be alive without suffering, I would agree with the decision to end it." Periodically over the years another family member has brought up the subject of withdrawal of life support with the social worker, but "nothing has been done about it." And at least a year ago a sibling expressed concern that "it's cruel to keep her alive in a body that is not able to respond." Now, at this last conference, the wheels are finally set in motion for the family to respond proactively.

Physician: She had a little bloody draining in the ear last month. More important is a gradual and inevitable decline of muscles and an inability to swallow saliva. She can't do that anymore. And increasingly problems in her chest. I don't know how much longer she can go on in this state, but with the care she receives it could be another year or two. It's a gradual, slow deterioration. [Various staff members make their reports.]

Social worker: She's a little more responsive lately. I don't know how purposeful it is.

Recreation therapist: The daughter e-mails once a month to ask, "How is Mom doing?" She appreciates the team conference letters. It was a big deal for Mrs. Peterson when the daughter found her job. We thought she was hanging on for that, but she's still here.

Friend (who regularly attends the meetings when Mrs. Peterson's condition is discussed): She hasn't been alert this whole week. She had her eyes closed during our whole last visit. Her sister wrote me her concern about tears, because she had noticed them. I don't know if they are purposeful or involuntary.

Physician: This has been a problem all along. So we haven't stopped the antidepressants. We don't know how much she doesn't want to communicate with us. Tears under those circumstances, when a visitor is present, seem to be entirely voluntary.

Recreation therapist: On some level she has declined. It's hard to put a definition on it.

Physician: Well, we've attempted to talk about this several times. We just had an annual review. Maybe I should try and call [family member] and see how he's feeling about it. Maybe we just need to get a dialogue going here. Now, at this particular time, at present, is this, now, what she wants? We all know she wanted to be on a ventilator and kept alive. She told us. But we couldn't paint a picture of how this is now. This is very difficult for me because she had always said she wanted to be alive as long as possible. Certainly, the quality of life she has now is not a quality of life most people would want. *(To social worker)* Maybe we should try and get people together to talk about this.

A few weeks after the conference the physician and the social worker succeed in drawing the family together to discuss Mrs. Peterson's condition and their feelings about her wishes to continue *living* in such a debilitated state. Family members' questions about prognosis are answered, but no decision is reached about a change in medical care or termination of treatment and life support. The physician asks the family to put into writing—if they can and will do so—their desire to discontinue life-supporting measures. A few days later the physician receives a letter signed by all the family members who have been involved with Mrs. Peterson during the past four years.

"To Dr. [X]: We, Maureen Peterson's close family, met together on [date] to confer about her current circumstances. We agree that it is time now to honor her written wish not to continue to be kept alive when she could no longer be active in decisions on her own behalf. We would like to have a private room in which to gather for a simple and sacred observance at the time of her release. Thank you for your help."

Two days later, "a time is set" for Mrs. Peterson's death.[33]

For Sylvia Sato's husband the facts about the person she was never changed. Though Mrs. Sato became permanently comatose, his hope and hands-on care both defined her as worthy of staying alive and invested her with a future that included the potential for increased agency. In contrast, for Maureen Peterson's family the "facts" about her changed when they were given medical information about her deterioration and when both they and staff determined that she could no longer indicate decisions or maintain an opinion about her own future. Two revelations shifted the interpretation of Mrs. Peterson from an active, knowing person who wanted life support to a pitiable and deteriorating being who was suffering now because her status as a person was questionable or who would probably suffer as she further declined: the physician questioned how long Mrs. Peterson could remain alive while supported by technology as her deterioration became extreme, and a family member expressed the wish for an end to an existence without agency and an end to suffering.

Of course there is no way that the nature and extent of such a patient's suffering—as both a state of being and an act involving reflexivity and engagement with the world—can be assessed. *Suffering* is often ascribed to comatose patients, yet subjectivity and agency are not. It is as though the person is perceived to be suffering because she can no longer consciously feel or experience. Yet suffering is a feeling itself, and conscious experience is intrinsic to many ideas of what suffering requires. This incongruity is irrelevant to the identification of *suffering* in the context of deteriorating conditions and to family debate about what to do.[34]

Maureen Peterson was perceived to be potentially or actually suffering only when she could no longer express the important facts about who she was and what she wanted, and at that point the value of continued life extension came into question. Her slow decline into a state of unresponsiveness was given context by the alert person who had four years earlier articulated her desire to prolong her life with biomedical support. When her deterioration progressed to the point where staff could foresee her approaching and inevitable death, and staff and family could acknowledge the disappearance of the spark of life and any vestige of an expressive self, an explicit conversation about death could finally occur, and the orchestration of her death could begin. But that particular way of imputing meaning and value, and thus of influencing or determining action, does not hold for all patients. No one spoke of Sylvia Sato as suffering, and her inability to express her *self* after the seizures did not diminish or change her in the eyes of her husband or the nursing staff. Mrs. Sato's lack of subjectivity, her inability to be her own person, was not a catalyst that altered the epistemological frame or created a moral shift from life preservation to death preparation. In the specialized unit, the boundaries of subjectivity and agency are fluid and open to multiple interpretations.

Sometimes, as in the case of Maureen Peterson, a reflexive, aware self is located in the patient. Sometimes, as in the case of Sylvia Sato, it is invested in the patient through staff and family interpretation.

Is There a Person There?: Paul Lenczyk

Occasionally a family finds the specialized hospital unit to be a kind of purgatory—a place that forces into relief their relative's grotesque condition. For such families, the strange person sustained by the institution unmakes their world.[35] They experience a palpably tragic anguish over what to do about their relative, over their quandary about how to construct their own lives in the face of what they perceive to be the patient's terrible state of lost identity in the zone of indistinction, and in their pursuit of a way out of the all-encompassing, all-consuming prison they feel themselves to be in. I watched three families cope with the untenable situation in which they felt trapped. None of them resolved the dilemma of what to do about their relative during my observations. The following story is emblematic of this situation. In it the question of medicine's purpose vis-à-vis patients at the zone of indistinction is brought to the surface and is articulated in a long debate, but medicine's pragmatic response with respect to "what can be done" satisfies no one.

Background: The New Relationship of "the Person" to "Life"

Paul Lenczyk came to the unit six months ago, following a traumatic head injury. I meet his family after a physician called for a hospital ethics committee meeting with them to discuss divergent opinions about his future treatment. I learn that the relatives want to withdraw all Mr. Lenczyk's medical care and life support so that he can, and will, die. The request is problematic because the physician thinks the patient is, slowly, improving. What attributes constitute "improvement" and whether the improvement means recovering the qualities that constitute the *person* can be questionable in the case of severely brain-damaged persons. Those attributes are the source of confusion and debate during the ethics consultation.

The Lenczyk family's request is unusual in this place, where most families ask that everything be done to keep their comatose or severely ill relatives alive indefinitely. The request is both practically and ethically complex. Practically, family members' requests to terminate life-sustaining treatments for patients *who have been comatose for months or years* are welcomed by the medical staff, who are extremely careful to make sure that all family members are in agreement (and who will not proceed unless they are in agreement). Staff expend considerable effort explaining to families what the withdrawal of treatments and technologies will, to the best of their knowledge, be like for the patient. Families are invited to be present at any time during the termination of treatments—when ventilators are turned off, while other treatments are discontinued, for religious services accompanying the dying, for discussions with staff. Each year only a few patients on the unit die as the result of such planning. Each year, most unit patients do not die.

Many discussions about "futile" treatment arise across the United States because doctors know that continuing to support *life* technologically will not, in any way, contribute to an improved condition.[36] Yet family demands for continued life-sustaining care in intensive care units and in specialized hospital units most often trump physicians' knowledge about inevitable physiologic decline and ineffective treatment. The potential always exists for the family to bring lawsuits. The request to terminate Mr. Lenczyk's care is entirely different. He is not entirely comatose—there is full agreement about that—and his condition is changing, medically at least, for the better. From the point of view of discrete bodily systems and specific physiological processes, his treatment is not *medically* futile. Nevertheless, the physician cannot ignore the Lenczyk family's request. She needs support, advice, and discussion about how to proceed.

Ethically, the request is difficult because though Mr. Lenczyk was apparently described in the medical records as unconscious immediately after the traumatic event, his condition has changed. He is no longer *clearly* without consciousness now. He has emerged from deep unconsciousness into a gray area, some kind of partial awareness, and members of the staff see his condition in different ways. The fundamental issue being examined at the conference is the patient's murky ontological status; the discussion highlights that medical science has no nuanced vocabulary and only awkward means for discerning and describing personhood. By what parameters can one approach and define Mr. Lenczyk *as a person* now that he is not in a vegetative state? Without awareness of himself as human, without self-identification and the ability to intentionally act in the world, how, the professionals gathered in this conference room wonder, could his life be meaningful?

Paul Lenczyk's condition provokes concerns about the role played by interpretations of quality of life in authorizing death, about the equation of *personhood* with *life* (and thus the loss of personhood with death), and about what one bioethicist has described as "what has to be lost before a person should be treated as dead." [37] These related concerns emerge from debates about the "higher-brain" versus "whole-brain" formulations of death that were taken up by a president's commission formed in 1980 to create a uniform definition of death across the United States. [38] Commission members' discussions focused on whether the definition of death should turn on the "higher-brain" formulation, that is, some notion of the permanent loss of consciousness, or on the "whole-brain" definition, which emphasized total disintegration of the organism. At stake in the controversy between whole-brain and higher-brain definitions was the question of whether consciousness or physiological integration is the fundamental criterion for human life. The commissioners settled on the whole-brain definition of death, though they never reached a consensus about the fundamental criterion for human life.[39]

Since then, proposals to shift to the higher-brain formulation of death continue to circulate. They result from a preoccupation among some neurologists, transplant surgeons, physicians who care for those with minimal or no consciousness, potential organ donors, bioethicists, and others with *which* brain functions, specifically, are significant to the nature of being human. In these proposals the capacity for reflexive experience (the ability to think, feel, and relate to others) is crucially important to what is significantly human, as is the related idea of personal identity.[40]

The debate about how much loss—of consciousness, personhood, bodily integration, self-sufficiency—is required to declare someone dead, and who should make the declaration, continues both in academic circles and at the bedside.[41] The following opinion, written together with a lawyer in 1987 by a leading clinician in the field of persistent vegetative state and minimal consciousness, expresses the growing emphasis on consciousness as the significant feature of the person, with consequences for declaring death: "Our major premise is that consciousness is the most critical moral, legal, and constitutional standard, not for human life itself, but for human personhood. . . . We believe that the permanent loss of all consciousness is just as significant as the loss of all cardiopulmonary functions (the cardiopulmonary standard for death), and all brain functions (the neurological standard for death), in determining the moral and legal status of a human being."[42]

Is He Suffering? Is He "Fully Human"?

Fourteen people representing different medical specialties and health professions are in the conference room with Paul Lenczyk's sister and brother-in-law, who have requested that treatment be withdrawn. The discussion is grounded in medical science, clinical politics, and the Western philosophical tradition. Once the door closes, we are insulated from the hospital's bustle and noise. The tone grows focused and intense as a tragic and emotionally disturbing story unfolds and envelops us. The physician who convened this consultation opens the meeting by summarizing the events that precipitated Mr. Lenczyk's present, perplexing condition: Six months ago, Mr. Lenczyk fell from a third-floor apartment window. He was taken to an acute care hospital and medically stabilized.

Because he was unconscious and required mechanical ventilation to survive, he was sent here. The acute care hospital records refer to him as "vegetative"; but staff at the long-term unit did not consider Mr. Lenczyk vegetative when he arrived here, as he was making "purposive" moves. Mr. Lenczyk has improved and become more responsive since his arrival. He sometimes acts intentionally. He can follow commands and can even walk with assistance. He is agitated. (It is not clear to me whether the agitation referred to is an emotional state or a bodily symptom of his impaired brain.) A CT scan has been done. He has extensive brain damage and there are no correctable lesions.

At the acute care hospital, the physician continues, the family requested that all life-sustaining care be given to the patient. At the time of his transfer to the specialized unit, the family asked for "no heroics" (no CPR) in the event of a cardiac arrest. Neither request was unusual. Yet now, six months later, the family has requested full withdrawal of therapy, saying he would not want to live *like this*.

The *like this*, in the physician's view, is a *person* showing signs both of increasing mental responsiveness and physical gain. The physician is not prepared to withdraw all therapy, including feedings (thus allowing the patient to die), because Mr. Lenczyk is now improving. The physician says also that the family members cannot act in the patient's best interest if they think he would be better off dead. The physician notes, somewhat ironically, that this is the first time in her long association with the specialized unit that she could not, ethically, withdraw care from a patient when the family requested her to do so. "Usually it's the opposite," she says. "Patients are there for a long time, years, and families want to keep going with care when the patient is comatose and not improving."

After these opening remarks, a free-flowing discussion ensues around the question of *what kind of a person* Mr. Lenczyk is now. How much responsiveness to other human beings and how much sense of self does he have? Are his movements truly intentional? Do they signify reflexive consciousness and the perception of an embodied self, that is, a sense of what one ethnographer calls "presence in the flesh"?[43] A second physician caring for Mr. Lenczyk comments—in contrast to the convening physician—that he has not seen any purposive moves: "Some of the medical chart notes say his movements are purposeful; others say they are not." He also notes that Mr. Lenczyk is no longer ventilator-dependent. "His tracheostomy care is minimal. He may be getting to the point where the tracheostomy can be safely removed, soon, even in the next few weeks." He also says that Mr. Lenczyk is on medication for agitation, and his hands are restrained with stocking tape so he cannot pull out his tracheostomy tube. A neurologist adds that the patient is not able to communicate with language and could have an aphasia[44] from the injury. He has not made eye contact. The convening physician responds that Mr. Lenczyk does make eye contact with the day-to-day staff and that he smiles reactively. "It feels like he follows what I'm saying. I asked him to show me his tongue, and he did."

Another doctor asks about removal of the feeding tube in the stomach. The convening physician replies that no one knows if Mr. Lenczyk would be able to eat, but it seems as though he would be safe without the tracheostomy tube. With traumatic brain injury (as opposed to hypoxic[45] injury), she continues, there is recovery, sometimes taking place over months and years, that cannot be predicted. The patient can continue to improve. The social worker adds, "He does make eye contact, but it's sporadic. The speech therapists have not been able to work out a communication system. He nods yes, slightly, when the doctor asks him to do so. But he's unable to communicate no."

The patient's sister, who has been silent up to this point, directs the conversation to the crux of the ontological problem in a poignant speech. It is she who asks direct questions: Can the patient experience life? Is he a person? She speaks plaintively, and everyone in the room turns toward her and concentrates intently. She guides the health professionals to consider the idea that the patient, whose *full* personhood is questionable, is capable of pain and suffering. These attributes of the patient's self, the sister insists, are still intact. She also articulates her own suffering and loss and her empathic identification with the patient. Some sort of person, or more precisely, some vestige of a person, she argues, may reside in the hospital unit, but her *brother,* as a sentient, relational human being whose qualities of *self* she could identify, is not there: "It seems to me like he's suffering. What can he do? What is his life? I don't know what's best for him—or for me. I don't know what I want really. It's up to God. I've been taking antidepressants these past few months, I'm so depressed about this. All the family has been waiting for God to take him. I don't want to see him this way. He's not alive. I speak Polish and German to him. He doesn't recognize anything. He speaks three languages and he doesn't understand anything. He looks at me and doesn't know who I am. I've lost him. I've been trying to recover from this depression. If I have the authority to do anything, I don't know what I'd do—you have my sympathy, Doctor. He can't enjoy anything. It seems he's in pain."

Doctors and other health professionals, of course, are no better equipped than anyone else to understand or talk about the essential qualities of being human, the existential condition of the patient, or the implications of a patient's loss of capacity to express himself for medical decision-making. The compassion expressed by Mr. Lenczyk's sister, who is visibly "suffering with"[46] the patient, allows her to come closer than the professionals to defining the parameters of *the human* in this case: suffering, recognition, agency. After her speech, only one of the physicians attempts to respond to the open question she posed: *What is it to be fully human, to be a person?* That doctor says, "Looking at a CT scan, he's lost a lot of brain tissue. But will he be able to read? Have a meaningful life? He will improve, but that's about removing the tracheostomy, taking steps. That's not a meaningful life." [47]

The patient's sister continues to articulate what personhood means to her by giving some background information, putting the patient's condition, and the source of that condition, into the context of his life so that those present can understand more fully her request to let her brother die. "He jumped out the window. He tried to commit suicide. He left notes. We are sure about that. He had also tried before. He's Catholic. He had talked to a priest. I wonder if he'd be better off if his soul could go. He can't go to heaven without dying. He left a note asking the Virgin Mary to have pity on him." The neurologist asks another physician if the patient seems depressed at present. The reply, "He's not alert enough so that depression can be noted," only adds to the ambiguity about Mr. Lenczyk's ontological status.

Mr. Lenczyk's brother-in-law attempts to spell out his and his wife's reasoning regarding their wish to withdraw therapies now, six months after the accident. As it is for all families faced with such an "option," this couple's decision is dependent on their understanding of a variety of factors, including the medical condition and prognosis, knowledge of how the patient wanted to live if dependent on technology to survive, and the power differential in their relationship with health care providers. He says, "Since January we were given hope that he may improve, and we didn't feel we had the authority to take out the tube, though the doctor almost asked us. We've never been involved with anything like this before. . . . If there's a chance he can improve and come back to the way he was, that would be incredible."

A physician who has not yet spoken pursues the theme of knowing the patient-as-person by asking, "Can you tell me about your brother?" Mr. Lenczyk's sister replies, "I raised him. He was younger. He was always difficult. I raised him like he was my son. I raised him, though I was young, because our parents were working. He was a very private person. Didn't talk much." The neurologist asks, "Would any of his friends be able to talk about him better?" and then, turning to the psychiatrist, "Does the fact that this happened during a suicide attempt color it differently?" The psychiatrist replies that it does not, and the neurologist's first question remains unanswered.

Another physician quickly summarizes, "I think all the physicians are reluctant to stop treatment while the patient, slowly, is getting better. And the family members here today now seem unsure about whether or not to stop everything." Mr. Lenczyk's sister replies, "If I listen to my brain, I say let him go. But it's painful. I'm between a rock and a hard place. I don't know what to do."

The convening physician attempts to clarify for the family that "letting go" has several components: "There are levels of withdrawal of care. It's progressive. First there is DNR and no treatment of a bad pneumonia. I'm okay with those. He's already not to get heroics. But the next level of withdrawing care involves two things. If you remove the tracheostomy tube, he could aspirate and get pneumonia and then die. And if you remove the feeding tube, he'll die within thirty days." The patient's sister, desperately wanting guidance from the physicians, responds, "If the doctor says this is the time to do it, it's okay. I'd be comfortable with it. But I'm not a doctor. Maybe I'll die before he does. It's very depressing. To begin with, I have no education. I don't know anything about medicine." The psychiatrist interjects, "But if the doctors say he may improve, what would you want?" "I don't know, he seems to be suffering," she replies.

The lawyer present asks the family who would provide care should Mr. Lenczyk continue to live, and a physician adds, "Would you feel better about the decision to keep giving care if he were closer [to where the family lives] and without the tracheostomy tube?" "That's no solution for me," the sister replies. Then, dramatically questioning the protean boundaries of the category *human* that is being invoked here but not pinned down, she says sadly, "There is no hope for him. This way it's terrible, depressing for me. I know he'll never be able to eat or think properly. He'll never be normal. What is he? An animal? I wish the doctor would make that decision for me." The convening physician replies, "I made myself clear. I can't do that now." Mr. Lenczyk's sister responds, "I sympathize with you." The doctor, who seems to me to be growing more sympathetic with the family, suggests a potential solution to this tragic impasse: "I'm willing to wait another month and see if he plateaus and then honor his Durable Power of Attorney for Health Care." Another physician comments to the family, "Then maybe the doctors will do what you request." But the neurologist quickly complicates that possible scenario: "It may take a year to see improvement. That's six months from now."

The physician who coordinates these ethics conferences and keeps track of the time asks everyone to make a closing comment to the family. Contradictions, both about how to proceed and who has the authority to make termination-of-life decisions, are now given voice.

A *medical student:* It seems no one is comfortable now with withdrawing all treatment. If he did reach a plateau, then the doctors would be more comfortable with removing treatment.

The *psychiatrist:* With some improvement we're required to wait and see and watch. I think everyone will feel more comfortable if we wait.

A *nurse:* I think we should wait for the plateau or wait for one year, whichever comes first.

Hospital chaplain: I would tend to wait and see because science is not everything. I would rely on the authority of your faith to give you guidance during this time.

The physician (who has spent quite a bit of time caring for Mr. Lenczyk): I know this is very difficult for you. Every visit I made, he was more capable of doing things, but he was not communicating. But there's been no improvement in the last three weeks. Perhaps this is a plateau, or only a temporary plateau. If the tracheostomy tube can come out, he will be more comfortable. And maybe it will be clearer for you to make a decision. Also if he can be moved closer to you and you can be around him more and learn maybe what he's feeling, perhaps a decision can come more naturally to you.

Hospital social worker: Our job is not to correct an unsuccessful suicide attempt. And that's uncomfortable. We all wish we could take your pain away. It's a regret you'll have to live with, that you didn't withdraw treatment at the other hospital. And now, if a window opens up,[48] and withdrawal seems appropriate, you need to take action, and do it firmly.

Lawyer (who identifies himself as a lawyer and as someone who thinks differently from physicians): I want to clarify that you do have the authority to make a decision. The people in this room can't make the decision for you. The lawyer part of me wants to reassure you that you can make a decision for him.

Another nurse (reinforcing, though specifying, the lawyer's remarks): This is your decision to make. But it isn't *your* decision. It is you speaking for your brother, what would he want? You are not *deciding* for him. You are *speaking* for him. What would he want? *(And then)* We have to work from the [Durable Power of Attorney for Health Care] form. *(She pauses and adds)* I have a concern with waiting. It will be harder for him to die, especially if he can't eat some.

The convening physician: I wanted to reiterate what [the lawyer] said. There is a doctor who will write the orders if you are sure. Personally I can't do it at this time. I can only do it if I feel it is the next thing to do.

Mr. Lenczyk's brother-in-law starts to speak, saying, "It seems that if everyone thinks we should wait—" His wife interrupts, "Let's talk it over. I can't make a decision." The doctor who serves as the ethics consultation coordinator has the last word and says to the family, "I should have said at the beginning and I'll say it now, this is not a decision-making body. That is for you to do after you've talked." He adjourns the meeting.

I never get to meet Mr. Lenczyk and thus can form no opinion about whether there is a *person* there. Even those who interact with him regularly do not know (as was obvious from the talk around the table) the extent to which or whether he is conscious of his own consciousness.[49] That is, can he both think about something in the world and be conscious of his own thinking? Can he act purposefully? Whether his sister can categorize him as a "person," as "human," and as "fully alive" depends in part on the hospital staff's ability to glean that knowledge, which, at the time of the conference, remains unfathomable.

Impossible Solutions

Contradictions and troubled reasoning about the value of living *like this* reigned at the ethics committee meeting. The health professionals seemed to agree that no one in the conference room wanted to discontinue treatment while there was "improvement," yet the convening physician, following the lawyer, told the family they could find a doctor elsewhere who would stop treatment and let Mr. Lenczyk die if they so desired. I do not know if, in this instance, there would actually be a physician "for hire" who would write an order to stop all medical treatment for the patient. It is important to recall that physicians have different opinions and thus different practices regarding treatments (or no treatments) for critically or terminally ill patients. There is no standardized medical approach to the end of life even when the patient's wishes have been clearly expressed. When the patient's *personhood* is questionable, things are more murky. The example of Mr. Lenczyk illustrates not a range of (potential) practices, but rather an unclear stance, the utter impossibility of "deciding" anything that is dependent on clearly knowing the qualities that comprise *the human.*

Mr. Lenczyk's medical prognosis is also murky. The social worker, expressing a different view, felt the family must wait for a "window" of opportunity, in the form of a "plateau," an unspecified amount of time during which no "improvement" was visible. That "window" would signal to them (and to everyone else as well) a morally appropriate moment in which to stop treatment. But how would one know when that plateau arrived? Perhaps Mr. Lenczyk was at a plateau now, as one physician remarked. The doctor who knew the patient best pondered whether it was "only a temporary plateau," however. The neurologist thought improvement could occur, regardless of temporary plateaus, for another six months. The lawyer stressed the autonomous decision-making capacity of the family, yet the gathered health professionals seemed to urge the family to follow the consensus of the group. Finally, a nurse qualified the lawyer's statement and reminded the couple that, according to the intent of the "living will" documents, they are supposed to enact only what *they know* the patient would have wanted *in this condition* and not what they want for him. That is, the family must abide by some hypothetical wish of the patient, not their own desire or the group consensus. Only this nurse raised the concern about the ramifications of waiting some unspecified time before authorizing death. What would it be like, her comment implied, if treatments were withdrawn and no food was given, yet the patient's level of consciousness increased? No one in the room took up that point.

The family knows that Mr. Lenczyk attempted to end his life. On the one hand, his sister does not want to be solely responsible for severing the ties to life of a recovering human being with whom she has the deepest of bonds. On the other hand, if the patient is no longer a person and could not become a person capable of having a meaningful relationship (in her terms), then she wants to allow his self-destruction to be complete, to allow an end to the story he started. That closure would, at least, acknowledge (and even honor) her brother's identity and agency and would complete his life, as he intended it.[50]

What Mr. Lenczyk assumed would be his final act has unfortunately led him to this unit. His sister's suffering results from her awareness that both the patient and she—through her empathy—are entirely dislocated from the narratives of life *and* suicide. She suffers with the betwixt and between patient in various ways: through her empathy, that is, her "suffering for the suffering of someone else";[51] through her own knowledge about the source of the patient's suffering, which must be viewed through the arc of his life; through her expectations for the patient's life *as a particular person;* and through her expectations of what a *life* is and should be like. Once the profound ambiguity of the patient's status as a thinking, feeling person become apparent to her and her husband in the public forum of the hospital ethics conference, Mr. Lenczyk's sister grows too perplexed to authorize—on her own— the completion of the sad story. If her brother's identity cannot be restored or will forever be questionable, she needs others to share her conviction about the appropriateness and necessity of the ending she proposes. Part of her wants to actualize what she knows her brother would want, but terminating treatment will only be ethically tenable for her with the support of the hospital committee or her brother's physician. However, she does not get an unequivocal response to her plea before the committee.

The fate of Mr. Lenczyk reveals that the clinical activities of the unit, while sustaining life, also raise the question of the sustainability and recoverability of *the person,* someone with identifiable features as an agent in the world; for an acknowledged continuity of at least some qualities of *the person* is necessary for patients to be recognizable to their families. But in this unit a patient's living body can exist, as we have seen, without a *lived body*, an embodied self. Some may variously interpret the self of another, when it is perceived to be severed from the body, as being alive, with agency, not human, or already dead. In those cases it is left to the local community of practitioners to come together and attempt, as a group, to define the moral appropriateness of dying, the specific clinical activities that will facilitate a death, and, perhaps most critically, the acceptable timing for ending a life. This particular ethics committee's deliberations about how to proceed in the presence of a troubling being at the zone of indistinction focused on what constitutes ethical practices vis-à-vis sustaining or ending life—and *this particular life*—when the qualities that signify and identify *the person* and *the human* cannot easily or clearly be apprehended.[52]

For some patients who reside in the specialized units, medical care effects a partial transformation—from injured or impaired personhood to a *person* whose subjectivity and agency are, to a greater or lesser degree, discernible yet open to interpretation. The qualities that make a patient with impaired consciousness (and in need of ongoing life-supporting technologies) a *person* are variable, debatable, and imputed, as we have seen in the cases of Sylvia Sato, Maureen Peterson, and Paul Lenczyk. But it is beyond debate that most patients on the specialized unit are *incomplete persons* in need of fabrication by others. This is a place of medical treatment that contains a crucial absence—of patients emplaced in embodied lives. That absence is both minimized and filled in during the day-to-day, routine interactions of staff and families with patients and in health care team discussions about care in which attributes of the *life* and the *person* are both proposed and inferred. For Mr. Lenczyk's sister, that absence is agonizing and intolerable. For us, that absence draws attention to the new relationships among hospital staff, families, persons at the zone of indistinction, and the larger hospital system that allows and fosters survival at the gray zone.

Persons sustained for long periods at the zone of indistinction are the consequence of the complex order of things in American health care delivery. The existence of specialized hospital units and the patients who reside there suspends us all between, on the one hand, older ideas about terminal illness, bodily deterioration, and their connection with the inevitability of death and, on the other, new, legitimating social and economic forces that have no clear and publicly articulated moral grounding. Persons in these units force a confrontation with the tension produced by doing for others what no one wants to "need" to have done for himself or herself.

Hospital staff, families, and sometimes patients—on any hospital unit— turn to the rhetoric about *quality of life, dignity,* and *suffering* when institutional imperatives insist that "something must be done." That rhetoric and its negotiated use are one piece of medicine's complicated ethical role in fabricating persons through its examinations, treatments, and decisions. Imputing the *person* who resides on one of the specialized units is merely the end point of a continuum of imputing the *person* (sometimes regardless of his ability to express his views) who may be near death in any hospital unit. Mr. Cline's family saw his suffering as temporary, was sure he could "get through this," and felt that his attitude about his condition could be improved with antidepressant medication. In the examples of Walter Cole, Constance Brady, Angela Stone, and Maureen Peterson, family, friends, and medical team chose a time for suffering to end based on their negotiated understanding of the *person*— in the contexts of life support and the deteriorating medical condition— and what he or she *wanted.* The politics and rhetoric that emerge in hospital culture when death seems near, that characterize the *person* and his or her desires, and that shape negotiations about what needs to be done are fundamental features of how death is made in any hospital setting.

9

CULTURE IN THE MAKING

One role of the anthropologist is to illustrate the ways in which "culture" works. I have tried to show how death is culturally shaped and organized in the American hospital, why the routine forms of dying there and the public's concern about them cannot easily be eradicated, and how the tensions created by the hospital system affect doctors, nurses, patients, and families. Everyone in the system that has been my focus, the natives and the strangers alike, must respond both to the constraints and demands that the medical bureaucracy sets up and to the difficult, contemporary fact that death can be, and is, brought into life in a myriad of ways.

The zone of indistinction is the moral and biotechnical frontier of contemporary hospital culture, and its existence demands that everyone in the system deliberate the value of *life itself* in its most vulnerable forms. Many of the stories I've presented exemplify this new frontier and the demands it imposes—Dorothy Mason's twelve days in the ICU prior to her death, the violent outcome of the Morrison family's refusal to "choose" death, Norman Cline's suffering and his children's hope, and Cynthia Graf, Jack Carter, Cathy Lewis, and Walter Cole being urged to facilitate their own deaths but being unable to make that extraordinary and historically unprecedented choice for themselves. The obligations and anguished politics that surrounded both Sylvia Sato's life and Paul Lenczyk's ambiguous condition are perhaps the most poignant illustrations of hospital culture in the making—the imperfect results of routine medical practices embodied in the most fragile forms of life our institutions and technologies produce.

The twenty-seven stories here convey the journeys of patients as they—both the patients and the journeys—are formed by hospital imperatives about time management and technology use and are understood through a rhetoric of person- and value-making. I have sought to show, on their example, why the problem of death exists and remains recalcitrant. This recalcitrance raises two compelling questions, each of which offers openings both for practical reform and for further ethnographic exploration.

The first is whether the hospital system is capable of responding to calls for change so that *hospital death is no longer considered a problem.* Based on my research, the answer is that while the system is, in part, responsive to calls for change, the "problem" of death will remain as long as people find themselves in the position of having to choose between life-prolonging/death-defying procedures and allowing death. As long as life-sustaining techniques and pathways exist, they will be wanted and chosen. The logic of the system shapes how everyone in it understands, first, the "rightness" of lifesaving treatments and, later, the "need" to allow death to come. Palliative care, now an institutionalized feature of many community and university hospitals, is a pragmatic attempt to introduce an alternative pathway that does not prolong dying for the patient, does not emphasize "decision-making" for the family, and does not encourage medical staff to use lifesaving strategies up until the moment of death. The palliative care option acknowledges the inevitability and appropriateness of death earlier in a patient's hospital journey, demonstrating clinical medicine's corrective to the stance that death can and should be avoided indefinitely. Yet even with the best intentions of palliative care practitioners and advocates, here, too, the question remains: At what stage of critical or terminal illness does one halt life-extending measures and move along to death instead? When is the time for death?

Dying today is characterized by the making of choices among procedures. Things must be done. The pathways, the pressures to decide, and the language that defines the patient and rationalizes the timing of death are not freestanding entities. They cannot easily be removed or changed by individual actors or by institutional decree. Each of these features of contemporary dying has emerged in its present form within the last half century and has a complex history. Hospital death will continue to be considered problematic precisely because the strands out of which it has been formed are anchored so deeply in that history, in a cluster of fundamental, linked assumptions including the power of clinical medicine and biomedical science to overcome disease and old age itself, even when death is imminent; the dominance of self-determination as the frame for ethics and thus for action; and the understanding that medicine's power can and should be employed to respond to the identity and needs of the patient-as-person.

Reflections offered by the SUPPORT investigators and others five years after the publication of that landmark study's first findings concede that the SUPPORT researchers' original gaze was misdirected.[1] The study's initial goal was to improve decision-making on the part of critically ill patients and their physicians by facilitating better lines of communication between them about patients' preferences for treatments. The researchers' hope was that patients would be able to express "what they wanted" and physicians would be able to hear and act on patients' desires. The study investigators assumed, based on the medical, nursing, legal, and bioethics literatures, that individual decisions drive treatment choices, and therefore outcomes, and that a study that sought to fine-tune the decision-making process within hospital walls would lead to treatments all would consider to be "better." When the intervention phase of the study did not impact the range or depth of doctor-patient dialogue, "decision-making," or physician treatment patterns and, in addition, did not lead to "better" deaths, a flood of additional studies of hospital death and medical practices for the critically ill poured forth.

The initial SUPPORT findings were published in 1995, and, in part, they inspired me to undertake the small-scale ethnographic inquiry that forms the core of this book. I wanted to learn why hospital culture was impervious to the SUPPORT interventions, and I sought answers in the journeys of individual patients, the perspectives and experiences of families and hospital staff, the waiting and moving along that are inherent in that culture, and the wide-ranging social underpinnings of the tensions, politics, and rhetoric that are found there. My discoveries proved to be similar to what the SUPPORT investigators noted as they reflected, five years later, on the findings of their own study.[2] But, in addition, my strategy of following the course of events for individual patients and the experiences of different players at the bedside allowed me to see features of the system that the SUPPORT investigators did not describe.

I saw, first, that the work of the hospital vis-à-vis death is dominated by the power of its pathways within a system of competing goals—the press of time, the foreshortening of dying, and the ambiguities of life support itself. Patients and families often have no tools with which to see the structure of the hospital world while they inhabit it. Second, my research revealed that the politics of moving things along and the rhetoric that has been institutionalized by bioethics shape knowledge of "what the patient wants" and characterize the patient's condition, including his or her aliveness. Importantly, I found that the rhetoric about dignity, suffering, and quality of life frames the way we consider the identity of persons who are near death. Third, the condition of death-brought-into-life is now normalized, expected, and far ranging. As such, it stands outside the reach of bureaucratic reform alone and confounds almost everyone's ability to imagine, and then choose, one kind of future over another.

These features of hospital culture "work" as background and they work invisibly. Certainly, they are not "seen" by hospital staff, preoccupied as they are with the responsibilities for clinical care and for moving things along. Nor are they seen by very sick patients or by worried families in the thick of decision-making about life and death and in the throes of discerning what the patient wants, whether he is suffering, whether there has been enough suffering. My task has been to make these features of hospital culture visible to those who stand outside the system, to those who work in it, and to those who pass through it. I contend that if these features can be widely recognized, then that awareness can lead, potentially, to a restructuring of action.

Given that the problem of death persists in the face of attempted reform, how, then, and in what direction, is the culture of hospital death evolving? What can an understanding of today's hospital culture lead us to expect in the future? This is the second of the compelling questions raised by the tenacity of the problem of death. Medicine provides and supports a view that humans can overcome disease and, in fact, can overcome nature through scientific discovery and its application and through sheer perseverance. In many quarters there is enormous enthusiasm for medicine's newest interventions—from reproductive technologies to artificial organs to gene therapies to treatments for cancer, Alzheimer's, AIDS, and heart disease. In fact, the biosciences and their clinical applications seem to suggest that *potential* solutions for much terminal illness and end-stage disease, indeed for old age itself, are just around the corner. This drive for optimum health and longer life is coupled with broad social support for experimental treatments, even for those who are critically ill, and together, these developments belie an underlying acceptance of and preparation for an inevitable time for death.

Since the 1980s there has been an explosion in biomedical research investigating the biological mechanisms of aging and the regeneration of cells, tissues, and organs. Biotechnologies that intervene in natural processes are shaping social as well as scientific understandings of what *aging* is, of what constitutes the *normal* aging of cells, tissues, and entire organisms, and, thus, of how *old* is evaluated. The ultimate goals of research in this area are to understand the basic mechanisms of biological aging while also thwarting or curing diseases that occur in later life—studies, for example, of telomerase (the enzyme that arrests cellular aging) and of stem cell and cloning technologies (which may lead to growth or repair of specific tissues and organs). Rapidly expanding knowledge of the human genome, together with advances in tissue engineering, the bioengineering of drugs, and the ability to manipulate cellular aging genetically, fuels societal expectations about medical treatments that can improve well-being, eradicate disease, and continually postpone death. That new knowledge also influences the strong public interest in clinical applications of genetic technologies to "cure" or alter *natural* aging.[3]

Increasingly, the boundaries are blurring between medicine's focus on cure and stabilization on the one hand and its more recent focus on life enhancement on the other hand. Today's biotechnologies are ushering in a new genre of medicine as they continue to investigate the molecular processes of *life itself* (rather than of disease) and to intervene in and manipulate bodily function. Called regenerative medicine by some, this new genre is conceived to be part cure, part prevention, and part experimental science, and it views the body—and especially the old body—

as simultaneously a diseased entity, a site for restoration, and a space for improvement.[4] While they have no direct application today, in the future biotechnological interventions will become implicated in clinical decision-making about life extension and life prolongation, even in advanced age. They already fuel the popular, though erroneous, idea that human aging, with its attendant frailties, can be eradicated or reversed.[5]

In the twentieth century better living conditions and treatments for infectious diseases enabled the majority of Americans to live to be old enough to suffer from cardiovascular disease, cancers, and degenerative conditions. The discoveries, inventions, and applications of late-twentieth- and early-twenty-first-century surgical techniques, drugs, and implantable devices will continue to impact those late-onset ailments, pushing death farther into the future for those able to access the newest treatments. Already, an increasing number and proportion of older patients are the beneficiaries of life-extending medical and surgical techniques. Coronary artery bypass graft surgery, commonplace for persons in their late eighties and not highly unusual now for persons in their nineties, is the most well known example. That procedure, along with a broad array of other interventions, expands the list of options for routine, safe, expected life-prolongation that hospital patients, nonhospitalized individuals, families, and physicians already encounter. Thus, "choosing death" becomes an even more daunting challenge simply because it is no longer remarkable to stave off death, even in advanced age.

Our notions of a *natural* old age are formed and supported by biomedicine's successes. We live in an era where routine and unquestioned life prolongation through medical technique (e.g., medications to lower blood pressure and regulate cholesterol, cardiac procedures, cancer treatments, organ transplantation) is coupled with many widely desired life-enhancement and modification interventions (e.g., designer drugs, hormone replacement, hip and knee replacement, cataract surgery, cosmetic surgery). It is ironic that in such times there is simultaneously a loud cry for a kind of dying in which medical intervention is minimal, if not entirely absent. Today, *natural* death stands as an abstract cultural ideal, and it is largely understood to be a somehow ethically neutral event that is unhampered by technological interference.[6] This vision becomes increasingly difficult to sustain in a society with insatiable demands for medical intervention—in more areas of life, in more of the body's vital processes, and in ever-older age—in order to achieve greater health, longevity, and "optimal well-being."

Our understandings of what is *natural* about human life, including the ways we respond to illness, grow older, and die, are forever being remade, and the zone of indistinction provides one of the most striking examples of how medical science and practice in American society manufacture *the natural* today. How the term is generally deployed these days can be seen in the politics surrounding the ongoing debates about what should be "done" about nature—debates about genetically modifying foods, using drugs to alter mood, sexuality, or physical strength, choosing abortion for a particular kind of fetus, selecting sperm for a particular kind of child, isolating stem cells and embryos for scientific research, replicating DNA in the laboratory, synthetically modifying human tissue for transplantation, or exploiting the earth's geological and biological resources for the commercial gain of a select few.[7] Nature, "a human idea with a long and complicated cultural history,"[8] has always been entangled with cultural values about fate and human agency, the uses of the body in life and death, and the essential, innate quality of things, including the human being.

Nature is perhaps most starkly revealed as a cultural construct at sites where routine medical practice and technology converge. Technologically assisted human reproduction, brain-dead bodies that are warm and breathing, transplant and implant recipients, and persons maintained in a prolonged comatose state all exemplify how malleable *nature* and the natural body can be in the hands of clinical practice. These hybrid forms embody the most current incarnation of the indeterminacy of both *culture* and *nature;* they subvert and redefine older understandings of *natural* to include the inventions of culture, especially biomedical technologies and the socioeconomic structures that support their development and use.

Anthropologist Marilyn Strathern aptly defines this contemporary situation as "the conceptual collapse of the differences between nature and culture when Nature cannot survive without Cultural intervention."[9] Thus brain death and persistent vegetative state, for example, can be said to represent new features of nature, sustained and made real by clinical (i.e., cultural) practices. Brain death redefines the biology of the cessation of life (as we have understood that biology for more than a hundred years) by locating death only in the brain. PVS marks a new life form—long-term existence, normalized through technology, in the absence of (autobiographical) subjectivity. PVS, as a category of knowledge, wrenches traditional ideas of life and death out of the realm of nature and places them in a new *cultural* location, one in which what is *natural* must be scrupulously maintained. All the forms of the zone of indistinction described in this book illustrate the multiple effects on patients, families, and health professionals of the blurring of the culture/nature boundary, the demise of a broadly assumed culture/nature dichotomy.

In the hospital, what is *natural* is negotiable, and that fact is, perhaps, the most fundamental feature of hospital practice today. My tales of the journeys of patients, families, and staff expose some of the ordinary forms that negotiation takes. Jack Carter, sustained in the ICU with a "dead" heart; Cynthia Graf's decaying body; Evelyn Barker, alive but "gone"; Sylvia Sato, "alive" but only on a ventilator—the journeys of these and other patients reveal the zone of indistinction to be a new kind of landscape in which nature must be maintained by culture for *life itself* to survive.

The concept of a nature "not in our own making,"[10] perceived as separate from the person and from society, has a grounding function. It provides a context for knowledge and for facts and thus serves as a moral imperative, shaping how reality is known and justifying the ways in which things are done. When nature is no longer viewed as natural, when it is known to be socially and culturally constructed, it can no longer provide the moral foundation for the good or correct life.[11] It is no longer available as a guiding concept, separate from the human, in which to situate and by which to compare and evaluate human activity. There is no longer a natural way to do things. And there is no longer a fundamental, apart-from-the-human essence about things. When the vision of an autonomous nature is exploded, as happens in the hospital when death enters the realm of clinical-bureaucratic control, an important ground for anchoring ideas of the moral is removed.

Another old idea is also removed in the hospital,[12] where biotechnologically created conditions and institutional options frame choice—the idea that human life has natural limits. It is no wonder that choice becomes a dilemma for those who confront and treat the denaturalized yet normalized body of a patient who is comatose or technologically supported in the ICU or whose end-stage disease can only be slowed, not reversed, or in whom the "spark of life" and the essence of "personhood" appear to be absent. *Choice* replaces *nature*[13] in such situations, but it is a specific kind of moral choice: the worth, potential, suffering, or vulnerable *life* of the patient-as-person must be balanced against both the comfort and finality of death. That choices are so difficult to make (indeed, are not always made) on hospital units that support death-in-life attests to the absence of moral guideposts in a world where nature, as one powerful moral arbiter, has disappeared. Nature has been replaced by the right and the obligation to choose, by the specter of litigation, the desire for control, the pressure of time, the quantification of disease and *dying,* and by debates about futility.

Death has entered the domain of choice, and today we inescapably think of death in terms of its control, quality, and timeliness. Technique and bureaucracy have expanded the range of choice, but in specific ways, as we have seen; and the rhetoric of individualism has made choice both valuable and necessary. I have tried to show how the hospital system organizes and constrains our choice-making to foster particular kinds of death and particular forms of death-in-life. At stake for us all in this culture-making is the character of our engagements with this normalized, naturalized order of things—dying is organized around the insidious power of bureaucratic imperatives to bring death into life in ever-expanding ways, the body is (almost) infinitely malleable and sustainable, and a cluster of rhetorical devices enables us to consider patients-as-persons to be either living or dying.

Change is possible, I think, but only through a widespread recognition of our own engagement with—and commitment to—how *naturalized* this contemporary order of things has become. The culture of death will not remain static. It, like all cultural forms, will both shape and be informed by other features of contemporary society, not the least of which is the kind of politics and ethics we want to strive for next, in making the end of life.

APPENDIX A: ABOUT THE RESEARCH

The Practice of Ethnography

In 1994 I attended a multidisciplinary working group on death at the Humanities Research Institute at the University of California, Irvine. Several colleagues there suggested it would be important for an anthropologist to study how patients die in the hospital and, more generally, what happens in the hospital at the end of life. They planted the seeds for this project, which is an ethnography—at once a report, cultural exploration, and interpretation—of hospital death. Ethnography, as a genre, is not well understood outside the field of anthropology, and in addition to its obscurity, it is also mutable—certainly, what constitutes an ethnography has been transformed dramatically during my own career in anthropology. Anthropologist Clifford Geertz succinctly describes ethnography as a record of "being there" that aims both to establish authority about the way things are and (in a recent development) to acknowledge the subjective terrain of the ethnographic encounter.[1] Ethnographies have always looked "at least as much like romances as they do like lab reports,"[2] Geertz notes, and this makes them difficult to describe and to define to those outside the social and humanistic sciences. In their contemporary incarnation, ethnographies may look, in part, like investigative journalism, philosophical meditations, literary criticism, biographies, and/or memoirs.

Traditionally, ethnographies were based on having gone to a place and spent a great deal of time there immersed, to whatever degree possible, in the language and daily life of a community. The goal was to characterize and categorize features of the cultural knowledge and social practices the anthropologist encountered there. Today, anthropologists generally still go to a particular place (or places), but they also supplement what they are learning on-site by seeking out individuals, institutions, social trends, kinds of knowledge, or events located elsewhere, anywhere, if they are related to their project. They may "go," also, to nonphysical locations (newspapers, novels, the Internet, scientific journals, government reports, archives) to find information that offers some conceptual relationship to the cultural object of study. Thus, anthropologists today make use of an expanded "field" because many contemporary objects of study are not located or fully accessible within one place. Objects of study—such as the actions of scientists, the doctor-patient relationship, the social impacts of biomedical technologies, discourses about birth and death, new forms of life, new forms of family, the troubled ethics surrounding reproductive and life-extending practices—are "located" in many kinds of places. Such topics are also undergoing rapid change and are thus never understood completely, either by study subjects or by the scrutinizing anthropologist.[3]

Ethnographies are the written reports, stories, and interpretations of what the anthropologist observed, of what happened in the field, how and why things occurred, and what people said and did. Ethnographies are not, however, the "truth" in any positivist or literal sense, and thus ethnographic texts are not "real." They are not exact portraits of actual events, people, relationships, or actions and are not meant to be. Rather, they are individual, intellectually informed accounts of social phenomena, interpreted and filtered through the subjective and personal experiences of the ethnographer. Ethnographies are therefore "partial truths,"[4] conceptually shaped and thematically organized by the anthropologist's experiences and by the goals of the project.

The research for this book was carried out within institutional walls by means of observations, conversations, and interviews about how death occurs. Because the places I went to were characterized by a distinctive culture, and because I stayed there a couple of years, talked with the natives, participated (to the extent I could) in the daily routines, and learned as much as I could about the social practices I wanted to investigate, my research reflects the kind of work anthropologists have traditionally done. Yet, my research is also about the widespread, distinctively American conversation about the "problem" of death, the fractured nature of the American health care delivery system, and the sociocultural and political sources of the hospital practices now associated with dying. Thus, the broader "field" of my research, the larger object of my investigation, is located beyond the confines of hospital walls and may be found in the structural fabric of the health care system and its institutions, the powerful and tenacious values and traditions that support individualism and biomedical progress, and the taken-for-granted, everyday activities that constitute bedside medicine. The objects of my inquiry were, therefore, both clearly delimited and open-ended. I sought to understand the work of hospital staff and the ways death is made. And I also wanted to describe why the pathways, the moving, the waiting, hospital time, and the patient's condition are patterned in particular ways.

The traditional starting point for ethnographic inquiry is the attempt to understand the world from "the natives' point of view."[5] More recently, ethnographic inquiries have also turned to what is new and emergent in social life (for example, cultural responses to the "risks" opened up by new biomedical interventions, the impacts of genetic knowledge, economic and structural arrangements among hospitals and clinics or science laboratories, the politics of AIDS research). Ethnography is predicated upon attention to the everyday and ordinary—the organization of social life, the structure of relationships, and the common understanding of things, as well as what is shared in the moral universe in which individual action is taken. Neither the traditional nor the newer forms of ethnographic inquiry test hypotheses or offer a causal model. Findings come not through explicit statements about specific, discrete variables, taken out of their context, but rather through concrete description of the everyday and ordinary and through interpretation of social processes and change. Importantly, findings emerge from the anthropologist's understanding of what the topics of investigation mean to the study subjects and how those meanings change over time.

Through ethnographic fieldwork, data are collected and a social world— of actors, actions, institutions, power relations, and moral positions—is understood. Ethnographic fieldwork is what distinguishes the anthropological approach to social analysis from approaches used by other disciplines. It differs from other methodologies used in the social and behavioral sciences in that it is both a technique for gathering information and an interpretive perspective. Fieldwork is labor intensive. It usually involves full-time or extensive involvement over a long time with the group, individuals, institutions, events, or social phenomena being studied.

Data are collected primarily in the form of field notes, and these are usually a mixture of diaries, observational notes, descriptions of settings, people, and activities, theoretical and methodological musings, interviews, conversations and reflections on them, and explorations of what various things mean, both to the "natives" in the setting and to the ethnographer. Field notes may be supplemented by other data-gathering techniques such as surveys, census data, questionnaires, archival materials, and by anything at all that seems pertinent for the understanding of the topic, from media reports to popular culture, from literature to science. There is no single way to collect ethnographic data, and no prescribed script or technique dictates how much or what kinds of information are necessary and important.

The fieldwork experience and ethnographic enterprise are shaped as much by accident and serendipity as by planning. In the field, certain events, processes, people, or lines of inquiry invariably emerge as more interesting to pursue than others; certain features of the data, or of the fieldwork experience, seem more central to the topic at hand. Thus the ethnographer must choose how to spend his or her time and which topics, events, or sites merit detailed focus. Whatever the object of study, it often changes or expands in scope as the ethnographer spends more time in the field. When I began this project, I did not foresee that about half my time would be devoted to observing activities in intensive care units. I did not know that units for chronic ventilator-dependent patients existed. But after participating in the daily routine on many hospital wards, I found that the dilemmas about prolonging life and the public conversation about the problem of death were most evident in those places.

Written texts are the medium through which ethnography joins the practice of fieldwork with the reconstruction of events and the representation of cultural worlds.[6] Geertz (along with others) has examined the complex terrain of cultural representation closely and summarized the central tension in contemporary anthropology—a tension created by the turn (beginning in the 1960s) from assuming that some kind of objectivity is possible to articulating the impact of literary processes on the understanding of cultural phenomena. He emphasizes the difficulty of "constructing texts ostensibly scientific out of experiences broadly biographical."[7] A challenge to the discipline today, he notes, is to create work that is "supposed to be at one and the same time an intimate view and a cool assessment," a balance, or reckoning, of the pull between intimacy and objectivity.[8] Ethnography today also faces additional challenges, perhaps especially that, often, both the anthropologist and the study subject are affected by social transformations happening beyond any demarcated "field."[9]

Ethnographies are also politically mediated and motivated, and the ethnographer is always situated in relationships of power to the groups and individuals who are study subjects. Those relationships often determine the ethnographer's access to people, documents, information, and behind-the-scene activities. Those relationships also influence the ways in which phenomena are witnessed and interpreted as well as the goals of ethnographic writing. The ethnographer's class, ethnic and cultural background, age, educational experience, and self-understandings are also brought to bear on the ethnographic enterprise, as is the degree of activism in which the ethnographer chooses to engage. The ethnographer's identity politics and level of activism both play important roles in shaping cultural accounts.

Thus the practice of ethnography is not straightforward. Cultural worlds, structures of power, and individual lives are experienced by a motivated ethnographer who decides which practices, information, and scenarios to portray and which to ignore, what kinds of details should be emphasized, which writing styles and conventions to employ, whose voices should speak and whose should speak at greatest length, and where to locate and how to express meaning. Ethnographies today are informed by a heightened awareness of all of these issues, and anthropologists work to engage and then describe their own field experience and their "data" in innovative ways, while at the same time retaining certain concepts, approaches, and sensibilities from the ethnographic tradition.

Development of the Research

The anthropological research on which this book is based was funded in two phases. The National Institute on Aging supported the first phase, from

1997 to 2000. The National Institute on Nursing Research supported the second phase, from 1999 to 2003. I spent a year, before the project was funded, meeting informally with physicians and nurses at different hospitals and discussing with them the possibility of conducting research on hospital practices surrounding death. I chose three community hospitals as the sites for my research, specifically because at each of them I had made contact with staff who were enthusiastic about the project and because each serves populations that represent a range of ethnic diversity, social class, and medical insurance coverage (including none). No observations for this project were carried out at any of the University of California teaching hospitals.

The research received Institutional Review Board (Human Subjects) approval at the University of California, San Francisco, as well as at the three hospitals in which I carried out my observations and interviews. I began my work by getting to know physicians, nurses, and social workers on the adult medical units and explaining that I wanted to follow them in their daily routines, sit in on staff and team meetings, and learn from them which patients were critically ill and possibly dying. I never approached a patient or family member until after it had been explained to them by a physician, nurse, or social worker that an anthropologist was in the hospital studying critical illness, decision-making, and patient and family responses to hospitalization. After each individual agreed to meet with me, I arranged to be personally introduced by a member of the hospital staff.

Throughout 1997 and then again from mid-1999 to mid-2000, I spent approximately thirty hours per week in the hospitals, gathering the data that form the core of this book. I always carried a notebook, and I took notes on much of what I saw and heard. Several times a day, I sequestered myself at the back of a cafeteria, or in an empty family waiting room, and filled in as many details as I could remember on my laptop computer. I took verbatim (to the extent possible), handwritten notes in family conferences with hospital staff and at team meetings. I used a tape recorder, when permission was granted to do so, when having one-to-one interviews with doctors, nurses, social workers, other hospital staff, and with patients and family members. Those conversations took place in doctors' offices, nurses' hospital offices, lunchrooms, hospital cafeterias, or quiet areas of the hospital and were later transcribed verbatim.

From 1996 through 2003, I attended medical rounds, ethics rounds, and lectures at my own university and at the three hospitals on topics broadly related to this project. Outside of the hospitals, I often spoke informally with doctors, nurses, social workers, medical students, nursing students, formerly hospitalized patients, and people whose family members had died in hospitals. Wherever I went, as soon as I mentioned my research topic, people began telling stories about their own involvement with hospital death. I also read widely in the medical, nursing, and bioethics literatures relevant to the topics included in this book and drew on the anthropological, sociological, and historical literatures for additional information about fieldwork, medicine, nursing, hospitals, nursing homes, patients, death, aging, biomedical science and technologies, ethics, rationality, and emotion.

This project is grounded in two specific theories from medical anthropology. The first of these suggests that medical practice and the varied responses to it are social enterprises, rooted in and influenced by cultural activities of all kinds. The second suggests that medicine—as art, science, and bureaucratic form—is, today, the most powerful framework for understanding the body, the person, dying, and most important, what to do.

Confidentiality

I have made every effort to maintain the anonymity of the hospitals in which I conducted this research and the confidentiality of the hospital staff and the patients and families whom I met. To that end, all names are pseudonyms; I have omitted or changed potentially identifying features of individuals; and I have not identified the hospitals. In several instances, I changed the gender of a health professional or a family member. In one example, I changed the gender of a patient. However, it is important to note that no person described here is a "composite" character—a strategy often employed by anthropologists to preserve anonymity.

Factual Representation

No one can accurately represent the many layers of an event that happened in real time, and I had to choose which patients' stories to describe and which details to highlight from each. Given that caveat, all of the events portrayed here are accurate to the best of my knowledge.[10] All quotations are based on taped conversations or on my verbatim note-taking.

Nothing I observed, and nothing I describe in these pages, fell outside the range of what was considered ordinary. I did not observe, and thus do not report, anything that was illegal or even highly unusual. In my years of observations, I never encountered a single instance of gross medical error or neglect, or anything that could be construed as malpractice. One goal of this book is to bring what ordinarily happens behind hospital doors—the mundane, the everyday, the routine and standard—to the attention of a wider public. So, I chose examples, from my hundreds of pages of notes and transcripts, that were representative of what could occur at many U.S. hospitals—examples of what happens to patients, how things are moved along, how decisions are made or not made, how the system works, and what hospital staff and families say. Many health professionals will recognize here the ways their own hospital works as well as their own practices and feelings of ambivalence. And many family members will find stories about hospitalization and dying that resonate with their own.

APPENDIX B: A NOTE ON DIVERSITY

While race, ethnicity, and other aspects of cultural diversity remain important considerations in any study of health care delivery, they are not—singly or together—the, or even a, major influence on how death is made. My observations on the role(s) elements of diversity play in the making of death lend additional support to my most important finding: it is the structure of the hospital system itself—along with the politics of hospital staff practice—that, more than anything else, affects how death is made. There is no question that a person's identity and identity politics shape the way he or she acts in the world—most importantly in situations of critical choice. However, identity labels, especially when applied by someone other than the actor, never represent a unilateral, determining "cause" for particular actions. This is particularly true in the hospital at the end of life, when the organizational features of the system so powerfully influence the unfolding of events. In my observations of several hundred hospitalized patients, and in following the hospital course of over one hundred of them, I found that the ethnic identity or religious affiliation listed in a patient's medical chart or reported to me by hospital staff was not predictive. They did not predict that patient's resistance, or that of his or her family, to making choices about the termination of life-prolonging treatments. Nor did they provide indicators of the degree of desire for aggressive procedures up to the moment of death, or of a wish to stop heroic interventions. Neither were English-language fluency, class, or insider knowledge of the culture of American health care delivery predictive, in and of themselves, of what patients or families "wanted." None of these "labels" described unique individuals' (often conflicting) values and motivations, and it was unique individuals whom I observed.

For example, people who identified themselves as "having a great deal of faith" sometimes wanted life-extending procedures to continue as long as possible and sometimes wanted treatments to be stopped when they realized that recovery would not occur. Family members who identified themselves or their ill relatives as "lapsed Catholics of many years" sometimes wanted priests to visit the bedside when death was near, and "nonpracticing" Jews sometimes wanted traditional religious services at the bedside of their dying relatives. Highly educated professionals, educated and uneducated citizens, old and new immigrants alike, sometimes wanted life support to be continued past the time hospital staff considered it appropriate. One thing was predictable: people from all walks of life resisted making impossible choices.

Racial and ethnic disparities in access to health care services, in treatments received, and in health outcomes and life expectancy in the United States are now well documented, as is the fact that in the U.S. racism is institutionalized and the poor receive less care and lower-quality care.[1] In addition, numerous studies in the last decade support the view that there are differences along ethnic lines, sometimes significant differences, regarding what people claim to want in terms of life support (whether in good health or critically ill) and especially regarding the relative importance of autonomy in "end-of-life decision-making."[2] Yet at least one comparative study that describes end-of-life choices of four ethnic groups (European-Americans, African-Americans, Chinese immigrants, and Hispanic immigrants) shows that, in *all* groups, some individuals want control over medical decision-making, and some prefer to defer decision-making to health professionals.[3]

This book is not a study of the ways in which diversity, per se, affects the range of responses to American hospital practices when death is near. I do not focus on the manner in which ethnic, class, or religious differences among patients and families affect their interpretations of events or their choices about medical treatments. Identifying study subjects by race or ethnic group, especially, is tricky, and a great deal of research in the social sciences shows those categories to be problematic when they are used to account for choice or behavior.[4] The U.S. population as a whole is more ethnically diverse than ever before. Twenty percent of the population (56 million people) is composed of first-generation residents.[5] In the urban metropolitan areas of California where I conducted my research, the extensive diversity that characterizes that state defies simple categorization, especially by the census categories.

Ethnic identity is far more complex than indicated by the five (current) U.S. census categories—Black, White, Asian/Pacific Islander, Native American/Eskimo, and Hispanic. "Hispanic," for example, does not differentiate among recent immigrants from rural backgrounds and war-torn countries, third-generation Mexican or Cuban Americans, college-educated professionals, non–English speakers, and those who were middle-class in their home countries but who have working-class jobs in the United States. "Asian" does not differentiate among rural Cambodian refugees, urban Vietnamese and Filipino immigrants and their American-born children, and third-generation, highly educated Chinese- and Japanese-Americans. And "White" includes, for example, English, Greek, French, Italian, Irish, Polish, Lebanese, Iranian, Russian, and Indian.

No discrete label used to designate race, ethnicity, or religion captures a point of view about serious illness or a response to hospitalization and dying. No single term describes the kinds of confusion and ambivalence people feel about end-of-life hospital treatment and the urge to prolong life. There is certainly no singular, definitive "Catholic" or "Jewish," "African-American" or "White," rich or poor, male or female, stance regarding what to do or what to want when choices must be made in the face of critical illness and death.

I found, too, that single labels were often inadequate as descriptors of "family," and I encountered examples of ethnic and religious diversity within many families whom I met. That diversity served to complicate, rather than explain, the kinds of opinion and action that emerged at the bedside. The former and current wives of an African-American patient shared decision-making about his treatments. The former wife was African-American; the current wife was white. Both had children at the bedside who wanted to be involved in deciding the time for death. Members of that family were Catholic, Protestant, and Baptist. Opinions varied about whether to keep the patient on life support or to remove the ventilator and allow the patient to die. A Chinese-American patient came to the hospital with end-stage cancer after two years of herbal treatments. Her African-American partner had begged her to use standard medical treatment. With death imminent, the partner, a health professional, had to decide whether the patient, now unconscious, "wanted" heroic interventions. The patient's brother, along with his white wife, was ambivalent about what should be done yet he hoped to help make treatment decisions as well. An elderly woman who had emigrated from Germany fifty years earlier was visited both by her first husband, a wealthy German immigrant, and by her second (current) husband, a much younger bricklayer from Central America. The men fought over whether to take her home to die. A Catholic, Italian-American patient with a great deal of religious faith who had slipped into a coma was married to a nonbelieving Irish-American who had to speak for him. His three adult children were conflicted about the role religion had played in his life and, thus, about what to do now. Elderly patients from Central America, Asia, India, Europe, and the Middle East sometimes were tended at the bedside by multihyphenated American grandchildren whose English-language fluency and education made them the primary "decision-makers," despite the fact that they inhabited a different cultural world from that of their grandparent patient.

Regardless of the extent of ethnic or cultural diversity within families, members of any family often have different approaches to religious observance, different degrees of faith, and differences of opinion regarding the relationship of God to life-extending medical techniques. Family members frequently disagree about the extent and duration of the life-supporting measures desired (a point of frustration mentioned regularly by health professionals), and their disagreements may not have anything to do with "religion" as it is designated in their relative's medical chart.

Until recently, scant attention was devoted to physician ethnicity and religion and the ways in which the identity of health professionals, especially physicians, also shape "doctor-patient communication" and medical decision-making. The demographics of physicians in the United States have changed a great deal in the last decade, with more women, ethnic minorities, and immigrants practicing in urban centers.[6] I talked with and followed in their daily routine African-American, Mexican-American, and Chinese-American doctors, as well as doctors who had come to the United States to work from Asia and Europe. And I observed among them a range of approaches to the uses of morphine, feeding tubes, DNR orders, and aggressive, life-prolonging care. Yet I could not isolate or characterize, from my conversations and observations, the degree to which ethnicity, religion, immigrant status, or gender (as isolated variables) played a part in individual physician choices about life prolongation.

Among physicians, the rules and norms of hospital culture—the ways in which specialists defer to one another and to lines of authority in the hospital, the need to move things along, and the mindful-of-potential-litigation style in which they work—far more than any single feature of "diversity," guide the kinds of dying that take place. This is equally true for families and patients—though they are subject to a different set of hospital rules and norms.

INTRODUCTION

Epigraph   Clifford Geertz, *Available Light* (Princeton: Princeton University Press, 2000), 84.

1. The ways people think about death and respond to the "dying process" are shaped as well by individual experience, including the ways in which race, ethnicity, class, and religion are central to experience. See appendix B, "A Note on Diversity."

2. To protect the anonymity of the institutions, hospital staff, patients, and their families, I do not describe the hospitals, all names have been changed, and identifying details have been changed or omitted. See appendix A, "About the Research," for greater detail.

3. Clifford Geertz, *Works and Lives: The Anthropologist as Author* (Stanford: Stanford University Press, 1988), 15.

4. For various discussions of the "double consciousness" of the ethnographic endeavor, see Edward M. Bruner, "Experience and Its Expressions," in *The Anthropology of Experience,* ed. Victor W. Turner and Edward M. Bruner (Urbana and Chicago: University of Illinois Press, 1986), 3–32; Geertz, *Works and Lives,* 14–15; Bruce M. Knauft, *Genealogies for the Present in Cultural Anthropology* (New York: Routledge, 1996), 57–61; Renato Rosaldo, *Culture and Truth: The Remaking of Social Analysis* (Boston: Beacon Press, 1989), 127–43.

5. The impact of nurses' vulnerability on patient care is enormous. See, for example, Linda H. Aiken et al., "Hospital Nurse Staffing and Patient Mortality, Nurse Burnout, and Job Dissatisfaction," *Journal of the American Medical Association* 288, no. 16 (October 23/30, 2002): 1987–93; Edward O'Neil and Jean Ann Seago, "Meeting the Challenge of Nursing and the Nation's Health," *Journal of the American Medical Association* 288, no. 16 (October 23/30, 2002): 2040–41; Abigail Zuger, "Prescription, Quite Simply, Was a Nurse," *New York Times,* November 19, 2002, D5.

6. I am indebted to Beverly Davenport for pointing this out so clearly to me.

7. Catherine A. Lutz, *Unnatural Emotions* (Chicago: University of Chicago Press, 1988), 76.

8. See Paul Rabinow, *French DNA* (Chicago: University of Chicago Press, 1999), 170–71, for a discussion of "disinterestedness," "conceptual activism," and

"engaged facilitation" when describing the subject position and complex role of ethnographers conducting research today. George Marcus describes the varieties of negotiated activism in fieldwork and how those changed over the twentieth century in the move from "rapport" to "complicity" in ethnographic engagement with informants and with multi-sited spaces of research. See "The Uses of Complicity in the Changing Mise-en-Scène of Anthropological Fieldwork," *Representations* 59 (1997):85–108. Reprinted in George E. Marcus, *Ethnography through Thick and Thin* (Princeton: Princeton University Press, 1998), 105–31.

PART I: THE PREDICAMENT:
DEATH BECOMES A NEW KIND OF PROBLEM
Epigraphs   Max Weber, "Science as a Vocation," in H. H. Gerth and C. Wright Mills, eds., *From Max Weber: Essays in Sociology* (New York: Oxford University Press [1919] 1958), 144. J. Lynn et al., "Capitated Risk-Bearing Managed Care Systems Could Improve End-of-Life Care," *Journal of the American Geriatrics Society* 46 (1998): 328. Elisabeth Hansot, "A Letter from a Patient's Daughter," *Annals of Internal Medicine* 125 (1996), 149–51.

CHAPTER 1. DEATH AND HOSPITAL CULTURE
Epigraph   Anthony Giddens, *Modernity and Self-Identity* (Stanford: Stanford University Press, 1991), 161–62.
1. In 1949, 49.5 percent of deaths occurred in hospitals and other medical institutions combined. By 1958, the figure had risen to 60.9 percent. U.S. mortality statistics for 1980 indicate that 60.5 percent of deaths occurred in hospitals; 13.5 percent occurred in other medical institutions. According to a 1997 Institute of Medicine report (*Approaching Death: Improving Care at the End of Life* [Washington, DC: National Academy Press, 1997], 37–39), 62 percent of deaths occurred in hospitals; 17 percent in nursing homes. A 2004 report of trends in death certificate data notes that 41 percent of Americans died in hospitals in 1998 (James Flory et al., "Places of Death: U.S. Trends Since 1980," *Health Affairs* 23, no. 8 [2004] 194–200).
    Patterns vary considerably across the nation, with fewest total hospital deaths in the state of Oregon (less than 40 percent) and most in New York City (more than 80 percent). Hospital mortality during 1995–96 for Medicare enrollees varied from below 20 percent in some areas of Western and Northwestern states to more than 50 percent in Eastern and Southern states (J. E. Wennberg, "The Likelihood of Being Admitted to an Intensive Care Unit during the Last Six Months of Life," in *Dartmouth Atlas of Health Care in the United States: A Report on the Medicare Program* [Chicago: AHA Press, 1999], 180–81). Location of death, however, like cause of death, also varies by race, age, and class.
2. Different studies report a range regarding percentages of patients who die in ICUs. In the most comprehensive study of end-of-life care in the hospital, 38 percent of patients died following an intensive care unit stay (see SUPPORT Principal Investigators, "A Controlled Trial to Improve Care for Seriously Ill Hospitalized Patients: The Study to Understand Prognoses and Preferences for Outcomes and Risks of Treatment (SUPPORT)," *Journal of the American Medical Association* 274 [1995]: 1591–98). Earlier reports show that 15 to 20 percent of hospital patients spend time in intensive care (Lis Dragsted and Jesper Qvist, "Epidemiology of Intensive Care," *International Journal of Technology Assessment*

in Health Care 8, no. 3 [1992]: 395–407). Nicholas A. Christakis cites studies that show that 25 to 35 percent of hospital patients receive intensive care or high-technology treatment of some kind before death, in *Death Foretold: Prophecy and Prognosis in Medical Care* (Chicago: University of Chicago Press, 1999), 24.

Calculations of mortality rates in the ICU vary enormously from study to study, and figures range from 10 to 69 percent. See, for example, John Luce and Thomas J. Prendergast, "The Changing Nature of Death in the ICU," in *Managing Death in the Intensive Care Unit,* ed. J. Randall Curtis and Gordon D. Rubenfeld (New York: Oxford University Press, 2001), 19–29. That article reports a 10 to 20 percent mortality rate in American ICUs. John F. Murray (*Intensive Care: A Doctor's Journal* [Berkeley: University of California Press, 2000]) and Dragsted and Qvist ("Epidemiology of Intensive Care") report an 11 to 29 percent mortality rate in the ICU for eight major U.S. hospitals. Others note a rate of up to 40 percent (W. A. Knaus et al., "Variations in Mortality and Length of Stay in Intensive Care Units," *Annals of Internal Medicine* 118 [1993]: 753–61). In a study of cancer patients admitted to ICUs, 67 percent of 377 who were on a mechanical ventilator died (J. S. Groeger et al., "Multicenter Outcome Study of Cancer Patients Admitted to the ICU: A Probability of Mortality Model," *Journal of Clinical Oncology* 16 [1998]: 761–70). A review of studies of death in the ICU notes mortality rates up to 69 percent for some diseases and circumstances (Kathleen Puntillo et al., "End-of-Life Issues in Intensive Care," *American Journal of Critical Care* 10 [2001]: 216–29).

3. See J. Lynn et al., "Capitated Risk-Bearing Managed Care Systems"; J. Lynn, "Serving Patients Who May Die Soon and Their Families: The Role of Hospice and Other Services," *Journal of the American Medical Association* 285 (2001): 925–32; J. Lynn, "Learning to Care for People with Chronic Illness Facing the End of Life, *Journal of the American Medical Association* 284 (2000): 2508–11; H. A. Huskamp et al., "Providing Care at the End of Life: Do Medicare Rules Impede Good Care?" *Health Affairs* 20 (2001): 204–11; C. K. Cassel, J. M. Ludden, and G. M. Moon, "Perceptions of Barriers to High-Quality Palliative Care in Hospitals," *Health Affairs* 19 (2000):166–72.

4. Disability rights activists are bringing to public awareness discussion of the "worth" of persons with certain medical conditions or diseases. See, for example, Harriet McBryde Johnson, "Should I Have Been Killed at Birth? The Case for My Life," *New York Times Magazine,* February 16, 2003, 50–79. Yet one physician I spoke with predicted that when aid-in-dying is legalized, it will be one more service that poor people will not have access to.

5. Autonomy, beneficence, avoiding harm (nonmaleficence), and justice (an obligation of fairness in the distribution of benefits and risks) are considered the four foundational principles of American bioethics. These are fully developed in Tom Beauchamp and James Childress, *Principles of Biomedical Ethics* (New York: Oxford University Press, 1979). In several editions over the past decades, this volume has become the leading text in bioethics. Taken together, the four foundational principles emerge from Western-American traditions of law, positivism, and individualism; they emphasize rules or procedures of reasoning and objective thinking; and they seek to develop prescriptive guidelines for human conduct. Many observers note that autonomy has become the centerpiece, or dominant principle, in contemporary views of how patients and health professionals should relate to one another. See Jessica H. Muller, "Anthropology,

Bioethics, and Medicine: A Provocative Trilogy," *Medical Anthropology Quarterly* 8 (1994): 448–67; Renée C. Fox, "The Evolution of American Bioethics: A Sociological Perspective," in *Social Science Perspectives on Medical Ethics,* ed. George Weisz (Philadelphia: University of Pennsylvania Press, 1990), 201–17; Barbara A. Koenig, "Cultural Diversity in Decision-Making about Care at the End of Life," in *Approaching Death: Improving Care at the End of Life,* ed. Institute of Medicine (Washington, DC: National Academy Press, 1997), 363–82; Deborah R. Gordon and Eugenio Paci, "Disclosure Practices and Cultural Narratives: Understanding Concealment and Silence around Cancer in Tuscany, Italy," *Social Science and Medicine* 44 (1997): 1433–52.

6. The mechanical ventilator, or "breathing machine," is described in chapter 2.

7. Cassel, Ludden, and Moon, "Perceptions of Barriers." They cite the World Health Organization definition of palliative care as "the active total care of patients whose disease is not responsive to curative treatment. Control of pain, of other symptoms, and of psychological, social, and spiritual problems is paramount. The goal of palliative care is achievement of the best possible quality of life for patients and their families" (World Health Organization, "WHO Definition of Palliative Care," www.who.int/cancer/palliative/definition/en, 1990, 166).

8. Though a diagnosis code was created in the Medicare scheme for identifying patients receiving palliative care services in the hospital, no reimbursement to hospitals is associated with the code (Melinda Beeuwkes Buntin and Haiden Huskamp, "What Is Known about the Economics of End-of-Life Care for Medicare Beneficiaries?" *The Gerontologist* 42 [2002]: *Special Issue III:* 40–48). If a diagnostic condition falls within the palliative-care code category, Medicare will review the case before payment. Medicare DRG (diagnostic-related group) payments to hospitals are based on the medical necessity of the treatment for the level of hospital acute care. And Medicare pays professional fees to palliative care consultants for acute care services they provide (Steven Pantilat, personal communication). Palliative care, by itself, does not meet the criteria for inpatient acute care. See also C. F. Capello, D. E. Meier, and C. K. Cassel, "Payment Code for Hospital-Based Palliative Care: Help or Hindrance?" *Journal of Palliative Medicine* 1 (1998): 155–63; and Cassel, Ludden, and Moon, "Perceptions of Barriers."

9. Haiden A. Huskamp et al., "Providing Care at the End of Life: Do Medicare Rules Impede Good Care?" *Health Affairs* 20 (2001): 204–11; Cassel, Ludden, and Moon, "Perceptions of Barriers"; J. Lynn et al., "Capitated Risk-Bearing Managed Care Systems."

10. I know many doctors who "creatively" make sure Medicare does pay for dying patients' hospital care, but the point is that they must be creative to give what they consider appropriate care to dying persons.

11. SUPPORT Principal Investigators, "A Controlled Trial."

12. The implications of these statistics about CPR and DNR are described later in this chapter.

13. SUPPORT Principal Investigators, "A Controlled Trial"; Bernard Lo, "Improving Care Near the End of Life: Why Is It So Hard?" *Journal of the American Medical Association* 274 (1995): 1634–36; E. H. Moskowitz and J. L. Nelson, "The Best Laid Plans," *Hastings Center Report* 25 (1995) (special supplement): S3–5; Nancy Freeborne, Joanne Lynn, and Norman A. Desbiens, "Insights about Dying from the SUPPORT Project," *Journal of the American Geriatrics Society* 48 (2000): S199–S205.

14. Medicine and nursing are gendered professions. It is well known that nurses do not have the power that physicians do to bring about institutional change. Perhaps if physicians had themselves spoken and listened more often to patients and families, the intervention phase of the study would have achieved its aims.

15. American Medical Association et al., *Physician and Public Attitudes on Health Care Issues* (Chicago: American Medical Association, 1989); Dan W. Brock, "Advance Directives: What Is It Reasonable to Expect from Them?" *Journal of Clinical Ethics* 5 (1994): 57–60.

16. Joan M. Teno et al., "Do Formal Advance Directives Affect Resuscitation Decisions and the Use of Resources for Seriously Ill Patients?" *Journal of Clinical Ethics* 5 (1994): 23–30.

17. Linda Emanuel, "Advance Directives: What Have We Learned So Far?" *Journal of Clinical Ethics* 4 (1993): 8–16; Rebecca Dresser, "Confronting the 'Near Irrelevance' of Advance Directives," *Journal of Clinical Ethics* 5 (1994): 55–56.

18. M. Danis et al., "A Prospective Study of Advance Directives for Life-Sustaining Care," *New England Journal of Medicine* 324 (1991): 882–88; A. Sehgal et al., "How Strictly Do Dialysis Patients Want Their Advance Directives Followed?" *Journal of the American Medical Association* 267 (1992): 59–63.

19. Nicholas A. Christakis, *Death Foretold: Prophecy and Prognosis in Medical Care* (Chicago, University of Chicago Press, 1999), xx. Christakis comments that he knows of "fewer than thirty published studies in the peer-reviewed literature that have compared physicians' predictions to observed outcomes for real patients" (p. 253, note).

20. J. Lynn et al., "Prognoses of Seriously Ill Hospitalized Patients on the Days before Death," *New Horizons* 5 (1997): 56–61. In the SUPPORT study, patients with congestive heart failure had optimistic prognoses up to the day before death. The median prognosis just prior to death was a 50 percent chance to live two months. See W. A. Knaus et al., "The SUPPORT Prognostic Model: Objective Estimates of Survival for Seriously Ill Hospitalized Patients," *Annals of Internal Medicine* 122 (1995): 191–203.

21. Ibid. See also Joanne Lynn et al., "Quality Improvements in End of Life Care," *The Joint Commission Journal on Quality Improvement* 26, no. 6 (2000): 254–67; J. Lynn, "Serving Patients Who May Die Soon and Their Families," *Journal of the American Medical Association* 285 (2001): 925–32.

22. See note 20.

23. See note 20. J. Lynn, "Serving Patients," 931. See also Institute of Medicine, *Approaching Death*; J. Lynn, "Caring at the End of Our Lives," *New England Journal of Medicine* 335 (1996): 201; and J. R. Lunney, J. Lynn, and C. Hogan, "Profiles of Elderly Medicare Decedents," *Journal of the American Geriatrics Society* 50 (2002): 1108–12.

24. T. J. Prendergast and J. M. Luce, "Increasing Incidence of Withholding and Withdrawal of Life Support from the Critically Ill," *American Journal of Respiratory and Critical Care Medicine* 155 (1997): 15–20; K. Faber-Langendoen and D. M. Bartels, "Process of Forgoing Life-Sustaining Treatment in a University Hospital: An Empirical Study," *Critical Care Medicine* 20 (1992): 570–77; K. A. Koch, H. D. Rodeffer, and R. L. Wears, "Changing Patterns of Terminal Care Management in an Intensive Care Unit," *Critical Care Medicine* 22 (1994): 233–43.
    One physician pointed out to me that, given the problems of prognosis (that is, knowing when a patient will die and which therapies will be ineffec-

tive), many patients will receive aggressive treatments shortly before they die. Those may be interpreted as "excessive" only in retrospect.

25. Despite that finding, the authors note that 22 percent of patients received full ICU care without a CPR attempt before death; 10 percent had life-sustaining technologies withheld; and 38 percent had life-supportive technologies withdrawn after they had been in use. The authors of the study conclude that most ICUs do limit life-sustaining treatment to some extent, but that the wide variation indicates a need to understand how medicine is actually practiced in different places around the United States. See especially Thomas J. Prendergast, Michael T. Claessens, and John M. Luce, "A National Survey of End-of-Life Care for Critically Ill Patients," *American Journal of Respiratory and Critical Care Medicine* 158 (1998): 1163–67.

A physician pointed out that a "CPR attempt," itself, is a highly malleable phenomenon. In addition, Stefan Timmermans, in *Sudden Death and the Myth of CPR* (Philadelphia: Temple University Press, 1999), notes that much CPR is done on already dead persons.

26. C. A. Marco et al., "Ethical Issues of Cardiopulmonary Resuscitation: Current Practice among Emergency Physicians," *Academic Emergency Medicine* 4 (1997): 898–904.

27. Louise Swig et al., "Physician Responses to a Hospital Policy Allowing Them to Not Offer Cardiopulmonary Resuscitation," *Journal of the American Geriatrics Society* 44 (1996): 1215–19.

28. Ann Hood, "Rage against the Dying of the Light," *New York Times,* August 2, 1997.

29. Bezalel Dantz, "Losing One's Bearings at the Life-Death Border," *New York Times,* December 7, 1999, D7.

30. Schuyler Bishop, "When Doctors Go Too Far," *New York Times,* February 27, 1999, A31. This opinion piece was followed, several days later, by several letters from physicians claiming that there are mechanisms for identifying and resolving ethical dilemmas, that more families than doctors demand "inappropriate" care, and that the likelihood of receiving overly aggressive care diminishes with the patient's age. See *New York Times,* March 2, 1999, A22.

31. *Near Death* (produced, directed, and edited by Frederick Wiseman; photography by John Davey; production company, Exit Films; a Zipporah Films Release) was shown in New York City in October 1989 and was first aired on public television on January 21, 1991. For reviews, see Janet Maslin, "Frederick Wiseman Views Life and Death," *New York Times,* October 7, 1989; and Susan M. Wolf, "*Near Death*—in the Moment of Decision," *New England Journal of Medicine* 322 (1990): 208–10.

32. Christakis, *Death Foretold,* 99.

33. Ibid., xx.

34. The articles in notes 20 and 21 make the same observation.

35. See also Jay Katz, *The Silent World of Doctor and Patient* (New York: Free Press, 1984).

36. For detailed discussion of the erosion of physician accountability, see Howard Brody, *The Healer's Power* (New Haven: Yale University Press, 1992); and Ronald Christie and C. Barry Hoffmaster, *Ethical Issues in Family Medicine* (New York: Oxford University Press, 1986). See also Sharon Kaufman, *The Healer's Tale* (Madison: University of Wisconsin Press, 1993).

37. David J. Garrow, "The Oregon Trail," *New York Times*, November 6, 1997.

38. Another designation is DNAR, or Do Not Attempt Resuscitation.

39. Jan C. Hoffmann et al., for the SUPPORT Investigators, "Patient Preferences for Communication with Physicians about End-of-Life Decisions," *Annals of Internal Medicine* 127 (1997): 1–12; B. Lo, G. A. McLeod, and G. Saika, "Patient Attitudes to Discussing Life-Sustaining Treatment," *Archives of Internal Medicine* 146 (1986): 1613–15; S. C. Johnston, M. P. Pfeifer, and R. McNutt, "The Discussion about Advance Directives: Patient and Physician Opinions regarding When and How It Should Be Conducted," *Archives of Internal Medicine* 155 (1995): 1025–30; C. J. Stolman et al., "Evaluation of Patient, Physician, Nurse, and Family Attitudes toward Do Not Resuscitate Orders," *Archives of Internal Medicine* 150 (1990): 653–58; J. A. Tulsky, M. A. Chesney, and B. Lo, "See One, Do One, Teach One? House Staff Experience Discussing Do-Not-Resuscitate Orders," *Archives of Internal Medicine* 156 (1996): 1285–89; B. M. Reilly et al., "Can We Talk? Inpatient Discussions about Advance Directives in a Community Hospital," *Archives of Internal Medicine* 154 (1994): 2299–2308; T. E. Quill, "Perspectives on Care at the Close of Life: Initiating End-of-Life Discussions with Seriously Ill Patients: Addressing the 'Elephant in the Room,'" *Journal of the American Medical Association* 284 (2000): 2502–7.

40. Morphine is frequently given to patients as part of a planned death. It provides respiratory comfort and pain reduction.

41. Several readers asked me why doctors did not discuss code status with the family for the first two weeks of Mrs. Jones's hospitalization. I do not know the answer, but "code status" designations are most frequently made only two days or less before death, showing that this example is not unusual. See SUPPORT, "A Controlled Trial."

42. Patients, families, and doctors can choose, before the fact, to implement only certain parts of a resuscitation procedure, in what one critical-care physician called "the Chinese menu approach." This is an unfortunate development in hospital bureaucracy because in practice one either attempts to resuscitate a person, or not.

43. Who, fully conscious and with any natural breath left in them, can let a machine take over the instinctive act of breathing? I had tried it myself a few weeks earlier, curious to experience how it felt to have the pressure of forced air "breathing" for me. When I placed the plastic tube in my mouth and tried to make sure that no air could get in around it, as the respiratory therapist had instructed me, I was apprehensive and could not allow the machine to fully breathe for me. It was too frightening to "stop" breathing. The therapist who was instructing me assured me that for patients who are extremely sick and weak, the machine simply takes over. It is much harder for a healthy person to let it do that. But, the therapist said, one can learn the technique.

44. Oxygen saturation level refers to the percentage of hemoglobin that is carrying oxygen. Desaturation occurs due to various problems of the heart or lungs that prevent enough oxygen being taken up by hemoglobin.

45. In *The Good Death: The New American Search to Reshape the End of Life* (New York: Bantam, 1999), Marilyn Webb writes, "The American Hospital Association estimates that 70 percent of the six thousand or so daily deaths are 'somehow timed or negotiated, with all concerned parties privately concurring on withdrawal of some death-delaying technology or not even starting it in the first place'" (p. 189).

46. Physicians are not required by law to obtain consent for emergency lifesaving procedures, nor are they required to ask if patients' families want procedures that they, the physicians, understand are nonbeneficial.

CHAPTER 2. DEATH IN LIFE:
THE "PERSON" AND THE EXPERIENCE OF DYING

Epigraph Giorgio Agamben, *Homo Sacer* (Stanford: Stanford University Press, 1998), 164.

1. I borrow the phrase from Giorgio Agamben, who in *Homo Sacer* uses the term *zone of indistinction* to refer to a point of intersection at which state politics and biological life converge. He uses the phrase to promote an argument about modern biopolitical forms of life and relationships among states of law and states of nature that can no longer be distinguished from one another. While his discussion is provocative, I use his phrase in a much simpler, more restrictive sense, to refer to a state of being in which forms of *life* and *death* "pass through one another" (p. 37) and thus cannot be distinguished from one another or separated.

2. These questions will be examined throughout the book and especially in chapter 8. Here, we focus on the evolution of the zone of indistinction as catalyst for the "problem of death."

3. Philippe Ariès, *The Hour of Our Death* (New York: Oxford University Press, 1981), 108.

4. Michel Foucault, *The Birth of the Clinic* (New York: Vintage Books, 1975).

5. William Osler, The Ingersoll Lecture, 1904. Published as *Science and Immortality* (Boston and New York: Houghton, Mifflin and Co., 1904), 19.

6. The cause of her condition remains debatable. She had been drinking and taking prescription drugs the evening she went into a coma. She had also sustained a head injury less than two weeks before the coma. Marilyn Webb, *The Good Death* (New York: Bantam Books, 1999), 126–53.

7. Anthony Giddens, *Modernity and Self-Identity* (Stanford: Stanford University Press, 1991). See especially pages 161–62.

8. William Ray Arney and Bernard J. Bergen, *Medicine and the Management of Living* (Chicago: University of Chicago Press, 1984).

9. Foucault, *Birth of the Clinic.*

10. Arney and Bergen, *Medicine,* 51.

11. Sharon R. Kaufman, *The Healer's Tale: Transforming Medicine and Culture* (Madison: University of Wisconsin Press, 1993).

12. T. R. Harrison et al., *Principles of Internal Medicine* (Philadelphia, PA: The Blakiston Company, 1950), 4, cited in Arney and Bergen, *Medicine,* 46. See also David Armstrong, "The Patient's View," *Social Science and Medicine* 18 (1984): 737–44.

13. The notion of the "whole patient" emerged in medical literature by the 1930s and was at least partly a reaction to the therapeutic nihilism that pervaded medicine in the early years of the twentieth century. See H. Brackenbury, *Patient and Doctor* (London: Hodder and Stoughton, 1935), cited in Armstrong, "Patient's View," 743. See also George Canby Robinson, *The Patient as a Person: The Study of the Social Aspects of Illness* (New York: Commonwealth Fund, 1939), which proposed the "treatment of the patient as a whole." Robinson stated, "I am now convinced that 'the human problems which surround the patient' are not apart from illness, but form an important component of illness, and it is therefore the doctor whose duty it is to understand them" (p. x).

14. London: Pitman Medical Publishing Co. Ltd., 1957. Revised and enlarged second edition, 1964. This book was translated into German, French, Italian, Hungarian, and Spanish.
15. See, for example, George L. Engel, "The Need for a New Medical Model: A Challenge for Biomedicine," *Science* 196 (1977): 129–36.
16. See Arney and Bergen, *Medicine and the Management of Living,* above, for a detailed Foucaultian exploration of medicine's changing "gaze" in the twentieth century:
    "The new language of medicine is summoning forth a new definition of medical practice and is reformulating the field of medical power. It provides new perspectives and postures, new prescriptions and proscriptions, new choices. The language is invoking the presence of the patient, calling him forward from the far side of what once appeared to be an unbridgeable gulf. It is ending the rule of silence. No longer is medical practice to confine itself to mobilizing all its resources against pain and suffering contained and visible in the body. Now, in a way that is not yet textbook clear, medical practice is called upon to disperse itself across the network of relationships between the patient and everything else" (p. 49).
17. Ibid., 107–15.
18. The logic that physicians should speak "the truth" about death does not refer to a requirement to announce that death is imminent. One physician colleague noted that the 1970s were a time of change mostly in the eyes of critics of medical practice. Changes in the physician/patient relationship appeared slowly during the last quarter of the twentieth century. Truth-speaking about death remains uneven in routine medical practice.
    The subject of the multiple kinds of disclosure regarding diagnosis and prognosis and physician strategies for communicating bad news to patients and families has been explored historically and cross-culturally by anthropologists and sociologists. See Nicholas A. Christakis, *Death Foretold: Prophecy and Prognosis in Medical Care* (Chicago: University of Chicago Press, 1999); Jay Katz, *The Silent World of Doctor and Patient* (New York: Free Press, 1984); David Armstrong, "Silence and Truth in Death and Dying," *Social Science and Medicine* 24 (1987): 651–57; Mary-Jo Del Vecchio Good et al., "American Oncology and the Discourse on Hope," *Culture, Medicine and Psychiatry* 14 (1990): 59–79; Kathryn M. Taylor, "Physicians and the Disclosure of Undesirable Information," in *Biomedicine Examined,* ed. Margaret Lock and Deborah Gordon (Dordrecht: Kluwer, 1988), 441–64; and the articles by Gordon and Paci, Good et al., and Frank et al. in note 32, below.
19. Barney G. Glaser and Anselm L. Strauss, *Awareness of Dying* (New York: Aldine, 1965); Barney G. Glaser and Anselm L. Strauss, *Time for Dying* (New York: Aldine, 1968); David Sudnow, *Passing On: The Social Organization of Dying* (Englewood Cliffs, NJ: Prentice-Hall, 1967).
20. *On Death and Dying* (London: Tavistock, 1969).
21. Kübler-Ross suggested that five psychological stages precede death: (1) denial and isolation, (2) anger, (3) bargaining, (4) depression, and (5) acceptance. Ibid.
22. Arney and Bergen, *Medicine,* 102–3. See also Clive Seale, *Constructing Death: The Sociology of Dying and Bereavement* (Cambridge: Cambridge University Press, 1998), 97.
23. See Seale, *Constructing Death,* and Tony Walter, *The Revival of Death* (London:

Routledge, 1994), for sociological analyses of the role of hospice in Anglo-American society.

24. In 1993, about 11 percent of the nearly 2.27 million people who died were in hospice programs. In 1995, data from the National Hospice Organization estimated the number of those served by hospice programs to be 390,000, about 17 percent of the 2.31 million deaths that year (Institute of Medicine, *Approaching Death: Improving Care at the End of Life* [Washington, DC: National Academy Press, 1997], 40). In 1999, U.S. hospice programs provided services to 700,000 patients, about one-quarter of all deaths that year (J. Lynn, "Serving Patients Who May Die Soon and Their Families: The Role of Hospice and Other Services," *Journal of the American Medical Association* 285 [2001]: 925–32). Cardiac or respiratory emergencies in which the patient dies shortly after arrival at a hospital would not be appropriate referrals for hospice. Many medical conditions do not have a trajectory in which physicians can accurately predict the timing of death.

25. A national poll conducted by the American Medical Association in 1997 found that 35 percent of respondents were not familiar with the term *hospice*. See M. J. Silveira et al., "Patients' Knowledge of Options at the End of Life: Ignorance in the Face of Death," *Journal of the American Medical Association* 284 (2000): 2483–88.

I noticed about this same proportion in my own research in community hospitals. When discharge planners or nurses mentioned to patients or their families that "it is time now to consider hospice care," about a quarter to a third of persons I observed either had never heard the word before or had heard of hospice but did not have any knowledge about its purpose. They did not have enough information about impending death or about hospice to "choose" it at the time considered appropriate by medical personnel.

26. Walter, *Revival of Death,* especially p. 59.

27. In the United States, 63 percent of Medicare patients in hospice have a diagnosis of cancer. Yet, the average hospice length of stay for those patients is less than three weeks (Lynn, "Serving Patients").

28. Those standards included the following:

"(1) Consent of the subject must be obtained. All subjects have been volunteers in the absence of coercion in any form. Before volunteering, the subjects have been informed of the hazards, if any.

"(2) The experiment to be performed must be so designed and based on the results of animal experimentation and the knowledge of the natural history of the disease . . . and must not be random and unnecessary in nature.

"(3) The experiment must be conducted only by scientifically qualified persons. . . . Such rules are required to insure the human rights of the individual, to avoid the debasement of a method for doing good, and the loss of the faith of the public in the profession" (Andrew C. Ivy, "The Brutalities of Nazi Physicians," *Journal of the American Medical Association* 132 [1946]: 714–15).

29. David J. Rothman, *Strangers at the Bedside* (New York: Basic Books, 1991), 31.

30. Ibid. Prior to 1960, there was "little law" in the United States that specifically concerned protecting the rights of the subjects of medical research (W. J. Curran, "Governmental Regulation of the Use of Human Subjects in Medical Research," *Daedalus* 98 [1969]: 542–94).

31. Henry Beecher, "Ethics and Clinical Research," *New England Journal of Medi-*

cine 274 (1966): 1354–60. Beecher cited twenty-two examples of medical research in which investigators had not informed research subjects about the nature of their participation, had not obtained their permission to participate, and had risked their health and, in some cases, their lives.

32. For a comparison of Western European and American approaches to the concept of "patient autonomy," see Deborah R. Gordon and Eugenio Paci, "Disclosure Practices and Cultural Narratives: Understanding Concealment and Silence around Cancer in Tuscany, Italy," *Social Science and Medicine* 44 (1997): 1433–52; and Paul Rabinow, *French DNA* (Chicago: University of Chicago Press, 1999). For a comparison of Japan and the United States regarding autonomy, see Mary-Jo Del Vecchio Good et al., "A Comparative Analysis of the Culture of Biomedicine," in *Health and Health Care in Developing Countries*, ed. P. Conrad and E. Gallagher (Philadelphia: Temple University Press, 1993), 180–210. For a discussion of divergent views within the United States regarding the value of autonomy, see Gelya Frank et al., "A Discourse of Relationships in Bioethics: Patient Autonomy and End-of-Life Decision-Making among Elderly Korean Americans," *Medical Anthropology Quarterly* 12 (1998): 403–23; Leslie J. Blackhall et al., "Ethnicity and Attitudes toward Patient Autonomy," *Journal of the American Medical Association* 274 (1995): 820–25; and Barbara A. Koenig and Jan Gates-Williams, "Understanding Cultural Difference in Caring for Dying Patients," *Western Journal of Medicine* 163 (1995): 244–49.

33. The Tuskegee syphilis study is the most famous twentieth-century example of morally abhorrent medical research conducted in the United States. See James H. Jones, *Bad Blood: The Tuskegee Syphilis Experiment* (New York: Free Press, 1981).

34. The President's Commission for the Study of Ethical Problems in Medicine and Biomedical and Behavioral Research. For a history of the government commissions, the topics covered, and the reports they issued, see Albert R. Jonsen, *The Birth of Bioethics* (New York: Oxford University Press, 1998). See especially chapter 4, "Commissioning Bioethics: The Government in Bioethics, 1974–1983," pp. 90–122. For a critique of the President's Commission focus on autonomy and self-determination, see Daniel Callahan, "Morality and Contemporary Culture: The President's Commission and Beyond," *Cardozo Law Review* 6 (1984): 223–42.

35. The report issued by the commission in 1979, *The Belmont Report,* cites autonomy as its first of three ethical principles (the other two were beneficence and justice): "Respect for persons incorporates at least two ethical convictions: first, that individuals should be treated as autonomous agents, and second, that persons with diminished autonomy are entitled to protection. The principle of respect for persons thus divides into two separate moral requirements: the requirement to acknowledge autonomy and the requirement to protect those with diminished autonomy. . . . An autonomous person is an individual capable of deliberation about personal goals and of acting under the direction of such deliberation. To respect autonomy is to give weight to autonomous persons' considered opinions and choices while refraining from obstructing their actions unless they are clearly detrimental to others. To show lack of respect for an autonomous agent is to repudiate the person's considered judgments, or to withhold information necessary to make a considered judgment, when there are no compelling reasons to do so" (National Commission for the Protection of Human Subjects in Biomedical

and Behavioral Research, *The Belmont Report*, Department of Health, Education, and Welfare publication No. [OS] 78–0013 and No. [OS] 78–0014 [Washington, DC: U.S. Government Printing Office, 1979]).

36. Jodi Halpern, *From Detached Concern to Empathy: Humanizing Medical Practice* (New York: Oxford University Press, 2001), 101.

37. Renée C. Fox, "The Evolution of American Bioethics: A Sociological Perspective," in *Social Science Perspectives on Medical Ethics*, ed. George Weisz (Philadelphia: University of Pennsylvania Press, 1991), 201–20 (quote is p. 206).

   Among social scientists and others a widespread critique finds bioethics too narrowly focused on individualism and rational decision-making. See Renee Anspach, *Deciding Who Lives* (Berkeley: University of California Press, 1993); Charles L. Bosk, "Professional Ethicist Available: Logical, Secular, Friendly," *Daedalus, Proceedings of the American Academy of Arts and Sciences* 128 (1999): 47–68. Barry Hoffmaster, ed., *Bioethics in Social Context* (Philadelphia: Temple University Press, 2001); Barry Hoffmaster, "Can Ethnography Save the Life of Medical Ethics?" *Social Science and Medicine* 35 (1992): 1421–31; and Arthur Kleinman, "Moral Experience and Ethical Reflection: Can Ethnography Reconcile Them? A Quandary for 'the New Bioethics,'" *Daedalus, Proceedings of the American Academy of Arts and Sciences* 128 (1999): 69–98. See also Gordon and Paci in note 32.

38. The Patient Self-Determination Act (PSDA) was drafted by Senator John Danforth (R-MO) as part of the Omnibus Budget Reconciliation Act (OBRA) of 1990. "The Act directed the Secretary of Health and Human Services to conduct a nationwide campaign to promote advance directives. Therefore, it was mandated that all health care institutions that receive Medicare/Medicaid funding must:
   • provide to each adult patient, on admission, written information regarding the individual's rights under state law to execute advance directives and make medical treatment decisions.
   • provide written information on institutional policies concerning such rights.
   • document in the medical record whether the individual has executed an advance directive.
   • avoid discrimination against any individual on the basis of whether an advance directive has been executed and provide education for staff and the community concerning advance directives" (http://www.afip.org/legalmed/jnrm2000/directives.htm, accessed January 19, 2001).

39. Mary Ann Glendon, *Rights Talk* (New York: The Free Press, 1991).

40. Barbara A. Koenig, "Cultural Diversity in Decision-Making about Care at the End of Life," in *Approaching Death: Improving Care at the End of Life*, ed., Institute of Medicine (Washington, DC: National Academy Press, 1997), 363–82. For a cogent discussion of the impact of the autonomy paradigm in particular and the discipline of bioethics in general on patient choice, see Theresa S. Drought and Barbara A. Koenig, "'Choice' in End-of-Life Decision-Making: Researching Fact or Fiction?" *The Gerontologist* 42, special issue no. 3 (2002): 114–28.

41. See note 32 and also appendix B, "A Note on Diversity."

42. Historian Charles E. Rosenberg writes, "In this historical and sociological sense, autonomy is a product, not a goal; it is a place-, time-, and system-specific outcome of the interaction between the microcosm of the clinical encounter and the macrocosm(s) of the larger society and the cognitive and institutional world of medicine. This needs hardly be elaborated at a moment in time when many

physicians find their clinical interactions limited by managed care providers to fifteen minutes and their diagnostic and therapeutic choices limited as well. Autonomy and agency are constructed and reconstructed in every healing context" (Charles E. Rosenberg, "Meanings, Policies, and Medicine: On the Bioethical Enterprise and History," *Daedalus, Proceedings of the American Academy of Arts and Sciences* 128, no. 4 [Fall 1999]: 27–46 [quote is p. 41]).

43. *Dignity*, like *rights*, was elevated to prominence in the Universal Declaration of Human Rights: "Whereas recognition of the inherent dignity and of the equal and inalienable rights of all members of the human family is the foundation of freedom, justice, and peace in the world . . . Article 1. All human beings are born free and equal in dignity and rights."

44. The Harvard committee report was published as Ad Hoc Committee of the Harvard Medical School to Examine the Definition of Brain Death, "A Definition of Irreversible Coma," *Journal of the American Medical Association* 205 (1968): 337–40. By the mid-1960s there were a variety of committees and commissions whose charge was to help solve practical problems of transplantation by redefining death. See Martin S. Pernick, "Brain Death in Cultural Context: The Reconstruction of Death, 1967–1981," in *The Definition of Death: Contemporary Controversies*, ed. S. J. Youngner, R. M. Arnold, and R. Schapiro (Baltimore: Johns Hopkins University Press, 1999), 3–33.

45. Pernick, in "Brain Death in Cultural Context," notes that the two technologies, transplantation and the mechanical respirator, were the only reasons that a new definition of death was needed. Yet the role of transplantation in shaping the Harvard committee criteria for brain death remains controversial. Some think that transplants were of peripheral concern to the committee deliberations. Others feel that the committee wanted to redefine death to make viable organs available (p. 9 and p. 27, note 17).

46. President's Commission for the Study of Ethical Problems in Medicine and Biomedical and Behavioral Research, *Defining Death: Medical, Legal and Ethical Issues in the Determination of Death* (Washington, DC: Government Printing Office, 1981).

47. Pernick, "Brain Death," 22. See also Alexander Capron, "The Report of the President's Commission on the Uniform Determination of Death Act," in *Death: Beyond Whole Brain Criteria*, ed. Richard M. Zaner (Dordrecht, Netherlands: Kluwer, 1988).

48. President's Commission, *Defining Death*. See Steven Miles, "Death in a Technological and Pluralistic Culture," and H. Tristram Engelhardt Jr., "Redefining Death," both in *Definition of Death*, ed. Youngner, Arnold, and Schapiro, 311–18, 320–31.

49. For the clinical distress and multiple meanings that the definition of brain death elicits, see S. J. Youngner et al., "Psychosocial and Ethical Implications of Organ Retrieval," *New England Journal of Medicine* 313 (1989): 321–24; S. J. Youngner et al., "'Brain Death' and Organ Retrieval: A Cross-Sectional Survey of Knowledge and Concepts among Health Professionals," *Journal of the American Medical Association* 261 (1989): 2205–10; Margaret Lock, "Death in Technological Time: Locating the End of Meaningful Life," *Medical Anthropology Quarterly* 10 (1996): 575–600; Margaret Lock, "On Dying Twice: Culture, Technology and the Determination of Death," in *Living and Working with the New Medical Technologies*, ed. Margaret Lock, Allan Young, and Alberto Cam-

brosio (Cambridge: Cambridge University Press, 2000), 233–62; and Lesley A. Sharp, "Organ Transplantation as a Transformative Experience," *Medical Anthropology Quarterly* 9 (1995): 357–89.

50. Agamben, *Homo Sacer,* 163.
51. For a discussion of the troublesome uses of technologies that prolong dying or keep the "dead" alive and the ambiguous obligations of contemporary clinical medicine, see Robert Arnold and Stuart Youngner, "The Dead Donor Rule: Should We Stretch It, Bend It, or Abandon It?" *Kennedy Institute of Ethics Journal* 3 (1993): 263–78; J. F. Childress, "Ethical Criteria for Procuring and Distributing Organs for Transplantation," in *Organ Transplantation Policy: Issues and Prospects,* ed. J. F. Blumstein and F. A. Sloan (Durham, NC: Duke University Press, 1989), 87–113; and Robert M. Veatch, "The Impending Collapse of the Whole-Brain Definition of Death," *Hastings Center Report* 23 (1993): 18–24.
    For a detailed historical and cross-cultural discussion of the making of the brain death definition and the debates it provokes about medical practice, responsibility and ethics, culture, nature, tradition, and modernity, see Margaret Lock, *Twice Dead: Organ Transplants and the Reinvention of Death* (Berkeley: University of California Press, 2002). For a popular discussion of physicians questioning the definition of brain death, see Gary Greenberg, "As Good as Dead," *New Yorker,* August 13, 2001, 36–41.
52. See David J. Rothman, *Beginnings Count* (New York: Oxford University Press, 1997); Thomas L. Petty, "The Modern Evolution of Mechanical Ventilation," *Clinics in Chest Medicine* 9 (1988): 1–10; and Gordon L. Snider, "Historical Perspective on Mechanical Ventilation: From Simple Life Support to Ethical Dilemma," *American Review of Respiratory Diseases* 140 (1982): S4–5.
53. Snider, "Historical Perspective."
54. Chapter 8 discusses "vegetative" and "comatose" persons in detail.
55. Martha Holstein, "Alzheimer's Disease and Senile Dementia, 1885–1920: An Interpretive History of Disease Negotiation," *Journal of Aging Studies* 11 (1997): 1–13; and Herman T. Blumenthal, "The Aging-Disease Dichotomy: True or False?" *Journals of Gerontology: Medical Sciences* 58A (2003): M138–45.
56. W. Andrew Achenbaum, *Old Age in the New Land* (Baltimore: Johns Hopkins University Press, 1978), 42–45; Lawrence Cohen, *No Aging in India* (Berkeley: University of California Press, 1998), 62–64.
57. Achenbaum, *Old Age,* 42–45.
58. Nascher's text (I. L. Nascher, *Geriatrics* [Philadelphia: P. Blakiston's Son and Co., 1914]) replaced that of French physician Jean-Martin Charcot, whose *Clinical Lectures on the Diseases of Old Age,* published in 1867, was the most authoritative work on the relationship of old age and disease in the preceding era (*Leçons cliniques sur les maladies des vieillards et les maladies chroniques* [Paris: A. Delahaye, 1867]). His work set forth the idea that one could understand diseases in old age only through clinical investigation of physical lesions and processes. That idea would become a foundation of modern geriatric medicine. See also, Achenbaum, *Old Age,* 42–43.
59. See Cohen, *No Aging in India,* 62–64.
60. Thomas R. Cole, *The Journey of Life: A Cultural History of Aging in America* (Cambridge: Cambridge University Press, 1992), 207.
61. G. W. Gray, "The Mystery of Aging," *Harper's* 182 (1941): 283, cited in Achenbaum, *Old Age,* 120.

62. Leonard Hayflick, *How and Why We Age* (New York: Ballantine Books, 1994). See also R. D. Adelman et al., "Issues in the Physician-Geriatric Patient Relationship," in *Communication, Health and the Elderly*, ed. H. Giles, N. Coupland, and J. M. Wiemann (Manchester, Great Britain: Manchester University Press, 1990), 126–34; Herman T. Blumenthal, "The Aging-Disease Dichotomy Is Alive, but Is It Well?" *Journal of the American Geriatrics Society* 41 (1993): 1272–73; and Herman T. Blumenthal, "'The Alzheimerization of Aging': A Response" (letter to the editor), *Gerontologist* 35 (1995): 721–23.

63. A. R. Somers and D. R. Fabian, *The Geriatric Imperative* (New York: Appleton-Century-Crofts, 1981).

64. Herman T. Blumenthal, "A View of the Aging-Disease Relationship from Age 85," *Journals of Gerontology: Biological Sciences* 54A (1999): B255–59; Herman T. Blumenthal, "Milestone or Genomania? The Relevance of the Human Genome Project to Biological Aging and the Age-Related Diseases," *Journals of Gerontology: Medical Sciences* 56A (2001): M529-37.

65. Andrea Sankar, "'It's Just Old Age': Old Age as Diagnosis in American and Chinese Medicine," in *Age and Anthropological Theory*, ed. D. Kertzer and J. Keith (Ithaca: Cornell University Press, 1984).

66. H. T. Blumenthal, "The Aging-Disease Dichotomy: True or False?" *Journal of Gerontology: Medical Sciences* 58A (2003): M138–45.

67. W. F. Forbes and J. P. Hirdes, "The Relationship between Aging and Disease: Geriatric Ideology and the Myths of Senility," *Journal of the American Geriatrics Society* 41 (1993): 1267–71.

68. Blumenthal, "Aging-Disease Dichotomy," M138–45.

69. Forbes and Hirdes, "Relationship between Aging and Disease"; Blumenthal, "View of the Aging-Disease Relationship"; D. Von Dras and H. T. Blumenthal, "Dementia of the Aged: Disease or Atypical-Accelerated Aging?" *Journal of the American Geriatrics Society* 40 (1992): 285–94.

70. Daniel Callahan, *The Troubled Dream of Life* (New York: Simon and Schuster, 1993). For a view from medicine of defying death, see J. H. Muller and B. Koenig, "On the Boundary of Life and Death: The Definition of Dying by Medical Residents," in *Biomedicine Examined*, ed. Lock and Gordon, 351–74. For a summary of popular and scientific views about postponing old age and death, see Jay Olshansky and Bruce A. Carnes, *The Quest for Immortality: Science at the Frontiers of Aging* (New York: Norton, 2001).

71. Daniel Callahan, *Setting Limits: Medical Goals in an Aging Society* (New York: Simon and Schuster, 1987); Callahan, *Troubled Dream*.

72. R. L. Barry and G. V. Bradley, eds., *Set No Limits* (Urbana: University of Illinois Press, 1991); R. H. Binstock and S. G. Post, eds., *Too Old for Health Care? Controversies in Medicine, Law, Economics, and Ethics* (Baltimore: Johns Hopkins University Press, 1991); C. L. Estes, "Cost Containment and the Elderly: Conflict or Challenge?" *Journal of the American Geriatrics Society* 36 (1988): 68–72; P. Homer and M. Holstein, eds., *A Good Old Age: The Paradox of Setting Limits* (New York: Simon and Schuster, 1990); N. S. Jecker and R. A. Pearlman, "Ethical Constraints on Rationing Medical Care by Age," *Journal of the American Geriatrics Society* 37 (1989): 1067–75; G. R. Winslow and J. W. Waters, eds., *Facing Limits: Ethics and Health Care for the Elderly* (Boulder, CO: Westview Press, 1993); N. R. Zweibel, C. K. Cassel, and T. Karrison, "Public Attitudes about the Use of Chronological Age as a Criterion for Allocating Health Care

Resources," *Gerontologist* 33 (1993): 74–80. For Callahan's response to the debate his work provoked, see Daniel Callahan, "Setting Limits: A Response," *Gerontologist* 34 (1994): 393–98.

73. Blumenthal, "'Alzheimerization of Aging'"; J. S. Goodwin, "Geriatric Ideology: The Myth of the Myth of Senility," *Journal of the American Geriatrics Society* 39 (1991): 627–31; Sherwin B. Nuland, *How We Die: Reflections on Life's Final Chapter* (New York: Knopf, 1994), 43–63.

74. Nuland, *How We Die*, 43–63.

75. Geoffrey C. Bowker and Susan Leigh Star, *Sorting Things Out—Classification and Its Consequences* (Cambridge: MIT Press, 2000). See especially pp. 90–91.

76. Ibid.

77. Surgeon and medical historian Sherwin Nuland writes critically about how death is categorized and argues that medicine has a "misplaced worldview" regarding clinical causes of death and thus a misguided approach toward how to act in the face of finitude (*How We Die*, 43–44).

PART II: THE HOSPITAL SYSTEM:
TIME AND THE POWER OF THE PATHWAY

CHAPTER 3. TRANSFORMING TIME:
FROM DEATHWATCH TO BILLABLE TREATMENTS

1. Julie Fairman and Joan E. Lynaugh, *Critical Care Nursing: A History* (Philadelphia: University of Pennsylvania Press, 1998), 15.

2. David Rothman, *Beginnings Count: The Technological Imperative in American Health Care* (New York: Oxford University Press), 1997. It was not until about 1970 that many hospitals had ICUs in which most patients were on ventilators. Those machines do not appear at all as protagonists in the sociologists' descriptions of the organization of medical work and death during the 1960s.

3. David Sudnow, *Passing On* (Englewood Cliffs, NJ: Prentice-Hall, 1967), 83.

4. Ruth Malone, personal communication.

5. Barney Glaser and Anselm Strauss, *Time for Dying* (New York: Aldine, 1968), 47.

6. One cannot "linger" in hospice care either. The Medicare hospice benefit specifies a time frame of six months or less, in the best medical judgment of the physician, during which it will pay for hospice care. Most health professionals do not want to refer a patient to hospice care "too soon," and most patients are designated as "hospice care" only a few days or weeks before death.

7. Sudnow, *Passing On*, 63.

8. Ibid., 68–69.

9. See Jessica Muller and Barbara Koenig, "On the Boundary of Life and Death: The Definition of Dying by Medical Residents," in *Biomedicine Examined*, ed. Margaret Lock and Deborah Gordon (Boston: Kluwer, 1988), 351–74.

10. Glaser and Strauss, *Time for Dying*, 197–99; Barney Glaser and Anselm Strauss, *Awareness of Dying* (New York: Aldine, 1965), 246–48; Sudnow, *Passing On*, 83–84. Of the three nurses I spoke with who worked on general hospital floors during the 1960s, two remembered the use of the term *deathwatch* and one did not. That latter nurse suggested that the term could have been put into use by the sociologists themselves. Reconstruction of a clinical sensibility during an earlier era is complex.

11. One physician recalled that during the 1970s he walked quickly past hospital

rooms in which patients were dying. "There was nothing to do for them," he said. "They were not in our purview."

12. Tony Walter, *The Revival of Death* (London: Routledge, 1994), 59.

13. Glaser and Strauss, *Awareness of Dying*.

14. Glaser and Strauss, *Time for Dying*, 47.

15. My italics. Ibid., 197.

CHAPTER 4. MOVING THINGS ALONG

Epigraph   Andrew Solomon, "A Death of One's Own," *New Yorker*, 1995, 69.

1. Some observers of managed hospital care claim that the reason "hospitalists"—those physicians who only care for hospitalized patients—are becoming more prominent in academic and community hospitals is that they are able to move patients out of the institution faster than community-based physicians. Hospitalists are paid by the hospital. They do not have long-term relationships with patients. They do not resist the pressure to "move things along" the way that community physicians do.

2. A Time/CNN poll found that seven out of ten Americans say they want to die at home (*Time*, September 18, 2000, 60). Yet about 75 percent die in acute care hospitals (55–60 percent) and nursing homes. That same article claims that about half of dying people spend some time on a mechanical ventilator before they die (p. 62), a figure that seems high from my personal observations and review of the medical literature. See also Gina Kolata, "Living Wills Aside, Dying Cling to Hope," *New York Times*, January 15, 1997.

3. Taken together, complaints about how death occurs that circulate in the media, popular books on dying well, and studies of hospital practices in the last decade suggest—whether through statistics, case studies, or organizational reform efforts—that unwanted medical treatments commonly accompany the end of life.

4. The SUPPORT study found that 38 percent of patients who died at five hospitals spent at least ten days in the ICU prior to death.

5. Philip Roth, *Patrimony* (New York: Vintage Books, 1991), 230.

6. Ibid., 232–33.

7. See, for example, Bernard Lo and Lois Snyder, "Care at the End of Life: Guiding Practices Where There Are No Easy Answers" (editorial), *Annals of Internal Medicine* 130, no. 9 (1999): 772–74; and Thomas J. Prendergast, Michael T. Claessens, and John M. Luce, "A National Survey of End-of-Life Care for Critically Ill Patients," *American Journal of Respiratory and Critical Care Medicine* 158 (1998): 1163–67.

8. See chapter 1, note 8.

9. Perhaps, with pressure from various sectors of society, a palliative care pathway will become more dominant. See especially Franklin G. Miller and Joseph J. Fins, "A Proposal to Restructure Hospital Care for Dying Patients, *New England Journal of Medicine* 334 (1996): 1740–42; C. K. Cassel and B. C. Vladeck, "ICD-9 Code for Palliative or Terminal Care," *New England Journal of Medicine* 335 (1996): 1232–33; C. K. Cassel, J. M. Ludden, and G. Moon, "Perceptions of Barriers to High-Quality Palliative Care in Hospitals," *Health Affairs* 19 (2000): 166–72; J. Lynn, "Serving Patients Who May Die Soon and Their Families: The Role of Hospice and Other Services," *Journal of the American Medical Association* 285 (2001): 925–32; and J. Lynn et al., "Quality Improvements in End of

Life Care: Insights from Two Collaboratives," *The Joint Commission Journal on Quality Improvement* 26 (2000): 254–67.

10. Kolata, "Living Wills Aside"; M. Danis et al., "Stability of Choices about Life-Sustaining Treatments," *Annals of Internal Medicine* 120 (1994): 567–73; Marion Danis et al., "A Prospective Study of the Impact of Patient Preferences on Life-Sustaining Treatment and Hospital Cost," *Critical Care Medicine* 24 (1996): 1811–17; J. M. Teno et al., "Preferences for Cardiopulmonary Resuscitation: Physician-Patient Agreement and Hospital Resource Use," *Journal of General Internal Medicine* 10 (1995): 179–86.

11. Joanne Lynn et al. for the SUPPORT investigators, "Perceptions by Family Members of the Dying Experience of Older and Seriously Ill Patients," *Annals of Internal Medicine* 126 (January 15, 1997): 97–106.

12. E. Somogyi-Zalud et al., "Elderly Persons' Last Six Months of Life: Findings from the Hospitalized Elderly Longitudinal Project," *Journal of the American Geriatrics Society* 48 (May 2000): S131–39.

13. David Frankl, Robert K. Oye, and Paul E. Bellamy, "Attitudes of Hospitalized Patients toward Life Support: A Survey of 200 Medical Inpatients," *American Journal of Medicine* 86 (June 1989): 645–48.

14. J. Tsevat et al. for the HELP investigators, "Health Values of Hospitalized Patients 80 Years or Older," *Journal of the American Medical Association* 279 (1998): 371–75.

15. M. Danis et al., "A Comparison of Patient, Family, and Physician Assessments of the Value of Medical Intensive Care," *Critical Care Medicine* 16 (1988): 594–600; M. Sonnenblick, Y. Friedlander, and A. Steinberg, "Dissociation between the Wishes of Terminally Ill Parents and Decisions by Their Offspring," *Journal of the American Geriatrics Society* 41 (1993): 599–604.

16. Sara Carmel and Elizabeth J. Mutran, "Stability of Elderly Persons' Expressed Preferences Regarding the Use of Life-Sustaining Treatments," *Social Science and Medicine* 49 (1999): 303–11.

17. Chronic obstructive pulmonary disease, that is, lung disease.

18. Mechanical ventilator.

19. Do not attempt resuscitation if she has a cardiac or respiratory arrest.

20. The percentage of patients who followed the heroic intervention pathway to death during the years of my observations is consistent with other accounts. Twenty to 25 percent of American hospital deaths occur following similar scenarios (John F. Murray, *Intensive Care: A Doctor's Journal* [Berkeley: University of California Press, 2000]).

    Although emergency room policies and practices regarding life prolongation can be considered truly age-blind, they are one important source of what has come to be regarded as "the problem of death" because the use of the mechanical ventilator, when it only prolongs dying, begins for many in the hospital emergency room. B. M. Singal, J. R. Hedges, and E. W. Rousseau, "Geriatric Patient Emergency Visits," *Annals of Emergency Medicine* 21 [1992]: 802–7.

21. The SUPPORT study found that for the 1,150 hospital patients enrolled in the first phase of the study, the average number of days spent in an ICU, comatose or receiving mechanical ventilation, was eight. More than one-third (38 percent) spent at least ten days in an ICU before death, and 46 percent received mechanical ventilation within three days of death (The SUPPORT Principal Investigators, "A Controlled Trial to Improve Care for Seriously Ill Hospital-

ized Patients," *Journal of the American Medical Association,* 274 [1995]: 1591–98).

22. This is hospital jargon for the gradual reduction of oxygen delivered through the machine to the lungs or removal of the machine for added hours each day so that the patient can learn to breathe again on his own. This is a routine procedure.

23. A flexible tube to administer oxygen.

24. Even an oxygen mask.

25. I learned that some physicians, at least at the hospital where Mr. Brown was a patient, are not clear about hospital policy regarding withholding and withdrawing life-sustaining treatments.

26. Such a written document allows the medical staff to stop life-sustaining treatment without fear of litigation.

27. The SUPPORT intervention nurses reported similarly that patients or families needed to be "ready" to "make decisions": P. Murphy et al., "Description of the SUPPORT Intervention," *Journal of the American Geriatric Society* 48 (2000): S154-61; and Joann Lynn et al., "Rethinking Fundamental Assumptions: SUPPORT's Implications for Future Reform," *Journal of the American Geriatric Society* 48 (2000): S214-21.

28. Although no laws in California require family approval to withdraw life-sustaining treatments, physicians are concerned about what families might do should treatments be withdrawn without specific consent. Thus physicians generally search for competent family members before withdrawing treatments.

29. American Heart Association, American Red Cross, Industrial Medical Association, U.S. Public Health Service, "The Closed-Chest Method of Cardiopulmonary Resuscitation—Revised Statement," *Circulation* 31 (1965): 641–43; G. D. Rubenfeld, "Do-Not-Resuscitate Orders: A Critical Review of the Literature," *Respiratory Care* 40 (1995): 528–35, discussion, 35–37; Stefan Timmermans, *Sudden Death and the Myth of CPR* (Philadelphia: Temple University Press, 1999), 56–62.

30. Joyce Coletta Leary, "Emotional Boundaries: The Physician's Experience of Patient Death" (master's thesis, Health and Medical Sciences, University of California, Berkeley, 2002); Jeanne Benoliel, RN, personal communication.

31. Rubenfeld, "Do-Not-Resuscitate Orders"; Clinical Care Committee of the Massachusetts General Hospital, "Optimum Care for Hopelessly Ill Patients," *New England Journal of Medicine* 295 (1976): 364–69; M. T. Rabkin, G. Gillerman, and N. R. Rice, "Orders Not to Resuscitate," *New England Journal of Medicine* 295 (1976): 367–69.

32. Rubenfeld, "Do-Not-Resuscitate Orders"; President's Commission for the Study of Ethical Problems in Medicine and Biomedical and Behavioral Research, "Deciding to Forgo Life-Sustaining Treatment: A Report on the Ethical, Medical, and Legal Issues in Treatment Decisions" (Washington, DC: U.S. Government Printing Office, 1983).

33. Elisabeth Rosenthal, "Rules on Reviving the Dying Bring Undue Suffering, Doctors Contend," *New York Times,* October 4, 1990, A1.

34. M. Hilberman et al., "Marginally Effective Medical Care: Ethical Analysis of Issues in Cardiopulmonary Resuscitation," *Journal of Medical Ethics* 23 (1997): 361–67; S. C. Schultz et al., "Predicting In-Hospital Mortality during Cardiopulmonary Resuscitation," *Resuscitation* 33 (1996): 13–17; H. Y. So, T. A. Buckley, and T. E. Oh, "Factors Affecting Outcome following Cardiopul-

monary Resuscitation," *Anesthesiology Intensive Care* 22 (1994): 647–58; C. F. Von Gunten, "CPR in Hospitalized Patients: When Is It Futile?" *American Family Physician* 44 (1991): 2130–34.

35. K. Faber-Langendoen, "Resuscitation of Patients with Metastatic Cancer," *Archives of Internal Medicine* 151 (1991): 235–39; Schultz et al., "Predicting In-Hospital Mortality," 13–17; M. H. Ebell et al., "Survival after In-Hospital Cardiopulmonary Resuscitation: A Meta-Analysis," *Journal of General Internal Medicine* 13 (1998): 805–16; T. W. Zoch et al., "Short- and Long-Term Survival after Cardiopulmonary Resuscitation," *Archives of Internal Medicine* 160 (2000): 1969–73; M. S. Eisenberg and T. J. Mengert, "Cardiac Resuscitation," *New England Journal of Medicine* 344 (2001): 1304–13.

36. Paul E. Marik and Michelle Craft, "Outcomes Analysis of In-Hospital Cardiopulmonary Resuscitation: The Futility Rationale for Do Not Resuscitate Orders," *Journal of Critical Care* 12 (1997): 142–46; Monroe Karetzky, M. Zubair, and Jayesh Parikh, "Cardiopulmonary Resuscitation in Intensive Care Unit and Non–Intensive Care Unit Patients," *Archives of Internal Medicine* 155 (1995): 1277–80.

37. Timmermans, *Sudden Death*, 79–82.

38. Katie Young, "In-Hospital CPR" (master's thesis, Health and Medical Sciences, University of California, Berkeley, 2002); R. J. Hamill, "Resuscitation: When Is Enough, Enough?" *Respiratory Care* 40 (1995): 515–24.

39. Timmermans, *Sudden Death*, 81. See also D. R. Miranda, "Quality of Life after Cardiopulmonary Resuscitation," *Chest* 106 (1994): 524–29.

40. Susan J. Diem, John D. Lantos, and James A. Tulsky, "Cardiopulmonary Resuscitation on Television—Miracles and Misinformation," *New England Journal of Medicine* 334 (1996): 1578–82; G. K. Jones, K. L. Brewer, and H. G. Garrison, "Public Expectations of Survival following Cardiopulmonary Resuscitation," *Academic Emergency Medicine* 7 (2000): 48–53.

41. One national survey demonstrated that fewer patients who die now undergo CPR. Yet there is great variability in resuscitation rates at American hospitals. CPR was attempted in only 4 percent of ICU patients in one hospital, but in 75 percent of ICU patients in another. See Prendergast, Claessens, and Luce, "A National Survey of End-of-Life Care," 1163–67. That variation points to a lack of standardized guidelines for CPR performed in the ICU (Young, "In-Hospital CPR").

42. See, for example, Tom Tomlinson and Howard Brody, "Futility and the Ethics of Resuscitation," *Journal of the American Medical Association* 264 (1990): 1276–80; J. Chris Hackler and F. Charles Hiller, "Family Consent to Orders Not to Resuscitate: Reconsidering Hospital Policy," *Journal of the American Medical Association* 264 (1990): 1281–83; Tom Tomlinson and Diane Czlonka, "Futility and Hospital Policy," *Hastings Center Report*, May–June 1995, 28–35; Teresa A. Hillier et al., "Physicians as Patients: Choices regarding Their Own Resuscitation," *Archives of Internal Medicine* 155 (1995): 1289–93; and Marguerite S. Lederberg, "Doctors in Limbo: The United States 'DNR' Debate," *Psycho-Oncology* 6 (1997): 321–28.

43. Even when hospital policy allows physicians to withdraw life-prolonging treatments that are not beneficial, they give patients/families a "choice." See chapter 1, note 27.

44. J. R. Lunney, J. Lynn, and C. Hogan, "Profiles of Older Medicare Decedents," *Journal of the American Geriatrics Society* 50 (2002): 1108–12.

45. Lynn, "Serving Patients Who May Die Soon" 285, 925–32; J. Lynn et al., "Defining the 'Terminally Ill': Insights from SUPPORT," *Duquesne Law Review,* 35 (1996): 311–36; J. Lynn et al., "Prognoses of Seriously Ill Hospitalized Patients on the Days before Death," *New Horizons* 5 (1997): 56–61.

46. See chapter 1, note 44.

47. That is, there is no medically indicated reason for her to be in the hospital right now.

48. Shortness of breath.

49. One physician who read the story of Mrs. Parker commented that the physician in charge of her care could have "made up a treatment plan," for example, treatment of severe dyspnea. Physicians and nurses are adept at creating treatment plans so that patients can remain hospitalized. But in this case, a treatment plan for keeping Mrs. Parker in the hospital never materialized.

50. Some physicians use morphine drips liberally; others refuse to use them. Some withdraw feeding tubes in anticipation of death; others do not. Some believe that aggressive treatment is indicated almost to the moment of death; others feel that aggressive treatment is not appropriate when patients with certain diseases are in declining health. There is no socially mandated "right" or "wrong" medical approach to the end of life, and doctors, patients, and families can and do make all kinds of choices about what to do. Much of that kind of decision-making does not involve the imperative of first interpreting the category of the person before acting.

51. The doctrine of double effect allows a clinician to administer high doses of opioid analgesics for the purpose of relieving severe pain and suffering in terminally ill patients, even though high amounts can cause the patient to die sooner than she otherwise would. The principle of double effect allows for death to be foreseen but not intended. In that way, death hastened by the administration of pain-relieving drugs is considered morally permissible (T. Quill, R. Dresser, and D. W. Brock, "The Rule of Double Effect—a Critique of Its Role in End-of-Life Decision Making," *New England Journal of Medicine* 337 [1997]: 1768–71). See also J. Garcia, "Double Effect," in W. T. Reich, ed., *Encyclopedia of Bioethics,* vol. 2 (New York: Simon and Schuster, 1995): 636–41; and H. Brody, "Causing, Intending, and Assisting Death," *Journal of Clinical Ethics* 4 (1993): 112–17.

52. A mask that goes over nose and mouth and that pushes oxygen into the patient's lungs.

53. U.S. Department of Health and Human Services, *Medicare Handbook* (Centers for Medicare and Medicaid Services, 2002, Publication No. CMS-10050); M. E. Gluck and K. W. Hanson, *Medicare Chart Book,* 2nd ed. (Menlo Park, CA: The Henry J. Kaiser Foundation, 2001).

54. The copayment required for days twenty-one to one hundred in 2001 was $99 per day. Gluck and Hanson, *Medicare Chart Book.*

55. http://www.medicare.gov/Nursing/payment.

56. That is, to reduce one's total assets.

57. Of elderly nursing home residents who rely on Medicare at the time of admission, approximately 40 percent shift to Medicaid. Of those who rely on private insurance, their own income, or family support at the time of admission, about 22 percent switch to Medicaid. See A. N. Dey, "Characteristics of Elderly Nursing Home Residents: Data from the 1995 National Nursing Home Survey, U.S. Dept. of Health and Human Services, National Center for Health Statistics,"

Advance Data 289 (July 2, 1997). See also Brenda C. Spillman and Peter Kemper, "Lifetime Patterns of Payment for Nursing Home Care," *Medical Care* 33 (1995): 280–96.

58. I am indebted to Charlene Harrington for her lucid explanation of the way Medicare and Medicaid policies actually affect nursing home and revolving door hospital patients. Dorothy Rice and Norman Fineman provided research support. See also H. A. Huskamp et al., "Providing Care at the End of Life," *Health Affairs* 20 (2001): 204–11; and J. Lynn et al., "Capitated Risk-Bearing Managed Care Systems Could Improve End-of-Life Care," *Journal of the American Geriatrics Society* 46 (1998): 322–30.

59. To the chagrin of many nurses, most doctors do not make hospice certifications often enough or soon enough, and nurses are not allowed to prescribe it (though they can and do suggest it to physicians). Family members, even if they have heard of hospice care for terminal illness, are not clear about how it works, when it is appropriate, when it starts, or what their role in it is. I was surprised to learn how many families had not heard of hospice care or had heard the term used but had no idea what it was. I never heard a family suggest the relevance of hospice care for their relative. Most important, families are extremely hesitant to name death, to label a relative as dying, before a health professional does.

60. SUPPORT Principal Investigators, "A Controlled Trial."

CHAPTER 5. WAITING

1. Albert Jonsen, *The Birth of Bioethics* (New York: Oxford University Press, 1998), 53, 259.

2. Standard intravenous pump, used to deliver medications.

3. A fistula is a tract or passage between two hollow organs (such as the intestine and the bladder). It is usually caused by an infection or inflammatory process or disease.

4. TPN stands for "total parenteral nutrition." It refers to total nutrition (everything needed to sustain life) given through an intravenous route.

5. One physician told me that doctors often make pronouncements about quality of life based on what they think they themselves would tolerate if they were in their patient's place.

6. Jane Weeks et al., "Relationship between Cancer Patients' Predictions of Prognosis and Their Treatment Preferences," *Journal of the American Medical Association* 279 (1998): 1709–14. The authors state, "Specifically, patients who believed that they would survive for at least six months favored life-extending therapy over comfort care at more than double the rate of those who believed that there was at least a small chance (as little as 10 percent) that they would not live six months. This association was most marked in patients who were optimistic about their probability of surviving six months despite physician estimates to the contrary" (p. 1712).

  Other studies also find that patients tend to overestimate the probability of survival. For example, L. A. Siminoff, J. H. Fetting, and M. D. Abeloff, "Doctor-Patient Communication about Breast Cancer Adjuvant Therapy," *Journal of Clinical Oncology* 7 (1989): 1192–1200; and R. N. Eidinger and D. V. Schapira, "Cancer Patients' Insight into Their Treatment, Prognosis and Unconventional Therapies," *Cancer* 53 (1984): 2736–40.

7. Nicholas Christakis, in *Death Foretold* (Chicago: University of Chicago Press,

1999), shows that physicians consistently overestimate length of survival, yet medical prognosis for cancer is considered to be relatively more accurate than for other conditions. See Joanne Lynn et al., "Prognoses of Seriously Ill Hospitalized Patients on the Days before Death," *New Horizons* 5 (1997): 56–61.

8. Researchers have documented changing attitudes among physicians in the second half of the twentieth century surrounding "truth-telling" and the disclosure of a terminal prognosis for cancer. Until the 1970s, surveys of U.S. physicians showed their almost unanimous preference for "protecting" patients from news of impending death (Donald Oken, "What to Tell Cancer Patients—a Study of Medical Attitudes," *Journal of the American Medical Association* 175 [1961]: 1120–28). A radical shift in physician attitudes and approaches occurred by the mid-1970s, when surveys indicated that the overwhelming majority of physicians reported that "disclosure" was their usual policy (D. H. Novack et al., "Changes in Physicians' Attitudes toward Telling the Cancer Patient," *Journal of the American Medical Association* 241 [1979]: 897–900). More recently anthropologists have shown that disclosure practices in the United States are quite varied and nuanced. They found that truth-telling is partial, takes place in stages and is not a single "event," and is based on what patients ask. They conclude that full disclosure is never possible and is not considered by physicians to be therapeutic (Kathryn M. Taylor, "Physicians and the Disclosure of Undesirable Information," in *Biomedicine Examined,* ed. M. Lock and D. Gordon [Boston: Kluwer, 1988], 441–63; Mary-Jo Del Vecchio Good et al., "American Oncology and the Discourse on Hope," *Culture, Medicine and Psychiatry* 14 [1990]: 59–79.) See also Kate Brown, "Information Disclosure, I: Attitudes toward Truth-Telling," in *Encyclopedia of Bioethics,* rev. ed., ed. Warren Thomas Reich (New York: Simon and Schuster, 1995).

9. A physician who read this account of Ms. Graf reported he was irritated by physicians or nurses who think they should "call the shots." He felt strongly that, in this case, there was a goal—to keep the patient alive per her wishes, while, at the same time, keeping her comfortable.

10. Congestive heart failure is one of the leading causes of death in the United States, and deaths caused by CHF are especially difficult to prognosticate. Institute of Medicine, ed., *Approaching Death: Improving Care at the End of Life* (Washington, DC: National Academy Press, 1997), 105. See also Lynn et al., "Prognoses of Seriously Ill Hospitalized Patients."

11. Those medications, called vasopressors, are muscle-constricting drugs that increase the tone of the lax layer of smooth muscle in arteries, thus restoring blood pressure. John F. Murray, *Intensive Care* (Berkeley: University of California Press, 2000), 39.

12. Also called an arteriogram, an angiogram is a picture of a blood vessel, specifically, of an artery or arteries. It is obtained by injecting a radio-opaque liquid (a "dye") into an artery, thus allowing the artery to be seen. It shows the state of things inside an artery or arteries. A coronary angiogram is used to see inside the arteries that feed the heart.

13. A procedure in which a small balloon is threaded into a coronary artery and inflated to clear away the blockage.

14. The line between cardioversion, a planned procedure, and emergency CPR is a fine one to me and to physicians as well. One doctor explained that cardioversion consists of a relatively low-intensity electric shock to the heart. It usually employs less electrical energy than full-blown emergency resuscitation and

does not include the other procedures that usually accompany CPR, such as the administration of intravenous medication or the delivery of oxygen via mechanical ventilation. The goal of each procedure is frequently the same, however: to reestablish heartbeat and rhythm or to regulate a dangerous rhythm. Paddles are applied to the chest to deliver the electric current in either case. Cardioversion is a routine part of CPR where an abnormal heart rhythm is life-threatening. But the procedure also stands alone. It is not considered part of CPR when it is used to treat a non-life-threatening condition.

15. A g-tube, or gastric tube, is put into the stomach. A j-tube is inserted in the jejunum. Both g- and j-tubes are methods of "enteral nutrition," to be distinguished from TPN, or "parenteral nutrition" (note 4, above). Medical opinion varies, but some think that a j-tube is less likely to lead to reflux of the feeding solution back into the stomach, up the esophagus, and then into the lungs, where it can cause aspiration.

16. Recent research shows that feeding tubes in persons with advanced dementia cause more problems than they relieve and do not contribute to the prolongation of life. See note 29, this chapter.

17. The definition of PVS is complex and problematic. See chapter 8.

18. She'd been medically supported before and had not died. The positive outcome of that past hospitalization perhaps made her more likely to think she would go home, to *live*, one more time.

19. Generally, families give permission to withdraw life-sustaining technologies when more than one health care professional tells them that death is inevitable and will come soon with or without life support.

20. I am indebted to Philippe Bourgois for drawing my attention to this point.

21. Alan Coleman and Guy Micco, personal communication. The term *failure to thrive* has crept into geriatrics, as it has into all of medicine, from pediatrics, where it was first used to describe newborns and infants who were not growing according to norms established for child development early in the twentieth century. In children, a specific rate of growth and development is expected. *Failure to thrive* refers to a generic condition, below normal, without a specific diagnosis, a state of suboptimal health. See also R. B. Verdery, "Failure to Thrive in Old Age," *Journal of Gerontology* 52A (1997): M333-36; and C. A. Sarkisian and M. S. Lachs, "'Failure to Thrive' in Older Adults," *Annals of Internal Medicine* 124 (1996): 1072–78. One physician told me that *failure to thrive* has come to be an entirely derogatory term in clinical medicine, like *gomer*, and refers to old patients for whom nothing can be done.

22. A narrowing of the lower spinal canal caused by degenerative changes of the spine that occur with aging. It can be asymptomatic or lead to pain and weakness in the legs.

23. A serious infection of a heart valve.

24. The physician is referring to the "double effect" of morphine. It slows respiration and can thus cause death, at the same time as it reduces pain. See chapter 4, note 51.

25. Permanent stomach tube to deliver fluid and nutrition.

26. The feeding tube, like the mechanical ventilator, can be considered heroic life support or ordinary medical treatment. The ambiguities of life-supporting procedures and technologies are discussed in chapter 7.

27. M. D. Grant, M. A. Rudberg, and J. A. Brody, "Gastrostomy Placement and Mor-

tality among Hospitalized Medicare Beneficiaries," *Journal of the American Medical Association* 279 (1998): 1973–76; L. Rabeneck, N. P. Wray, and N. J. Petersen, "Long-Term Outcomes of Patients Receiving Percutaneous Endoscopic Gastrostomy Tubes," *Journal of General Internal Medicine* 11 (1996): 287–93.

28. M. O. Hodges and S. W. Tolle, "Tube-Feeding Decisions in the Elderly," *Clinics in Geriatric Medicine* 10 (1994): 475–88; J. Kayser-Jones, "The Use of Nasogastric Feeding Tubes in Nursing Homes," *The Gerontologist* 30 (1990): 469–79; C. L. Sprung, "Changing Attitudes and Practices in Forgoing Life-Sustaining Treatments," *Journal of the American Medical Association* 263 (1990): 2211–15; Joanne Lynn, ed., *By No Extraordinary Means: The Choice to Forgo Life-Sustaining Food and Water,* expanded ed. (Bloomington: Indiana University Press, 1989).

29. T. E. Finucane, C. Christmas, and K. Travis, "Tube Feeding in Patients with Advanced Dementia: A Review of the Evidence," *Journal of the American Medical Association* 282 (1999): 1365–70; Muriel R. Gillick, "Rethinking the Role of Tube Feeding in Patients with Advanced Dementia," *New England Journal of Medicine* 342 (2000): 206–10.

30. I do not know the circumstances that made it possible for that ninety-seven-year-old woman to move toward death without days of life-prolonging treatments.

31. Yet one physician told me that larger doses of morphine rarely "kill" patients.

32. Without a written order in the chart, nurses on the unit would have to attempt to resuscitate the patient if she had a cardiac arrest, despite the fact that she was actively dying.

33. Several days before this incident, I witnessed a resuscitation attempt on the oncology unit. Eight people rushed to a man's room after his heart stopped and spent about twenty minutes unsuccessfully trying to bring him "back to life." The man had a terminal diagnosis, and some thought he would die quite soon from his disease. An oncologist said, "We should have let him go a month ago." Two nurses, another doctor, and a social worker remarked that they "do too many codes." "Perhaps," the social worker said, "if more people saw them, there would be less of them. And if the patient survives, he isn't in as good shape [neurologically] as before." A doctor said, "If it's very advanced disease, maybe they won't do CPR, because it isn't medically indicated, even when 'Full Code' is written in the chart. But if a patient is not imminently dying, he will be coded."

34. Diagnostic work frequently continues until death, per institutional routines, as does the administration of fluids.

PART III: THE POLITICS AND RHETORIC OF THE PATIENT'S CONDITION: "SUFFERING," "DIGNITY," AND THE "QUALITY OF LIFE"

CHAPTER 6. DEATH BY DESIGN

1. Thanks to Vincanne Adams for her help in clarifying this point.

2. The phrase was used by a critical care physician at Beth Israel Hospital, Boston, in Frederick Wiseman's 1989 documentary film, *Near Death,* which is described in chapter 1, including note 31. The phrase is instructive in that it drew my attention to the manner in which "ethical decision-making" takes place in a complex institutional world of differential power relations in which different things are at stake for different players. In that way, it is a political activity, organized and negotiated through various rhetorical strategies.

3. This distinction is described also in Jacquelyn Slomka, "The Negotiation of

Death: Clinical Decision Making at the End of Life," *Social Science and Medicine* 35 (1992): 251–59.

4. For a comprehensive history of those debates, see Albert R. Jonsen, *The Birth of Bioethics* (New York: Oxford University Press, 1998).

5. Robert A. Pearlman and Albert Jonsen, "The Use of Quality-of-Life Considerations in Medical Decision Making," *Journal of the American Geriatrics Society* 33 (1985): 344–50.

6. Ibid., 348.

7. Ibid. See also D. C. Thomasma, "Ethical Judgments of Quality of Life in the Care of the Aged," *Journal of the American Geriatrics Society* 32 (1984): 525; R. A. Pearlman and J. B. Speer, "Quality-of-Life Considerations in Geriatric Care," *Journal of the American Geriatrics Society* 31 (1983): 113.

8. Pearlman and Jonsen, "Use of Quality-of-Life Considerations"; Thomasma, "Ethical Judgments."

9. Bruce Jennings, "A Life Greater than the Sum of Its Sensations: Ethics, Dementia, and the Quality of Life," *Journal of Mental Health and Aging* 5 (1999): 95–106.

10. Leon R. Kass, "Death with Dignity and the Sanctity of Life," in *A Time to Be Born and a Time to Die: The Ethics of Choice,* ed. Barry S. Kogan (New York: Aldine deGruyter, 1991); Kurt Bayertz, *Sanctity of Life and Human Dignity* (Dordrecht/Boston: Kluwer, 1996). See also Ronald Dworkin, *Life's Dominion* (New York: Knopf, 1993).

11. Jonsen, *Birth of Bioethics*, 337–38; Daniel Callahan, "The Sanctity of Life," in *Updating Life and Death*, ed. Donald Cutler (Boston: Beacon Press, 1969); Edward Shils, "The Sanctity of Life," in *Life or Death: Ethics and Options*, ed. Daniel Labby (Seattle: University of Washington Press, 1968).

12. Philosopher Peter Singer claims that modern medical practice has rendered that traditional view no longer tenable. See his *Rethinking Life and Death* (New York: St. Martin's Griffin, 1994).

13. This point is made by K. Dan Clouser, " 'The Sanctity of Life': An Analysis of a Concept," *Annals of Internal Medicine* 78 (1973): 119–25.

14. Toxic shock is a severe illness caused by a bacterial infection.

15. The physician's use of the word *successfully* means that the patient did not die.

16. Supplemental Social Security Insurance.

17. A doctor who read this story commented, "It wasn't his [the physician's] job to adjust the IV morphine," and that perhaps he did not know how to make the adjustment, either.

CHAPTER 7. LIFE SUPPORT

1. Thanks to Robert Brody for emphasizing this point.

2. See J. M. Teno et al., "Medical Care Inconsistent with Patients' Treatment Goals," *Journal of the American Geriatrics Society* 50 (2002): 496–500.

3. Neither the patient's age nor the ethnicity nor the religion of the patient and family seemed to make a difference in my small sample.

4. In a study of the relationship at one institution of formal hospital policy to actual physician practices regarding CPR, the authors found that, despite a policy that allows physicians to withhold the offer of CPR, most offered CPR to patients, regardless of benefit. The authors conclude that respect for patient autonomy prevails at the hospital studied and that doctors do not act uniformly on their authority to withhold CPR from patients whom they consider

unlikely to benefit. Louise Swig et al., "Physician Responses to a Hospital Policy Allowing Them to Not Offer Cardiopulmonary Resuscitation," *Journal of the American Geriatrics Society* 44 (1996): 1215–19. In his film *Near Death,* filmmaker Frederick Wiseman documented similar hospital staff practices.

5. See chapter 6, note 10.
6. This phrase is taken from Margaret Pabst Battin, *The Least Worst Death* (New York: Oxford University Press, 1994).
7. In a study of dialysis patients who received emergency CPR, 95 percent were on mechanical ventilation in an ICU at the time of death. See A. H. Moss, J. L. Holley, and M. B. Upton, "Outcomes of Cardiopulmonary Resuscitation in Dialysis Patients," *Journal of the American Society of Nephrology* 3 (1992): 1238–43.
8. The question of whether treatments are "futile" or beneficial looms large in the bioethics discourse and is debated at bedsides continually. For a description of both sides of the futility debate in clinical medicine, see Lawrence Sniderman, Nancy Jecker, and Albert A. Jonsen, "Medical Futility: Response to Critiques," *Annals of Internal Medicine* 125 (1996): 669–74; Susan B. Rubin, *When Doctors Say NO: The Battleground of Medical Futility* (Bloomington: Indiana University Press, 1998); and Laurie Zoloth-Dorfman and Susan B. Rubin, "'Medical Futility': Managed Care and the Powerful New Vocabulary for Clinical and Public Policy Discourse," *Healthcare Forum Journal,* March-April, 1997. For a discussion about the constraints perceived by gastroenterologists regarding the placement of feeding tubes, see Sharon R. Kaufman, "Construction and Practice of Medical Responsibility: Dilemmas and Narratives from Geriatrics," *Culture, Medicine and Psychiatry* 21 (1997): 1–26.
9. Mr. Morrison has also become "a placement problem" in the larger health care system. Long-term facilities that accept comatose, ventilator-dependent patients generally do not accept them if they need kidney dialysis as well.
10. See Stefan Timmermans, *Sudden Death and the Myth of CPR* (Philadelphia: Temple University Press, 1999).
11. Mr. Morrison's primary care physician agreed with my rendition of events and noted in retrospect that he might have done more to end things (by stopping some treatments) if he had more "strongly held" the staff position.
12. This device works like a ventilator, but without a tube down the trachea. Physicians refer to it as "noninvasive mechanical ventilation."
13. *Unweanable* implies that the person will be on the ventilator for life.
14. A bedsore, or pressure sore, is an ulceration of the skin that occurs because of immobility and pressure (decubitus ulcer).
15. See Jodi Halpern, *From Detached Concern to Empathy: Humanizing Medical Practice* (New York: Oxford University Press, 2001), for a recent discussion.
16. P. S. Appelbaum, C. W. Lidz, and A. Meisel, "Patients Who Refuse Treatment," in *Informed Consent: Legal Theory and Clinical Practice* (New York: Oxford University Press, 1987), 90–207; J. Katz, *The Silent World of Doctor and Patient* (New York: Free Press, 1984).
17. Halpern, *From Detached Concern,* 101.
18. Sam Martin (chapter 2) was in a similar situation in which only certain parts of the resuscitation procedure were authorized.
19. Received more blood, and thus more oxygen.
20. Oxygen saturation levels.
21. Systemic lupus erythematosus.

22. One physician commented to me that the existence of and emphasis on advance directives in American society makes people feel guilty if they change their minds.

CHAPTER 8. HIDDEN PLACES:
THE ZONE OF INDISTINCTION AS A WAY OF *LIFE*

Opening Epigraph   Paul Rabinow, *French DNA* (Chicago: University of Chicago Press, 1999), 16.
Epigraph, p. 296   David Armstrong, "Silence and Truth in Death and Dying," *Social Science & Medicine* 24 (1987): 655.

1. Persons in PVS who reside in their own homes or in nursing homes are not usually in need of mechanical ventilation.
2. See discussion of Medicare payment schemes, and note 8, in chapter 1.
3. Sandeep Jauhar, "As Technology Improves, More People Breathe with Machines," *New York Times,* April 24, 2001, D7; S. S. Carson et al., "Outcomes after Long-Term Acute Care," *American Journal of Respiratory and Critical Care Medicine* 159 (1999): 1568–73.
4. Marilyn Strathern, *After Nature* (Cambridge: Cambridge University Press, 1992). See especially pages 177–84.
5. My knowledge of the place, and of the patients in the place, is grounded more firmly in staff perspectives and actions than in family (or patient) orientations. This is because staff were always present, family members were mostly not present, and patients were mostly noncommunicative. Thus my greatest access was to staff knowledge and practices.
6. See Jean-Dominique Bauby, *The Diving Bell and the Butterfly* (New York: Knopf, 1997), for an extraordinary memoir of a man afflicted with locked-in syndrome.
7. See Deborah R. Gordon, "Tenacious Assumptions in Western Medicine," in *Biomedicine Examined,* ed. M. Lock and D. Gordon (Boston: Kluwer, 1988), 19–56, for elaboration of this point.
8. According to the fundamental division between mind and body that Western societies and Western medicine still largely assume.
9. R. E. Cranford and D. R. Smith, "Consciousness: The Most Critical Moral (Constitutional) Standard for Human Personhood," *American Journal of Law and Medicine* 13 (1987): 233–48; Antonio Damasio, *The Feeling of What Happens: Body and Emotion in the Making of Consciousness* (New York: Harcourt, 1999).
10. Multi-Society Task Force on PVS, "Medical Aspects of the Persistent Vegetative State (Part I)," *New England Journal of Medicine* 330 (1994): 1499–1508. This statement was approved by the governing bodies of the American Academy of Neurology, American Neurological Association, American Association of Neurological Surgeons, Child Neurology Society, and American Academy of Pediatrics.
11. Ibid.
12. Marcia Angell, "After Quinlan: The Dilemma of the Persistent Vegetative State," *New England Journal of Medicine* 330 (1994): 1524–25.
13. Multi-Society Task Force, "Medical Aspects," 1500–1502.
14. Raphael Cohen-Almagor, "Some Observations on Post-Coma Unawareness Patients and on Other Forms of Unconscious Patients: Policy Proposals," *Medicine and Law* 16 (1997): 451–71.
15. It is not known how many people in PVS reside outside of institutions, in their own homes. In addition, the national prevalence of PVS is not known because

of the lack of accepted diagnostic criteria. However, there are estimated to be ten thousand to twenty-five thousand adults and four thousand to ten thousand children in PVS in the United States, residing in private residences and institutions (Multi-Society Task Force, "Medical Aspects").

See especially Keith Andrews, "Vegetative State—Background and Ethics," *Journal of the Royal Society of Medicine* 90 (1997): 593–96; D. Bates, "Persistent Vegetative State and Brain Stem Death," *Current Opinion in Neurology* 10 (1997): 502–5; Adam Zeman, "Persistent Vegetative State," *Lancet* 350 (1997): 795–99.

16. Christian J. Borthwick, "The Permanent Vegetative State: Ethical Crux, Medical Fiction?" *Issues in Law & Medicine* 12 (1996): 167–85; Christian J. Borthwick, "The Proof of the Vegetable: A Commentary on Medical Futility," *Journal of Medical Ethics* 21 (1995): 205–8; A. A. Howsepian, "The 1994 Multi-Society Task Force Consensus Statement on the Persistent Vegetative State: A Critical Analysis," *Issues in Law & Medicine* 12 (1996): 3–29.

17. Kirk Payne et al., "Physicians' Attitudes about the Care of Patients in the Persistent Vegetative State: A National Survey," *Annals of Internal Medicine* 125 (1996): 104–10.

18. Ibid.; Eric Cassell, "Clinical Incoherence about Persons: The Problem of the Persistent Vegetative State," *Annals of Internal Medicine* 125 (1996): 146–47.

19. For a discussion of the relationship of the notion of "person" to the idea of brain death, see Margaret Lock, "On Dying Twice: Culture, Technology and the Determination of Death," in *Living and Working with the New Medical Technologies,* ed. M. Lock, A. Young, and A. Cambrosio (Cambridge: Cambridge University Press, 2000), 233–62.

20. D. A. Cusack, A. A. Sheikh, and J. L. Hyslop-Westrup, "'Near PVS': A New Medico-Legal Syndrome?" *Medicine, Science and the Law* 40 (2000): 133–42.

21. Ibid., 140.

22. Cranford and Smith, "Consciousness." The authors state, "Medicine cannot preserve and maintain health because there is no health for a patient in persistent vegetative state, only life in terms of the most primitive vegetative functions . . . health is an empty concept for a patient without consciousness" (p. 242).

23. Claude Levi-Strauss, *The Savage Mind* (Chicago: University of Chicago Press, 1966).

24. See especially Robert N. Bellah et al., *Habits of the Heart* (Berkeley: University of California Press, 1985); Michel Foucault, *The Order of Things* (New York: Vintage, 1973); Michel Foucault, *Discipline and Punish* (New York: Pantheon Books, 1977); Anthony Giddens, *Modernity and Self-Identity* (Stanford: Stanford University Press, 1991); and Unni Wikan, "The Self in a World of Urgency and Necessity," *Ethos* 23 (1995): 259–85.

25. George Herbert Mead, *Mind, Self and Society* (Chicago: University of Chicago Press, 1934); Michel Foucault, *Order of Things*; Foucault, *The History of Sexuality, Vol. 1: An Introduction* (New York: Vintage Books, 1980); Gordon, "Tenacious Assumptions."

26. Gordon, "Tenacious Assumptions," 40; Wikan, "Self in a World."

27. Charles Taylor, "The Person," in *The Category of the Person,* ed. Michael Carrithers, Steven Collins, and Steven Lukes (Cambridge: Cambridge University Press, 1985), 257–81; Charles Taylor, *Sources of the Self: The Making of Modern Identity* (Cambridge: Harvard University Press, 1989).

28. Sarah Franklin, *Embodied Progress* (London and New York: Routledge, 1997);

Sarah Franklin, "Making Miracles: Scientific Progress and the Facts of Life," in *Reproducing Reproduction,* ed. Sarah Franklin and Helena Ragone (Philadelphia: University of Pennsylvania Press, 1998), 102–17; Gordon, "Tenacious Assumptions"; Sharon R. Kaufman, "Toward a Phenomenology of Boundaries in Medicine," *Medical Anthropology Quarterly* 2 (1988): 338–54.

29. Arthur Frank, *The Wounded Storyteller* (Chicago: University of Chicago Press, 1995).

30. *Cyanotic* means "blue." It refers to a blueness of the skin due to a low oxygen content in the blood.

31. Studies that point to religion or ethnicity, as though they were discrete variables that can, by themselves, influence or determine end-of-life "decision-making," ignore the complexity of those notions in any individual experience as well as the immense variability in how they are lived. Neither religion nor ethnicity, when employed as defining labels, can capture or predict the ways in which those mutable constructs are felt over a lifetime and how they impact particular medical "decisions."

32. Scholarship on the making of the modern subject and the ways in which subjectivity is produced is vast. The works of Michel Foucault, Nikolas Rose, and Charles Taylor (among others) are foundational to much recent work (including my own) in the medical social sciences on the "practices in which persons are understood and acted upon" (Nikolas Rose, *Inventing Our Selves: Psychology, Power, and Personhood* [Cambridge, U.K.: Cambridge University Press, 1998], 23).

33. By bringing the family together at that moment, the hospital staff may have brought pressure, coaxed, or suggested to the family that it was appropriate, now, for the patient's life to end.

34. I am indebted to an anonymous reviewer for pointing out this incongruity.

35. Elaine Scarry, *The Body in Pain* (New York: Oxford University Press, 1985).

36. Debates about what constitutes futile treatment in medical care have been lively for over twenty years. For recent reviews and summaries of that debate, see Ethics Committee of the Society of Critical Care Medicine, "Consensus Statement of the Society of Critical Care Medicine's Ethics Committee regarding Futile and Other Possibly Inadvisable Treatments," *Critical Care Medicine* 25 (1997): 887–91; and P. Helft, M. Siegler, and J. Lantos, "The Rise and Fall of the Futility Movement," *New England Journal of Medicine* 343 (2000): 293–96. See also chapter 7, note 8.

37. Robert Veatch, *Death, Dying, and the Biological Revolution: Our Last Quest for Responsibility,* rev. ed. (New Haven: Yale University Press, 1989), 30.

38. President's Commission for the Study of Ethical Problems in Medicine and Biomedical and Behavioral Research, *Defining Death: Medical, Legal and Ethical Issues in the Determination of Death* (Washington, DC: Government Printing Office, 1981). The commission was formed in response to the Ad Hoc Harvard Committee's definition of *brain death.* The Harvard committee's impact is discussed in chapter 2.

39. Martin S. Pernick, "Back from the Grave: Recurring Controversies over Defining and Diagnosing Death in History," in *Death: Beyond Whole-Brain Criteria,* ed. Richard M. Zaner (Boston: Kluwer, 1988), 59; President's Commission, *Defining Death,* especially pp. 38–40.

The definition of death proposed by the president's commission did not move very far from ordinary clinical practice, public attitudes, or legal under-standings of the day. See Albert Jonsen, *The Birth of Bioethics* (New York: Oxford University Press, 1998), 243.

40. Veatch, *Death, Dying*, 27. See also Damasio, *Feeling of What Happens.*
41. Robert M. Veatch, "The Impending Collapse of the Whole-Brain Definition of Death," *Hastings Center Report* 23 (1993): 18–24; Stuart Youngner, "Defining Death: A Superficial and Fragile Consensus," *Archives of Neurology* 49 (1992): 570–72; S. Youngner et al., "'Brain Death' and Organ Retrieval: A Cross-Sectional Survey of Knowledge and Concepts among Health Professionals," *Journal of the American Medical Association* 261 (1989): 2205–10; Margaret Lock, *Twice Dead* (Berkeley: University of California Press, 2002); Gary Green-berg, "As Good as Dead," *New Yorker,* August 13, 2001, 36–41.
42. Cranford and Smith, "Consciousness."
43. Katharine Young, *Presence in the Flesh* (Cambridge: Harvard University Press, 1997).
44. Aphasia is the loss of the ability to speak or comprehend spoken or written lan-guage, resulting from brain damage.
45. *Hypoxic* means "low on oxygen." Hypoxia in the brain is usually the result of lack of blood flow to the brain. A typical cause of hypoxic brain injury is car-diac arrest with delayed resuscitation—if the heart does not pump for several minutes, blood does not flow to the brain.
46. Drew Leder, *The Absent Body* (Chicago: University of Chicago Press, 1990), 161.
47. For a recent discussion of the question of "meaningful life" in the context of pro-found disability, see Harriet McBryde Johnson, "Should I Have Been Killed at Birth? The Case for My Life," *New York Times Magazine,* February 16, 2003, 50. Johnson's article is a response to the work of controversial ethicist Peter Singer.
48. One cannot help but compare the "window" of opportunity that the social worker articulates with the window that Mr. Lenczyk jumped from. Her use of that word is symbolically loaded. It implies that maybe there will be an appro-priate moment in which the family can, with support from the hospital staff, push him through a (symbolic) window again.
49. Jean-Paul Sartre, *The Transcendence of the Ego: An Existentialist Theory of Con-sciousness,* trans. Forrest Williams and Robert Kirkpatrick (New York: Farrar, Straus and Giroux, 1956).
50. Physician and philosopher Drew Leder reminds us that the term *compassion* "is derived from the Latin *cum* and *patior,* which together can be literally translated as 'to suffer with.'" We speak of compassion in relation to someone whom we feel is suffering. To be compassionate is thus to "enter into the experience of others through a process of empathic identification." Leder, *Absent Body,* 161.
51. Emmanuel Levinas, "Useless Suffering," in *The Provocation of Levinas,* ed. R. Bernasconi and D. Wood (London: Routledge, 1988), 156–67.
52. Philosopher Ed Casey suggests that the qualities that comprise *the person* and *the human* may be impossible to definitively characterize or apprehend in any context (personal communication).

CHAPTER 9. CULTURE IN THE MAKING

1. Joanne Lynn et al., "Rethinking Fundamental Assumptions: SUPPORT's Implications for Future Reform," *Journal of the American Geriatrics Society* 48 (2000): S214–21.

2. The SUPPORT study is introduced in chapter 1. In their reflections five years later, the researchers realized, first, that the course of hospitalized patients' care is guided not by individual "preferences" or shared decision-making, but rather by institutional patterns and routines and by health care delivery arrangements specific to regional health care systems. Second, many patients would not or could not articulate "preferences" about "what they wanted" in the way of specific treatments when they were at risk of death. Some patients who did state preferences for certain kinds of care changed their minds later. Importantly, neither patients nor families could imagine a particular future of specific medical symptoms, evaluate whether "life" or "death" is desirable given those symptoms, and then choose between such a life or death. The investigators found that neither patients nor families wanted the responsibility for such decision-making and that they "often delayed or dodged making a choice" at all or they simply went along with usual hospital practice. In addition, neither patients nor health care providers wanted to talk about death, and, indeed, death was not discussed in most cases, with one result being that DNR orders were not written until very shortly before death. Third, and most ironic in light of the enormous weight given to the value of patient "decision-making," the investigators learned that the range of actual choices for hospitalized patients is highly constrained; in fact, it is often limited to the timing of DNR orders. Finally, most patients involved in the study could not be classified as *dying* "in the sense that they—or anyone else—would have found it appropriate to accept death and be treated for symptoms at home. Instead, they were thought to have a substantial chance to leave the hospital and do well for a while if treatments were successful." Patients enrolled in the study mostly had uncertain prognoses, "bad enough to be at risk of death but good enough to hope for longer survival with the appropriate treatment" (ibid., S218).

3. Titia de Lange, "Telomeres and Senescence: Ending the Debate," *Science* 279 (1998): 334–35; Andrew Pollack, "The Promise of Selling Stem Cells," *New York Times,* August 26, 2001, sec. 3, p. 1; Richard A. Miller, "Extending Life: Scientific Prospects and Political Obstacles," *The Milbank Quarterly* 80 (2002): 155–74. For examples of popular books on the (potential) impacts of the genetic sciences on aging, see Stephen S. Hall, *Merchants of Immortality: Chasing the Dream of Human Life Extension* (Boston: Houghton Mifflin Company, 2003); and Nicholas Wade, *Life Script: How the Human Genome Discoveries Will Transform Medicine and Enhance Your Health* (New York: Simon & Schuster, 2001).

4. Sherwin Nuland, "Medicine Isn't Just for the Sick Anymore," *New York Times,* May 10, 1998, Week in Review, 1; Thomas B. Okarma, "Symposium, Human Primordial Stem Cells," *Hastings Center Report,* March-April 1999, 30; Lisa Sowle Cahill, "The New Biotech World Order," *Hastings Center Report,* March-April 1999, 45–48; President's Council on Bioethics, *Beyond Therapy: Biotechnology and the Pursuit of Happiness,* October 2003, http:// www.bioethics.gov/ reports/beyond therapy; Carl Elliott, *Better than Well: American Medicine Meets the American Dream* (New York: Norton, 2003).

5. R. N. Butler et al., "Is There an Antiaging Medicine?" *Journal of Gerontology: Biological Sciences* 57A (2002): B333–38; S. Jay Olshansky and Bruce A. Carnes, *The Quest for Immortality: Science at the Frontiers of Aging* (New York: Norton, 2001). But see Aubrey D. N. J. de Grey et al., "Time to Talk SENS: Critiquing the

Immutability of Human Aging," *Annals of the New York Academy of Sciences* 959 (2002): 452–62, for a provocative discussion of "reversing" aging.

6. Nancy Johnson et al., "Towards a 'Good' Death: End-of-Life Narratives Constructed in an Intensive Care Unit," *Culture, Medicine and Psychiatry* 24 (2000): 275–95.

7. A recent example of the politics of intervening, beyond the therapeutic, in the "normal," "natural" workings of the human body is the report of the President's Council on Bioethics, *Beyond Therapy.*

8. William Cronon, ed., *Uncommon Ground: Rethinking the Human Place in Nature* (New York: Norton, 1996), 20. Nature has been considered to be both part of us and separate from us, and our descriptions and understanding of it are linked to concepts of God, fate and human agency, culture, society, science, and the body. See, for example, Peter Coates, *Nature: Western Attitudes Since Ancient Times* (Berkeley: University of California Press, 1998); Bill McKibben, *The End of Nature* (New York: Random House, 1989); and Carolyn Merchant, *The Death of Nature* (New York: HarperCollins, 1990).

9. Marilyn Strathern, *After Nature* (Cambridge: Cambridge University Press, 1992), 174.

10. Cronon, *Uncommon Ground,* 34.

11. Strathern, *After Nature;* Phil Macnaghten and John Urry, *Contested Natures* (London: Sage, 1998), 30.

12. It is similarly removed in other clinical realms (such as assisted reproduction) and in the new genetic sciences.

13. Sarah Franklin, *Embodied Progress* (London and New York: Routledge, 1997), 166.

APPENDIX A: ABOUT THE RESEARCH

1. Clifford Geertz, perhaps the leading senior anthropologist in the United States today, writes, "The ability of anthropologists to get us to take what they say seriously has less to do with either a factual look or an air of conceptual elegance than it has with their capacity to convince us that what they say is a result of their having actually penetrated (or, if you prefer, been penetrated by) another form of life, of having, one way or another, truly 'been there.'" (Clifford Geertz, *Works and Lives: The Anthropologist as Author* [Stanford: Stanford University Press, 1988], 4–5).

2. Ibid., 8.

3. George E. Marcus, *Ethnography through Thick and Thin* (Princeton: Princeton University Press, 1998); Paul Rabinow, *Essays on the Anthropology of Reason* (Princeton: Princeton University Press, 1996). See also Akhil Gupta and James Ferguson, eds., *Anthropological Locations: Boundaries and Grounds of a Field Science* (Berkeley: University of California Press, 1997).

4. James Clifford, "Introduction: Partial Truths," in *Writing Culture,* ed. James Clifford and George E. Marcus (Berkeley: University of California Press, 1986), 1–26.

5. Clifford Geertz, *The Interpretation of Cultures* (New York: Basic Books, 1973).

6. John Van Maanen, *Tales of the Field: On Writing Ethnography* (Chicago: University of Chicago Press, 1988); Clifford and Marcus, *Writing Culture;* Ruth Behar and Deborah A. Gordon, eds., *Women Writing Culture* (Berkeley: University of California Press, 1995); Marcus, *Ethnography through Thick and Thin.*

7. Geertz, *Works and Lives,* 10.

8. Ibid., 15.

9. Marcus, "The Uses of Complicity in the Changing Mise-en-Scène of Anthro-pological Fieldwork," chapter 4 in *Anthropology through Thick and Thin*, 118.
10. Psychotherapist, novelist, and newcomer to ethnography Amy Bloom captures the anthropological meaning of "partial truths," the ways in which details are portrayed accurately, when she reflects on how she conducted research for her book *Normal: Transsexual CEOs, Cross-Dressing Cops, and Hermaphrodites with Attitude* (New York: Random House, 2002). She states, "I chose: whom to talk to, whom to quote, whom to describe, whom to pass over. And they chose: where we met, what they said, whom they introduced me to, which pho-tographs and scars and articles they showed me. I wanted to tell the truth, and so did they, and it was impossible for us to do so without choosing which truths to tell, and knowing that when you leave something out, you may come pretty damned close to lying" (*New York Times*, November 18, 2002, B1).

A physician who read an earlier version of one of my chapters commented to me, "Well, Sharon, you didn't exactly get the facts wrong. But you've taken things out of context, distorted things."

APPENDIX B: A NOTE ON DIVERSITY

1. Institute of Medicine, *Unequal Treatment: Confronting Racial and Ethnic Dis-parities in Health Care*, ed. Brian D. Smedley, Adrian Y. Stith, and Alan R. Nel-son (Washington, DC: National Academy Press, 2002); Mary-Jo Del Vecchio Good et al., "The Culture of Medicine and Racial, Ethnic, and Class Disparities in Health Care," in *Unequal Treatment*, 594–625 (CD-ROM).
2. Leslie J. Blackhall et al., "Ethnicity and Attitudes toward Patient Autonomy," *Journal of the American Medical Association* 274 (1995): 820–25; Gelya Frank et al., "A Discourse of Relationships in Bioethics: Patient Autonomy and End-of-Life Decision-Making among Elderly Korean Americans," *Medical Anthropology Quarterly* 12 (1998): 403–23; Sheila T. Murphy et al., "Ethnicity and Advance Care Directives," *Journal of Law, Medicine & Ethics* 24 (1996): 108–17; H. M. Spiro, M. G. McCrea Curnen, and L. P. Wandel, *Facing Death: Where Culture, Religion, and Medicine Meet* (New Haven: Yale University Press, 1996); and Catherine M. Waters, "Understanding and Supporting African-Americans' Per-spectives of End-of-Life Care Planning and Decision-Making," *Qualitative Health Research* 11 (2001): 385–99.
3. Theresa S. Drought and Barbara A. Koenig, "'Choice' in End-of-Life Decision-Making: Researching Fact or Fiction?" *Gerontologist* 42, special issue no. 3 (2002): 114–28.
4. Barbara A. Koenig and Jan Gates-Williams, "Understanding Cultural Differ-ences in Caring for Dying Patients," *Western Journal of Medicine* 163 (1995): 244–49; Barbara A. Koenig and Elizabeth Davies, "Cultural Dimensions of Care at Life's End for Children and Their Families," in Institute of Medicine, *When Children Die: Improving Palliative and End-of-Life Care for Children and Their Families* (Washington, DC: National Academy Press, 2003), appendix D; Mar-garet Lock, "Education and Self-Reflection: Teaching about Culture, Health and Illness," in *Health and Cultures: Exploring the Relationships*, ed. R. Masi and L. Mensha (Oakland, Ontario, Canada: Mosaic Press, 1993), 139; Rayna Rapp, *Testing Women, Testing the Fetus* (New York: Routledge, 1999).
5. Koenig and Davies, "Cultural Dimensions of Care."
6. Good et al., "Culture of Medicine."

BIBLIOGRAPHY

Achenbaum, W. Andrew. *Old Age in the New Land: The American Experience since 1790.* Baltimore: Johns Hopkins University Press, 1978.

Adelman, R. D., et al. "Issues in the Physician–Geriatric Patient Relationship." In *Communication, Health and the Elderly.* Ed. H. Giles, N. Coupland, and J. M. Wiemann. Manchester, Great Britain: Manchester University Press, 1990, 126–34.

Ad Hoc Committee of the Harvard Medical School to Examine the Definition of Brain Death. "A Definition of Irreversible Coma." *Journal of the American Medical Association* 205, no. 6 (1968): 337–40.

Agamben, Giorgio. *Homo Sacer.* Stanford: Stanford University Press, 1998.

Aiken, L. H., et al. "Hospital Nurse Staffing and Patient Mortality, Nurse Burnout, and Job Dissatisfaction." *Journal of the American Medical Association* 288, no. 16 (2002): 1987–93.

American Medical Association et al. *Physician and Public Attitudes on Health Care Issues.* Chicago: American Medical Association, 1989.

Andrews, K. "Vegetative State—Background and Ethics." *Journal of the Royal Society of Medicine* 90, no. 11 (1997): 593–96.

Angell, M. "After Quinlan: The Dilemma of the Persistent Vegetative State." *New England Journal of Medicine* 330, no. 21 (1994): 1524–25.

Anspach, Renee R. *Deciding Who Lives: Fateful Choices in the Intensive-Care Nursery.* Berkeley: University of California Press, 1993.

Appelbaum, Paul S., Charles W. Lidz, and Alan Meisel. "Patients Who Refuse Treatment." In *Informed Consent: Legal Theory and Clinical Practice.* Ed. Paul S. Appelbaum, Charles W. Lidz, and Alan Meisel. New York: Oxford University Press, 1987, 90–207.

Ariès, Philippe. *The Hour of Our Death.* New York: Oxford University Press, 1981.

Armstrong, David. "The Patient's View." *Social Science & Medicine* 18, no. 9 (1984): 737–44.

———. "Silence and Truth in Death and Dying." *Social Science & Medicine* 24, no. 8 (1987): 651–57.

Arney, William Ray, and Bernard J. Bergen. *Medicine and the Management of Living: Taming the Last Great Beast.* Chicago: University of Chicago Press, 1984.

Arnold, Robert M., and Stuart J. Youngner. "The Dead Donor Rule: Should We Stretch It, Bend It, or Abandon It?" *Kennedy Institute of Ethics Journal* 3, no. 2 (1993): 263–78.

Balint, Michael. *The Doctor, His Patient and the Illness.* London: Pitman Medical Publishing Co. Ltd., 1957.

Barry, Robert Laurence, and Gerard V. Bradley, eds. *Set No Limits.* Urbana: University of Illinois Press, 1991.

Bates, D. "Persistent Vegetative State and Brain Stem Death." *Current Opinion in Neurology* 10, no. 6 (1997): 502–5.

Battin, M. Pabst. *The Least Worst Death: Essays in Bioethics on the End of Life.* New York: Oxford University Press, 1994.

Bauby, Jean-Dominique. *The Diving Bell and the Butterfly.* New York: Knopf, 1997.

Bayertz, Kurt. *Sanctity of Life and Human Dignity.* Boston: Kluwer, 1996.

Beauchamp, Tom, and James Childress. *Principles of Biomedical Ethics.* New York: Oxford University Press, 1979.

Beecher, H. K. "Ethics and Clinical Research." *New England Journal of Medicine* 274, no. 24 (1966): 1354–60.

Behar, Ruth, and Deborah A. Gordon, eds. *Women Writing Culture.* Berkeley: University of California Press, 1995.

Bellah, Robert, et al. *Habits of the Heart: Individualism and Commitment in American Life.* Berkeley: University of California Press, 1985.

Binstock, Robert H., Stephen G. Post, and Laurel S. Mills, eds. *Too Old for Health Care? Controversies in Medicine, Law, Economics, and Ethics.* The Johns Hopkins Series in Contemporary Medicine and Public Health. Baltimore: Johns Hopkins University Press, 1991.

Bishop, Schuyler. "When Doctors Go Too Far." *New York Times,* February 27, 1999.

Blackhall, Leslie J., et al. "Ethnicity and Attitudes toward Patient Autonomy." *Journal of the American Medical Association* 274, no. 10 (1995): 820–25.

Bloom, Amy. *Normal: Transsexual CEOs, Cross-Dressing Cops, and Hermaphrodites with Attitude.* New York: Random House, 2002.

————. "Writers on Writing: Trading Fiction's Comfort for a Chance to Look Life in the Eye." *New York Times,* November 18, 2002.

Blumenthal, Herman T. "The Aging-Disease Dichotomy Is Alive, but Is It Well?" *Journal of the American Geriatrics Society* 41, no. 11 (1993): 1272–73.

————. "The Aging-Disease Dichotomy: True or False?" *Journals of Gerontology: Medical Sciences* 58A, no. 2 (2003): M138–45.

————. "The Alzheimerization of Aging: A Response." *Gerontologist* 35, no. 6 (1995): 721–23.

————. "Milestone or Genomania? The Relevance of the Human Genome Project to Biological Aging and the Age-Related Diseases." *Journals of Gerontology: Medical Sciences* 56, no. 9 (2001): M529–37.

————. "A View of the Aging-Disease Relationship from Age 85." *Journals of Gerontology: Biological Sciences* 54, no. 6 (1999): B255–59.

Borthwick, Christian J. "The Permanent Vegetative State: Ethical Crux, Medical Fiction?" *Issues in Law & Medicine* 12, no. 2 (1996): 167–85.

————. "The Proof of the Vegetable: A Commentary on Medical Futility." *Journal of Medical Ethics* 21, no. 4 (1995): 205–8.

Bosk, Charles L. "Professional Ethicist Available: Logical, Secular, Friendly." *Daedalus* 128, no. 4 (1999): 47–68.

Bowker, Geoffrey C., and Susan Leigh Star. *Sorting Things Out—Classification and Its Consequences.* Cambridge: MIT Press, 2000.

Brackenbury, H. *Patient and Doctor.* London: Hodder and Stoughton, 1935.

Brock, Dan W. "Advance Directives: What Is It Reasonable to Expect from Them?" *Journal of Clinical Ethics* 5, no. 1 (1994): 57–60.

Brody, Howard. "Causing, Intending, and Assisting Death." *Journal of Clinical Ethics* 4, no. 2 (1993): 112–17.

———. *The Healer's Power.* New Haven: Yale University Press, 1992.

Brown, Kate. "Information Disclosure." In *Encyclopedia of Bioethics.* Ed. Warren T. Reich. New York: Simon & Schuster, 1995, 636–41.

Bruner, Edward M. "Experience and Its Expressions." In *The Anthropology of Experience.* Ed. Victor W. Turner and Edward M. Bruner. Urbana: University of Illinois Press, 1986, 3–32.

Buntin, M. B., and H. Huskamp. "What Is Known about the Economics of End-of-Life Care for Medicare Beneficiaries?" *Gerontologist* 42, special issue no. 3 (2002): 40–48.

Butler, R. N., et al. "Is There an Antiaging Medicine?" *Journals of Gerontology: Biological Sciences* 57, no. 9 (2002): B333–38.

Cahill, Lisa Sowle. "The New Biotech World Order." *Hastings Center Report* 29, no. 2 (1999): 45–48.

Callahan, Daniel. "Morality and Contemporary Culture: The President's Commission and Beyond." *Cardozo Law Review* 6 (1984): 223–42.

———. "The Sanctity of Life." In *Updating Life and Death: Essays in Ethics and Medicine.* Ed. Donald R. Cutler. Boston: Beacon Press, 1969, 181–251.

———. "Setting Limits: A Response." *Gerontologist* 34, no. 3 (1994): 393–98.

———. *Setting Limits: Medical Goals in an Aging Society.* New York: Simon & Schuster, 1987.

———. *The Troubled Dream of Life.* New York: Simon & Schuster, 1993.

Capello, C. F., D. E. Meier, and C. K. Cassel. "Payment Code for Hospital-Based Palliative Care: Help or Hindrance?" *Journal of Palliative Medicine* 1 (1998): 155–63.

Capron, Alexander. "Report on the President's Commission on the Uniform Determination of Death Act." In *Death: Beyond Whole-Brain Criteria.* Ed. Richard M. Zaner. Dordrecht: Kluwer, 1988.

Carmel, Sara, and Elizabeth J. Mutran. "Stability of Elderly Persons' Expressed Preferences regarding the Use of Life-Sustaining Treatments." *Social Science & Medicine* 49, no. 3 (1999): 303–11.

Carson, S. S., et al. "Outcomes after Long-Term Acute Care: An Analysis of 133 Mechanically Ventilated Patients." *American Journal of Respiratory and Critical Care Medicine* 159, no. 5, pt. 1 (1999): 1568–73.

Cassel, Christine K., John M. Ludden, and Grace M. Moon. "Perceptions of Barriers to High-Quality Palliative Care in Hospitals." *Health Affairs* 19, no. 5 (2000): 166–72.

Cassel, Christine K., and B. C. Vladeck. "ICD-9 Code for Palliative or Terminal Care." *New England Journal of Medicine* 335, no. 16 (1996): 1232–34.

Cassell, Eric. "Clinical Incoherence about Persons: The Problem of the Persistent Vegetative State." *Annals of Internal Medicine* 125, no. 2 (1996): 146–47.

Charcot, Jean-Martin. *Leçons cliniques sur les maladies des vieillards et les maladies chroniques.* Paris: A. Delahaye, 1867.

Childress, J. F. "Ethical Criteria for Procuring and Distributing Organs for Transplantation." In *Organ Transplantation Policy: Issues and Prospects.* Ed. James F. Blumstein and Frank A. Sloan. Durham, NC: Duke University Press, 1989, 87–113.

Christakis, Nicholas A. *Death Foretold: Prophecy and Prognosis in Medical Care.* Chicago: University of Chicago Press, 1999.

Christie, Ronald J., and C. Barry Hoffmaster. *Ethical Issues in Family Medicine.* New York: Oxford University Press, 1986.

Clifford, James. "Introduction: Partial Truths." In *Writing Culture: The Poetics and Politics of Ethnography.* Ed. James Clifford and George E. Marcus. Berkeley: University of California Press, 1986, 1–26.

Clifford, James, and George E. Marcus, eds. *Writing Culture: The Poetics and Politics of Ethnography.* Berkeley: University of California Press, 1986.

Cloud, John, and Harriet Barovick. "A Kinder, Gentler Death." *Time,* September 18, 2000, 60.

Clouser, K. D. " 'The Sanctity of Life' ": An Analysis of a Concept." *Annals of Internal Medicine* 78, no. 1 (1973): 119–25.

Coates, Peter A. *Nature: Western Attitudes Since Ancient Times.* Berkeley: University of California Press, 1998.

Cohen, Lawrence. *No Aging in India: Alzheimer's, the Bad Family, and Other Modern Things.* Berkeley: University of California Press, 1998.

Cohen-Almagor, Raphael. "Some Observations on Post-Coma Unawareness Patients and on Other Forms of Unconscious Patients: Policy Proposals." *Medicine and Law* 16, no. 3 (1997): 451–71.

Cole, Thomas R. *The Journey of Life: A Cultural History of Aging in America.* Cambridge: Cambridge University Press, 1992.

Cranford, R. E., and D. R. Smith. "Consciousness: The Most Critical Moral (Constitutional) Standard for Human Personhood." *American Journal of Law & Medicine* 13, no. 2–3 (1987): 233–48.

Cronon, William. *Uncommon Ground: Rethinking the Human Place in Nature.* New York: Norton, 1996.

Curran, W. J. "Governmental Regulation of the Use of Human Subjects in Medical Research: The Approach of Two Federal Agencies." *Daedalus* 98 (1969): 542–94.

Cusack, D. A., A. A. Sheikh, and J. L. Hyslop-Westrup. " 'Near PVS': A New Medico-Legal Syndrome?" *Medicine, Science and the Law* 40, no. 2 (2000): 133–42.

Damasio, Antonio R. *The Feeling of What Happens: Body and Emotion in the Making of Consciousness.* New York: Harcourt Brace, 1999.

Danis, Marion, et al. "A Comparison of Patient, Family, and Physician Assessments of the Value of Medical Intensive Care." *Critical Care Medicine* 16, no. 6 (1988): 594–600.

———. "A Prospective Study of Advance Directives for Life-Sustaining Care." *New England Journal of Medicine* 324, no. 13 (1991): 882–88.

———. "A Prospective Study of the Impact of Patient Preferences on Life-Sustaining Treatment and Hospital Cost." *Critical Care Medicine* 24, no. 11 (1996): 1811–17.

———. "Stability of Choices about Life-Sustaining Treatments." *Annals of Internal Medicine* 120, no. 7 (1994): 567–73.

Dantz, Bezalel. "Losing One's Bearings at the Life-Death Border." *New York Times,* December 7, 1999.

de Grey, Aubrey, et al. "Time to Talk SENS: Critiquing the Immutability of Human Aging." *Annals of the New York Academy of Sciences* 959 (2002): 452–62.

de Lange, Titia. "Telomeres and Senescence: Ending the Debate." *Science* 279, no. 5349 (1998): 334–35.

Dey, A. N. "Characteristics of Elderly Nursing Home Residents: Data from the 1995 National Nursing Home Survey." *Advance Data from Vital and Health Statistics* 289. Hyattsville, MD: National Center for Health Statistics, 1997.

Diem, Susan J., John D. Lantos, and James A. Tulsky. "Cardiopulmonary Resuscitation on Television—Miracles and Misinformation." *New England Journal of Medicine* 334, no. 24 (1996): 1578–82.

Dragsted, Lis, and Jesper Qvist. "Epidemiology of Intensive Care." *International Journal of Technology Assessment in Health Care* 8, no. 3 (1992): 395–407.

Dresser, Rebecca. "Confronting the 'Near Irrelevance' of Advance Directives." *Journal of Clinical Ethics* 5, no. 1 (1994): 55–56.

Drought, Theresa S., and Barbara A. Koenig. " 'Choice' in End-of-Life Decision-Making: Researching Fact or Fiction?" *Gerontologist* 42, special issue no. 3 (2002): 114–28.

Dworkin, R. M. *Life's Dominion: An Argument about Abortion, Euthanasia, and Individual Freedom.* New York: Knopf, 1993.

Ebell, M. H., et al. "Survival after In-Hospital Cardiopulmonary Resuscitation. A Meta-Analysis." *Journal of General Internal Medicine* 13, no. 12 (1998): 805–16.

Eidinger, R. N., and D. V. Schapira. "Cancer Patients' Insight into Their Treatment, Prognosis, and Unconventional Therapies." *Cancer* 53, no. 12 (1984): 2736–40.

Eisenberg, M. S., and T. J. Mengert. "Cardiac Resuscitation." *New England Journal of Medicine* 344, no. 17 (2001): 1304–13.

Elliott, Carl. *Better than Well: American Medicine Meets the American Dream.* New York: Norton, 2003.

Emanuel, Linda. "Advance Directives: What Have We Learned So Far?" *Journal of Clinical Ethics* 4, no. 1 (1993): 8–16.

Engel, G. L. "The Need for a New Medical Model: A Challenge for Biomedicine." *Science* 196, no. 4286 (1977): 129–36.

Engelhardt, H. Tristram, Jr. "Redefining Death." In *The Definition of Death: Contemporary Controversies.* Ed. Stuart J. Youngner, Robert M. Arnold, and Renie Schapiro. Baltimore: Johns Hopkins University Press, 1999, 320–31.

Estes, C. L. "Cost Containment and the Elderly: Conflict or Challenge?" *Journal of the American Geriatrics Society* 36, no. 1 (1988): 68–72.

Ethics Committee of the Society of Critical Care Medicine. "Consensus Statement of the Society of Critical Care Medicine's Ethics Committee regarding Futile and Other Possibly Inadvisable Treatments." *Critical Care Medicine* 25, no. 5 (1997): 887–91.

Faber-Langendoen, K. "Resuscitation of Patients with Metastatic Cancer: Is Transient Benefit Still Futile?" *Archives of Internal Medicine* 151, no. 2 (1991): 235–39.

Faber-Langendoen, K., and D. M. Bartels. "Process of Forgoing Life-Sustaining Treatment in a University Hospital: An Empirical Study." *Critical Care Medicine* 20, no. 5 (1992): 570–77.

Fairman, Julie, and Joan E. Lynaugh. *Critical Care Nursing: A History.* Philadelphia: University of Pennsylvania Press, 1998.

Finucane, T. E., C. Christmas, and K. Travis. "Tube Feeding in Patients with Advanced Dementia: A Review of the Evidence." *Journal of the American Medical Association* 282, no. 14 (1999): 1365–70.

Flory, James, et al. "Places of Death: U.S. Trends Since 1980." *Health Affairs* 23, no. 3 (2004): 194–200.

Foley, G. E., et al. "The Closed-Chest Method of Cardiopulmonary Resuscitation—Revised Statement." *Circulation* 31 (1965): 641–43.

Forbes, W. F., and J. P. Hirdes. "The Relationship between Aging and Disease: Geriatric Ideology and Myths of Senility." *Journal of the American Geriatrics Society* 41, no. 11 (1993): 1267–71.

Foucault, Michel. *The Birth of the Clinic: An Archaeology of Medical Perception.* New York: Vintage Books, 1975.

———. *Discipline and Punish: The Birth of the Prison.* New York: Pantheon Books, 1977.

———. *The History of Sexuality, Vol. I: An Introduction.* New York: Vintage Books, 1980.

———. *The Order of Things.* New York: Vintage Books, 1973.

Fox, Renée C. "The Evolution of American Bioethics: A Sociological Perspective." In *Social Science Perspectives on Medical Ethics.* Ed. George Weisz. Philadelphia: University of Pennsylvania Press, 1991, 201–20.

Frank, Arthur W. *The Wounded Storyteller: Body, Illness, and Ethics.* Chicago: University of Chicago Press, 1995.

Frank, Gelya, et al. "A Discourse of Relationships in Bioethics: Patient Autonomy and End-of-Life Decision-Making among Elderly Korean Americans." *Medical Anthropology Quarterly* 12, no. 4 (1998): 403–23.

Frankl, David, Robert K. Oye, and Paul E. Bellamy. "Attitudes of Hospitalized Patients toward Life Support: A Survey of 200 Medical Inpatients." *American Journal of Medicine* 86, no. 6 (1989): 645–48.

Franklin, Sarah. *Embodied Progress: A Cultural Account of Assisted Conception.* London and New York: Routledge, 1997.

———. "Making Miracles: Scientific Progress and the Facts of Life." In *Reproducing Reproduction: Kinship, Power, and Technological Innovation.* Ed. Sarah Franklin and Helena Ragone. Philadelphia: University of Pennsylvania Press, 1998, 102–17.

Freeborne, Nancy, Joanne Lynn, and Norman A. Desbiens. "Insights about Dying from the SUPPORT Project. The Study to Understand Prognoses and Preferences for Outcomes and Risks of Treatments." *Journal of the American Geriatrics Society* 48, no. 5 supp. (2000): S199–205.

Garcia, J. "Double Effect." In *Encyclopedia of Bioethics.* Ed. Warren T. Reich. New York: Simon & Schuster, 1995, 636–41.

Garrow, David J. "The Oregon Trail." *New York Times,* November 6, 1997.

Geertz, Clifford. *The Interpretation of Cultures: Selected Essays.* New York: Basic Books, 1973.

———. *Works and Lives: The Anthropologist as Author.* Stanford: Stanford University Press, 1988.

Giddens, Anthony. *Modernity and Self-Identity: Self and Society in the Late Modern Age.* Stanford: Stanford University Press, 1991.

Gillick, M. R. "Rethinking the Role of Tube Feeding in Patients with Advanced Dementia." *New England Journal of Medicine* 342, no. 3 (2000): 206–10.

Glaser, Barney G., and Anselm L. Strauss. *Awareness of Dying.* New York: Aldine, 1965.

———. *Time for Dying.* New York: Aldine, 1968.

Glendon, Mary Ann. *Rights Talk.* New York: Free Press, 1991.

Gluck, M. E., and K. W. Hanson. *Medicare Chart Book.* Menlo Park, CA: The Henry J. Kaiser Foundation, 2001.

Good, Mary-Jo Del Vecchio, et al. "American Oncology and the Discourse on Hope." *Culture, Medicine and Psychiatry* 14, no. 1 (1990): 59–79.

———. "A Comparative Analysis of the Culture of Biomedicine." In *Health and Health Care in Developing Countries: Sociological Perspectives.* Ed. Peter Conrad and Eugene B. Gallagher. Philadelphia: Temple University Press, 1993, 180–93.

———. "The Culture of Medicine and Racial, Ethnic, and Class Disparities in Health Care." In *Unequal Treatment: Confronting Racial and Ethnic Disparities in Health Care.* Ed. Institute of Medicine. Washington, DC: National Academy Press, 2002, 594–625.

Goodwin, J. S. "Geriatric Ideology: The Myth of the Myth of Senility." *Journal of the American Geriatrics Society* 39, no. 6 (1991): 627–31.

Gordon, Deborah R. "Tenacious Assumptions in Western Medicine." In *Biomedicine Examined.* Ed. Margaret M. Lock and Deborah Gordon. Dordrecht: Kluwer, 1988, 19–56.

Gordon, Deborah R., and Eugenio Paci. "Disclosure Practices and Cultural Narratives: Understanding Concealment and Silence around Cancer in Tuscany, Italy." *Social Science & Medicine* 44, no. 10 (1997): 1433–52.

Grant, M. D., M. A. Rudberg, and J. A. Brody. "Gastrostomy Placement and Mortality among Hospitalized Medicare Beneficiaries." *Journal of the American Medical Association* 279, no. 24 (1998): 1973–76.

Gray, G. W. "The Mystery of Aging." *Harper's,* 1941, 283.

Greenberg, Gary. "As Good as Dead." *New Yorker,* August 13, 2001, 36–41.

Groeger, J. S., et al. "Multicenter Outcome Study of Cancer Patients Admitted to the Intensive Care Unit: A Probability of Mortality Model." *Journal of Clinical Oncology* 16, no. 2 (1998): 761–70.

Gupta, Akhil, and James Ferguson. *Anthropological Locations: Boundaries and Grounds of a Field Science.* Berkeley: University of California Press, 1997.

Hackler, J. C., and F. C. Hiller. "Family Consent to Orders Not to Resuscitate: Reconsidering Hospital Policy." *Journal of the American Medical Association* 264, no. 10 (1990): 1281–83.

Hall, Stephen S. *Merchants of Immortality: Chasing the Dream of Human Life Extension.* Boston: Houghton Mifflin, 2003.

Halpern, Jodi. *From Detached Concern to Empathy: Humanizing Medical Practice.* New York: Oxford University Press, 2001.

Hamill, R. J. "Resuscitation: When Is Enough, Enough?" *Respiratory Care* 40, no. 5 (1995): 515–24; discussion 24–27.

Harrison, Tinsley Randolph, et al. *Principles of Internal Medicine.* Philadelphia: The Blakiston Company, 1950.

Hayflick, Leonard. *How and Why We Age.* New York: Ballantine Books, 1994.

Helft, P. R., M. Siegler, and J. Lantos. "The Rise and Fall of the Futility Movement." *New England Journal of Medicine* 343, no. 4 (2000): 293–96.

Hilberman, M., et al. "Marginally Effective Medical Care: Ethical Analysis of Issues in Cardiopulmonary Resuscitation (CPR)." *Journal of Medical Ethics* 23, no. 6 (1997): 361–67.

Hillier, Teresa A., et al. "Physicians as Patients: Choices regarding Their Own Resuscitation." *Archives of Internal Medicine* 155, no. 12 (1995): 1289–93.

Hodges, M. O., and S. W. Tolle. "Tube-Feeding Decisions in the Elderly." *Clinics in Geriatric Medicine* 10, no. 3 (1994): 475–88.

Hoffman, Jan C., et al. "Patient Preferences for Communication with Physicians about

End-of-Life Decisions. SUPPORT Investigators. Study to Understand Prognoses and Preference for Outcomes and Risks of Treatment." *Annals of Internal Medicine* 127, no. 1 (1997): 1–12.

Hoffmaster, Barry, ed. *Bioethics in Social Context.* Philadelphia: Temple University Press, 2001.

———. "Can Ethnography Save the Life of Medical Ethics?" *Social Science & Medicine* 35, no. 12 (1992): 1421–31.

Holstein, Martha. "Alzheimer's Disease and Senile Dementia, 1885–1920: An Interpretive History of Disease Negotiation." *Journal of Aging Studies* 11, no. 1 (1997): 1–13.

Homer, P., and M. Holstein, eds. *A Good Old Age: The Paradox of Setting Limits.* New York: Simon & Schuster, 1990.

Hood, Ann. "Rage against the Dying of the Light." *New York Times,* August 2, 1997.

Howsepian, A. A. "The 1994 Multi-Society Task Force Consensus Statement on the Persistent Vegetative State: A Critical Analysis." *Issues in Law & Medicine* 12, no. 1 (1996): 3–29.

Huskamp, Haiden A., et al. "Providing Care at the End of Life: Do Medicare Rules Impede Good Care?" *Health Affairs* 20, no. 3 (2001): 204–11.

Institute of Medicine. *Approaching Death: Improving Care at the End of Life.* Washington, DC: National Academy Press, 1997.

———. *Unequal Treatment: Confronting Racial and Ethnic Disparities in Health Care,* Committee on Understanding and Eliminating Racial and Ethnic Disparities in Health Care. Washington, DC: National Academy Press, 2002.

Ivy, Andrew C. "The Brutalities of Nazi Physicians." *Journal of the American Medical Association* 132 (1946): 714–15.

Jauhar, Sandeep. "As Technology Improves, More People Breathe with Machines." *New York Times,* April 24, 2001.

Jecker, N. S., and R. A. Pearlman. "Ethical Constraints on Rationing Medical Care by Age." *Journal of the American Geriatrics Society* 37, no. 11 (1989): 1067–75.

Jennings, Bruce. "A Life Greater than the Sum of Its Sensations: Ethics, Dementia, and the Quality of Life." *Journal of Mental Health & Aging* 5, no. 1 (1999): 95–106.

Johnson, Harriet McBryde. "Should I Have Been Killed at Birth? The Case for My Life." *New York Times Magazine,* February 16, 2003.

Johnson, Nancy, et al. "Towards a 'Good' Death: End-of-Life Narratives Constructed in an Intensive Care Unit." *Culture, Medicine & Psychiatry* 24, no. 3 (2000): 275–95.

Johnston, S. C., M. P. Pfeifer, and R. McNutt. "The Discussion about Advance Directives. Patient and Physician Opinions regarding When and How It Should Be Conducted. End of Life Study Group." *Archives of Internal Medicine* 155, no. 10 (1995): 1025–30.

Jones, G. K., K. L. Brewer, and H. G. Garrison. "Public Expectations of Survival following Cardiopulmonary Resuscitation." *Academic Emergency Medicine* 7, no. 1 (2000): 48–53.

Jones, James H. *Bad Blood: The Tuskegee Syphilis Experiment.* New York: Free Press, 1981.

Jonsen, Albert. *The Birth of Bioethics.* New York: Oxford University Press, 1998.

Karetzky, Monroe, M. Zubair, and Jayesh Parikh. "Cardiopulmonary Resuscitation in Intensive Care Unit and Non–Intensive Care Unit Patients: Immediate and Long-Term Survival." *Archives of Internal Medicine* 155, no. 12 (1995): 1277–80.

Kass, Leon R. "Death with Dignity and the Sanctity of Life." In *A Time to Be Born and a Time to Die: The Ethics of Choice.* Ed. Barry S. Kogan. Hawthorne, N.Y.: Aldine, 1991, 117–45.

Katz, Jay. *The Silent World of Doctor and Patient.* New York: Free Press, 1984.

Kaufman, Sharon R. "Construction and Practice of Medical Responsibility: Dilemmas and Narratives from Geriatrics." *Culture, Medicine & Psychiatry* 21, no. 1 (1997): 1–26.

———. *The Healer's Tale: Transforming Medicine and Culture.* Madison, WI: University of Wisconsin Press, 1993.

———. "Toward a Phenomenology of Boundaries in Medicine: Chronic Illness Experience in the Case of Stroke." *Medical Anthropology Quarterly* 2, no. 4 (1988): 338–54.

Kayser-Jones, J. "The Use of Nasogastric Feeding Tubes in Nursing Homes: Patient, Family and Health Care Provider Perspectives." *Gerontologist* 30, no. 4 (1990): 469–79.

Kleinman, A. "Moral Experience and Ethical Reflection: Can Ethnography Reconcile Them? A Quandary for 'the New Bioethics.'" *Daedalus* 128, no. 4 (1999): 69–97.

Knauft, Bruce M. *Genealogies for the Present in Cultural Anthropology.* New York: Routledge, 1996.

Knaus, W. A., et al. "The SUPPORT Prognostic Model. Objective Estimates of Survival for Seriously Ill Hospitalized Adults. Study to Understand Prognoses and Preferences for Outcomes and Risks of Treatments." *Annals of Internal Medicine* 122, no. 3 (1995): 191–203.

———. "Variations in Mortality and Length of Stay in Intensive Care Units." *Annals of Internal Medicine* 118, no. 10 (1993): 753–61.

Koch, K. A., H. D. Rodeffer, and R. L. Wears. "Changing Patterns of Terminal Care Management in an Intensive Care Unit." *Critical Care Medicine* 22, no. 2 (1994): 233–43.

Koenig, Barbara A. "Cultural Diversity in Decision-Making about Care at the End of Life." In *Approaching Death: Improving Care at the End of Life.* Institute of Medicine. Washington, DC: National Academy Press, 1997, 363–82.

Koenig, Barbara A., and Elizabeth Davies. "Cultural Dimensions of Care at Life's End for Children and Their Families." In *When Children Die: Improving Palliative and End-of-Life Care for Children and Their Families.* Institute of Medicine. Washington, DC: National Academy Press, 2003, appendix D, 509–52.

Koenig, Barbara A., and Jan Gates-Williams. "Understanding Cultural Difference in Caring for Dying Patients." *Western Journal of Medicine* 163, no. 3 (1995): 244–49.

Kogan, Barry S., ed. *A Time to Be Born and a Time to Die: The Ethics of Choice.* Hawthorne, NY: Aldine, 1991.

Kolata, Gina. "Living Wills Aside, Dying Cling to Hope." *New York Times,* January 15, 1997.

Kübler-Ross, Elisabeth. *On Death and Dying.* London: Tavistock, 1969.

Leary, Joyce Coletta. "Emotional Boundaries: The Physician's Experience of Patient Death." Master's thesis, University of California, Berkeley, 2002.

Leder, Drew. *The Absent Body.* Chicago: University of Chicago Press, 1990.

Lederberg, Marguerite S. "Doctors in Limbo: The United States 'DNR' Debate." *Psycho-Oncology* 6, no. 4 (1997): 321–28.

Levinas, Emmanuel. "Useless Suffering." In *The Provocation of Levinas.* Ed. Robert Bernasconi and David Wood. London: Routledge, 1988, 156–67.

Levi-Strauss, Claude. *The Savage Mind.* Chicago: University of Chicago Press, 1966.

Lo, Bernard. "Improving Care Near the End of Life. Why Is It So Hard?" *Journal of the American Medical Association* 274, no. 20 (1995): 1634–36.

Lo, Bernard, G. A. McLeod, and G. Saika. "Patient Attitudes to Discussing Life-Sustaining Treatment." *Archives of Internal Medicine* 146, no. 8 (1986): 1613–15.

Lo, Bernard, and Lois Snyder. "Care at the End of Life: Guiding Practice Where There Are No Easy Answers" (editorial). *Annals of Internal Medicine* 130, no. 9 (1999): 772–74.

Lock, Margaret. "Death in Technological Time: Locating the End of Meaningful Life." *Medical Anthropology Quarterly* 10, no. 4 (1996): 575–600.

———. "On Dying Twice: Culture, Technology and the Determination of Death." In *Living and Working with the New Medical Technologies: Intersections of Inquiry*. Ed. Margaret Lock, Allan Young, and Alberto Cambrosio. Cambridge: Cambridge University Press, 2000, 233–62.

———. *Twice Dead: Organ Transplants and the Reinvention of Death*. Berkeley: University of California Press, 2002.

Luce, John, and Thomas J. Prendergast. "The Changing Nature of Death in the ICU." In *Managing Death in the Intensive Care Unit*. Ed. Randall Curtis and Gordon D. Rubenfeld. New York: Oxford University Press, 2001, 19–29.

Lunney, J. R., J. Lynn, and C. Hogan. "Profiles of Older Medicare Decedents." *Journal of the American Geriatrics Society* 50, no. 6 (2002): 1108–12.

Lutz, Catherine. *Unnatural Emotions: Everyday Sentiments on a Micronesian Atoll and Their Challenge to Western Theory*. Chicago: University of Chicago Press, 1988.

Lynn, Joanne. *By No Extraordinary Means: The Choice to Forgo Life-Sustaining Food and Water*. Bloomington: Indiana University Press, 1989.

———. "Caring at the End of Our Lives." *New England Journal of Medicine* 335, no. 3 (1996): 201–2.

———. "Learning to Care for People with Chronic Illness Facing the End of Life." *Journal of the American Medical Association* 284 (2000): 2508–11.

———. "Serving Patients Who May Die Soon and Their Families: The Role of Hospice and Other Services." *Journal of the American Medical Association* 285 (2001): 925–32.

Lynn, Joanne, et al. "Capitated Risk-Bearing Managed Care Systems Could Improve End-of-Life Care." *Journal of the American Geriatrics Society* 46, no. 3 (1998): 322–30.

———. "Defining the 'Terminally Ill': Insights from SUPPORT." *Duquesne Law Review* 35, no. 1 (1996): 311–36.

———. "Perceptions by Family Members of the Dying Experience of Older and Seriously Ill Patients." *Annals of Internal Medicine* 126, no. 2 (1997): 97–106.

———. "Prognoses of Seriously Ill Hospitalized Patients on the Days before Death: Implications for Patient Care and Public Policy." *New Horizons* 5, no. 1 (1997): 56–61.

———. "Quality Improvements in End of Life Care: Insights from Two Collaboratives." *Joint Commission Journal on Quality Improvement* 26, no. 6 (2000): 254–67.

———. "Rethinking Fundamental Assumptions: SUPPORT's Implications for Future Reform." *Journal of the American Geriatrics Society* 48, no. 5 supp. (2000): S214–21.

Macnaghten, Phil, and John Urry. *Contested Natures*. London: Sage, 1998.

Marco, C. A., et al. "Ethical Issues of Cardiopulmonary Resuscitation: Current Practice among Emergency Physicians." *Academic Emergency Medicine* 4, no. 9 (1997): 898–904.

Marcus, George. *Ethnography through Thick and Thin.* Princeton: Princeton University Press, 1998.

―――. "The Uses of Complicity in the Changing Mise-en-Scène of Anthropological Fieldwork." In *Ethnography through Thick and Thin.* Princeton: Princeton University Press, 1998, 105–31.

Marik, Paul E., and Michelle Craft. "An Outcomes Analysis of In-Hospital Cardiopulmonary Resuscitation: The Futility Rationale for Do Not Resuscitate Orders." *Journal of Critical Care* 12, no. 3 (1997): 142–46.

Maslin, Janet. "Fredrick Wiseman Views Life and Death." *New York Times,* October 7, 1989.

McKibben, Bill. *The End of Nature.* New York: Random House, 1989.

Mead, George Herbert. *Mind, Self and Society from the Standpoint of a Social Behaviorist.* Chicago: University of Chicago Press, 1934.

Merchant, Carolyn. *The Death of Nature: Women, Ecology, and the Scientific Revolution.* New York: HarperCollins, 1990.

Miles, Steven. "Death in a Technological and Pluralistic Culture." In *The Definition of Death: Contemporary Controversies.* Ed. Stuart J. Youngner, Robert M. Arnold, and Renie Schapiro. Baltimore: Johns Hopkins University Press, 1999, 311–18.

Miller, Franklin G., and Joseph J. Fins. "A Proposal to Restructure Hospital Care for Dying Patients." *New England Journal of Medicine* 334, no. 26 (1996): 1740–42.

Miller, Richard A. "Extending Life: Scientific Prospects and Political Obstacles." *Milbank Quarterly* 80, no. 1 (2002): 155–74.

Miranda, D. R. "Quality of Life after Cardiopulmonary Resuscitation." *Chest* 106, no. 2 (1994): 524–30.

Moskowitz, E. H., and J. L. Nelson. "The Best Laid Plans." *Hastings Center Report* 25, no. 6 (1995): S3–5.

Moss, A. H., J. L. Holley, and M. B. Upton. "Outcomes of Cardiopulmonary Resuscitation in Dialysis Patients." *Journal of the American Society of Nephrology* 3, no. 6 (1992): 1238–43.

Muller, Jessica H. "Anthropology, Bioethics, and Medicine: A Provocative Trilogy." *Medical Anthropology Quarterly* 8 (1994): 448–67.

Muller, Jessica H., and Barbara A. Koenig. "On the Boundary of Life and Death: The Definition of Dying by Medical Residents." In *Biomedicine Examined.* Ed. Margaret Lock and Deborah R. Gordon. Boston: Kluwer, 1988, 351–74.

Multi-Society Task Force on PVS. "Medical Aspects of the Persistent Vegetative State (Part I)." *New England Journal of Medicine* 330, no. 21 (1994): 1499–1508.

Murphy, Sheila T., et al. "Ethnicity and Advance Care Directives." *Journal of Law, Medicine and Ethics* 24, no. 2 (1996): 108–17.

Murray, John F. *Intensive Care: A Doctor's Journal.* Berkeley: University of California Press, 2000.

Nascher, Ignatz Leo. *Geriatrics.* Philadelphia: P. Blakiston's Son & Co., 1914.

National Commission for the Protection of Human Subjects of Biomedical and Behavioral Research. "The Belmont Report: Ethical Principles and Guidelines for the Protection of Human Subjects of Research." Washington, DC: U.S. Government Printing Office, 1979.

Novack, D. H., et al. "Changes in Physicians' Attitudes toward Telling the Cancer Patient." *Journal of the American Medical Association* 241, no. 9 (1979): 897–900.

Nuland, Sherwin B. *How We Die: Reflections on Life's Final Chapter.* New York: Knopf, 1994.

————. "Medicine Isn't Just for the Sick Anymore: The Rush to Enhancement." *New York Times,* May 10, 1998.

Okarma, Thomas B. "Human Primordial Stem Cells." *Hastings Center Report* 29, no. 2 (1999): 30.

Oken, D. "What to Tell Cancer Patients—a Study of Medical Attitudes." *Journal of the American Medical Association* 175 (1961): 1120–28.

Olshansky, S. Jay, and Bruce A. Carnes. *The Quest for Immortality: Science at the Frontiers of Aging.* New York: Norton, 2001.

O'Neil, E., and J. A. Seago. "Meeting the Challenge of Nursing and the Nation's Health." *Journal of the American Medical Association* 288, no. 16 (2002): 2040–41.

Osler, William. *Science and Immortality.* Boston: Houghton, Mifflin and Co., 1904.

Payne, K., et al. "Physicians' Attitudes about the Care of Patients in the Persistent Vegetative State: A National Survey." *Annals of Internal Medicine* 125, no. 2 (1996): 104–10.

Pearlman, R. A., and A. Jonsen. "The Use of Quality-of-Life Considerations in Medical Decision Making." *Journal of the American Geriatrics Society* 33, no. 5 (1985): 344–52.

Pearlman, R. A., and J. B. Speer Jr. "Quality-of-Life Considerations in Geriatric Care." *Journal of the American Geriatrics Society* 31, no. 2 (1983): 113–20.

Pernick, Martin S. "Back from the Grave: Recurring Controversies over Defining and Diagnosing Death in History." In *Death: Beyond Whole-Brain Criteria.* Ed. Richard M. Zaner. Dordrecht: Kluwer, 1988, 17–74.

————. "Brain Death in Cultural Context: The Reconstruction of Death, 1967–1981." In *The Definition of Death: Contemporary Controversies.* Ed. S. J. Youngner, R. M. Arnold, and R. Schapiro. Baltimore: Johns Hopkins University Press, 1999, 3–33.

Petty, Thomas L. "The Modern Evolution of Mechanical Ventilation." *Clinics in Chest Medicine* 9, no. 1 (1988): 1–10.

Pollack, Andrew. "The Promise in Selling Stem Cells." *New York Times,* August 26, 2001.

Prendergast, Thomas J., M. T. Claessens, and John M. Luce. "A National Survey of End-of-Life Care for Critically Ill Patients." *American Journal of Respiratory and Critical Care Medicine* 158, no. 4 (1998): 1163–67.

Prendergast, Thomas J., and John M. Luce. "Increasing Incidence of Withholding and Withdrawal of Life Support from the Critically Ill." *American Journal of Respiratory and Critical Care Medicine* 155, no. 1 (1997): 15–20.

President's Commission for the Study of Ethical Problems in Medicine and Biomedical and Behavioral Research. "Deciding to Forgo Life-Sustaining Treatment: A Report on the Ethical, Medical and Legal Issues in Treatment Decisions." Washington, DC: U.S. Government Printing Office, 1983.

————. *Defining Death: Medical, Legal and Ethical Issues in the Determination of Death.* Washington, DC: U.S. Government Printing Office, 1981.

President's Council on Bioethics. *Beyond Therapy: Biotechnology and the Pursuit of Happiness.* http://www.bioethics.gov/reports/beyondtherapy/index.html, 2003.

Puntillo, Kathleen, et al. "End-of-Life Issues in Intensive Care Units: A National Random Survey of Nurses' Knowledge and Beliefs." *American Journal of Critical Care* 10, no. 4 (2001): 216–29.

Quill, T. E. "Perspectives on Care at the Close of Life. Initiating End-of-Life Discussions with Seriously Ill Patients: Addressing the 'Elephant in the Room.'" *Journal of the American Medical Association* 284, no. 19 (2000): 2502–7.

Quill, T. E., R. Dresser, and D. W. Brock. "The Rule of Double Effect—a Critique of Its Role in End-of-Life Decision Making." *New England Journal of Medicine* 337, no. 24 (1997): 1768–71.

Rabeneck, L., N. P. Wray, and N. J. Petersen. "Long-Term Outcomes of Patients Receiving Percutaneous Endoscopic Gastrostomy Tubes." *Journal of General Internal Medicine* 11, no. 5 (1996): 287–93.

Rabinow, Paul. *Essays on the Anthropology of Reason.* Princeton: Princeton University Press, 1996.

———. *French DNA.* Chicago: University of Chicago Press, 1999.

Rapp, Rayna. *Testing Women, Testing the Fetus: The Social Impact of Amniocentesis in America.* New York: Routledge, 1999.

Reilly, B. M., et al. "Can We Talk? Inpatient Discussions about Advance Directives in a Community Hospital. Attending Physicians' Attitudes, Their Inpatients' Wishes, and Reported Experience." *Archives of Internal Medicine* 154, no. 20 (1994): 2299–2308.

Robinson, George Canby. *The Patient as a Person: The Study of the Social Aspects of Illness.* New York: Commonwealth Fund, 1939.

Rosaldo, Renato. *Culture and Truth: The Remaking of Social Analysis.* Boston: Beacon Press, 1989.

Rose, Nikolas S. *Inventing Our Selves: Psychology, Power, and Personhood.* Cambridge: Cambridge University Press, 1998.

Rosenberg, Charles E. "Meanings, Policies, and Medicine: On the Bioethical Enterprise and History." *Daedalus* 128, no. 4 (1999): 27–46.

Rosenthal, Elisabeth. "Rules on Reviving the Dying Bring Undue Suffering, Doctors Contend." *New York Times,* October 4, 1990.

Roth, Philip. *Patrimony.* New York: Vintage Books, 1991.

Rothman, David J. *Beginnings Count.* New York: Oxford University Press, 1997.

———. *Strangers at the Bedside: A History of How Law and Bioethics Transformed Medical Decision Making.* New York: Basic Books, 1991.

Rubenfeld, G. D. "Do-Not-Resuscitate Orders: A Critical Review of the Literature." *Respiratory Care* 40, no. 5 (1995): 528–35; discussion 35–37.

Rubin, Susan B. *When Doctors Say No: The Battleground of Medical Futility.* Bloomington: Indiana University Press, 1998.

Sankar, Andrea. "'It's Just Old Age': Old Age as Diagnosis in American and Chinese Medicine." In *Age and Anthropological Theory.* Ed. David I. Kertzer and Jennie Keith. Ithaca, NY: Cornell University Press, 1984, 250–80.

Sarkisian, C. A., and M. S. Lachs. "'Failure to Thrive' in Older Adults." *Annals of Internal Medicine* 124, no. 12 (1996): 1072–78.

Sartre, Jean-Paul. *The Transcendence of the Ego: An Existentialist Theory of Consciousness.* Trans. Forrest Williams and Robert Kirkpatrick. New York: Farrar, Straus and Giroux, 1956.

Scarry, Elaine. *The Body in Pain: The Making and Unmaking of the World.* New York: Oxford University Press, 1985.

Schneiderman, Lawrence, Nancy Jecker, and Albert Jonsen. "Medical Futility: Response to Critiques." *Annals of Internal Medicine* 125, no. 8 (1996): 669–74.

Schultz, S. C., et al. "Predicting In-Hospital Mortality during Cardiopulmonary Resuscitation." *Resuscitation* 33, no. 1 (1996): 13–17.

Seale, Clive. *Constructing Death: The Sociology of Dying and Bereavement.* Cambridge: Cambridge University Press, 1998.

Sehgal, A., et al. "How Strictly Do Dialysis Patients Want Their Advance Directives Followed?" *Journal of the American Medical Association* 267, no. 1 (1992): 59–63.

Sharp, Lesley A. "Organ Transplantation as a Transformative Experience—Anthropological Insights into the Restructuring of the Self." *Medical Anthropology Quarterly* 9, no. 3 (1995): 357–89.

Shils, Edward. "The Sanctity of Life." In *Life or Death: Ethics and Options*. Ed. Daniel Labby. Seattle: University of Washington Press, 1968, 2–38.

Silveira, M. J., et al. "Patients' Knowledge of Options at the End of Life: Ignorance in the Face of Death." *Journal of the American Medical Association* 284, no. 19 (2000): 2483–88.

Siminoff, L. A., J. H. Fetting, and M. D. Abeloff. "Doctor-Patient Communication about Breast Cancer Adjuvant Therapy." *Journal of Clinical Oncology* 7, no. 9 (1989): 1192–1200.

Singal, B. M., et al. "Geriatric Patient Emergency Visits." *Annals of Emergency Medicine* 21, no. 7 (1992): 802–7.

Singer, Peter. *Rethinking Life and Death: The Collapse of Our Traditional Ethics*. New York: St. Martin's Press, 1994.

Slomka, J. "The Negotiation of Death: Clinical Decision Making at the End of Life." *Social Science & Medicine* 35, no. 3 (1992): 251–59.

Snider, Gordon L. "Historical Perspective on Mechanical Ventilation: From Simple Life Support System to Ethical Dilemma." *American Review of Respiratory Diseases* 140, no. 2, pt. 2 (1989): S2–7.

So, H. Y., T. A. Buckley, and T. E. Oh. "Factors Affecting Outcome following Cardiopulmonary Resuscitation." *Anaesthesia and Intensive Care* 22, no. 6 (1994): 647–58.

Somers, Anne Ramsay, and Dorothy R. Fabian. *The Geriatric Imperative: An Introduction to Gerontology and Clinical Geriatrics*. New York: Appleton-Century-Crofts, 1981.

Somogyi-Zalud, E., et al. "Elderly Persons' Last Six Months of Life: Findings from the Hospitalized Elderly Longitudinal Project." *Journal of the American Geriatrics Society* 48, no. 5 supp. (2000): S131–39.

Sonnenblick, M., Y. Friedlander, and A. Steinberg. "Dissociation between the Wishes of Terminally Ill Parents and Decisions by Their Offspring." *Journal of the American Geriatrics Society* 41, no. 6 (1993): 599–604.

Spillman, Brenda C., and Peter Kemper. "Lifetime Patterns of Payment for Nursing Home Care." *Medical Care* 33, no. 3 (1995): 280–96.

Spiro, Howard M., Mary G. McCrea Curnen, and Lee Palmer Wandel. *Facing Death: Where Culture, Religion, and Medicine Meet*. New Haven: Yale University Press, 1996.

Sprung, C. L. "Changing Attitudes and Practices in Forgoing Life-Sustaining Treatments." *Journal of the American Medical Association* 263, no. 16 (1990): 2211–15.

Stolman, C. J., et al. "Evaluation of Patient, Physician, Nurse, and Family Attitudes toward Do Not Resuscitate Orders." *Archives of Internal Medicine* 150, no. 3 (1990): 653–58.

Strathern, Marilyn. *After Nature*. Cambridge: Cambridge University Press, 1992.

Sudnow, David. *Passing On: The Social Organization of Dying*. Englewood Cliffs, NJ: Prentice-Hall, 1967.

SUPPORT Principal Investigators. "A Controlled Trial to Improve Care for Seriously Ill

Hospitalized Patients. The Study to Understand Prognoses and Preferences for Outcomes and Risks of Treatments (SUPPORT)." *Journal of the American Medical Association* 274, no. 20 (1995): 1591–98.

Swig, Louise, et al. "Physician Responses to a Hospital Policy Allowing Them to Not Offer Cardiopulmonary Resuscitation." *Journal of the American Geriatrics Society* 44, no. 10 (1996): 1215–19.

Taylor, Charles. "The Person." In *The Category of the Person: Anthropology, Philosophy, History.* Ed. Michael Carrithers, Steven Collins, and Steven Lukes. Cambridge: Cambridge University Press, 1985, 257–81.

———. *Sources of the Self: The Making of the Modern Identity.* Cambridge: Harvard University Press, 1989.

Taylor, Kathryn M. "Physicians and the Disclosure of Undesirable Information." In *Biomedicine Examined.* Ed. Margaret Lock and Deborah Gordon. Dordrecht: Kluwer, 1988, 441–64.

Teno, Joan M., et al. "Do Formal Advance Directives Affect Resuscitation Decisions and the Use of Resources for Seriously Ill Patients?" *Journal of Clinical Ethics* 5, no. 1 (1994): 23–30.

———. "Medical Care Inconsistent with Patients' Treatment Goals: Association with 1-Year Medicare Resource Use and Survival." *Journal of the American Geriatrics Society* 50, no. 3 (2002): 496–500.

———. "Preferences for Cardiopulmonary Resuscitation: Physician-Patient Agreement and Hospital Resource Use. The SUPPORT Investigators." *Journal of General Internal Medicine* 10, no. 4 (1995): 179–86.

Thomasma, David C. "Ethical Judgments of Quality of Life in the Care of the Aged." *Journal of the American Geriatrics Society* 32, no. 7 (1984): 525–27.

Timmermans, Stefan. *Sudden Death and the Myth of CPR.* Philadelphia: Temple University Press, 1999.

Tomlinson, Tom, and Howard Brody. "Futility and the Ethics of Resuscitation." *Journal of the American Medical Association* 264, no. 10 (1990): 1276–80.

Tomlinson, Tom, and Diane Czlonka. "Futility and Hospital Policy." *Hastings Center Report* 25, no. 3 (1995): 28–35.

Tsevat, J., et al. "Health Values of Hospitalized Patients 80 Years or Older." *Journal of the American Medical Association* 279, no. 5 (1998): 371–75.

Tulsky, J. A., M. A. Chesney, and B. Lo. "See One, Do One, Teach One? House Staff Experience Discussing Do-Not-Resuscitate Orders." *Archives of Internal Medicine* 156, no. 12 (1996): 1285–89.

U.S. Department of Health and Human Services. *Medicare Handbook.* Centers for Medicare and Medicaid Services, 2002.

Van Maanen, John. *Tales of the Field: On Writing Ethnography.* Chicago: University of Chicago Press, 1988.

Veatch, Robert M. *Death, Dying, and the Biological Revolution: Our Last Quest for Responsibility.* New Haven: Yale University Press, 1989.

———. "The Impending Collapse of the Whole-Brain Definition of Death." *Hastings Center Report* 23, no. 4 (1993): 18–24.

Verdery, R. B. "Failure to Thrive in Old Age: Follow-Up on a Workshop." *Journals of Gerontology: Medical Sciences* 52, no. 6 (1997): M333–36.

Von Dras, D. D., and H. T. Blumenthal. "Dementia of the Aged: Disease or Atypical-Accelerated Aging? Biopathological and Psychological Perspectives." *Journal of the American Geriatrics Society* 40, no. 3 (1992): 285–94.

Von Gunten, C. F. "CPR in Hospitalized Patients: When Is It Futile?" *American Family Physician* 44, no. 6 (1991): 2130–34.

Wade, Nicholas. *Life Script: How the Human Genome Discoveries Will Transform Medicine and Enhance Your Health.* New York: Simon & Schuster, 2001.

Walter, Tony. *The Revival of Death.* London: Routledge, 1994.

Waters, C. M. "Understanding and Supporting African-Americans' Perspectives of End-of-Life Care Planning and Decision Making." *Qualitative Health Research* 11, no. 3 (2001): 385–98.

Webb, Marilyn. *The Good Death: The New American Search to Reshape the End of Life.* New York: Bantam Books, 1999.

Weeks, Jane, et al. "Relationship between Cancer Patients' Predictions of Prognosis and Their Treatment Preferences." *Journal of the American Medical Association* 279, no. 21 (1998): 1709–14.

Wennberg, J. E. "The Likelihood of Being Admitted to an Intensive Care Unit during the Last Six Months of Life." In *Dartmouth Atlas of Health Care in the United States: A Report on the Medicare Program.* Chicago: AHA Press, 1999.

Wikan, Unni. "The Self in a World of Urgency and Necessity." *Ethos* 23, no. 3 (1995): 259–85.

Winslow, Gerald R., and James W. Walters, eds. *Facing Limits: Ethics and Health Care for the Elderly.* Boulder, CO: Westview Press, 1993.

Wiseman, Frederick. *Near Death.* Directed by Frederick Wiseman. Zipporah Films, 1989.

Wolf, Susan M. "*Near Death*—in the Moment of Decision." *New England Journal of Medicine* 322, no. 3 (1990): 208–10.

World Health Organization. "WHO Definition of Palliative Care." http://www.who.int/cancer/palliative/definition/en/, 1990.

Young, Katharine. *Presence in the Flesh: The Body in Medicine.* Cambridge: Harvard University Press, 1997.

Young, Katie. "In-Hospital CPR." Master's thesis, University of California, Berkeley, 2002.

Youngner, S. J. "Defining Death. A Superficial and Fragile Consensus." *Archives of Neurology* 49, no. 5 (1992): 570–72.

Youngner, S. J., et al. " 'Brain Death' and Organ Retrieval: A Cross-Sectional Survey of Knowledge and Concepts among Health Professionals." *Journal of the American Medical Association* 261, no. 15 (1989): 2205–10.

———. "Psychosocial and Ethical Implications of Organ Retrieval." *New England Journal of Medicine* 313, no. 5 (1985): 321–24.

Zeman, A. "Persistent Vegetative State." *Lancet* 350, no. 9080 (1997): 795–99.

Zoch, T. W., et al. "Short- and Long-Term Survival after Cardiopulmonary Resuscitation." *Archives of Internal Medicine* 160, no. 13 (2000): 1969–73.

Zoloth-Dorfman, L., and S. B. Rubin. " 'Medical Futility': Managed Care and the Powerful New Vocabulary for Clinical and Public Policy Discourse." *Healthcare Forum Journal* 40, no. 2 (1997): 28–33.

Zuger, Abigail. "Prescription, Quite Simply, Was a Nurse." *New York Times,* November 19, 2002.

Zweibel, N. R., C. K. Cassel, and T. Karrison. "Public Attitudes about the Use of Chronological Age as a Criterion for Allocating Health Care Resources." *Gerontologist* 33, no. 1 (1993): 74–80.

ACKNOWLEDGMENTS

Two federal agencies supported this project—the National Institute on Aging and the National Institute of Nursing Research—and my first debt is to them. The National Institute on Aging has funded my work since 1983. I received my first National Institute of Nursing Research award in 1999. I have great respect for the peer review process at these agencies, and I thank the anthropologists, sociologists, psychologists, physicians, nurses, and others who have evaluated my proposals over the years and who have spent considerable energy thinking about my research. My project officers at the National Institute on Aging have guided me well over the past twenty-two years and have offered important suggestions for conceptualizing my work. I thank Marcia Ory, in particular, for her long engagement with my work, as well as Jared Jobe and Sidney Stahl for their advice and guidance on this project. My thanks also to the National Institute of Nursing Research director Patricia Grady for her vision, commitment, and inspiration, and to her colleague June Lunney, who started the End of Life Initiative. The research for this book was funded by NIA Grant #AG13636 and NINR Grant #NR05109.

On the very day we met in 1994, Guy Micco suggested that I study hospital death. Over the years he has proven to be a stimulating interlocutor and important guide through the maze of hospital policies, federal law, medical procedures, and terminology. We talked a great deal about death, hospitals, and the role of the physician, and our conversations have helped shape this work.

This project would never have been possible without the acceptance, support, and guidance from key physicians, nurses, and administrators at the hospitals I observed. I hope my intrusive questions and presence in their daily activities were not too burdensome, and I hope they feel it was worthwhile to have an anthropologist following them around with a notebook and laptop for nearly two years. I spoke with some physicians and nurses on an almost daily basis during the years of this research and interviewed a few of them formally—they know who they are—and I thank them all for their time and efforts on my behalf. I also thank the many hospital social workers and chaplains and respiratory, speech, occupational, and physical therapists whom I observed in their work with patients and families. I admire health professionals who work in hospitals today. The challenges they face are enormous, the frustrations unrelenting, and suffering surrounds them.

Many hospitalized patients, their families, and their friends consented to talk with me and I spent considerable time with some of them. The family members and friends, especially, put their fears and anxiety aside to try to articulate answers to my questions. I thank them all for speaking so candidly with an anthropologist who could offer them little except conversation.

I began writing this book in the fall of 2000 as a fellow at the Humanities Research Institute, University of California, Irvine. Ruth Malone convened the working group, "Health Services and Place," and I thank her and the fellows and guests—Carolyn Cartier, Nancy Stoller, Sara Shostak, Ed Casey, and Jeff Malpas—for lively discussions and for their engagement with my project. They read my earliest chapter drafts and offered important suggestions. Director David Theo Goldberg and the entire HRI staff made my three-month stay there enjoyable and comfortable.

Valuable discussions with three nurse colleagues helped me think through transformations in nursing practice since the 1960s. Jeanne Benoliel, Patricia Benner, and Ruth Malone reflected thoughtfully on changes in hospital culture and the work of nurses, and I am most grateful to them. Thanks also to physicians Alan Coleman and Elizabeth Herskovits, who talked with me about hospitals and the way they shape doctors, the challenges of geriatrics, the pressures to treat and reasons not to, and shifts in treatments over the years. And my colleagues Doris Francis, Charlene Harrington, and Bob Brody offered crucial information about Medicare, nursing homes, patient autonomy, physician authority, and family worry and powerlessness.

Many of my colleagues at the Department of Anthropology, History and Social Medicine, the Department of Social and Behavioral Sciences, and the Institute for Health and Aging at the University of California, San Francisco, offered support, encouragement, and provocative conversation at all phases of this project. Special thanks go to Gay Becker and Philippe Bourgois for their insights and for conversations about research and anthropology. I thank the staff at the Institute for Health and Aging for their attention to grants management and for their always cheery help with proposal and report writing. Regina Gudelunas, Melinda Gorospe, and Annabel Paragas were especially helpful during the years of this project. I am also indebted to Dorothy Rice for her endless enthusiasm and wealth of knowledge about health care delivery in the United States, to Norman Fineman for helping me with information about Medicare, and to Ann Russ for her thorough research assistance and careful thinking about the project.

Kudos also to Lynn Watts for her always perfect tape transcription, Ann Magruder for assembling the bibliography, and Polly Coote for proofreading.

Readers of various manuscript drafts offered important comments and criticisms along the way. Shirley Daleski, Bill Daleski, Gelya Frank, Sandra Gilbert, Walter Kent, and Ann Russ read the earliest chapters and offered significant suggestions that I have incorporated. The students in my spring 2002 dissertation writing seminar asked to read my chapter drafts while they were working on their own, and I thank Angela Beattie, Beverly Davenport, Jennifer Fishman, Amy Gardner, Karen Greene, Fannie Norwood, Rashmi Sadana, and Lupe Salazar for their comments on what, eventually, became the first three chapters.

Vincanne Adams, Warwick Anderson, Gay Becker, Philippe Bourgois, Bob Brody, Adele Clarke, Lawrence Cohen, Alan Coleman, Bob Coote, and Guy Micco each generously read some or all of the manuscript and offered corrections and critiques that helped shape the ideas presented here. Most of all, I thank them for their friendship, interest, and good humor over the years. I admire them for their own outstanding scholarship and practice. I owe a special debt to Tom Laqueur, whose suggestions at various stages of the project helped move it forward. He, more than anyone else, advised me on the manuscript as a whole, which helped shape the book's final form.

Jill Hannum entered my life when I had completed a first draft of the manuscript. Her outstanding editorial skills and gentle coaxing improved my writing. I also thank her for the title and her advice about trade publishing. I offer my unending gratitude to my agent, Liza Dawson, for her enthusiasm and work on my behalf, and to my editor at Scribner, Lisa Drew, for her belief in this book and her guidance through the world of commercial publishing. Thanks also to her capable assistants, Erin Curler and Samantha Martin.

I have often joked with friends that the daughter of a physician and a poet had no choice but to become a medical anthropologist, and certainly there is no doubt that my parents' life work served as the foundation for my own commitment to undertake this research and write a book about what I found. My ongoing conversations with my father about medicine and with my mother about literature and writing seep into much of what I do. I dedicate this book to them with love.

There are all kinds of deaths, and during the years I worked on this project I was acutely aware of how preoccupied Americans are with control over the end of life. In an era marked by exceptional violence and violent death, I often think it ironic, or perhaps misplaced, to have spent so much time investigating the cultural complaint about hospital death. Three people dear to me died while this project was under way—none of them died in a hospital. This book is dedicated, in part, to their memory. My oldest friend, Joan Edelstein Davenny, died violently in Jerusalem in 1995 when the bus she was riding was blown up by a suicide bomber. My cousin, Debra Ruth Plotkin, died of cancer in 2000, in her own bed, with her family and friends at her side. Margaret Clark, my teacher and mentor, died suddenly in a movie theater in 2003, following years of heart disease. Her work on the anthropology of aging and the culture of medicine, her commitment to the development of a broadly humanistic medicine, and her passionate engagement with probing questions about technological innovation and ethics have inspired my career.

Finally, I offer my heartfelt thanks to Seth, for being there, and to Jacob, Sarah, and now Avrami, for making me laugh, keeping me honest, and leading me into the future.

CREDITS

Portions of Chapter 1 first appeared in "Narrative, Death, and the Uses of Anthropology," in *Handbook of the Humanities and Aging*, 2nd edition, editors T. Cole, T. Kastenbaum, and R. Ray, New York: Springer, 1999, 342–64. Portions of Chapters 2 and 5 appeared in "Senescence, Decline, and the Quest for a Good Death: Contemporary Dilemmas and Historical Antecedents," *Journal of Aging Studies* 14 (2000): 1–23. Portions of Chapter 4 appeared in "Intensive Care, Old Age, and the Problem of Death in America," *The Gerontologist*, 38 (1998): 715–25. Portions of Chapter 7 appeared in "Ethnography of the Particular: The Individual Case and the Culture of Death in America," in *Qualitative Gerontology: A Contemporary Perspective*, editors G. Rowles and N. Schoenberg, New York: Springer, 2002, 68–92. Portions of Chapter 8 appeared in "In the Shadow of 'Death with Dignity': Medicine and Cultural Quandaries of the Vegetative State," *American Anthropologist* 102 (2000): 69–83, and in "Hidden Places, Uncommon Persons," *Social Science and Medicine* 56 (2003): 2249–61.

INDEX

ABOUT THE AUTHOR

SHARON R. KAUFMAN is professor of medical anthropology at the University of California, San Francisco, where she teaches students in anthropology, sociology, medicine, and nursing. Her research explores the culture of medicine and the anthropology of aging. She is the author of numerous articles, book chapters, and two previous books—*The Ageless Self: Sources of Meaning in Late Life* and *The Healer's Tale: Transforming Medicine and Culture*. She lives with her husband in the San Francisco Bay Area.